VOLUME 5
BY RIE TAKADA

TOKYOPOP®
LOS ANGELES • TOKYO • LONDON

ALSO AVAILABLE FROM TOKYOPOP

**For more
information visit
www.TOKYOPOP.com**

01.09.04T

MANGA

.HACK//LEGEND OF THE TWILIGHT
@LARGE
ABENOBASHI
A.I. LOVE YOU
AI YORI AOSHI
ANGELIC LAYER
ARM OF KANNON
BABY BIRTH
BATTLE ROYALE
BATTLE VIXENS
BRAIN POWERED
BRIGADOON
B'TX
CANDIDATE FOR GODDESS, THE
CARDCAPTOR SAKURA
CARDCAPTOR SAKURA - MASTER OF THE CLOW
CHOBITS
CHRONICLES OF THE CURSED SWORD
CLAMP SCHOOL DETECTIVES
CLOVER
COMIC PARTY
CONFIDENTIAL CONFESSIONS
CORRECTOR YUI
COWBOY BEBOP
COWBOY BEBOP: SHOOTING STAR
CRESCENT MOON
CULDCEPT
CYBORG 009
D.N. ANGEL
DEMON DIARY
DEMON ORORON, THE
DEUS VITAE
DIGIMON
DIGIMON ZERO TWO
DIGIMON TAMERS
DOLL
DRAGON HUNTER
DRAGON KNIGHTS
DREAM SAGA
DUKLYON: CLAMP SCHOOL DEFENDERS
ERICA SAKURAZAWA COLLECTED WORKS
EERIE QUEERIE!
ET CETERA
ETERNITY
EVIL'S RETURN
FAERIES' LANDING
FAKE
FLCL
FORBIDDEN DANCE
FRUITS BASKET
G GUNDAM
GATE KEEPERS

GETBACKERS
GIRL GOT GAME
GRAVITATION
GTO
GUNDAM SEED ASTRAY
GUNDAM WING
GUNDAM WING: BATTLEFIELD OF PACIFISTS
GUNDAM WING: ENDLESS WALTZ
GUNDAM WING: THE LAST OUTPOST (G-UNIT)
HAPPY MANIA
HARLEM BEAT
I.N.V.U.
IMMORTAL RAIN
INITIAL D
ISLAND
JING: KING OF BANDITS
JULINE
KARE KANO
KILL ME, KISS ME
KINDAICHI CASE FILES, THE
KING OF HELL
KODOCHA: SANA'S STAGE
LAMENT OF THE LAMB
LES BIJOUX
LEGEND OF CHUN HYANG, THE
LOVE HINA
LUPIN III
MAGIC KNIGHT RAYEARTH I
MAGIC KNIGHT RAYEARTH II
MAHOROMATIC: AUTOMATIC MAIDEN
MAN OF MANY FACES
MARMALADE BOY
MARS
MINK
MIRACLE GIRLS
MIYUKI-CHAN IN WONDERLAND
MODEL
ONE
PARADISE KISS
PARASYTE
PEACH GIRL
PEACH GIRL: CHANGE OF HEART
PET SHOP OF HORRORS
PITA-TEN
PLANET LADDER
PLANETES
PRIEST
PRINCESS AI
PSYCHIC ACADEMY
RAGNAROK
RAVE MASTER
REALITY CHECK
REBIRTH

01.09.04T

Translator - Ben Axia Hirayama
English Adaptation - Jodi Bryson
Copy Editors - Alexis Kirsch, Carol Fox
Retouch and Lettering - Jennifer Nunn-Iwai
Cover Layout - Patrick Hook
Graphic Designer - James Lee

Editor - Bryce P. Coleman
Managing Editor - Jill Freshney
Production Coordinator - Antonio DePietro
Production Managers - Jennifer Miller, Mutsumi Miyazaki
Art Director - Matt Alford
Editorial Director - Jeremy Ross
VP of Production - Ron Klamert
President & C.O.O. - John Parker
Publisher & C.E.O. - Stuart Levy

Email: editor@TOKYOPOP.com

Come visit us online at www.TOKYOPOP.com

A  Manga

TOKYOPOP Inc.
5900 Wilshire Blvd. Suite 2000
Los Angeles, CA 90036

Wild Act Vol. 5

ISBN: 1-59182-563-6

First TOKYOPOP printing: March 2004

10 9 8 7 6 5 4 3 2 1

Printed in the USA

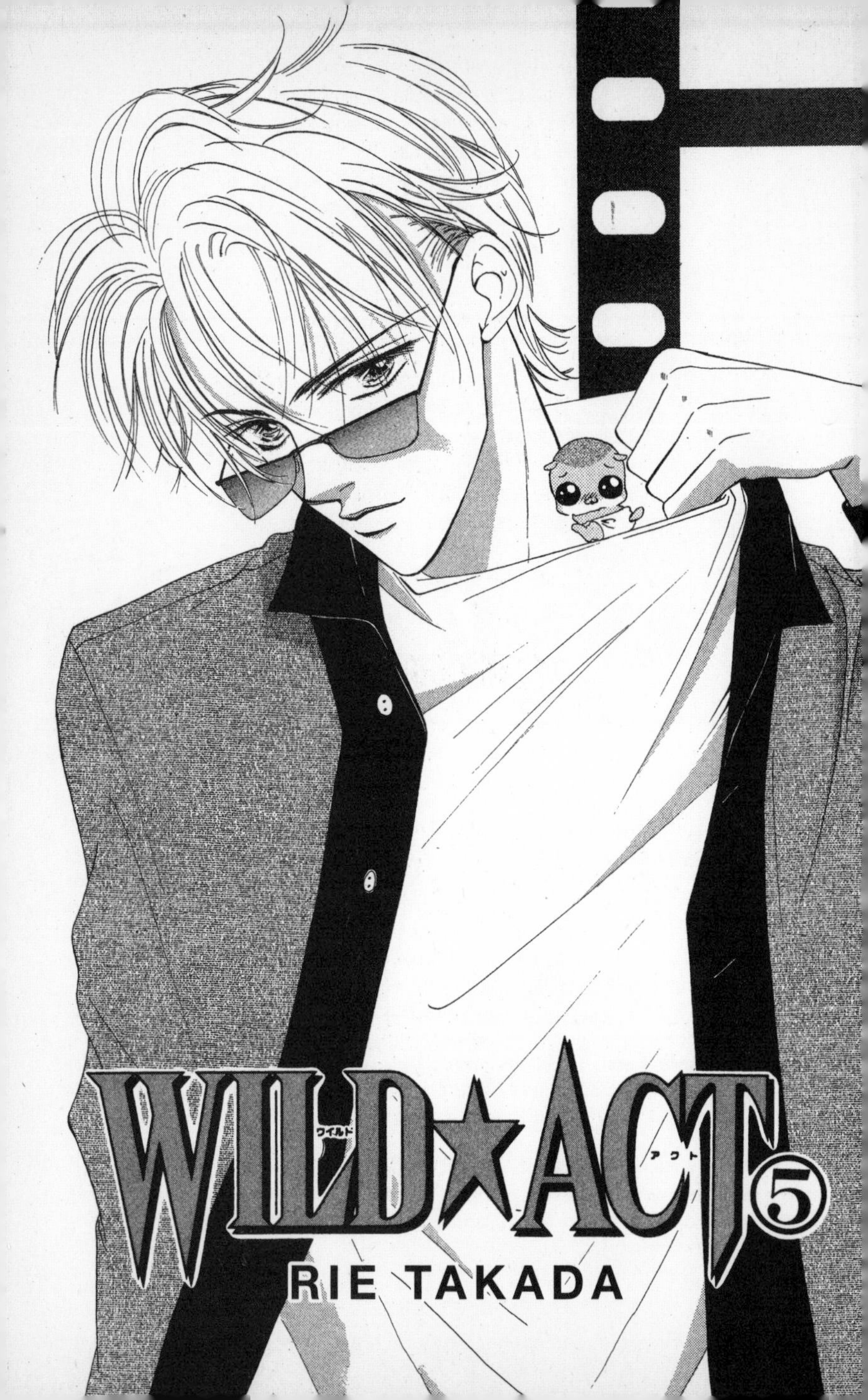
WILD★ACT
ワイルド
アクト
5
RIE TAKADA

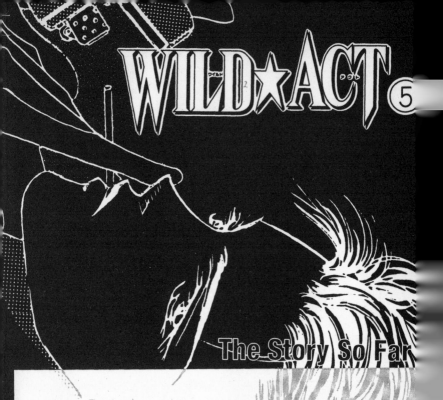

WILD★ACT ⑤

The Story So Far

Yuniko Sakuraba is a 15 year-old girl who's just started high school. She's also a huge fan of the great actor, Akira Nanae, who died sixteen years ago. She is so into him that she became a thief to collect his stolen mementos while being raised among actors at the theater company where Akira and her mother, Maiko, worked. Yuniko never met her mother until recently—but meanwhile, love is blooming for Yuniko and Ryu Eba, an up-and-coming actor who is frequently compared to Akira Nanae (He hates it!).

Thanks to Ryu's help, Yuniko gets her hands on a recording of a conversation which proves she's Akira's daughter! However, suspicions arise that Ryu is also Akira Nanae's son! This could mean he's...Yuniko's big brother?! To make matters worse, the press learns of Ryu and Akira's alleged connection because of Maki Tatsumi, a high-schooler who wants to follow in his father's paparazzi footsteps.

The only way to clear this suspicion and carry on with their love is through Maiko, who happens to be hospitalized for amnesia. Yuniko and Ryu find old photographs of Maiko and Akira, and hope that these are the key to bringing back Maiko's memory!

Meet the Characters

Akira Nanae
He was the first Japanese actor to succeed in Hollywood and the international film scene. He died in a tragic accident at the young age of 25.

Yuniko Sakuraba
A huge fan and the daughter of Akira Nanae. She loves Ryu, and is currently trying to prove that she and Ryu are not brother and sister.

Ryu Eba
A popular 17-year-old actor who is often compared to Akira, which he can't stand. He loves Yuniko, and will do almost anything to help her. Is he really Akira's son?!

Maki Tatsumi
Classmate of Yuniko's and Ryu's. He's the son of a ruthless paparazzi photographer. He's trying to get the scoop on Ryu before anyone to make a name for himself as a paparazzi.

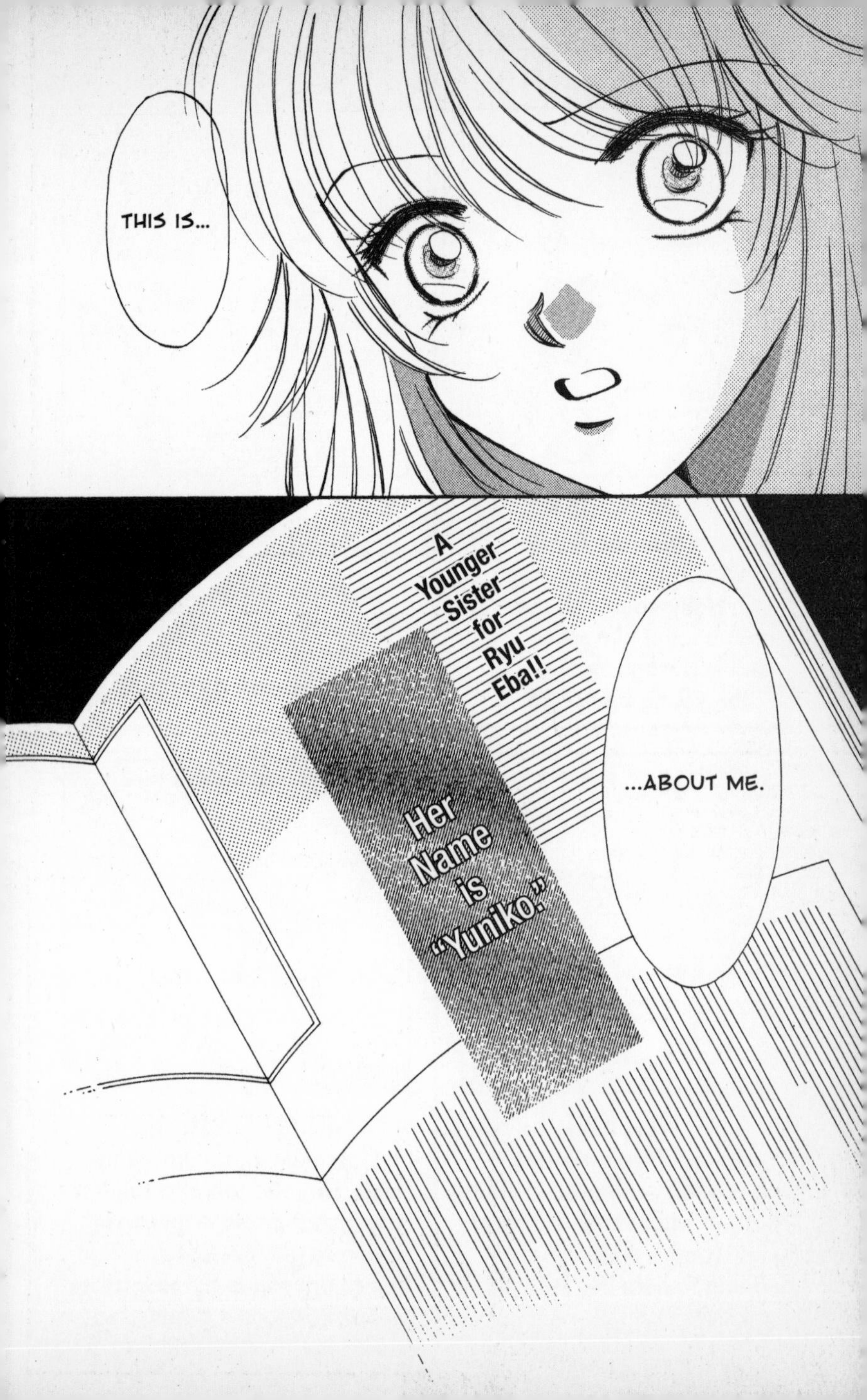
THIS IS...
A Younger Sister for Ryu Eba!!
...ABOUT ME.
Her Name is "Yuniko."

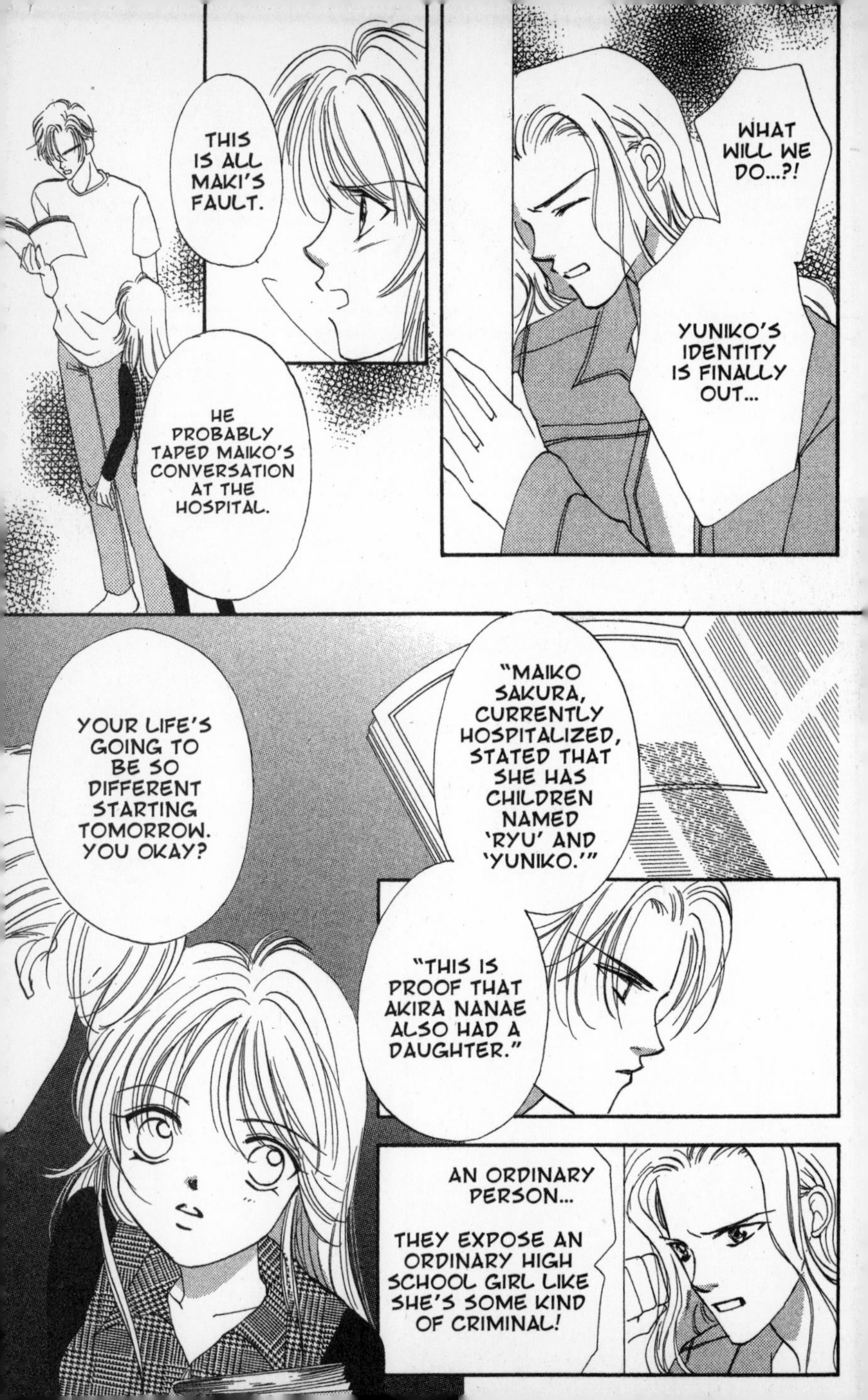
WHAT WILL WE DO...?!
YUNIKO'S IDENTITY IS FINALLY OUT...
THIS IS ALL MAKI'S FAULT.
HE PROBABLY TAPED MAIKO'S CONVERSATION AT THE HOSPITAL.
"MAIKO SAKURA, CURRENTLY HOSPITALIZED, STATED THAT SHE HAS CHILDREN NAMED 'RYU' AND 'YUNIKO.'"
"THIS IS PROOF THAT AKIRA NANAE ALSO HAD A DAUGHTER."
AN ORDINARY PERSON...
THEY EXPOSE AN ORDINARY HIGH SCHOOL GIRL LIKE SHE'S SOME KIND OF CRIMINAL!
YOUR LIFE'S GOING TO BE SO DIFFERENT STARTING TOMORROW. YOU OKAY?

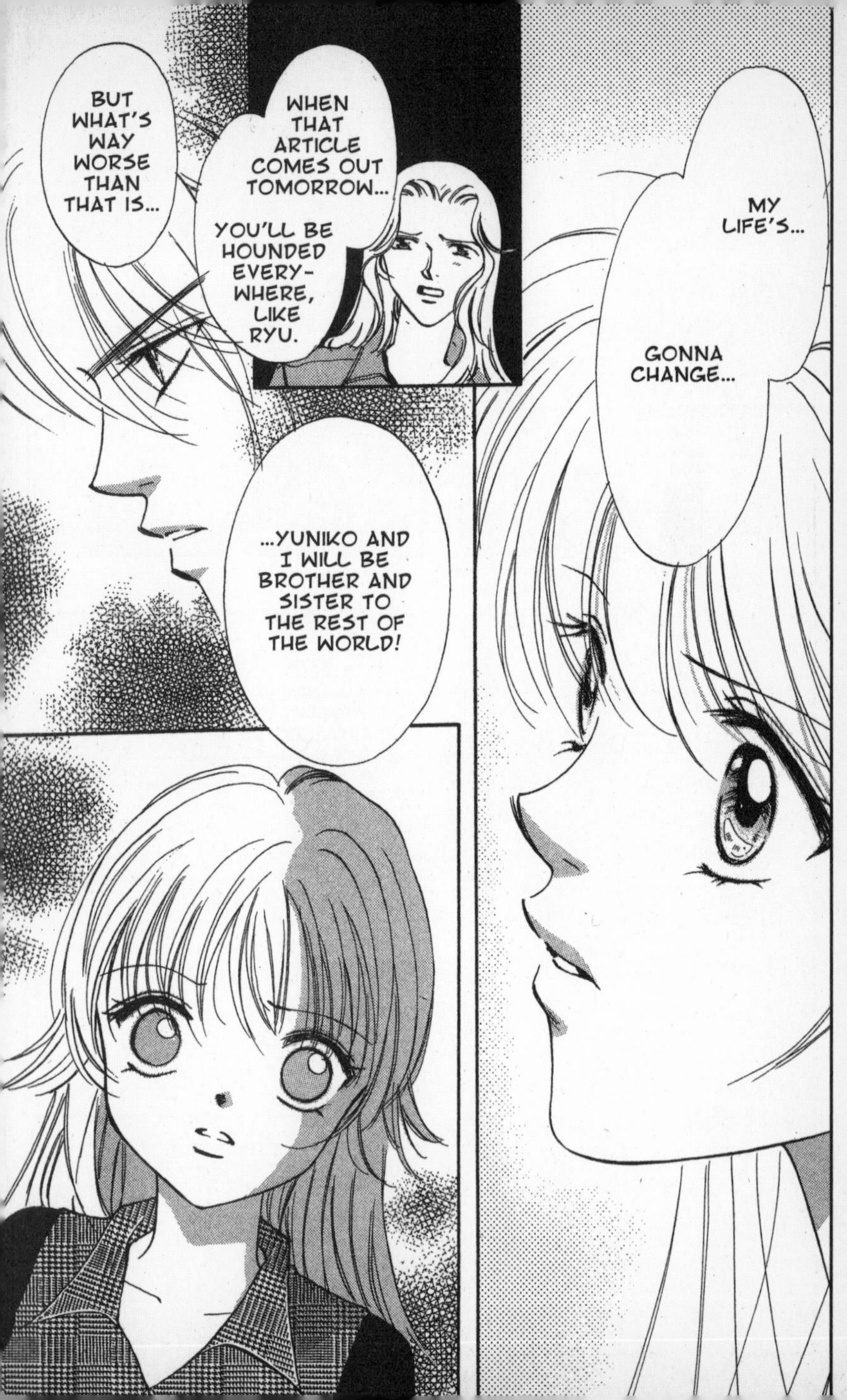
MY LIFE'S...
GONNA CHANGE...
WHEN THAT ARTICLE COMES OUT TOMORROW...
YOU'LL BE HOUNDED EVERY-WHERE, LIKE RYU.
BUT WHAT'S WAY WORSE THAN THAT IS...
...YUNIKO AND I WILL BE BROTHER AND SISTER TO THE REST OF THE WORLD!

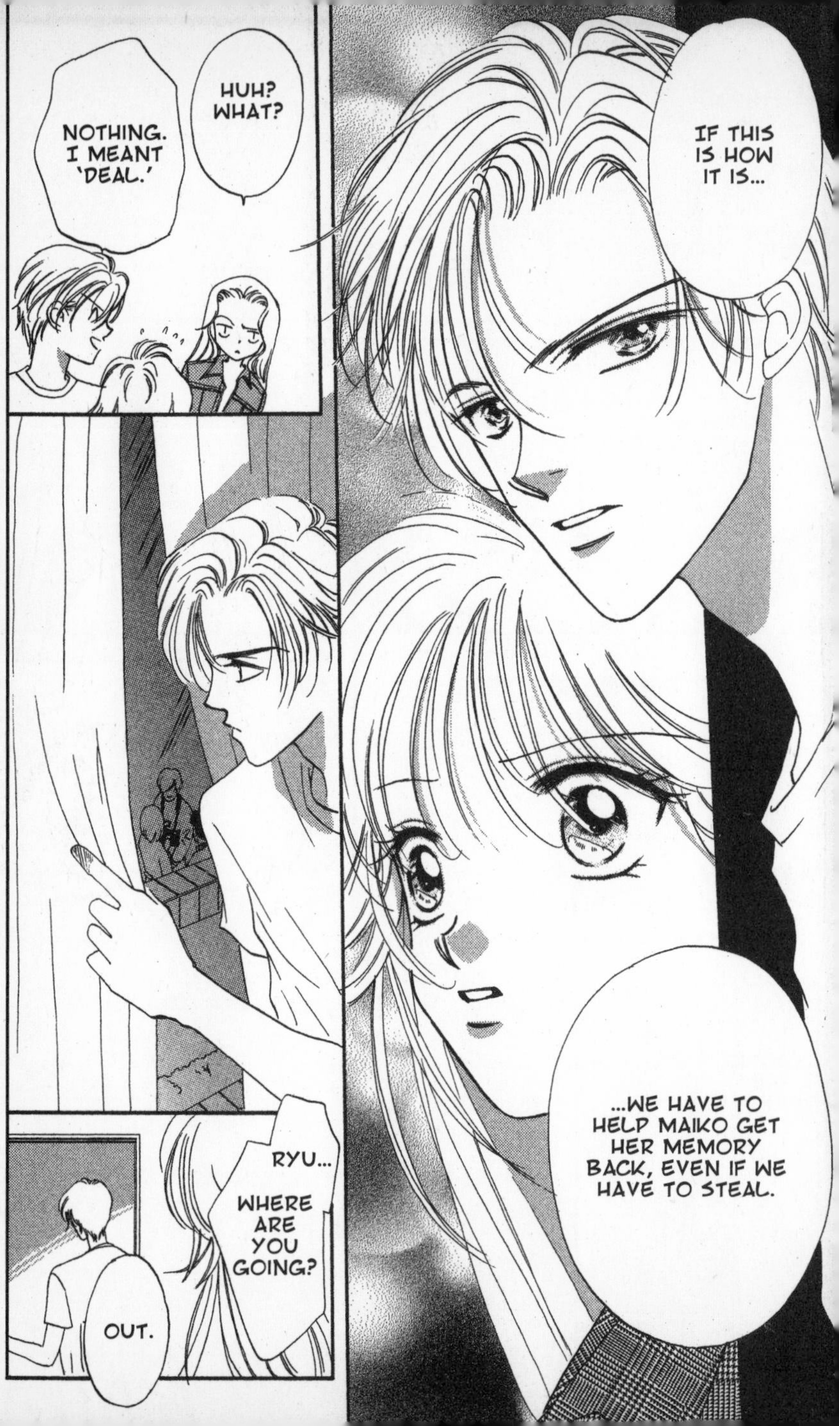
IF THIS IS HOW IT IS...
...WE HAVE TO HELP MAIKO GET HER MEMORY BACK, EVEN IF WE HAVE TO STEAL.
HUH? WHAT?
NOTHING. I MEANT 'DEAL.'
RYU...
WHERE ARE YOU GOING?
OUT.

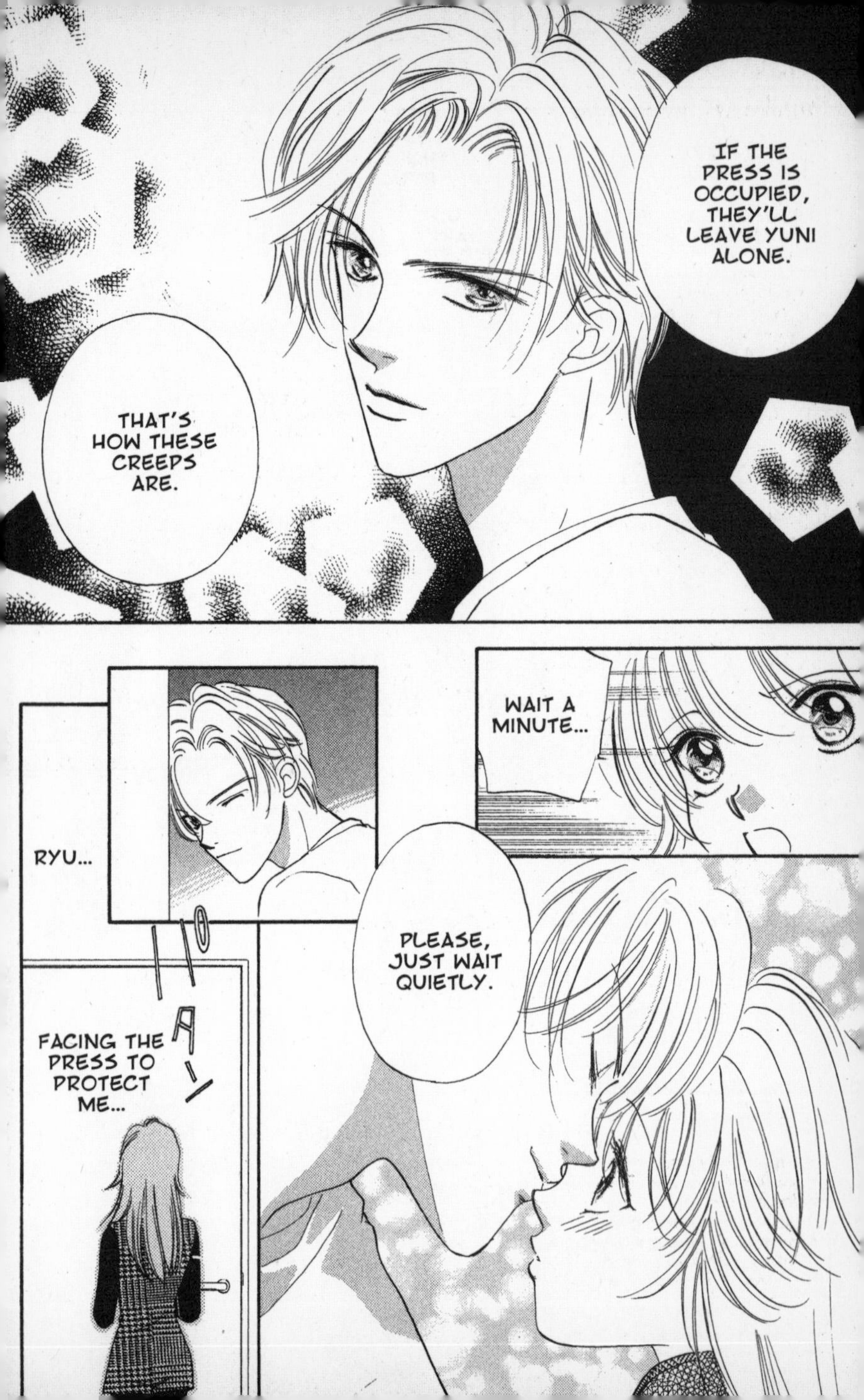
IF THE PRESS IS OCCUPIED, THEY'LL LEAVE YUNI ALONE.
THAT'S HOW THESE CREEPS ARE.
WAIT A MINUTE...
RYU...
PLEASE, JUST WAIT QUIETLY.
FACING THE PRESS TO PROTECT ME...

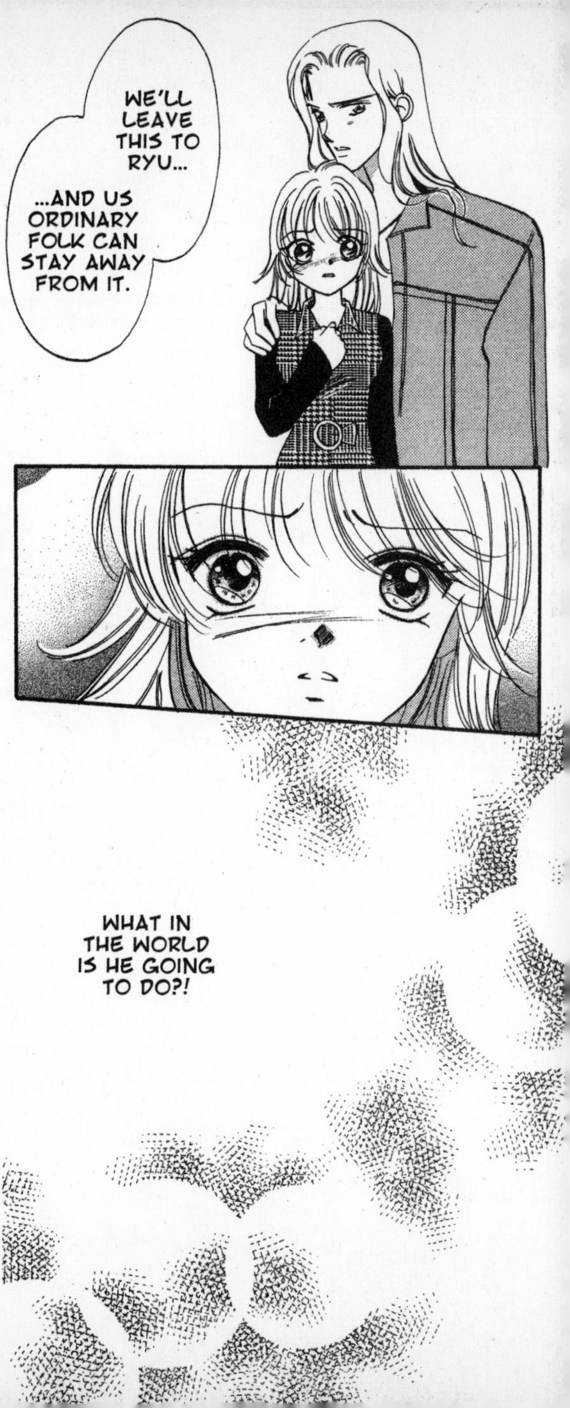
WE'LL LEAVE THIS TO RYU...
...AND US ORDINARY FOLK CAN STAY AWAY FROM IT.
WHAT IN THE WORLD IS HE GOING TO DO?!

Yuniko Sakuraba Data

Big Illustrated Book

1. Eyes: Intense eyes, inherited from Akira Nanae, make Ryu a captive.
2. Hair that curls out. It droops when she's not energetic.
3. Chest: It's in the process of growing!
4. Hips: A tight and lean butt-kicker!

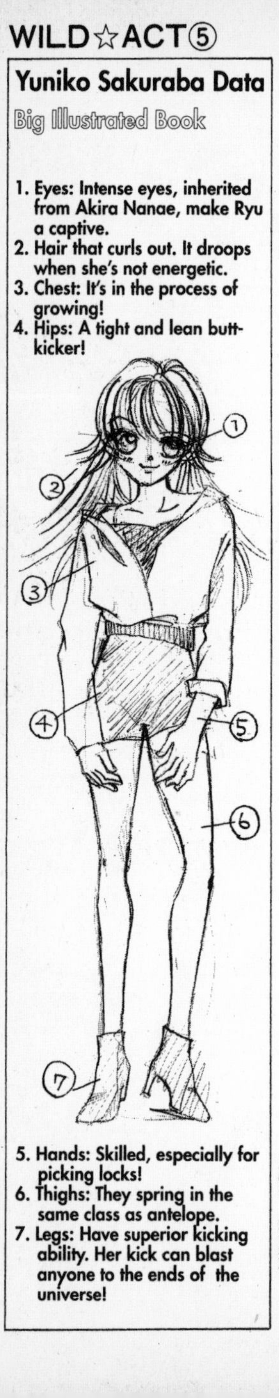
1
2
3
4
5
6
7

5. Hands: Skilled, especially for picking locks!
6. Thighs: They spring in the same class as antelope.
7. Legs: Have superior kicking ability. Her kick can blast anyone to the ends of the universe!

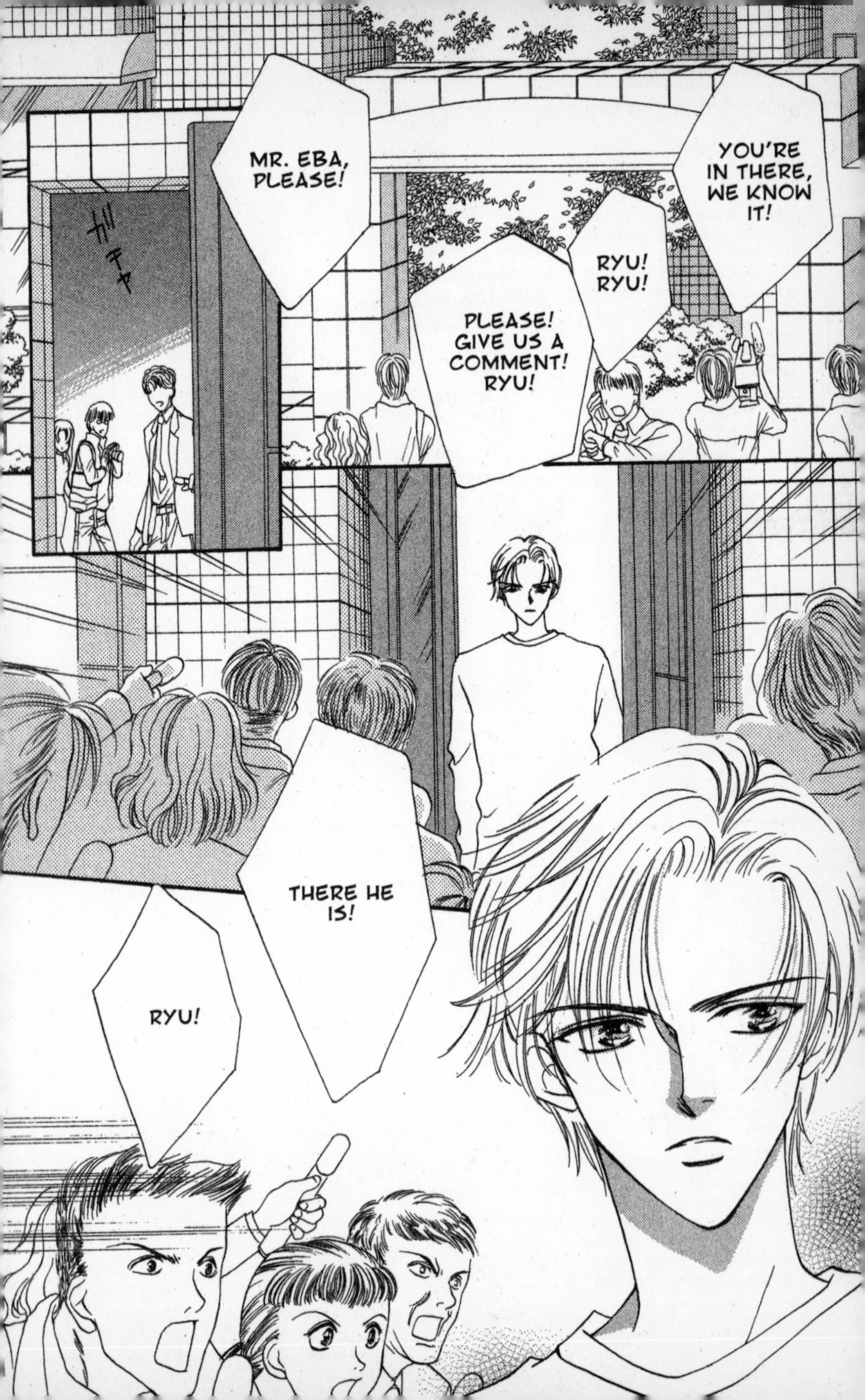
YOU'RE IN THERE, WE KNOW IT!
RYU! RYU!
PLEASE! GIVE US A COMMENT! RYU!
MR. EBA, PLEASE!
ガチャ
THERE HE IS!
RYU!

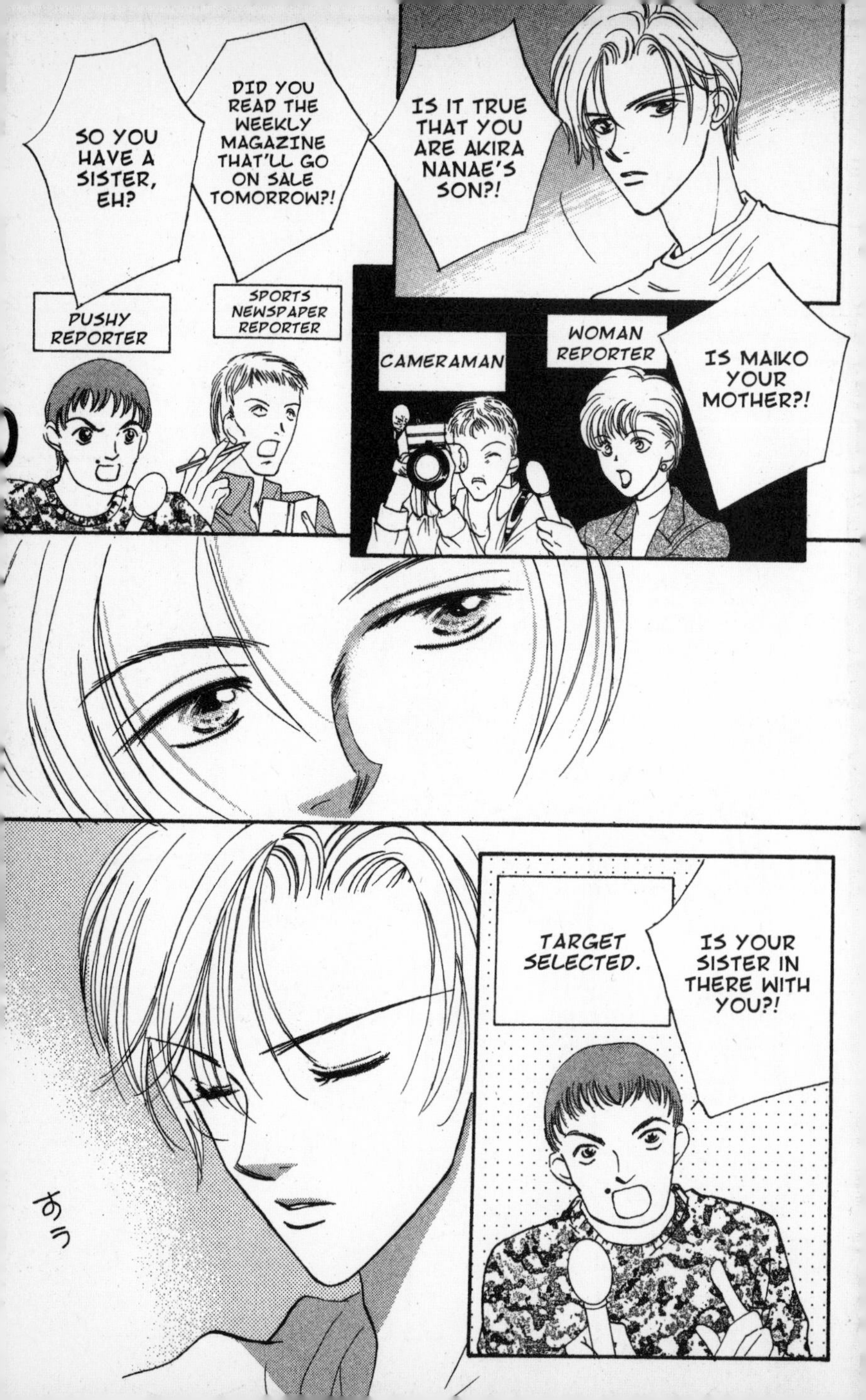
IS IT TRUE THAT YOU ARE AKIRA NANAE'S SON?!
IS MAIKO YOUR MOTHER?!
WOMAN REPORTER
CAMERAMAN
DID YOU READ THE WEEKLY MAGAZINE THAT'LL GO ON SALE TOMORROW?!
SO YOU HAVE A SISTER, EH?
SPORTS NEWSPAPER REPORTER
PUSHY REPORTER
IS YOUR SISTER IN THERE WITH YOU?!
TARGET SELECTED.
すう

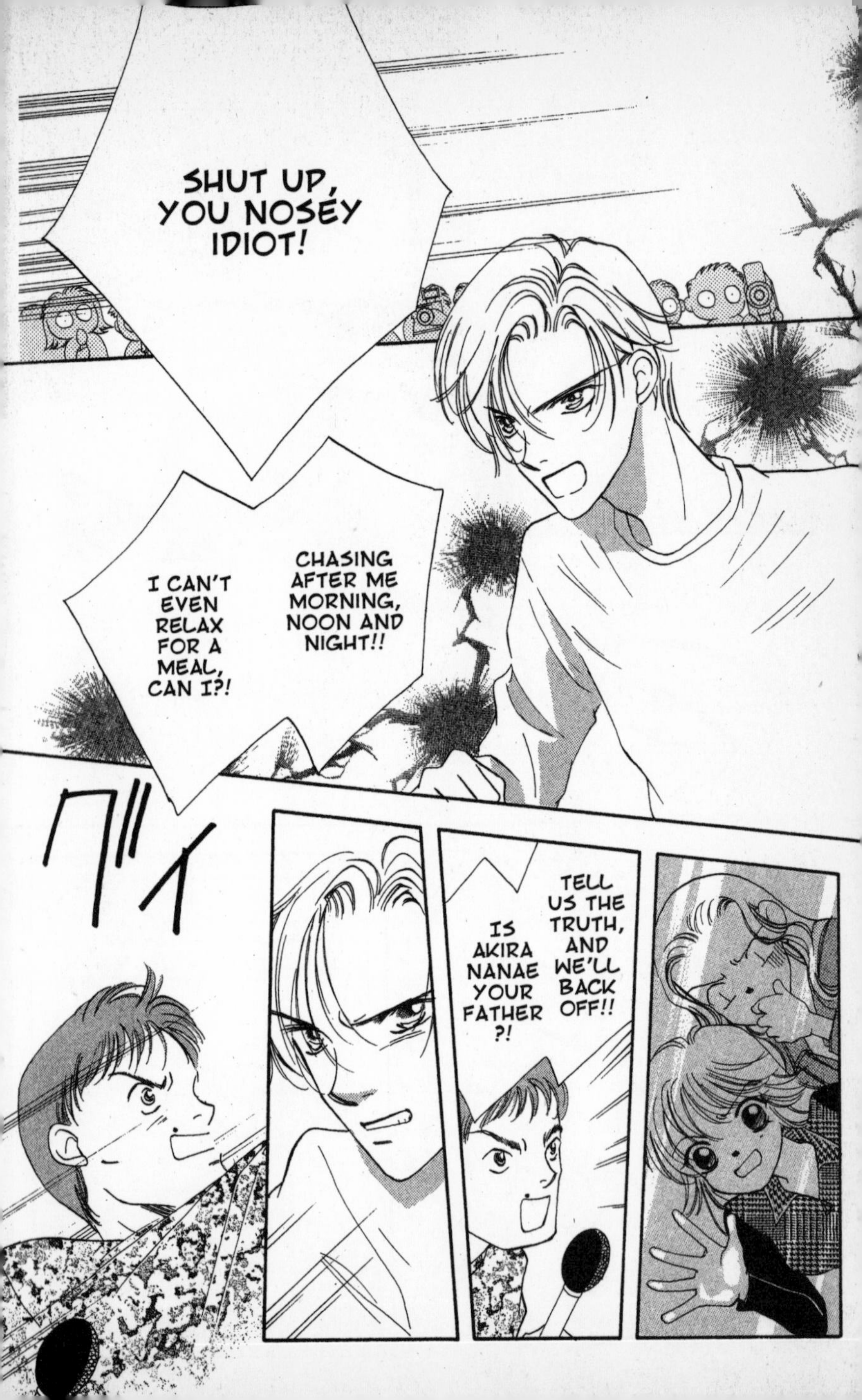
SHUT UP, YOU NOSEY IDIOT!
CHASING AFTER ME MORNING, NOON AND NIGHT!!
I CAN'T EVEN RELAX FOR A MEAL, CAN I?!
TELL US THE TRUTH, AND WE'LL BACK OFF!!
IS AKIRA NANAE YOUR FATHER?!
グイ

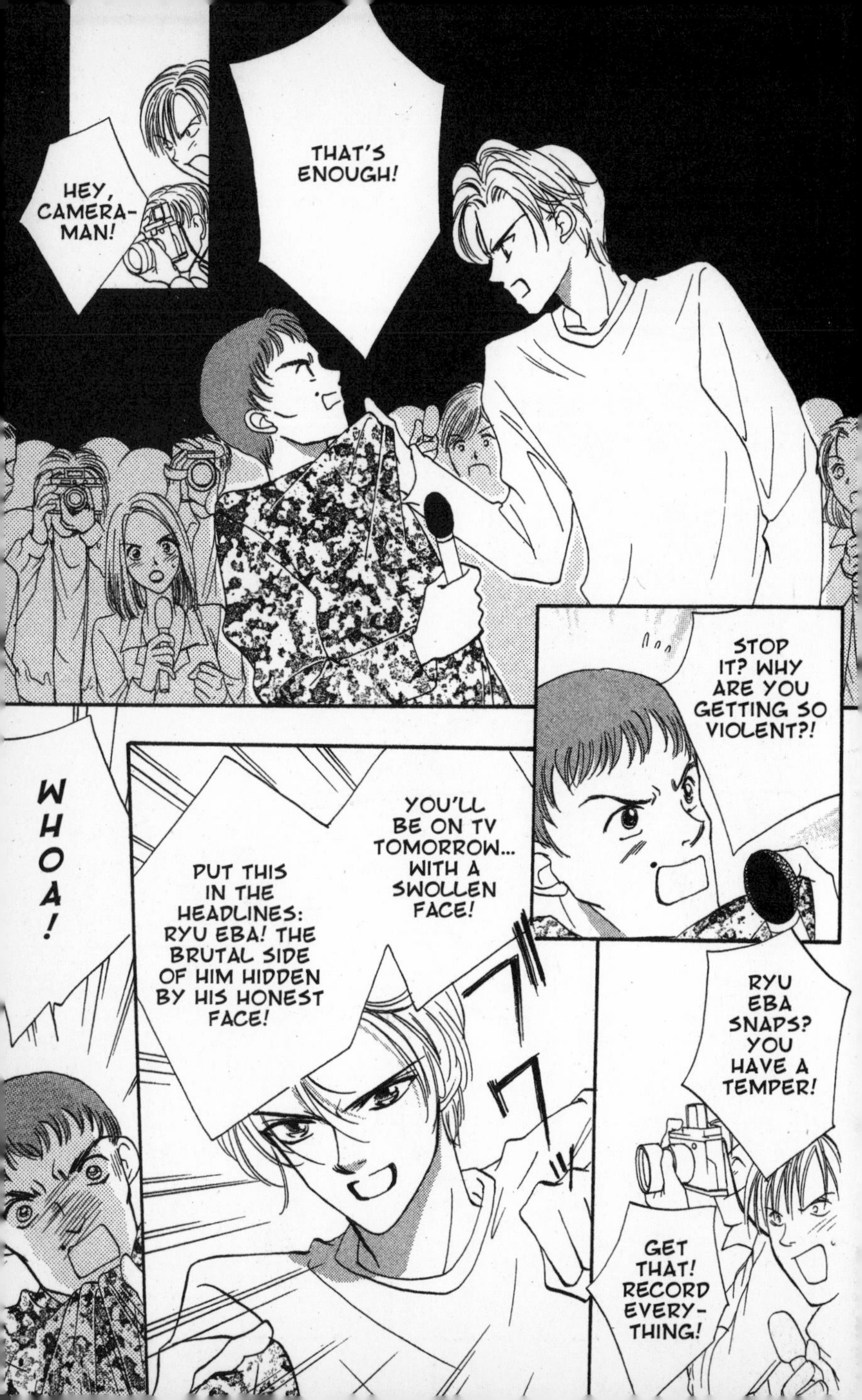
THAT'S ENOUGH!
HEY, CAMERA-MAN!
STOP IT? WHY ARE YOU GETTING SO VIOLENT?!
RYU EBA SNAPS? YOU HAVE A TEMPER!
GET THAT! RECORD EVERY-THING!
YOU'LL BE ON TV TOMORROW... WITH A SWOLLEN FACE!
PUT THIS IN THE HEADLINES: RYU EBA! THE BRUTAL SIDE OF HIM HIDDEN BY HIS HONEST FACE!
WHOA!

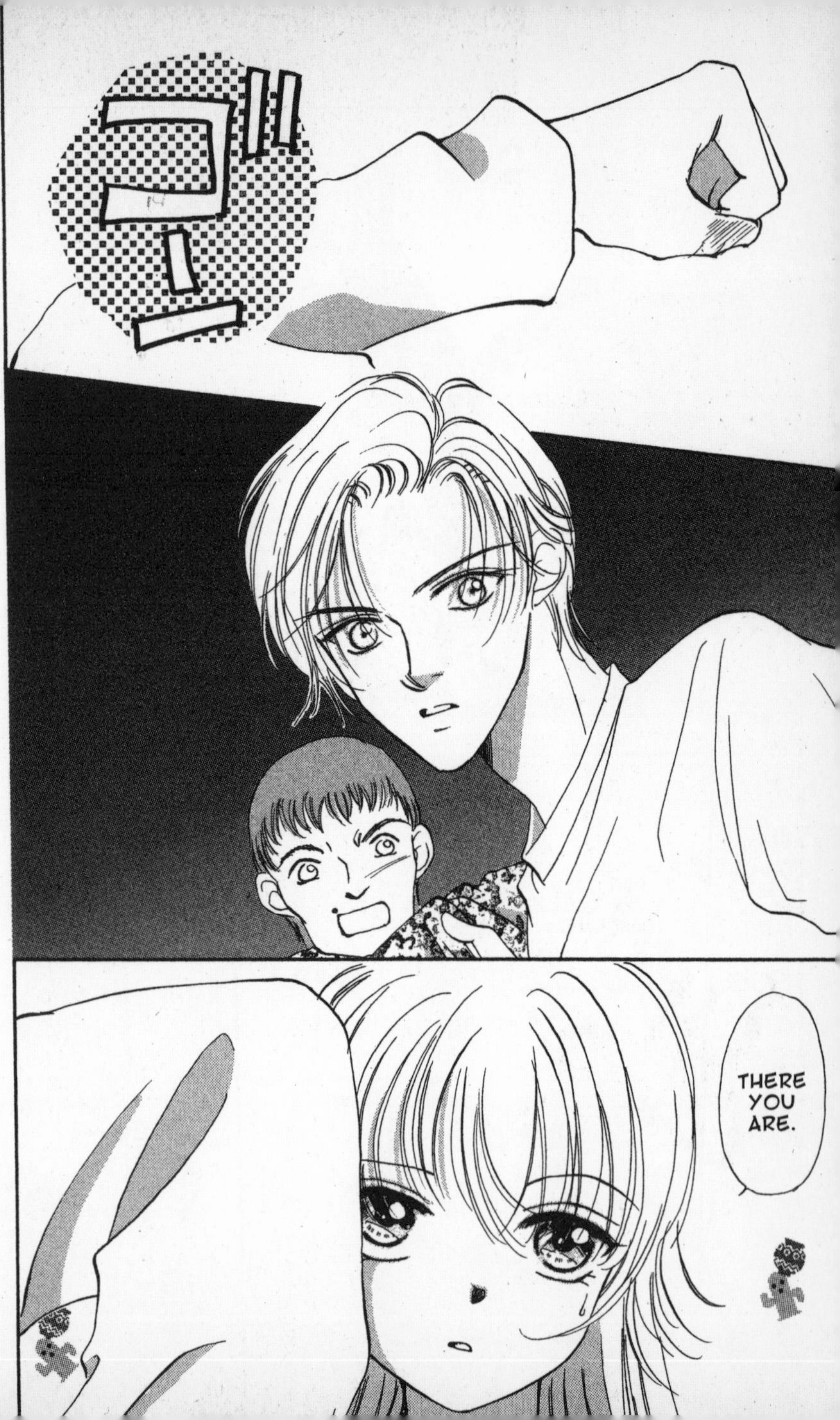
ゴーー
THERE YOU ARE.

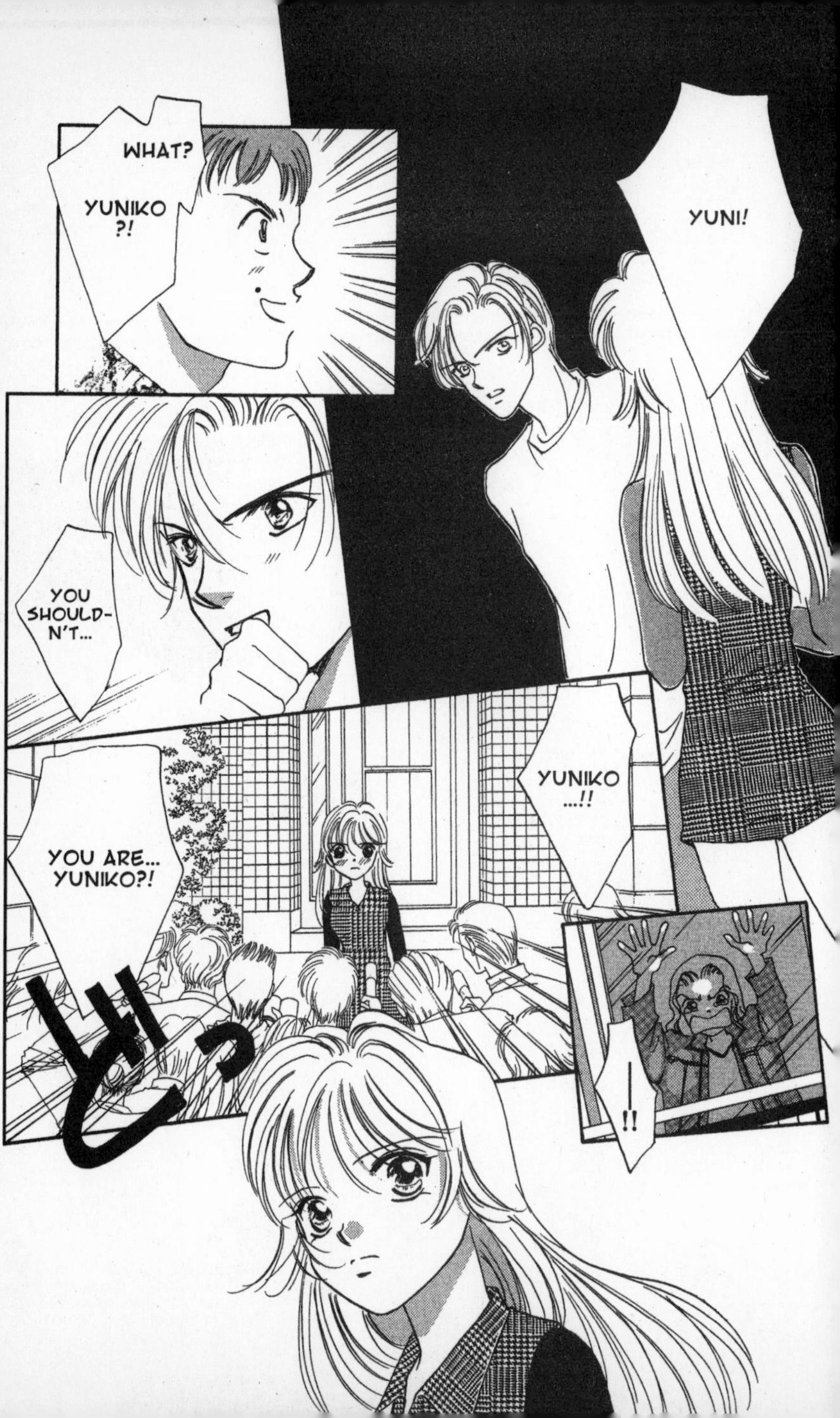
YUNI!
WHAT?
YUNIKO ?!
YOU SHOULDN'T...
YUNIKO ...!!
—!!
YOU ARE... YUNIKO?!
どっ

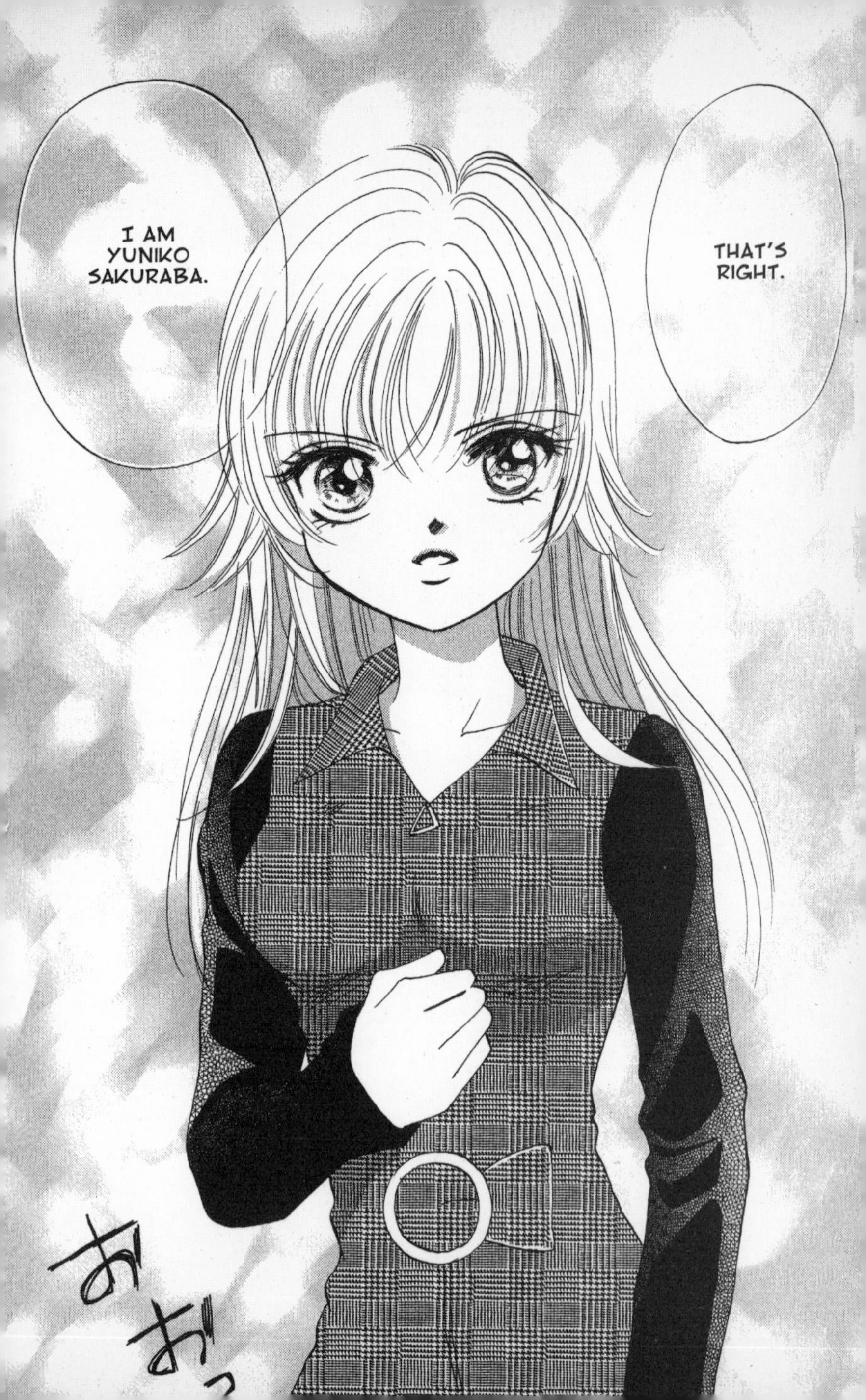
THAT'S RIGHT.
I AM YUNIKO SAKURABA.
おおっ

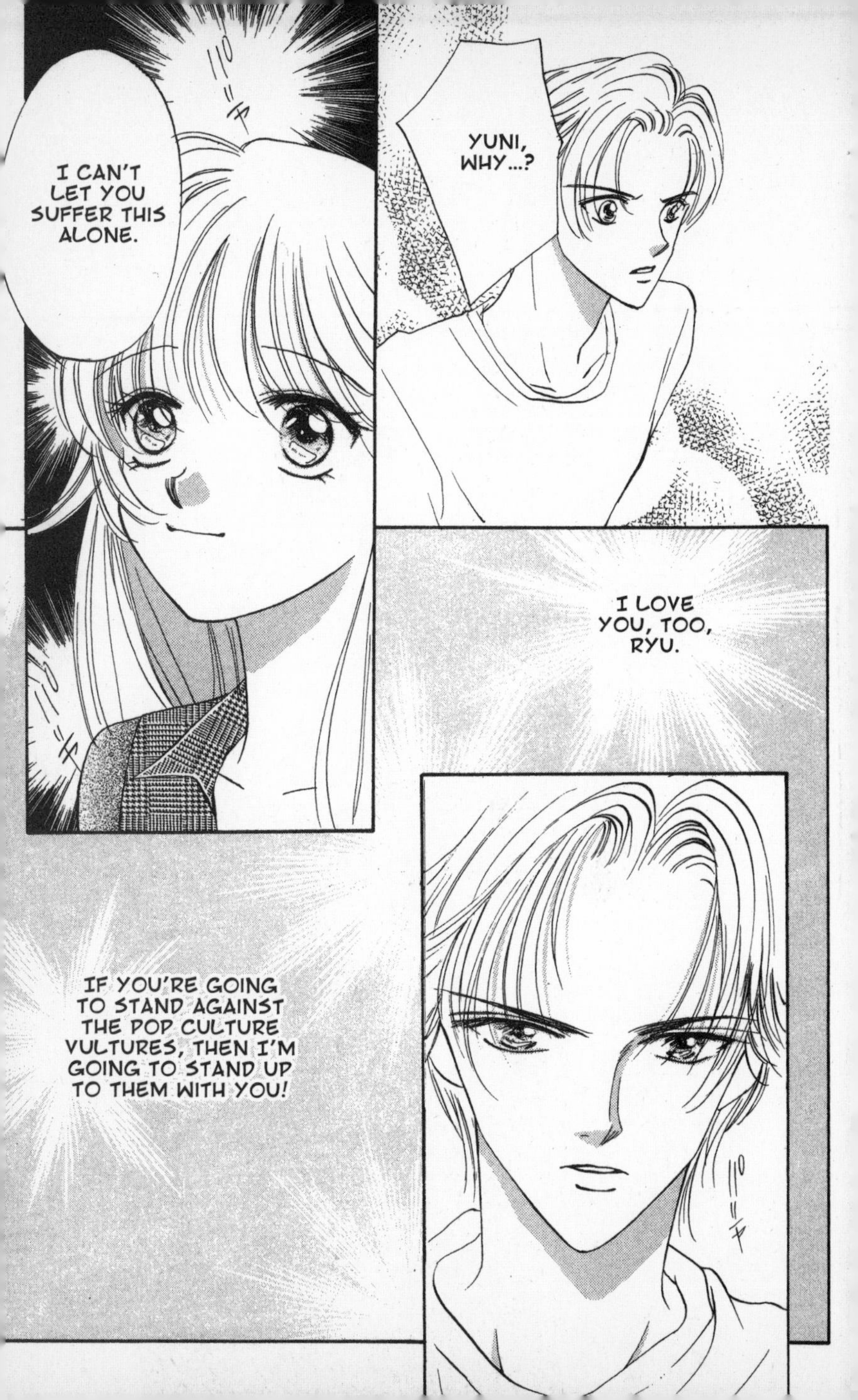
YUNI, WHY...?
I CAN'T LET YOU SUFFER THIS ALONE.
I LOVE YOU, TOO, RYU.
IF YOU'RE GOING TO STAND AGAINST THE POP CULTURE VULTURES, THEN I'M GOING TO STAND UP TO THEM WITH YOU!

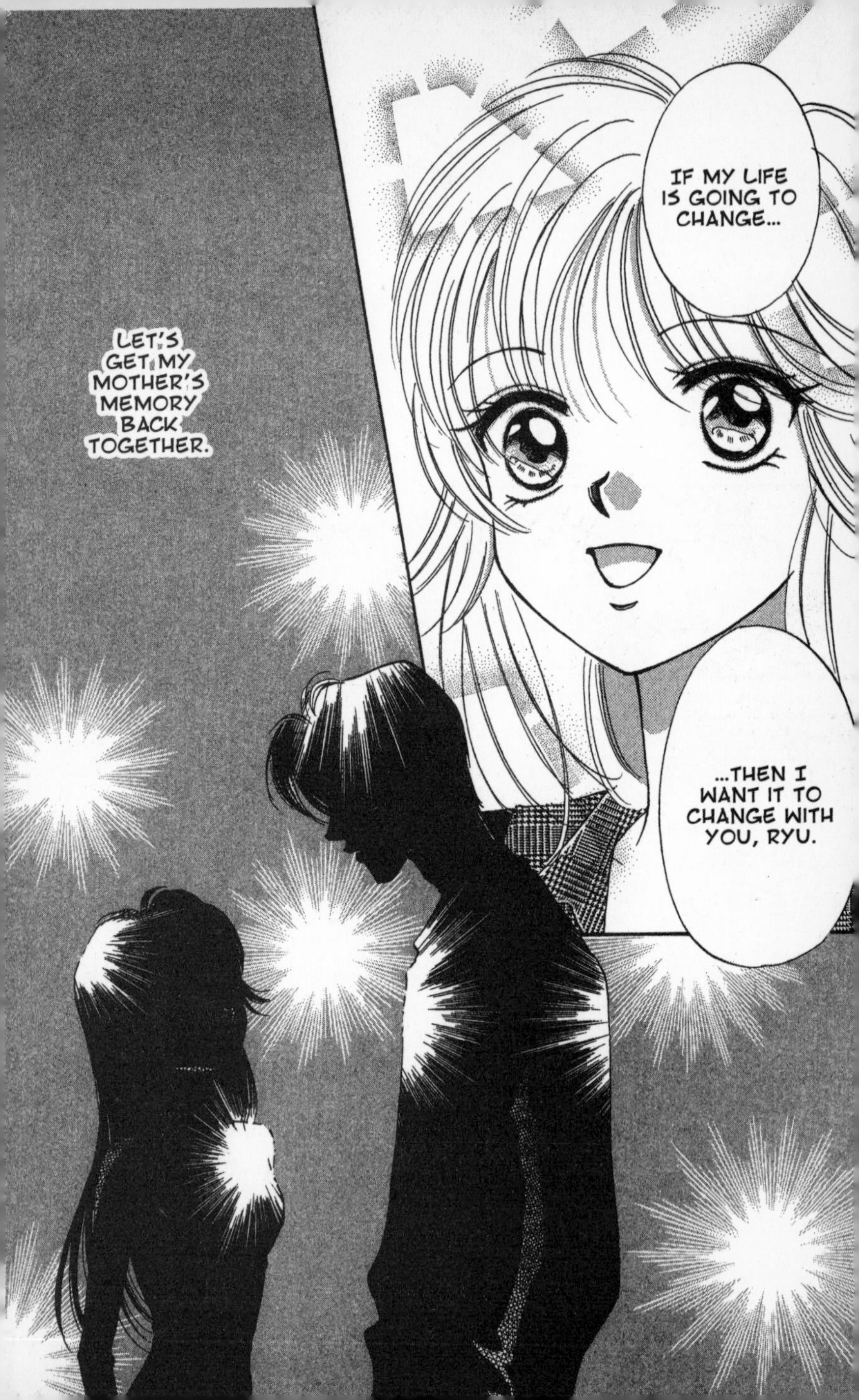
IF MY LIFE IS GOING TO CHANGE...
...THEN I WANT IT TO CHANGE WITH YOU, RYU.
LET'S GET MY MOTHER'S MEMORY BACK TOGETHER.

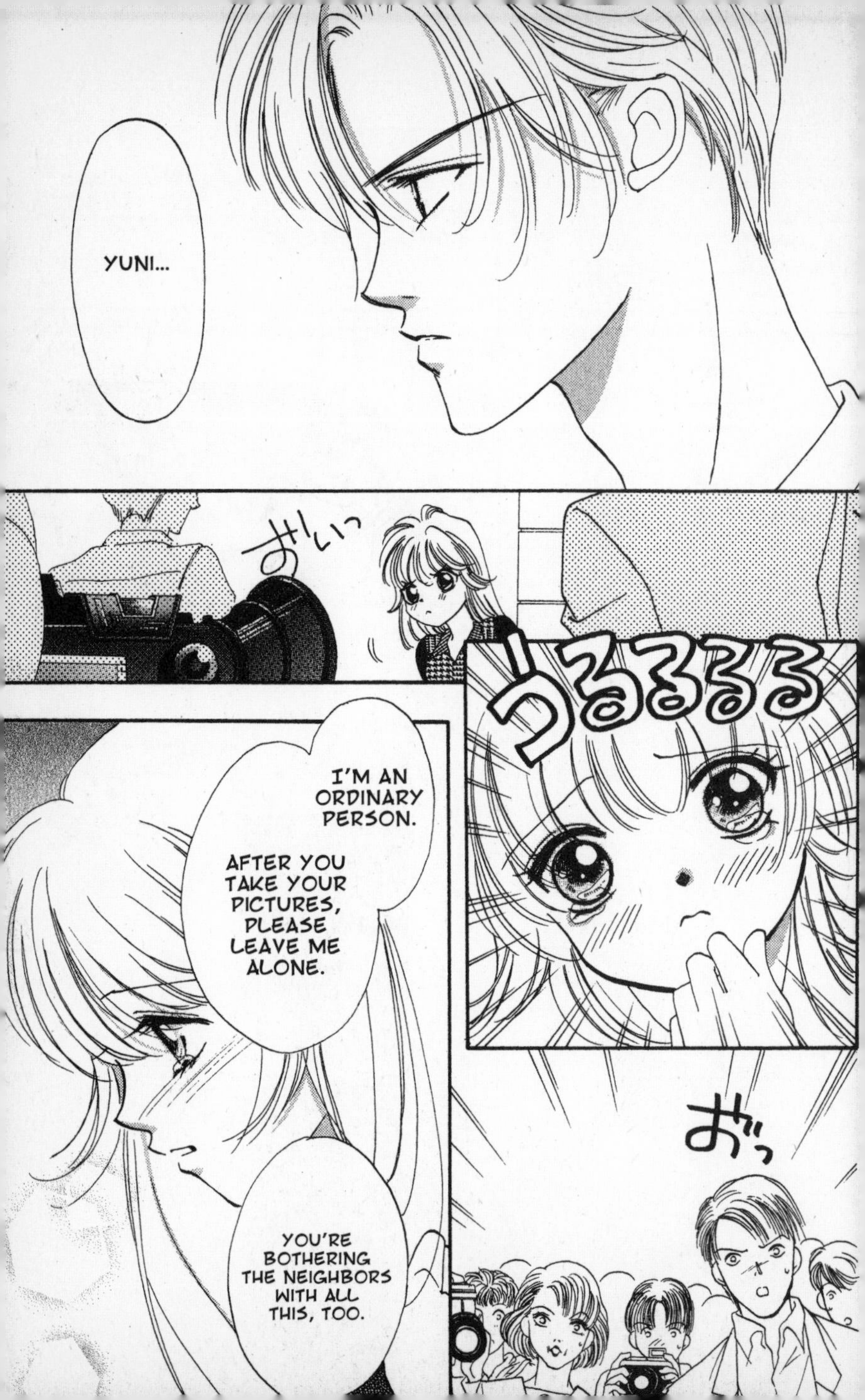
YUNI...
おいっ
うるるるる
おっ
I'M AN ORDINARY PERSON.
AFTER YOU TAKE YOUR PICTURES, PLEASE LEAVE ME ALONE.
YOU'RE BOTHERING THE NEIGHBORS WITH ALL THIS, TOO.

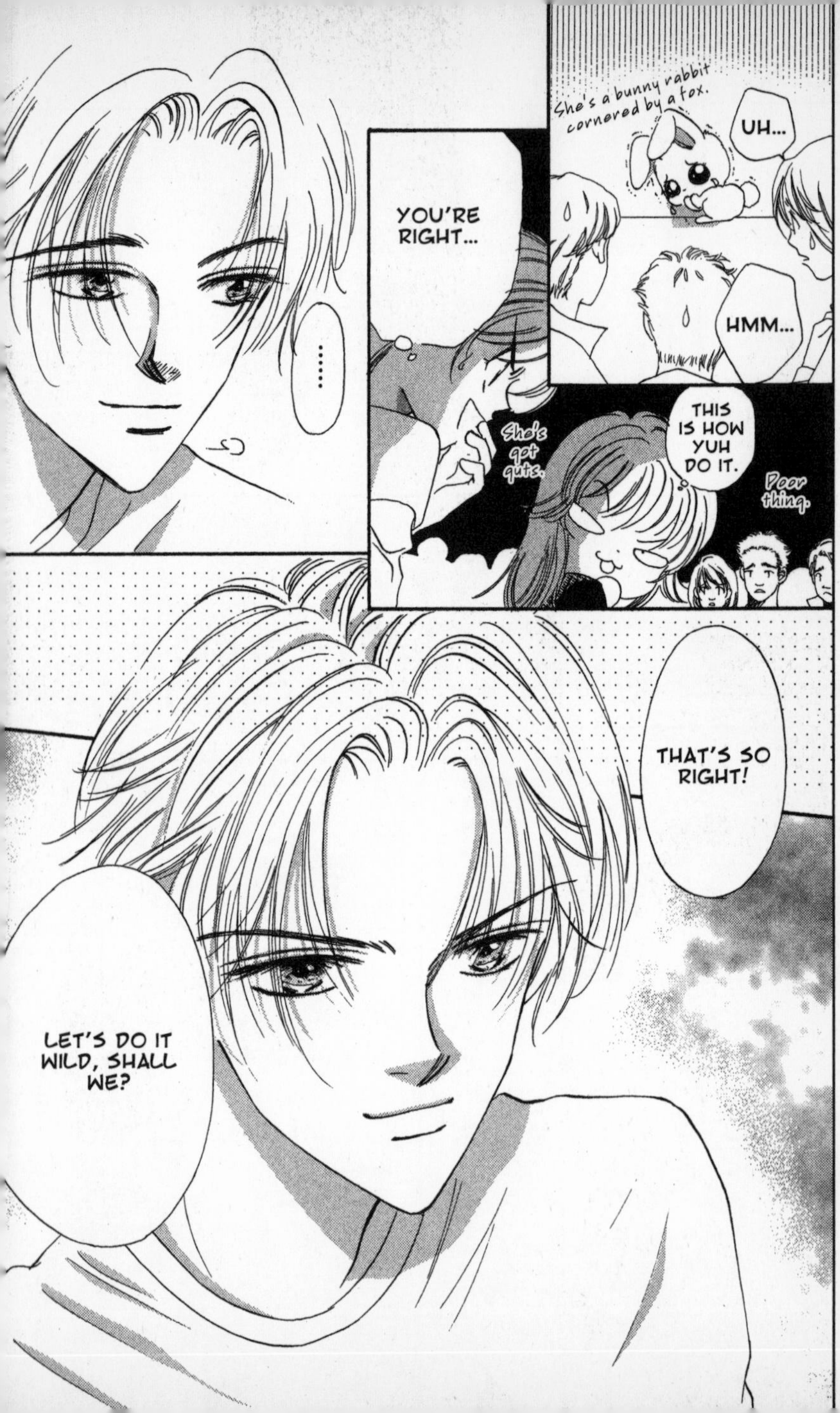
She's a bunny rabbit cornered by a fox.
UH...
HMM...
YOU'RE RIGHT...
THIS IS HOW YUH DO IT.
Poor thing.
She's got guts.
......
THAT'S SO RIGHT!
LET'S DO IT WILD, SHALL WE?

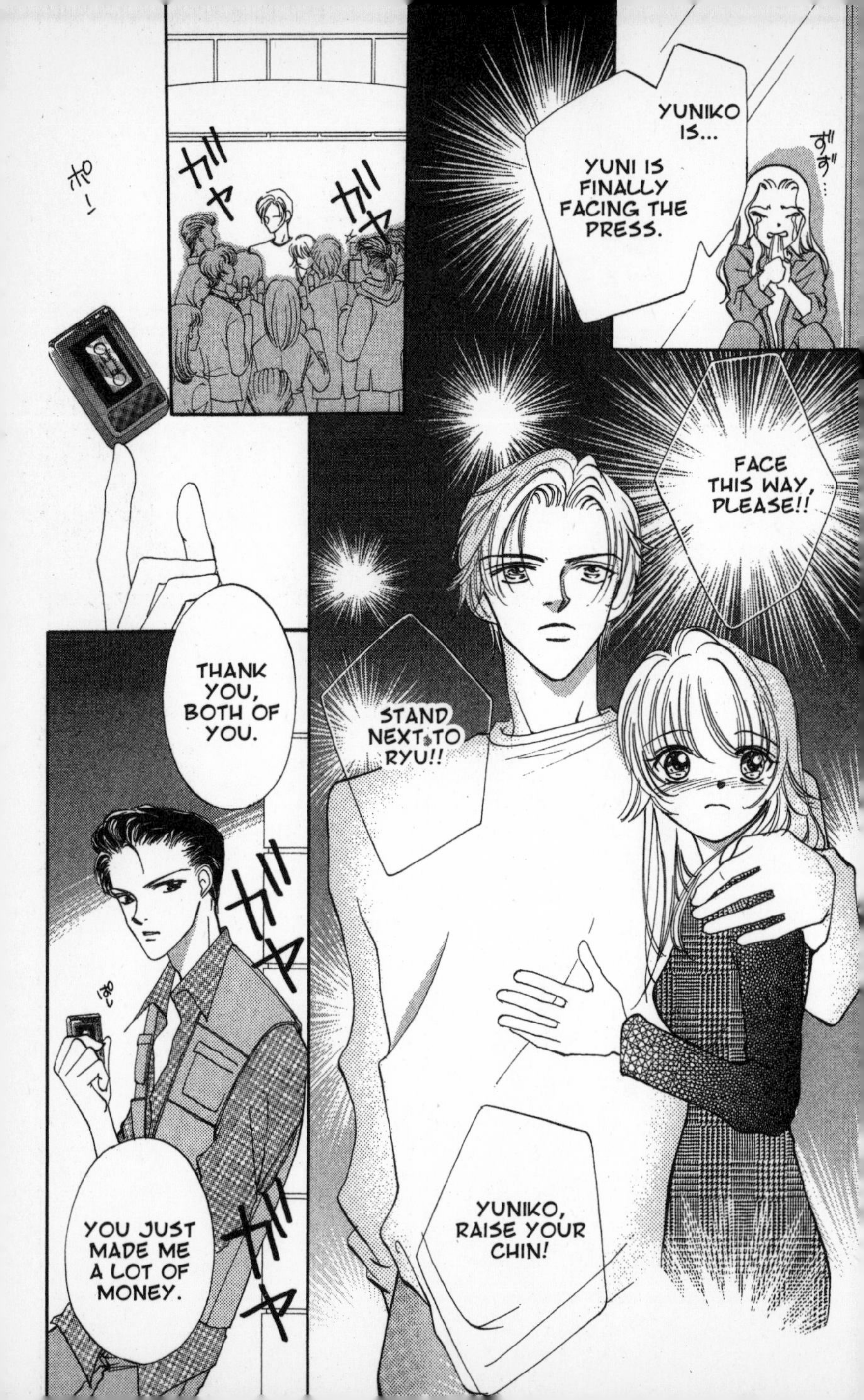
YUNIKO IS...
YUNI IS FINALLY FACING THE PRESS.
ガヤ
ガヤ
ポイ!
FACE THIS WAY, PLEASE!!
STAND NEXT TO RYU!!
YUNIKO, RAISE YOUR CHIN!
THANK YOU, BOTH OF YOU.
ガヤ
YOU JUST MADE ME A LOT OF MONEY.
ガヤ

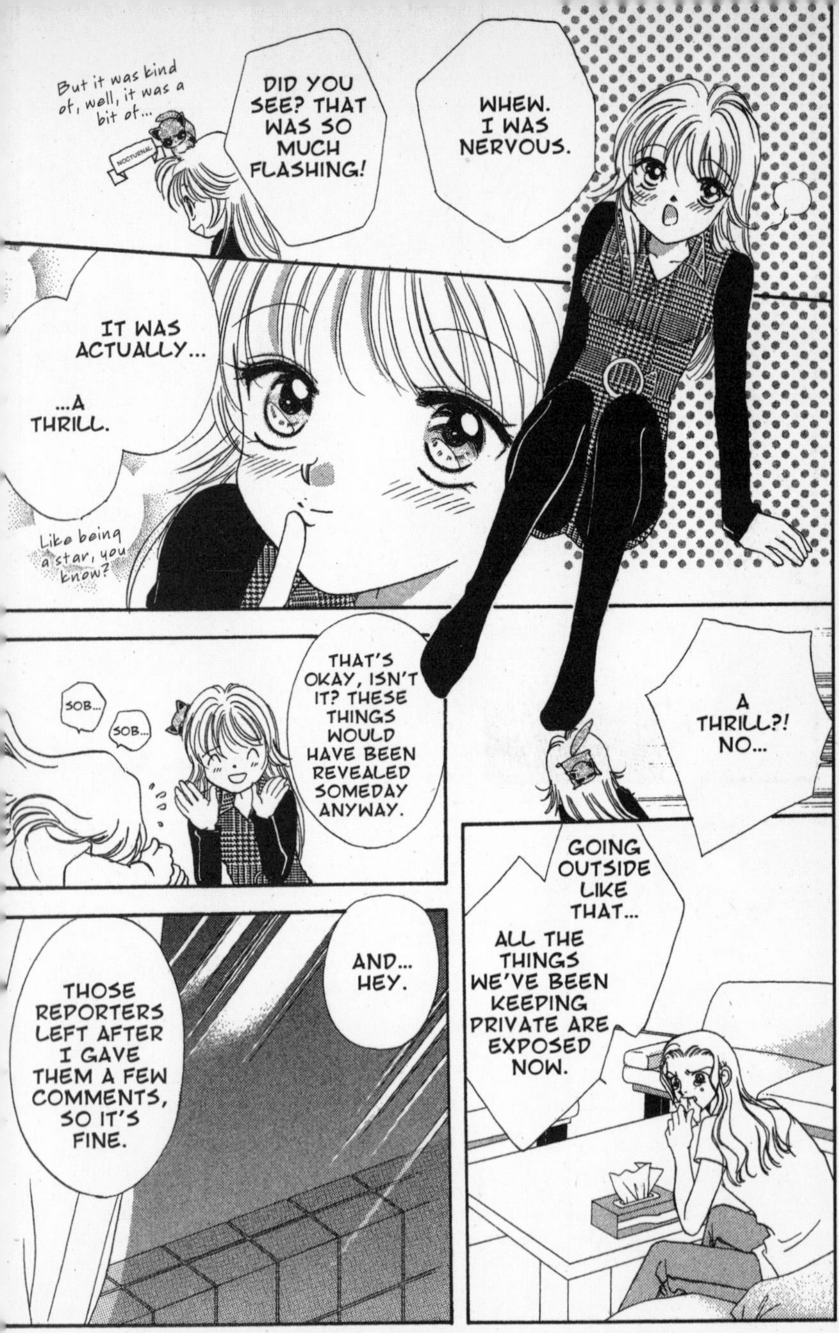
WHEW. I WAS NERVOUS.
DID YOU SEE? THAT WAS SO MUCH FLASHING!
But it was kind of, well, it was a bit of...
NOCTURNAL
IT WAS ACTUALLY...
...A THRILL.
Like being a star, you know?
A THRILL?! NO...
THAT'S OKAY, ISN'T IT? THESE THINGS WOULD HAVE BEEN REVEALED SOMEDAY ANYWAY.
SOB...
SOB...
GOING OUTSIDE LIKE THAT...
ALL THE THINGS WE'VE BEEN KEEPING PRIVATE ARE EXPOSED NOW.
AND... HEY.
THOSE REPORTERS LEFT AFTER I GAVE THEM A FEW COMMENTS, SO IT'S FINE.

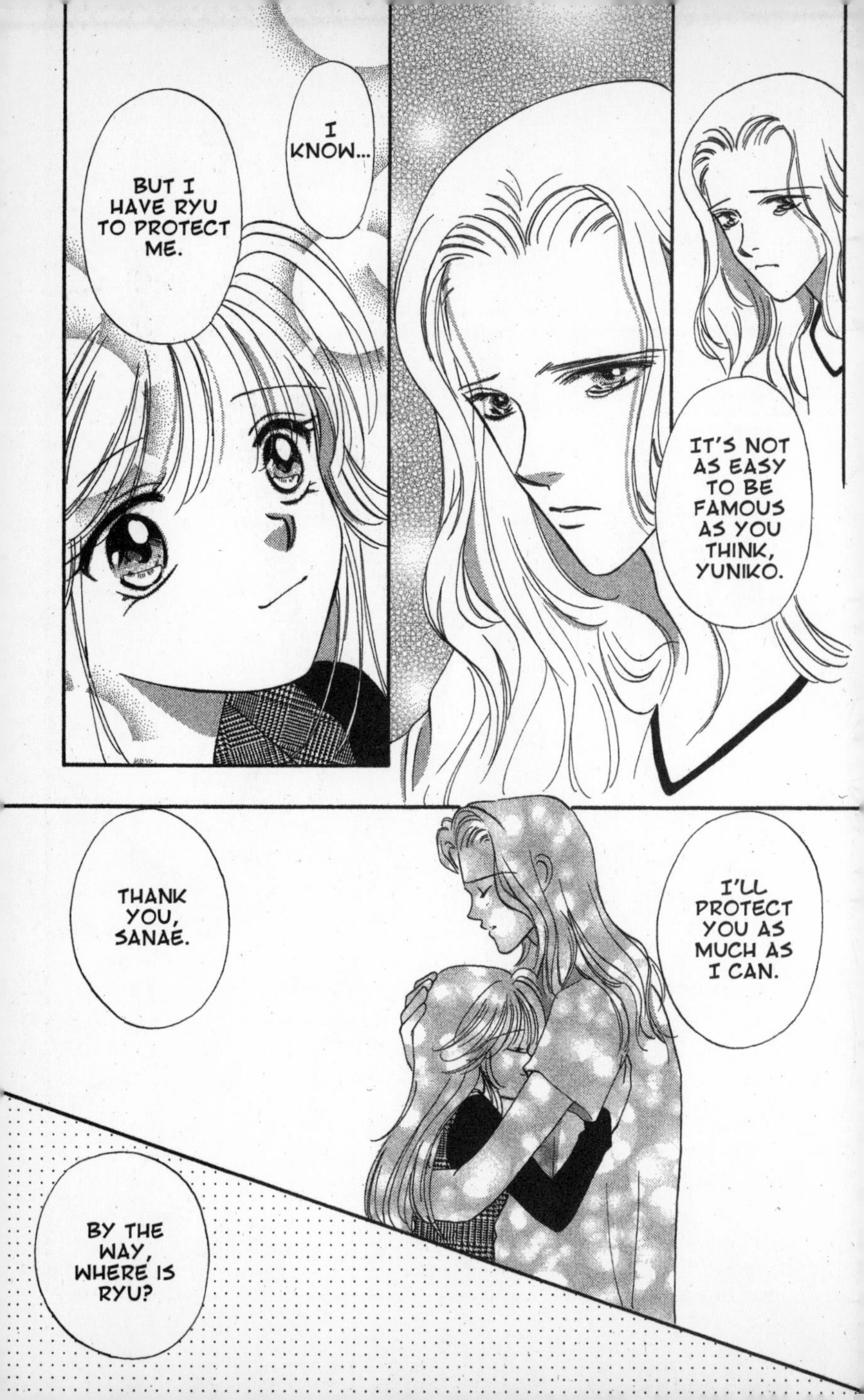
IT'S NOT AS EASY TO BE FAMOUS AS YOU THINK, YUNIKO.
I KNOW...
BUT I HAVE RYU TO PROTECT ME.
I'LL PROTECT YOU AS MUCH AS I CAN.
THANK YOU, SANAE.
BY THE WAY, WHERE IS RYU?

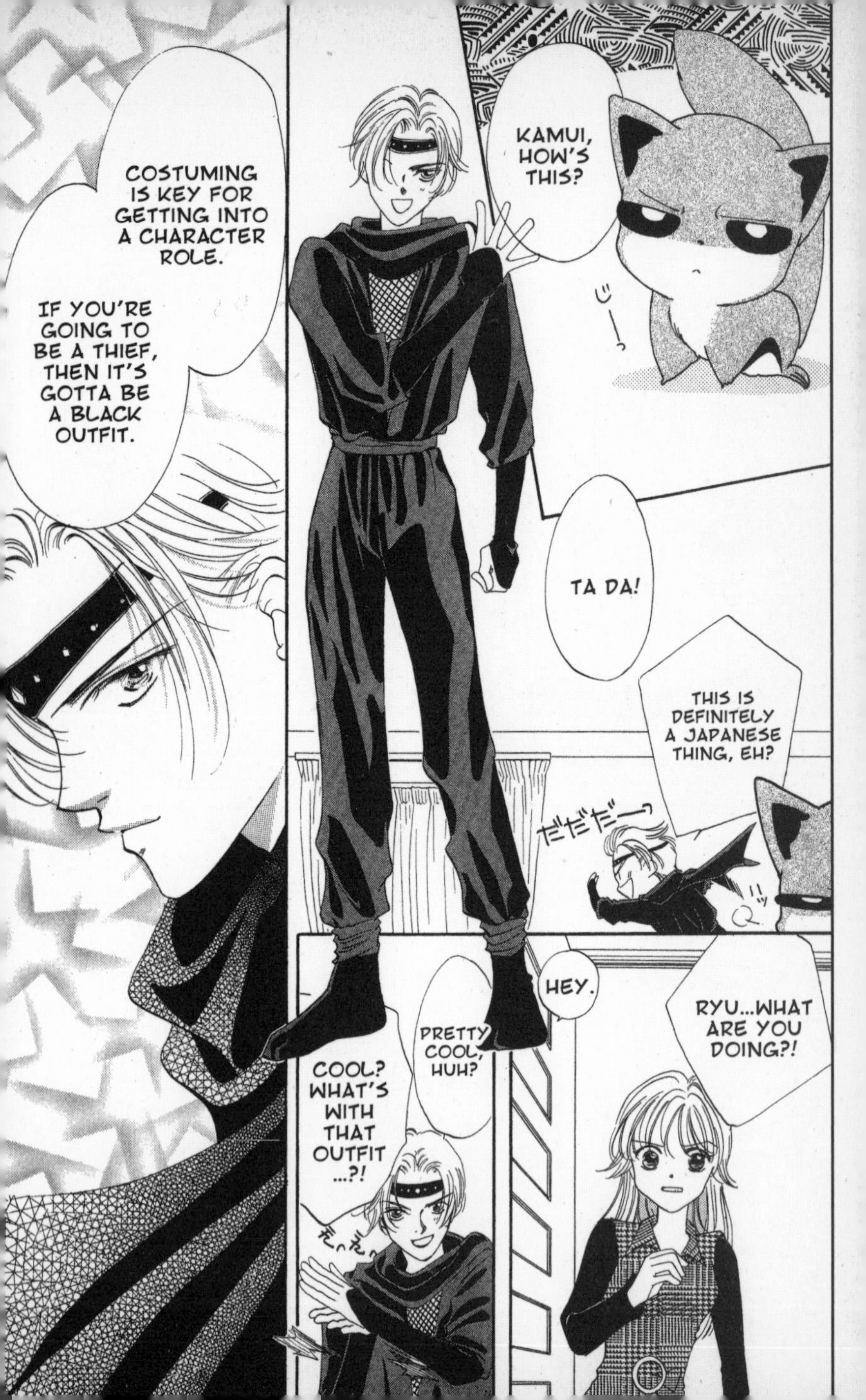
KAMUI, HOW'S THIS?
TA DA!
THIS IS DEFINITELY A JAPANESE THING, EH?
RYU...WHAT ARE YOU DOING?!
HEY.
PRETTY COOL, HUH?
COOL? WHAT'S WITH THAT OUTFIT ...?!
COSTUMING IS KEY FOR GETTING INTO A CHARACTER ROLE.
IF YOU'RE GOING TO BE A THIEF, THEN IT'S GOTTA BE A BLACK OUTFIT.

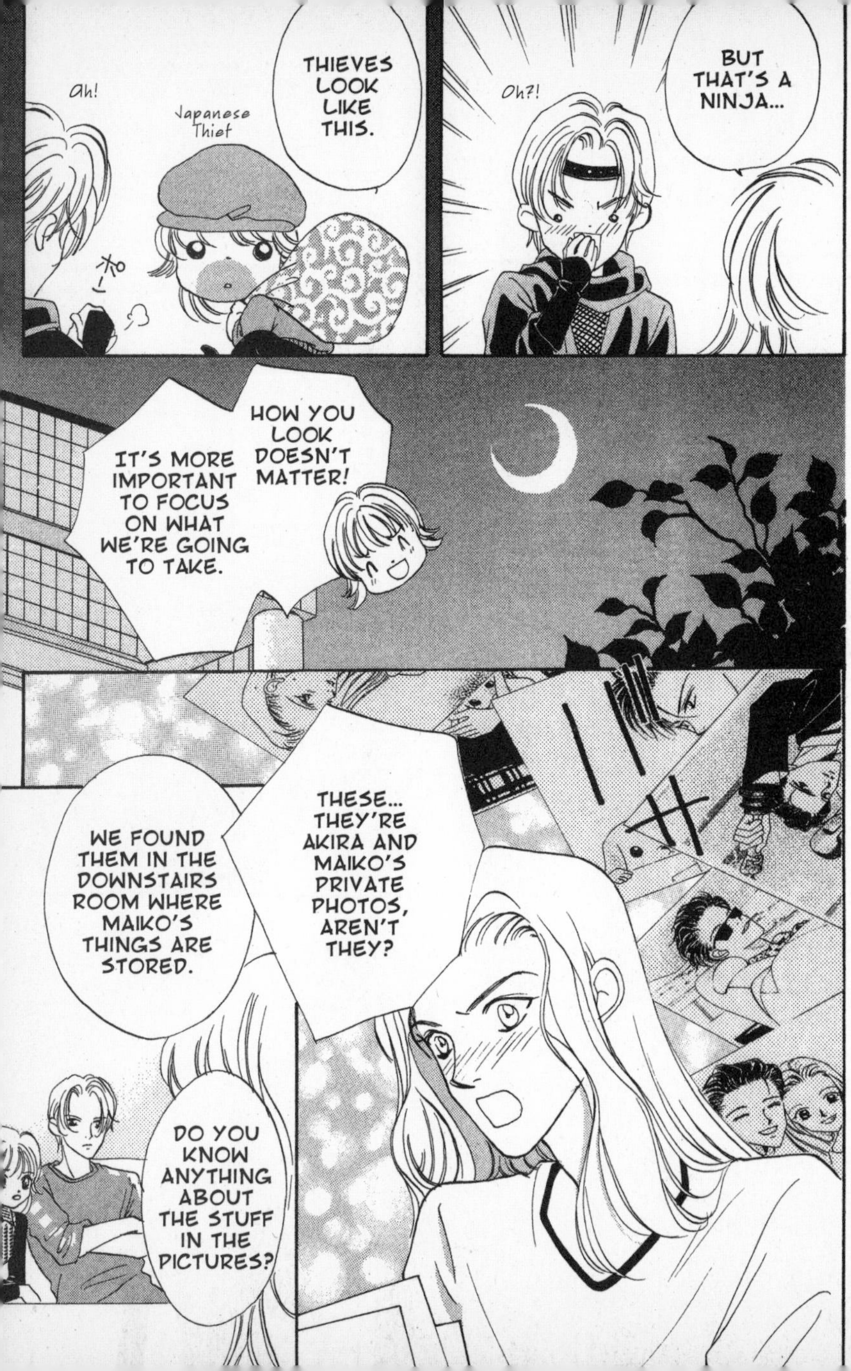
BUT THAT'S A NINJA...
Oh?!
THIEVES LOOK LIKE THIS.
Japanese Thief
Ah!
HOW YOU LOOK DOESN'T MATTER!
IT'S MORE IMPORTANT TO FOCUS ON WHAT WE'RE GOING TO TAKE.
THESE... THEY'RE AKIRA AND MAIKO'S PRIVATE PHOTOS, AREN'T THEY?
WE FOUND THEM IN THE DOWNSTAIRS ROOM WHERE MAIKO'S THINGS ARE STORED.
DO YOU KNOW ANYTHING ABOUT THE STUFF IN THE PICTURES?

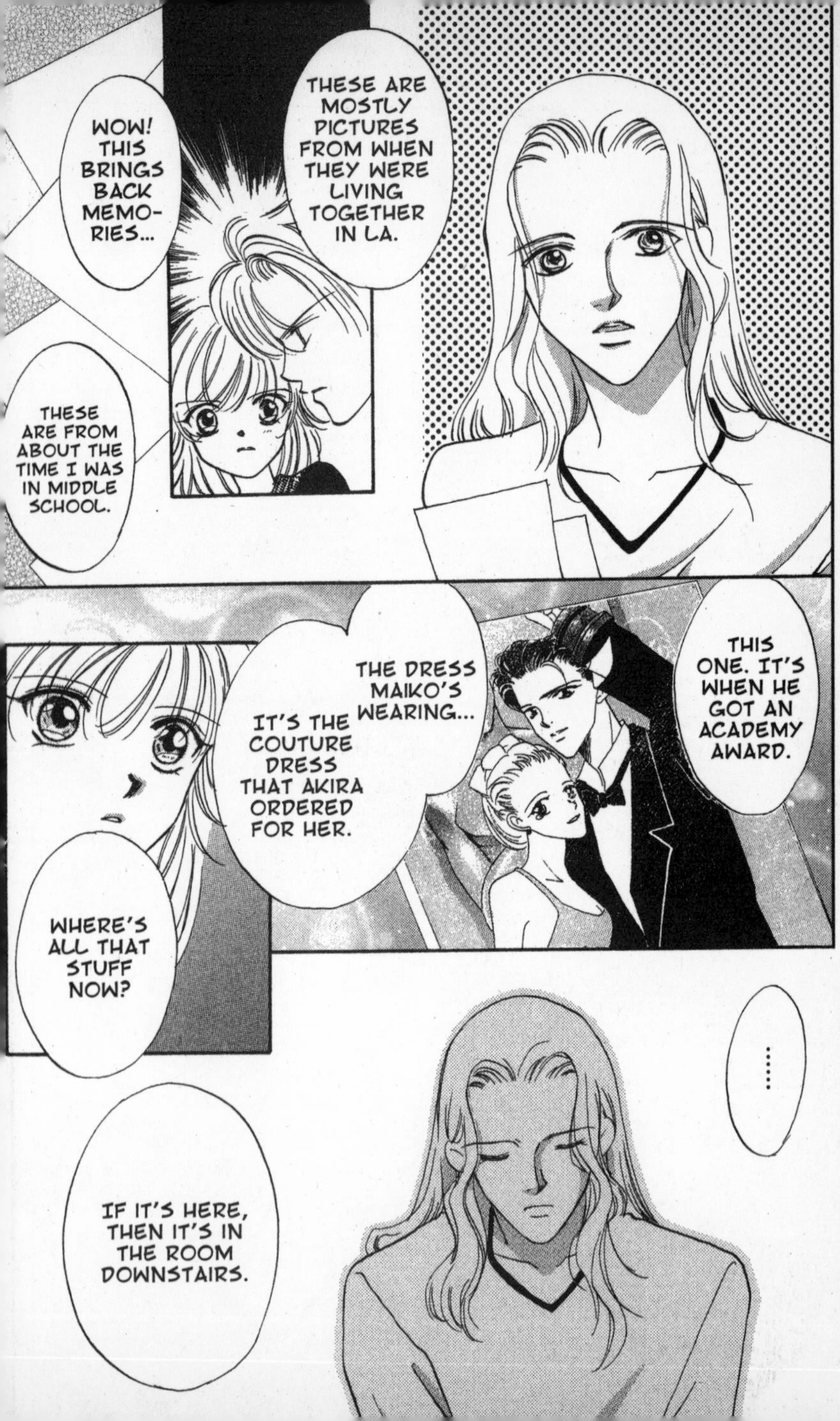
THESE ARE MOSTLY PICTURES FROM WHEN THEY WERE LIVING TOGETHER IN LA.
WOW! THIS BRINGS BACK MEMO-RIES...
THESE ARE FROM ABOUT THE TIME I WAS IN MIDDLE SCHOOL.
THIS ONE. IT'S WHEN HE GOT AN ACADEMY AWARD.
THE DRESS MAIKO'S WEARING...
IT'S THE COUTURE DRESS THAT AKIRA ORDERED FOR HER.
WHERE'S ALL THAT STUFF NOW?
......
IF IT'S HERE, THEN IT'S IN THE ROOM DOWNSTAIRS.

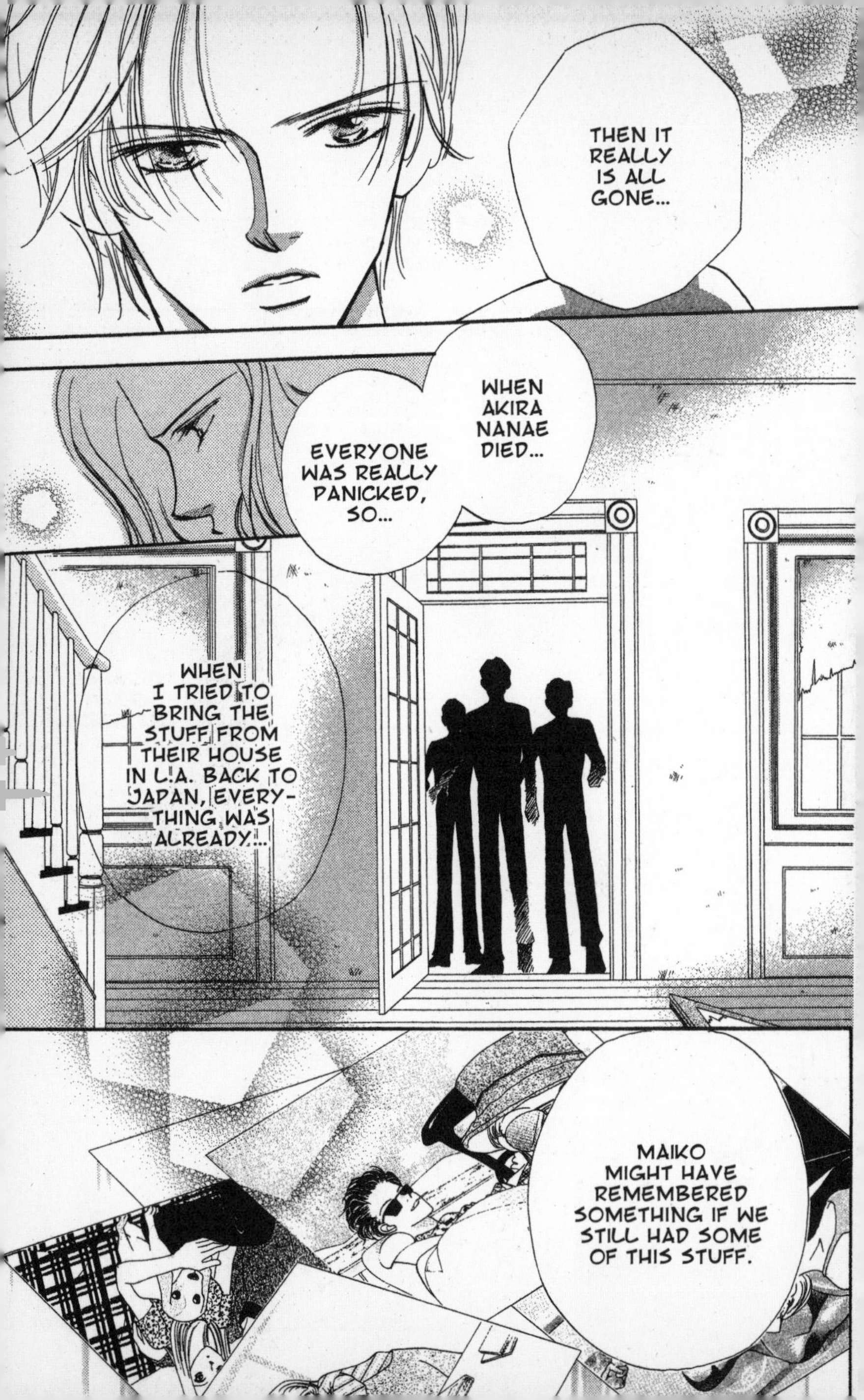
THEN IT REALLY IS ALL GONE...
WHEN AKIRA NANAE DIED...
EVERYONE WAS REALLY PANICKED, SO...
WHEN I TRIED TO BRING THE STUFF FROM THEIR HOUSE IN L.A. BACK TO JAPAN, EVERY-THING WAS ALREADY...
MAIKO MIGHT HAVE REMEMBERED SOMETHING IF WE STILL HAD SOME OF THIS STUFF.

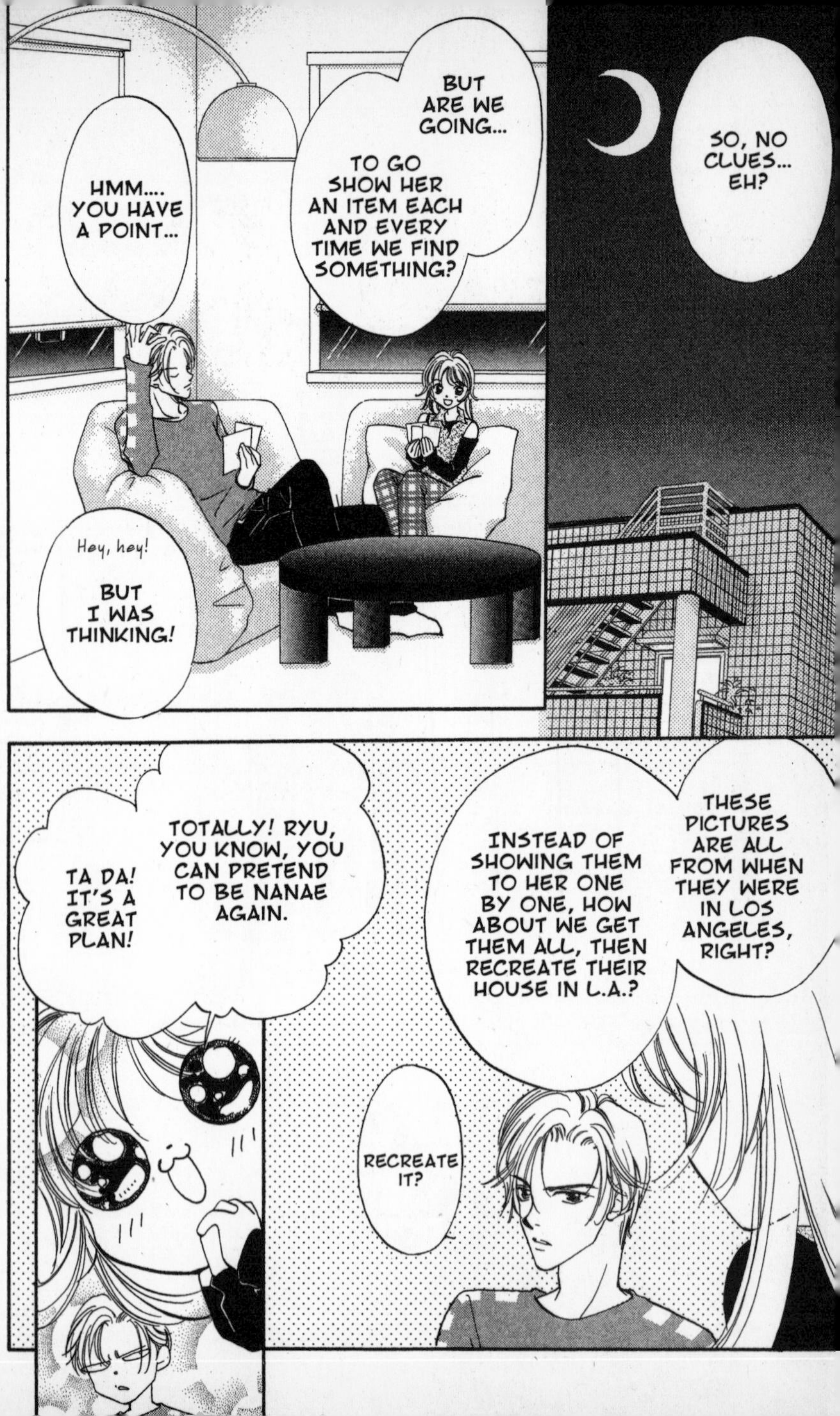
SO, NO CLUES... EH?
BUT ARE WE GOING...
TO GO SHOW HER AN ITEM EACH AND EVERY TIME WE FIND SOMETHING?
HMM.... YOU HAVE A POINT...
Hey, hey!
BUT I WAS THINKING!
THESE PICTURES ARE ALL FROM WHEN THEY WERE IN LOS ANGELES, RIGHT?
INSTEAD OF SHOWING THEM TO HER ONE BY ONE, HOW ABOUT WE GET THEM ALL, THEN RECREATE THEIR HOUSE IN L.A.?
RECREATE IT?
TOTALLY! RYU, YOU KNOW, YOU CAN PRETEND TO BE NANAE AGAIN.
TA DA! IT'S A GREAT PLAN!

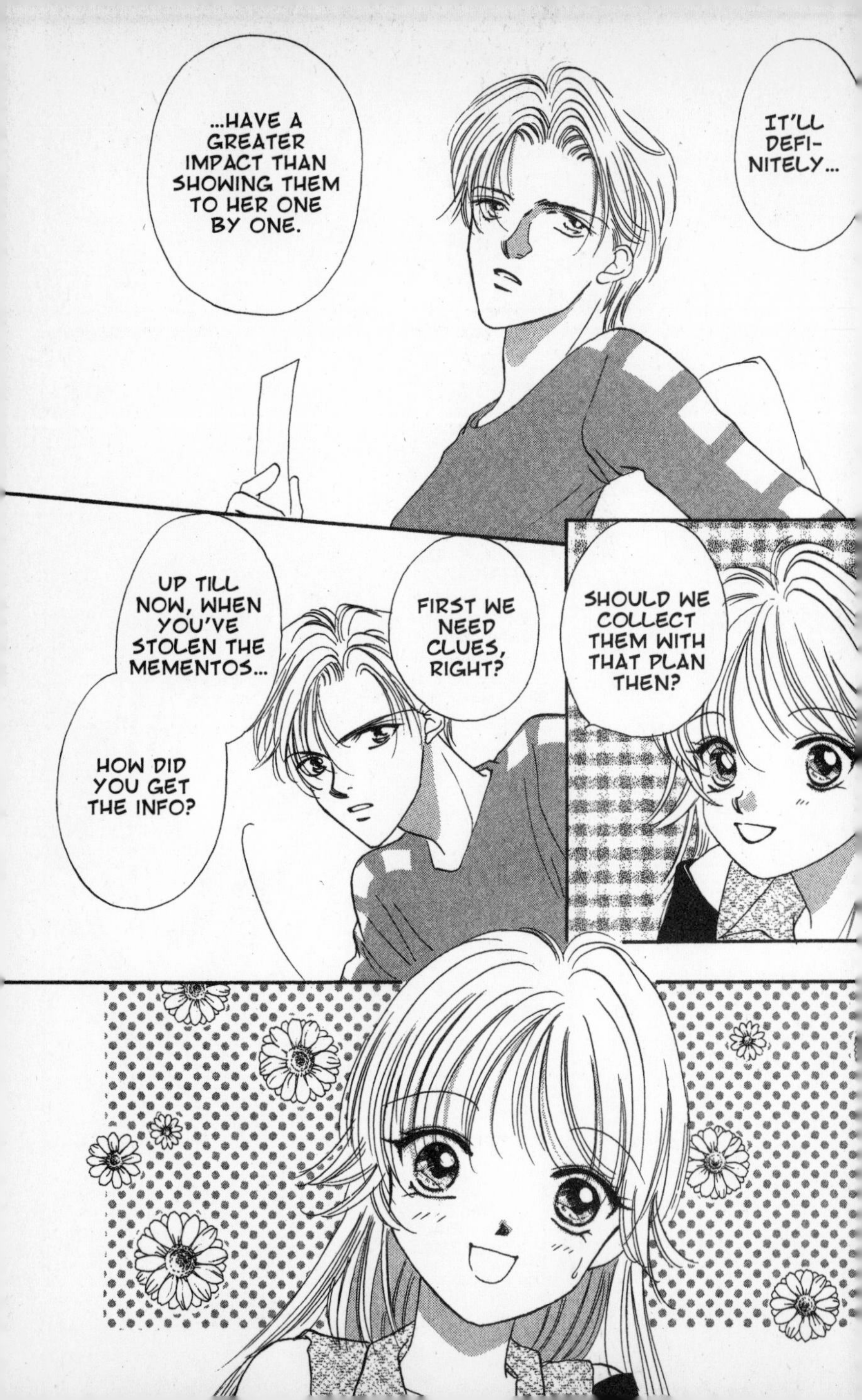
IT'LL DEFI-NITELY...
...HAVE A GREATER IMPACT THAN SHOWING THEM TO HER ONE BY ONE.
SHOULD WE COLLECT THEM WITH THAT PLAN THEN?
FIRST WE NEED CLUES, RIGHT?
UP TILL NOW, WHEN YOU'VE STOLEN THE MEMENTOS...
HOW DID YOU GET THE INFO?

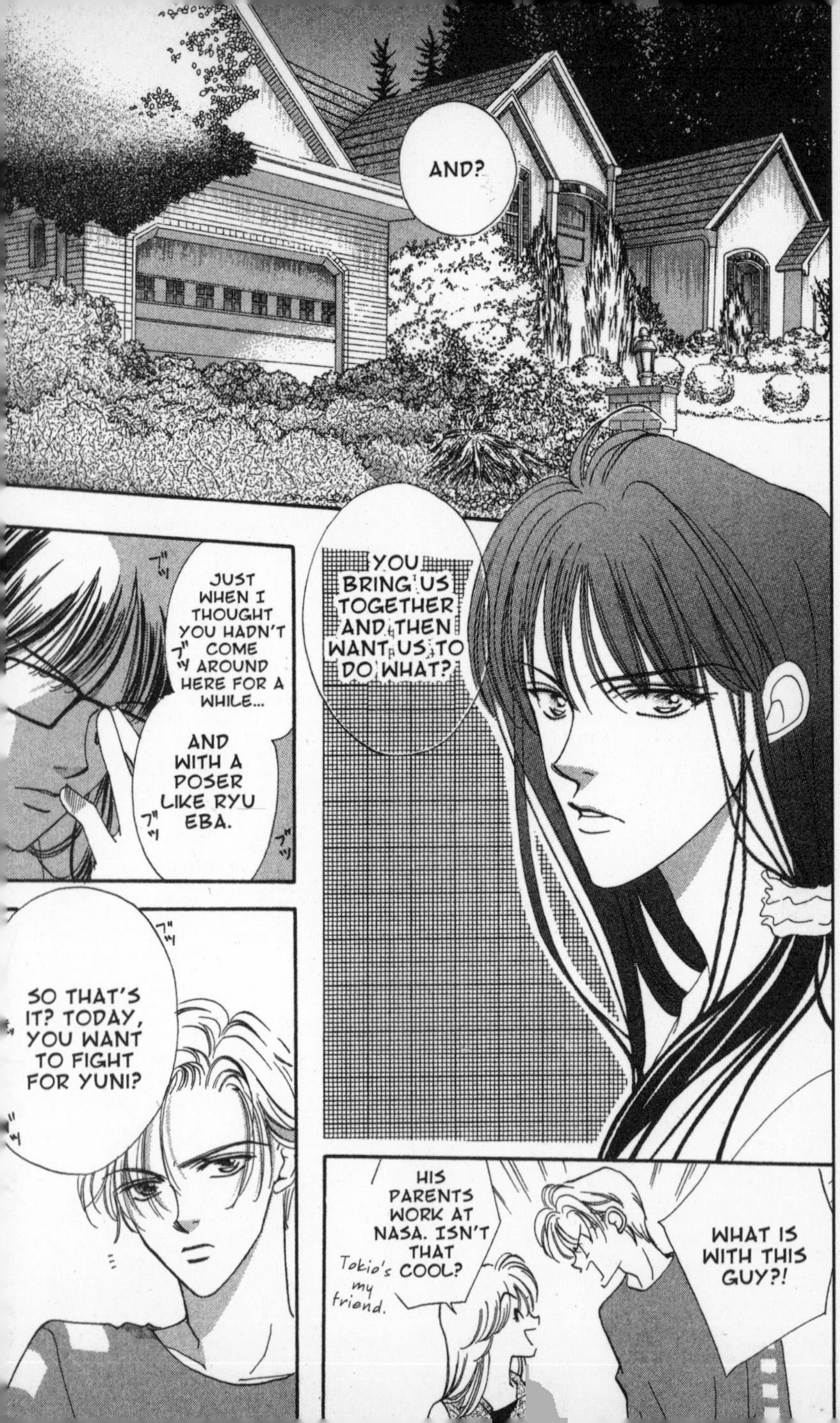
AND?
YOU BRING US TOGETHER AND THEN WANT US TO DO WHAT?
JUST WHEN I THOUGHT YOU HADN'T COME AROUND HERE FOR A WHILE...
AND WITH A POSER LIKE RYU EBA.
SO THAT'S IT? TODAY, YOU WANT TO FIGHT FOR YUNI?
WHAT IS WITH THIS GUY?!
HIS PARENTS WORK AT NASA. ISN'T THAT COOL?
Tokio's my friend.

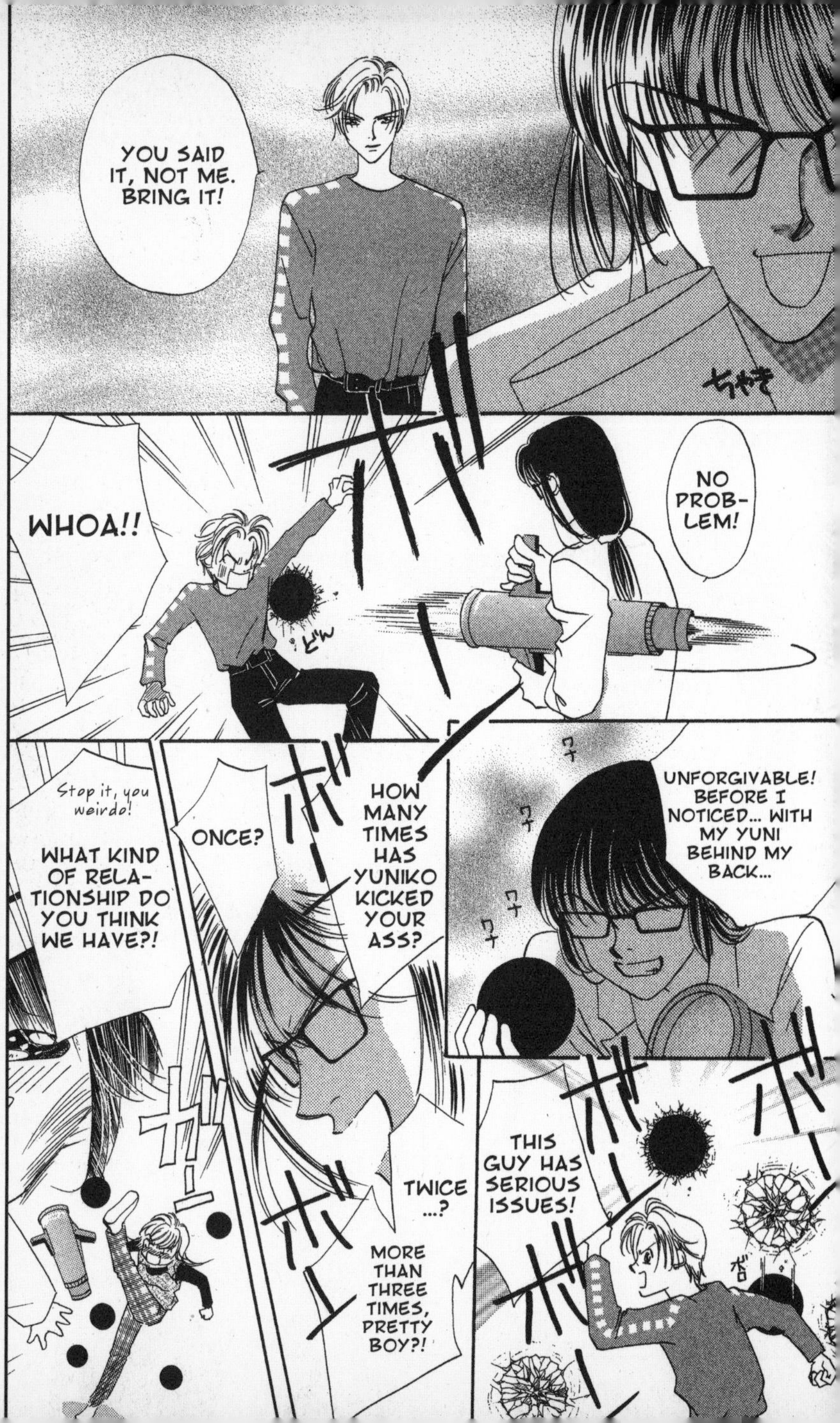
YOU SAID IT, NOT ME. BRING IT!
NO PROBLEM!
WHOA!!
UNFORGIVABLE! BEFORE I NOTICED... WITH MY YUNI BEHIND MY BACK...
THIS GUY HAS SERIOUS ISSUES!
HOW MANY TIMES HAS YUNIKO KICKED YOUR ASS?
ONCE?
TWICE ...?
MORE THAN THREE TIMES, PRETTY BOY?!
WHAT KIND OF RELATIONSHIP DO YOU THINK WE HAVE?!
Stop it, you weirdo!

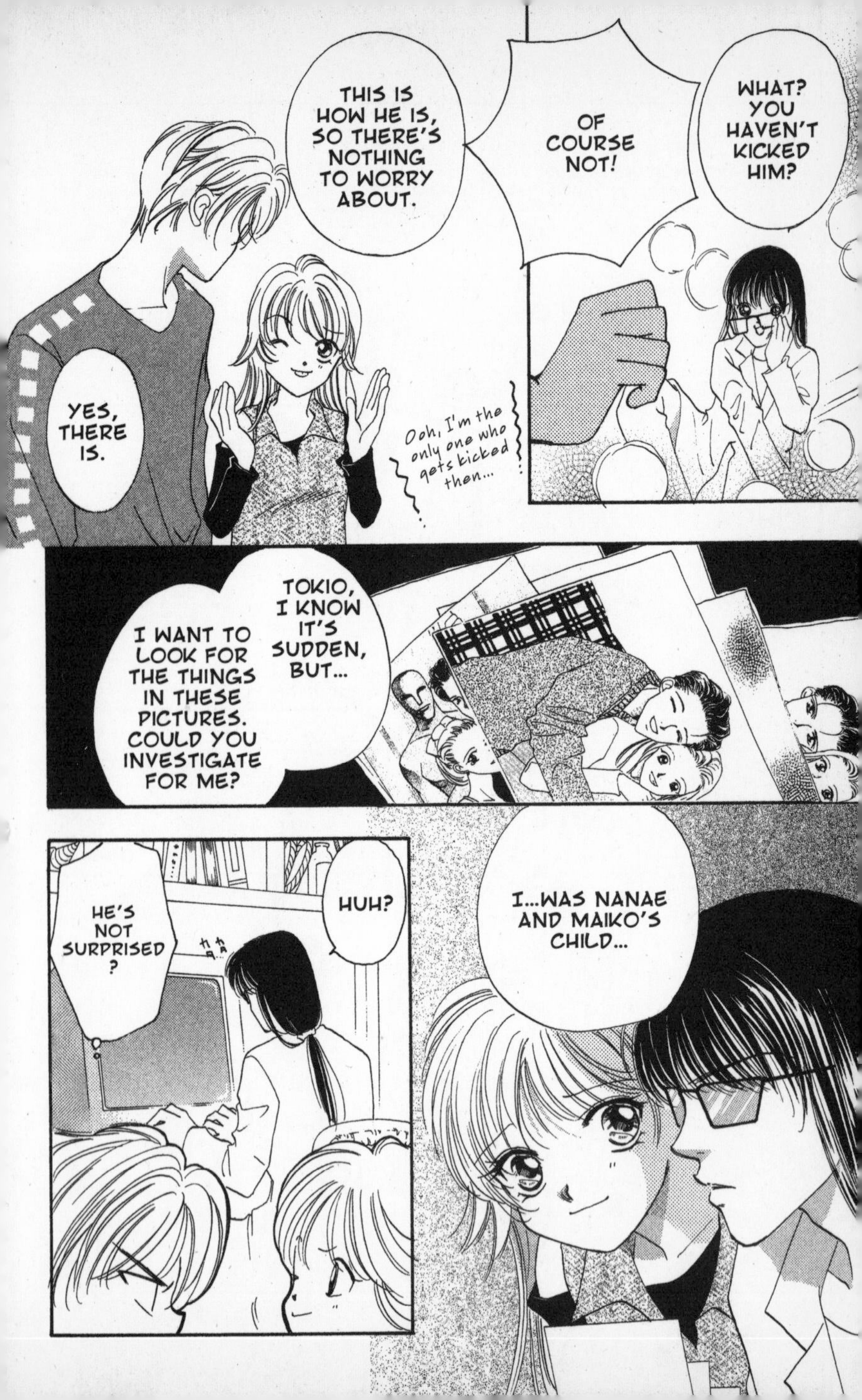
WHAT? YOU HAVEN'T KICKED HIM?
OF COURSE NOT!
THIS IS HOW HE IS, SO THERE'S NOTHING TO WORRY ABOUT.
Ooh, I'm the only one who gets kicked then...
YES, THERE IS.
TOKIO, I KNOW IT'S SUDDEN, BUT...
I WANT TO LOOK FOR THE THINGS IN THESE PICTURES. COULD YOU INVESTIGATE FOR ME?
I...WAS NANAE AND MAIKO'S CHILD...
HUH?
HE'S NOT SURPRISED?

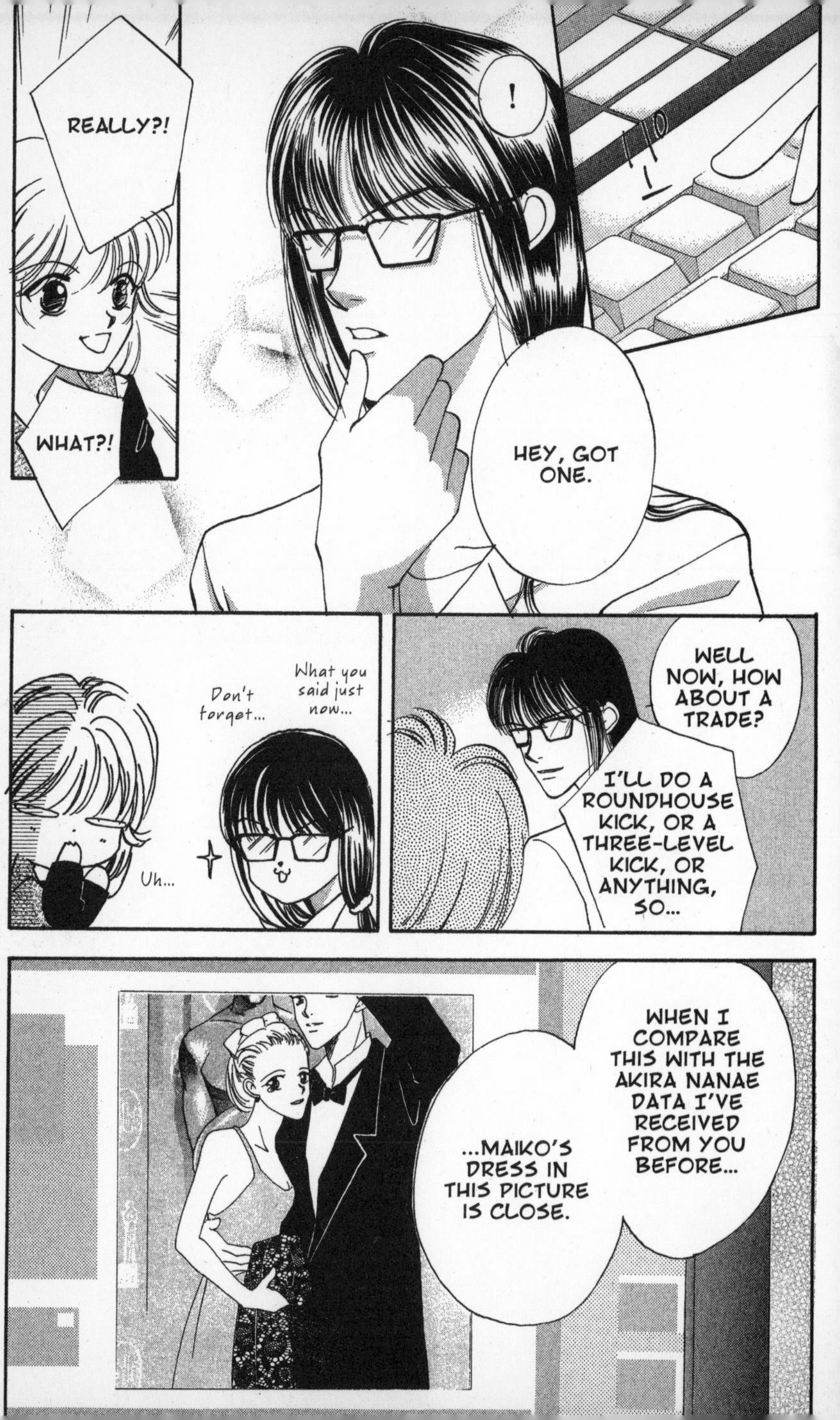
!
HEY, GOT ONE.
REALLY?!
WHAT?!
WELL NOW, HOW ABOUT A TRADE?
I'LL DO A ROUNDHOUSE KICK, OR A THREE-LEVEL KICK, OR ANYTHING, SO...
What you said just now...
Don't forget...
Uh...
WHEN I COMPARE THIS WITH THE AKIRA NANAE DATA I'VE RECEIVED FROM YOU BEFORE...
...MAIKO'S DRESS IN THIS PICTURE IS CLOSE.

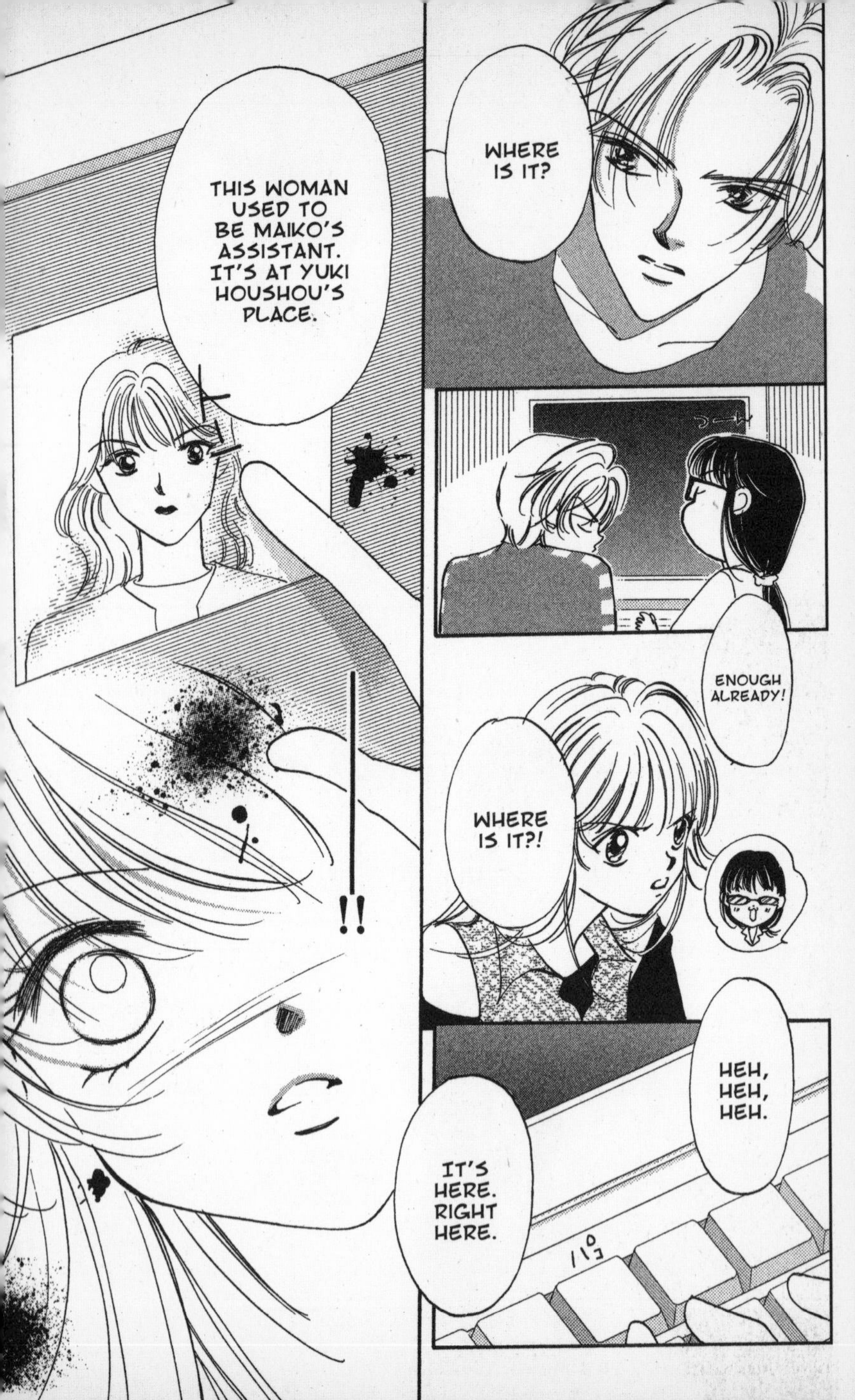
WHERE IS IT?
ENOUGH ALREADY!
WHERE IS IT?!
HEH, HEH, HEH.
IT'S HERE. RIGHT HERE.
THIS WOMAN USED TO BE MAIKO'S ASSISTANT. IT'S AT YUKI HOUSHOU'S PLACE.
!!

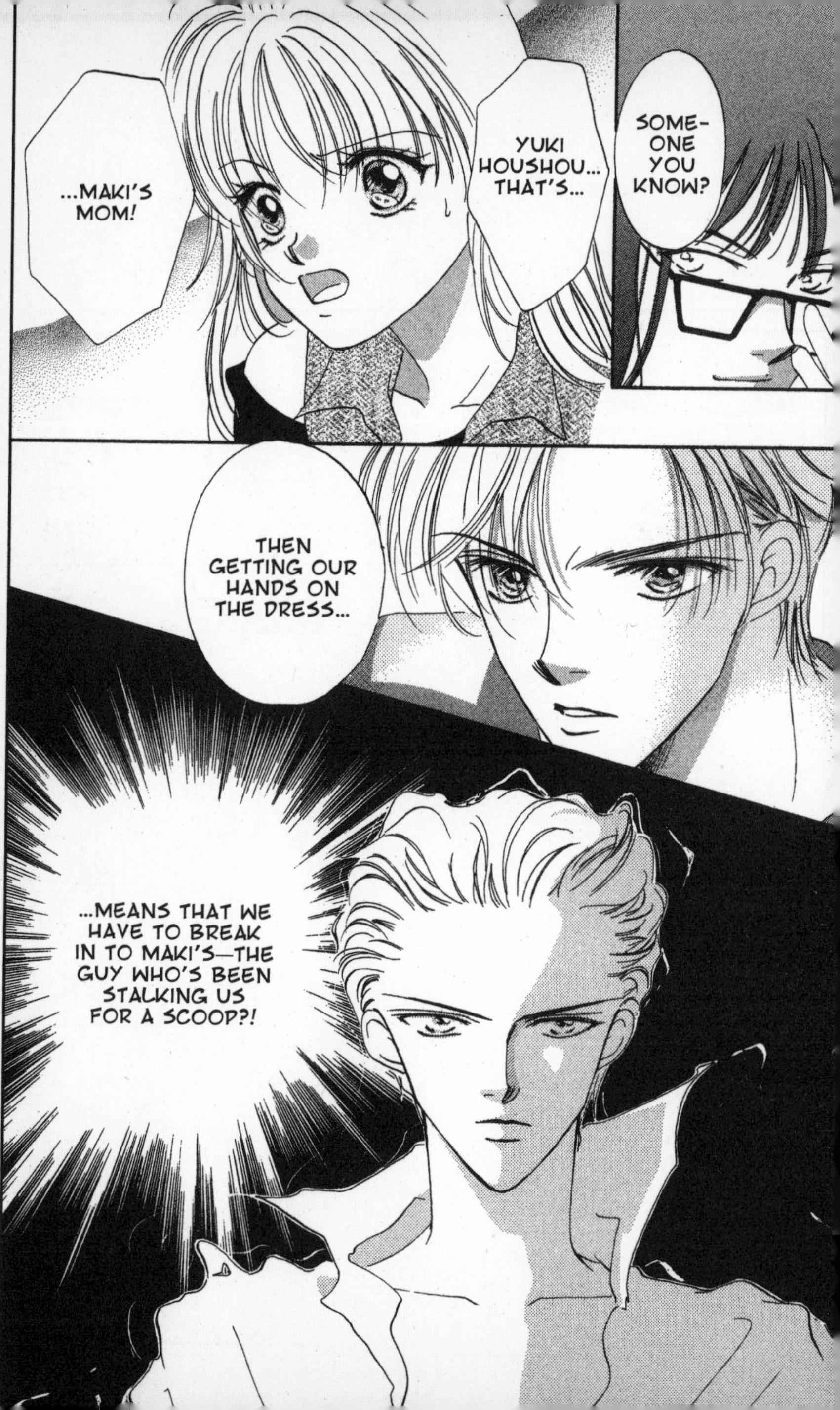
SOME-ONE YOU KNOW?
YUKI HOUSHOU... THAT'S...
...MAKI'S MOM!
THEN GETTING OUR HANDS ON THE DRESS...
...MEANS THAT WE HAVE TO BREAK IN TO MAKI'S—THE GUY WHO'S BEEN STALKING US FOR A SCOOP?!

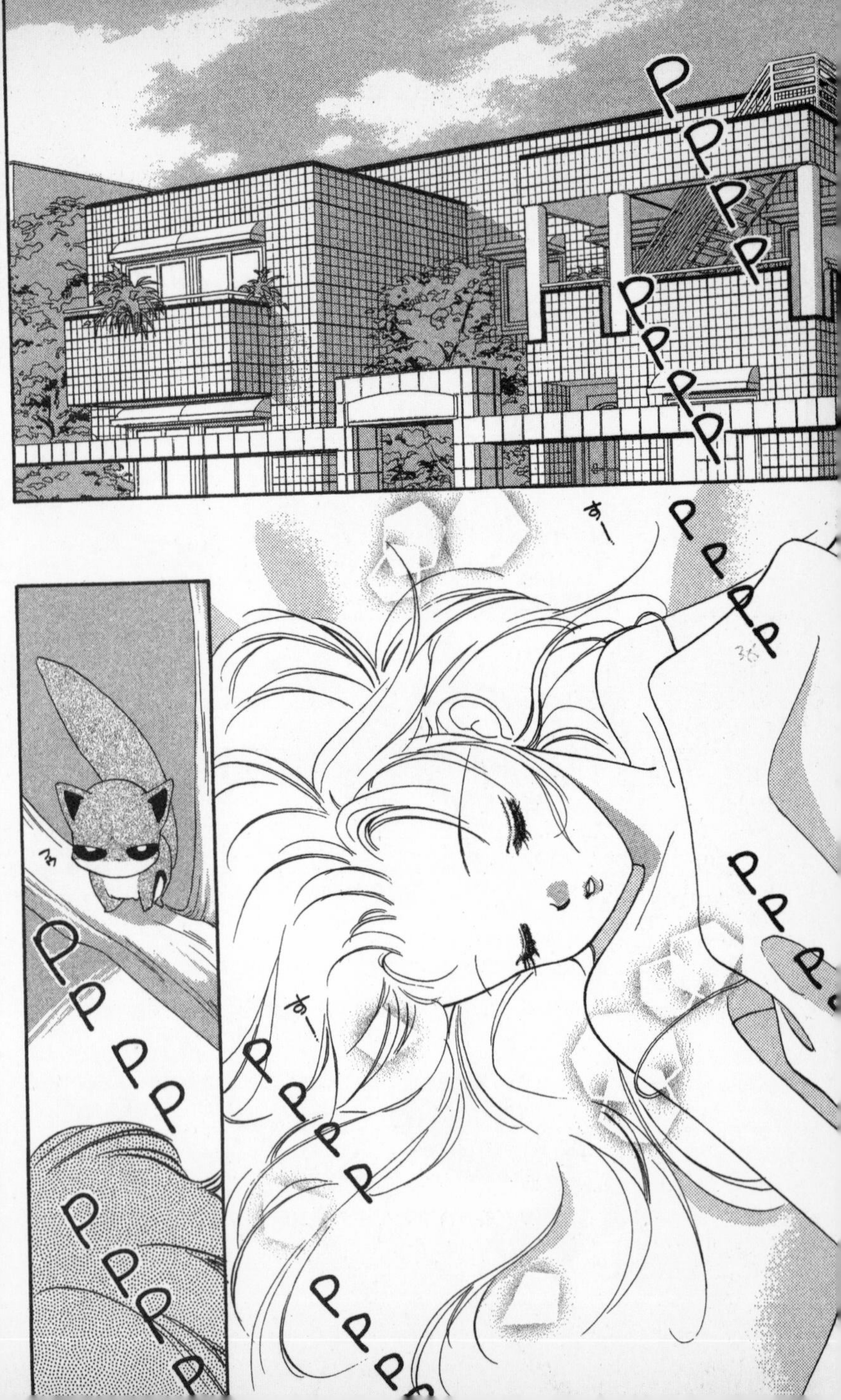
PPPPPPPP
すー
PPPPP
PPP...
すー…
PPPPP
PPPP
ふ
PPPP
PPPP

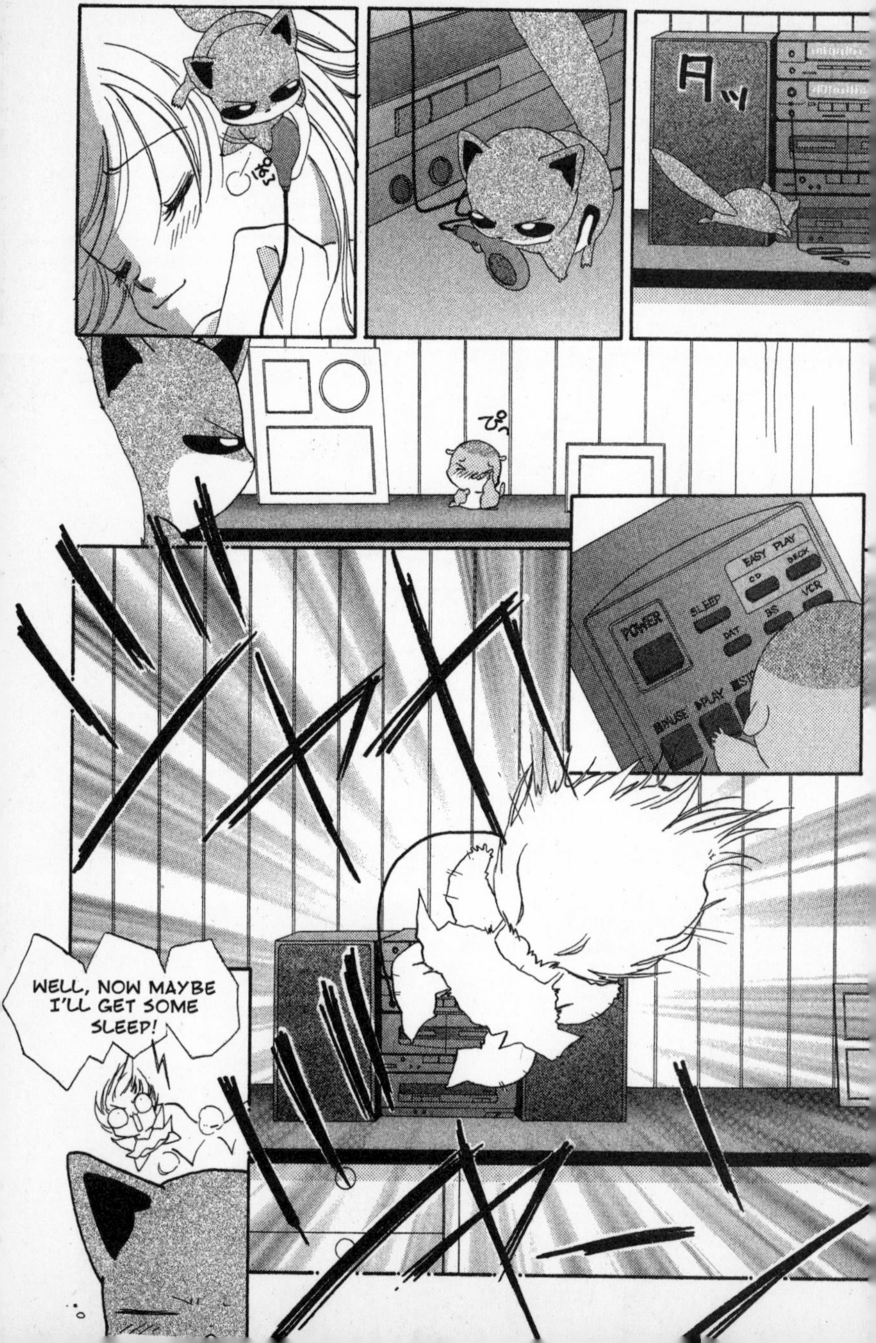
ガッ
EASY PLAY
DECK
CD
VCR
POWER
SLEEP
BS
PAUSE
PLAY
WELL, NOW MAYBE I'LL GET SOME SLEEP!

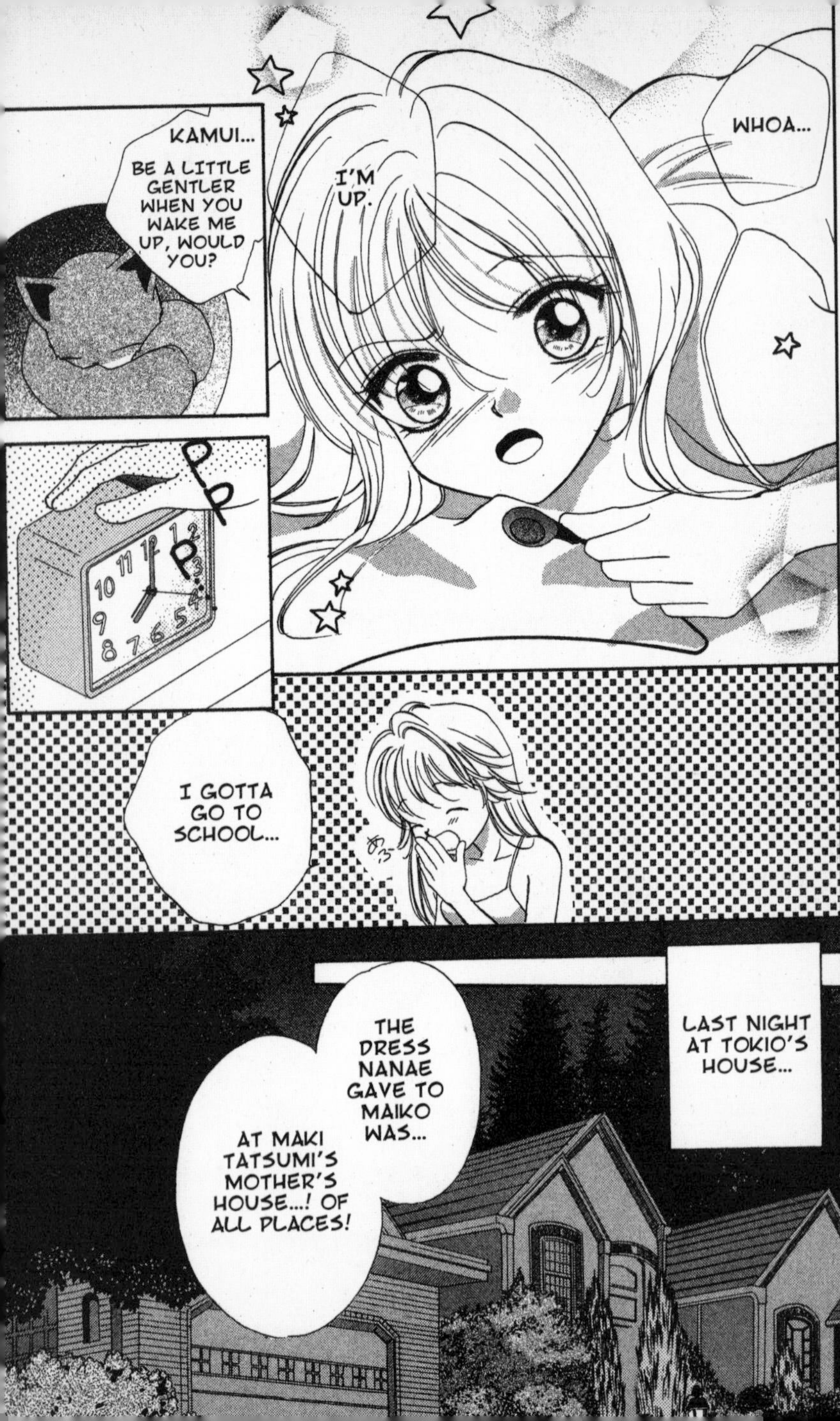
WHOA...
I'M UP.
KAMUI... BE A LITTLE GENTLER WHEN YOU WAKE ME UP, WOULD YOU?
PPP
I GOTTA GO TO SCHOOL...
LAST NIGHT AT TOKIO'S HOUSE...
THE DRESS NANAE GAVE TO MAIKO WAS...
AT MAKI TATSUMI'S MOTHER'S HOUSE...! OF ALL PLACES!

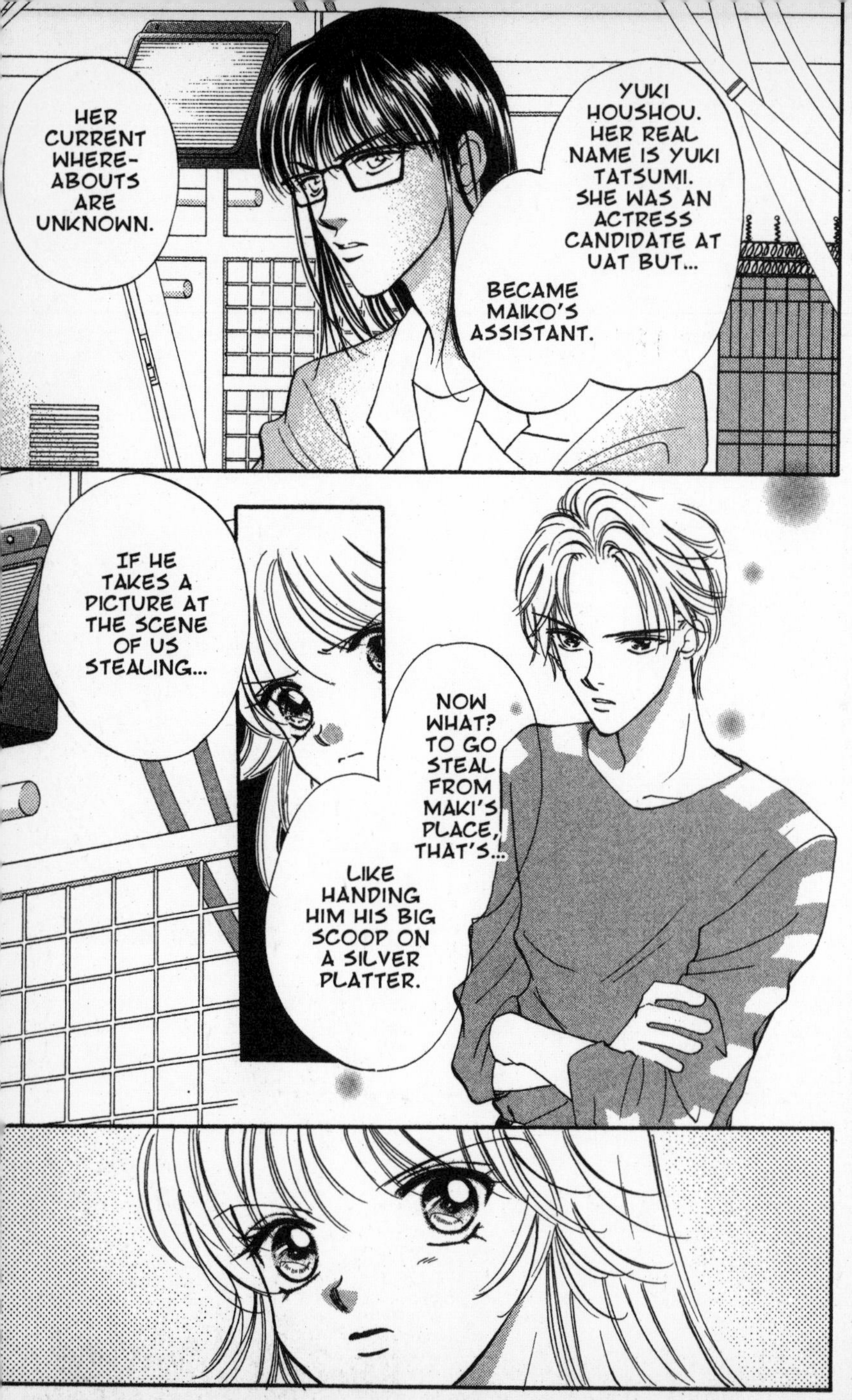
YUKI HOUSHOU. HER REAL NAME IS YUKI TATSUMI. SHE WAS AN ACTRESS CANDIDATE AT UAT BUT...
BECAME MAIKO'S ASSISTANT.
HER CURRENT WHERE-ABOUTS ARE UNKNOWN.
NOW WHAT? TO GO STEAL FROM MAKI'S PLACE, THAT'S...
LIKE HANDING HIM HIS BIG SCOOP ON A SILVER PLATTER.
IF HE TAKES A PICTURE AT THE SCENE OF US STEALING...

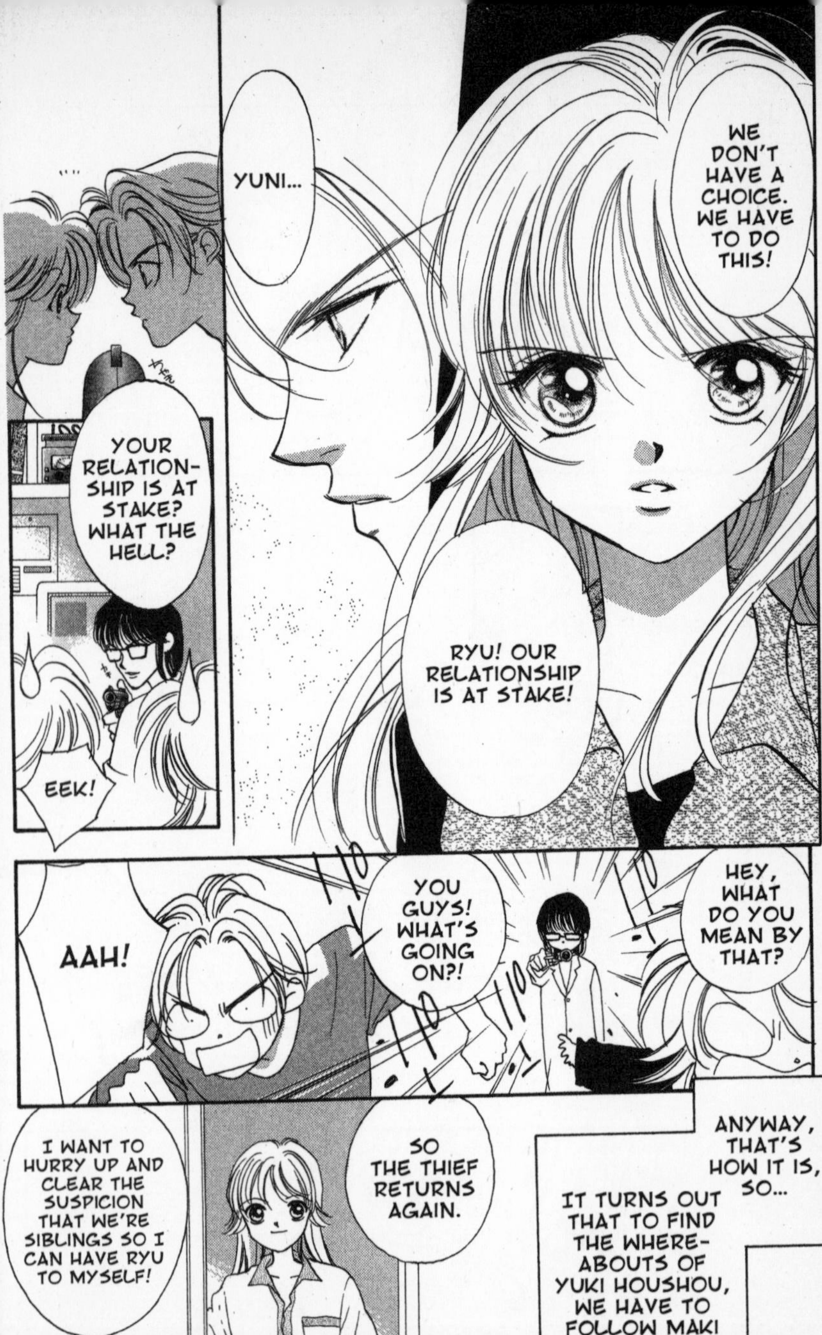
WE DON'T HAVE A CHOICE. WE HAVE TO DO THIS!
YUNI...
RYU! OUR RELATIONSHIP IS AT STAKE!
YOUR RELATIONSHIP IS AT STAKE? WHAT THE HELL?
EEK!
HEY, WHAT DO YOU MEAN BY THAT?
YOU GUYS! WHAT'S GOING ON?!
AAH!
ANYWAY, THAT'S HOW IT IS, SO...
IT TURNS OUT THAT TO FIND THE WHEREABOUTS OF YUKI HOUSHOU, WE HAVE TO FOLLOW MAKI TATSUMI.
SO THE THIEF RETURNS AGAIN.
I WANT TO HURRY UP AND CLEAR THE SUSPICION THAT WE'RE SIBLINGS SO I CAN HAVE RYU TO MYSELF!

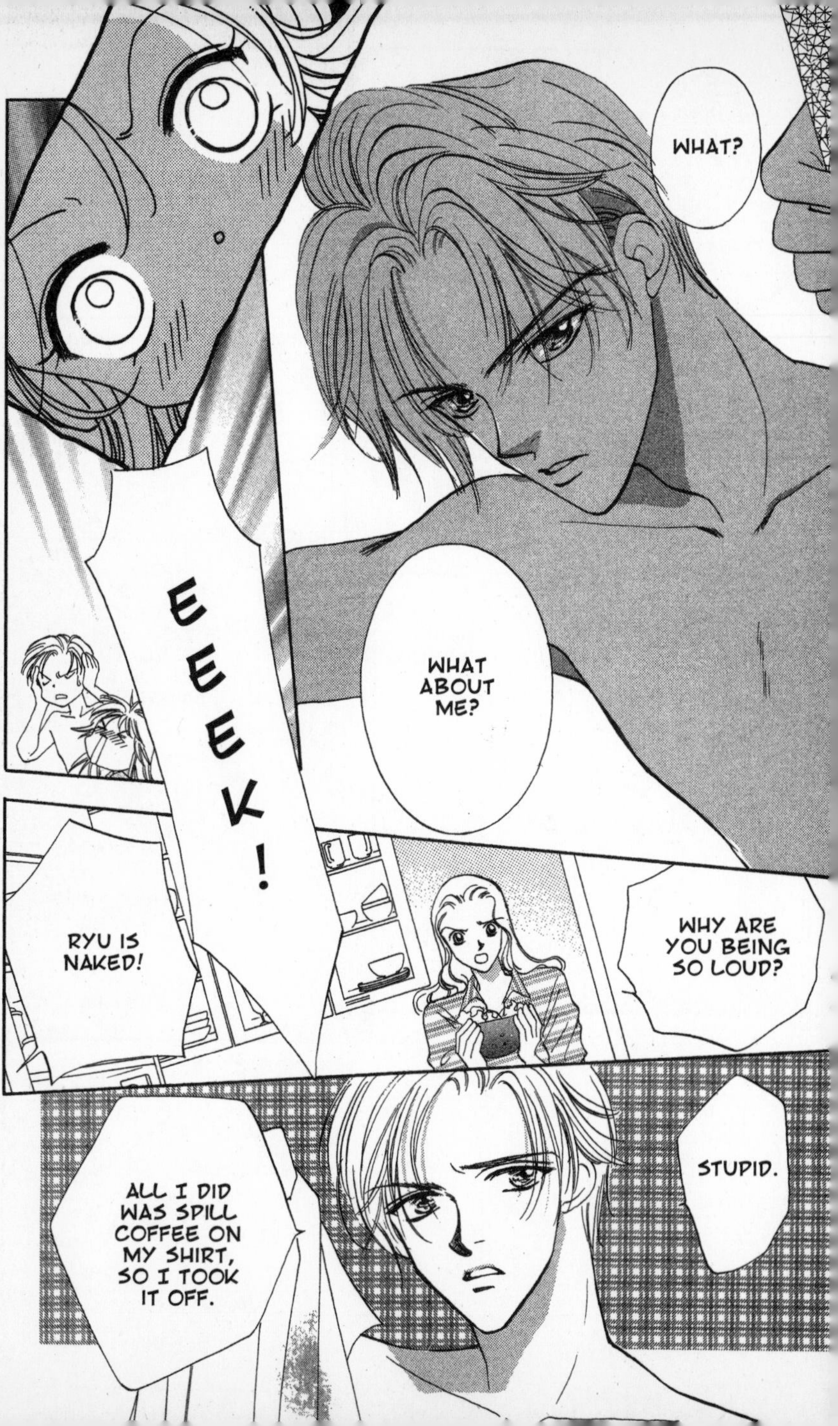
WHAT?
WHAT ABOUT ME?
EEEK!
WHY ARE YOU BEING SO LOUD?
RYU IS NAKED!
STUPID.
ALL I DID WAS SPILL COFFEE ON MY SHIRT, SO I TOOK IT OFF.

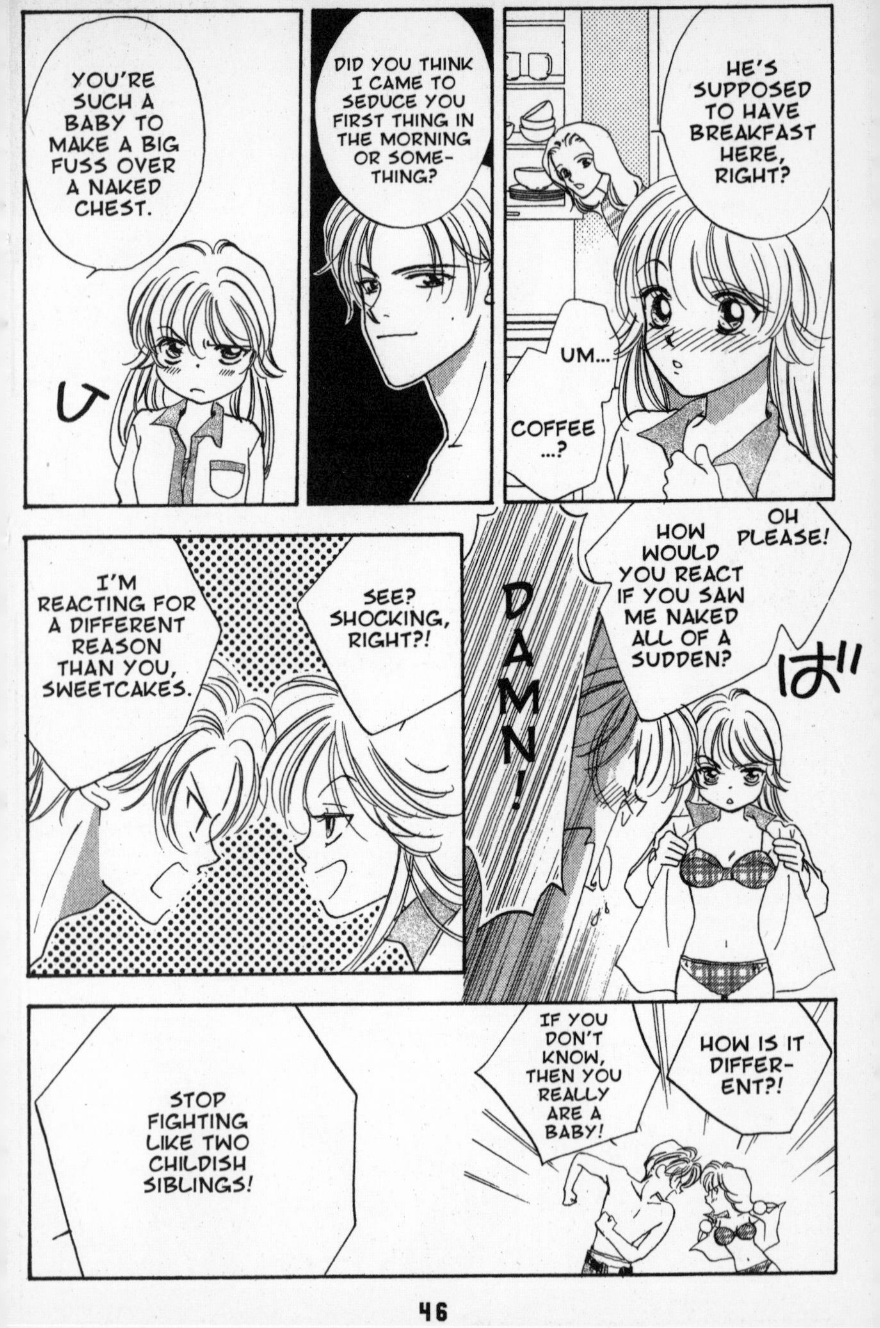

HE'S SUPPOSED TO HAVE BREAKFAST HERE, RIGHT?
UM...
COFFEE ...?
DID YOU THINK I CAME TO SEDUCE YOU FIRST THING IN THE MORNING OR SOME-THING?
YOU'RE SUCH A BABY TO MAKE A BIG FUSS OVER A NAKED CHEST.
ひ
OH PLEASE!
HOW WOULD YOU REACT IF YOU SAW ME NAKED ALL OF A SUDDEN?
ば"
DAMN!
SEE? SHOCKING, RIGHT?!
I'M REACTING FOR A DIFFERENT REASON THAN YOU, SWEETCAKES.
HOW IS IT DIFFER-ENT?!
IF YOU DON'T KNOW, THEN YOU REALLY ARE A BABY!
STOP FIGHTING LIKE TWO CHILDISH SIBLINGS!

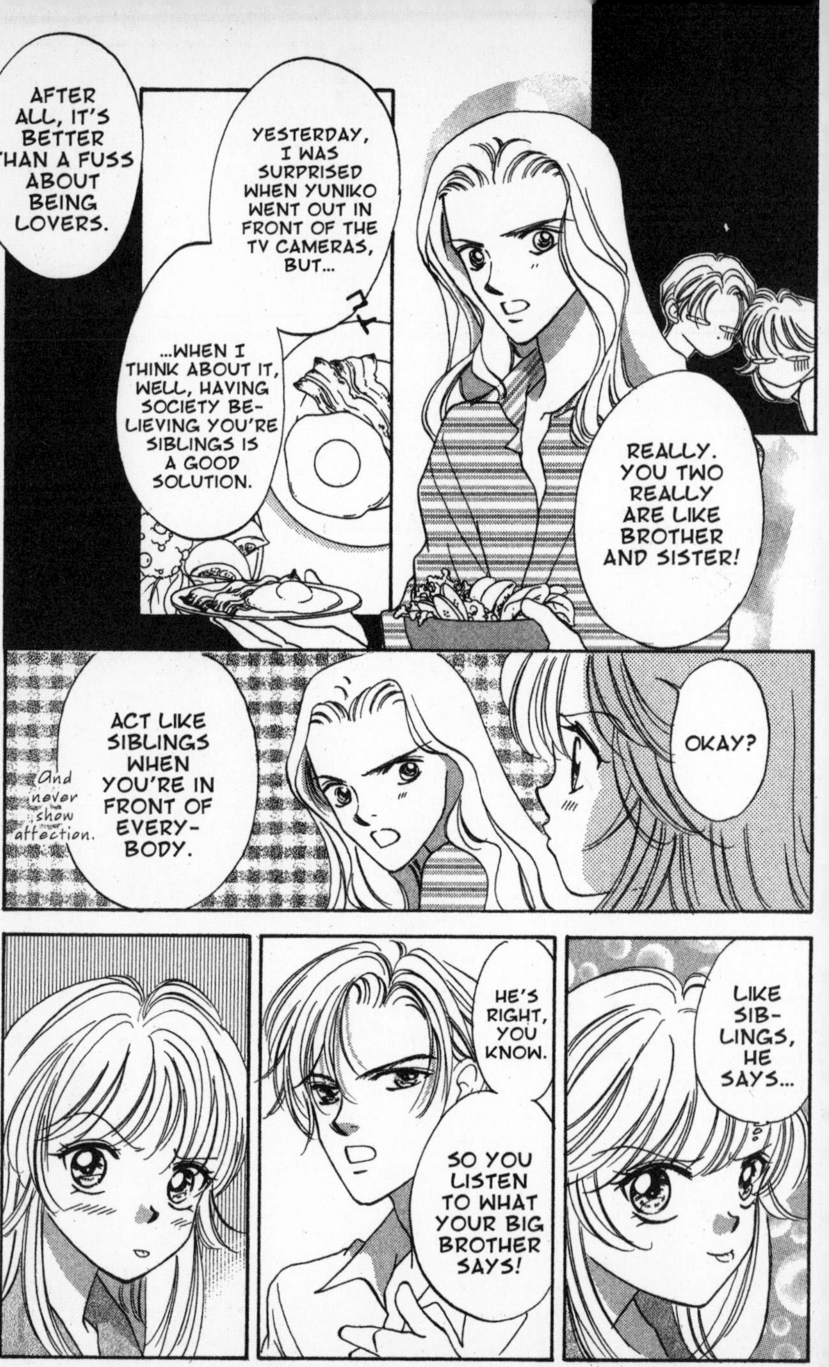
YESTERDAY, I WAS SURPRISED WHEN YUNIKO WENT OUT IN FRONT OF THE TV CAMERAS, BUT...
...WHEN I THINK ABOUT IT, WELL, HAVING SOCIETY BE-LIEVING YOU'RE SIBLINGS IS A GOOD SOLUTION.
AFTER ALL, IT'S BETTER THAN A FUSS ABOUT BEING LOVERS.
REALLY. YOU TWO REALLY ARE LIKE BROTHER AND SISTER!
OKAY?
ACT LIKE SIBLINGS WHEN YOU'RE IN FRONT OF EVERY-BODY.
And never show affection.
LIKE SIB-LINGS, HE SAYS...
HE'S RIGHT, YOU KNOW.
SO YOU LISTEN TO WHAT YOUR BIG BROTHER SAYS!

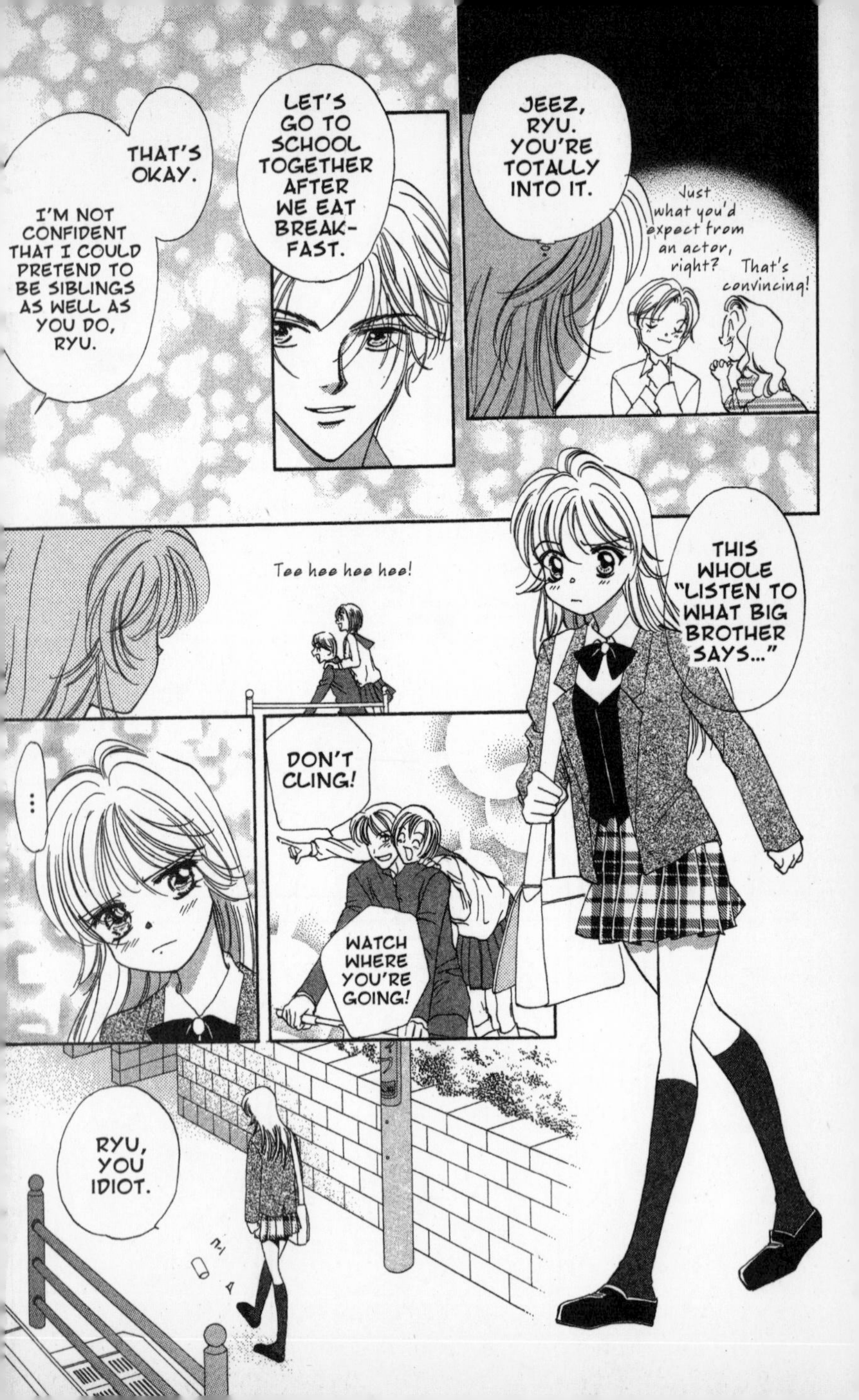
JEEZ, RYU. YOU'RE TOTALLY INTO IT.
Just what you'd expect from an actor, right?
That's convincing!
LET'S GO TO SCHOOL TOGETHER AFTER WE EAT BREAK-FAST.
THAT'S OKAY.
I'M NOT CONFIDENT THAT I COULD PRETEND TO BE SIBLINGS AS WELL AS YOU DO, RYU.
THIS WHOLE "LISTEN TO WHAT BIG BROTHER SAYS..."
Tee hee hee hee!
DON'T CLING!
WATCH WHERE YOU'RE GOING!
...
RYU, YOU IDIOT.

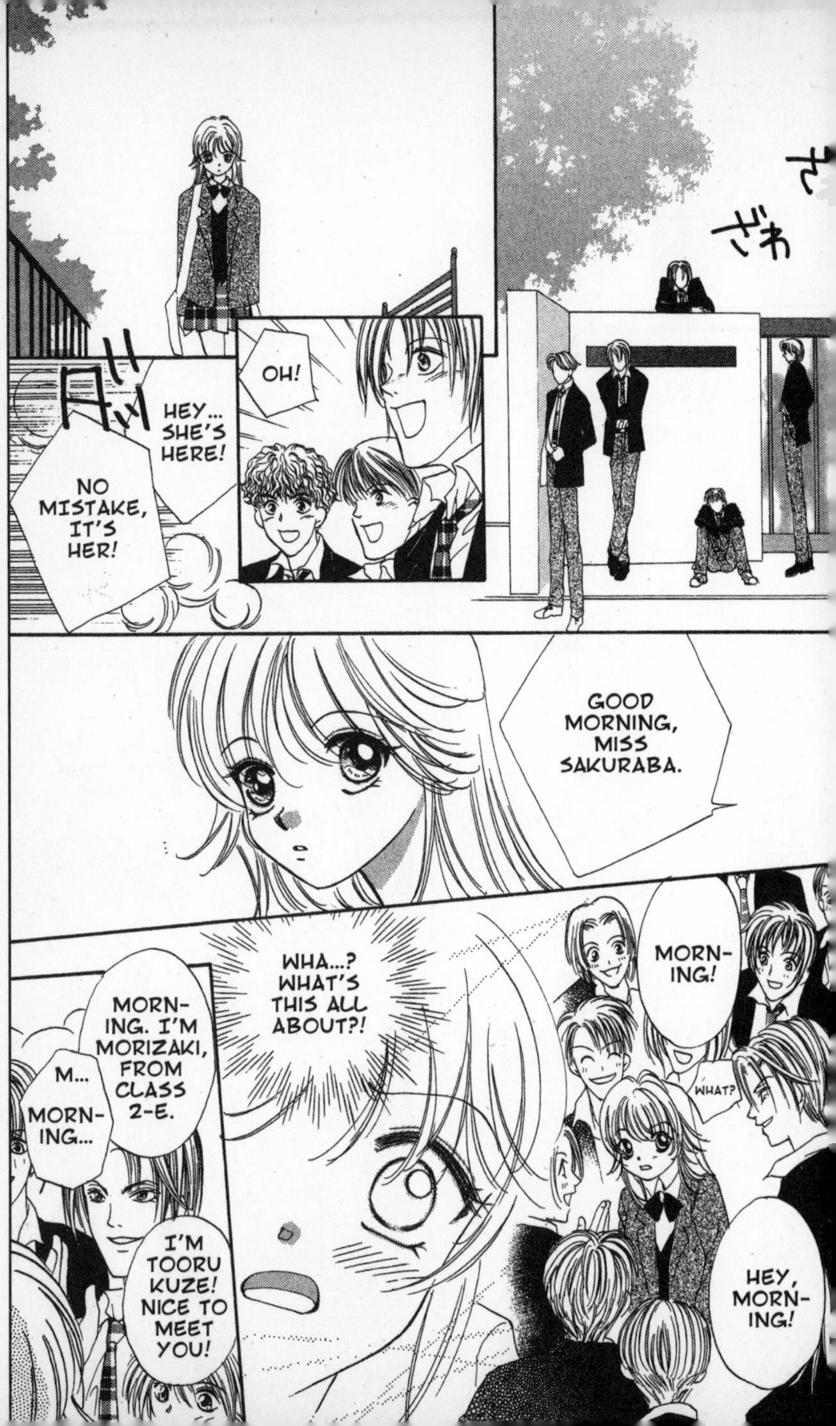
さ
ざわ
OH!
HEY... SHE'S HERE!
NO MISTAKE, IT'S HER!
GOOD MORNING, MISS SAKURABA.
MORN-ING!
WHAT?
HEY, MORN-ING!
WHA...? WHAT'S THIS ALL ABOUT?!
MORN-ING. I'M MORIZAKI, FROM CLASS 2-E.
M... MORN-ING...
I'M TOORU KUZE! NICE TO MEET YOU!

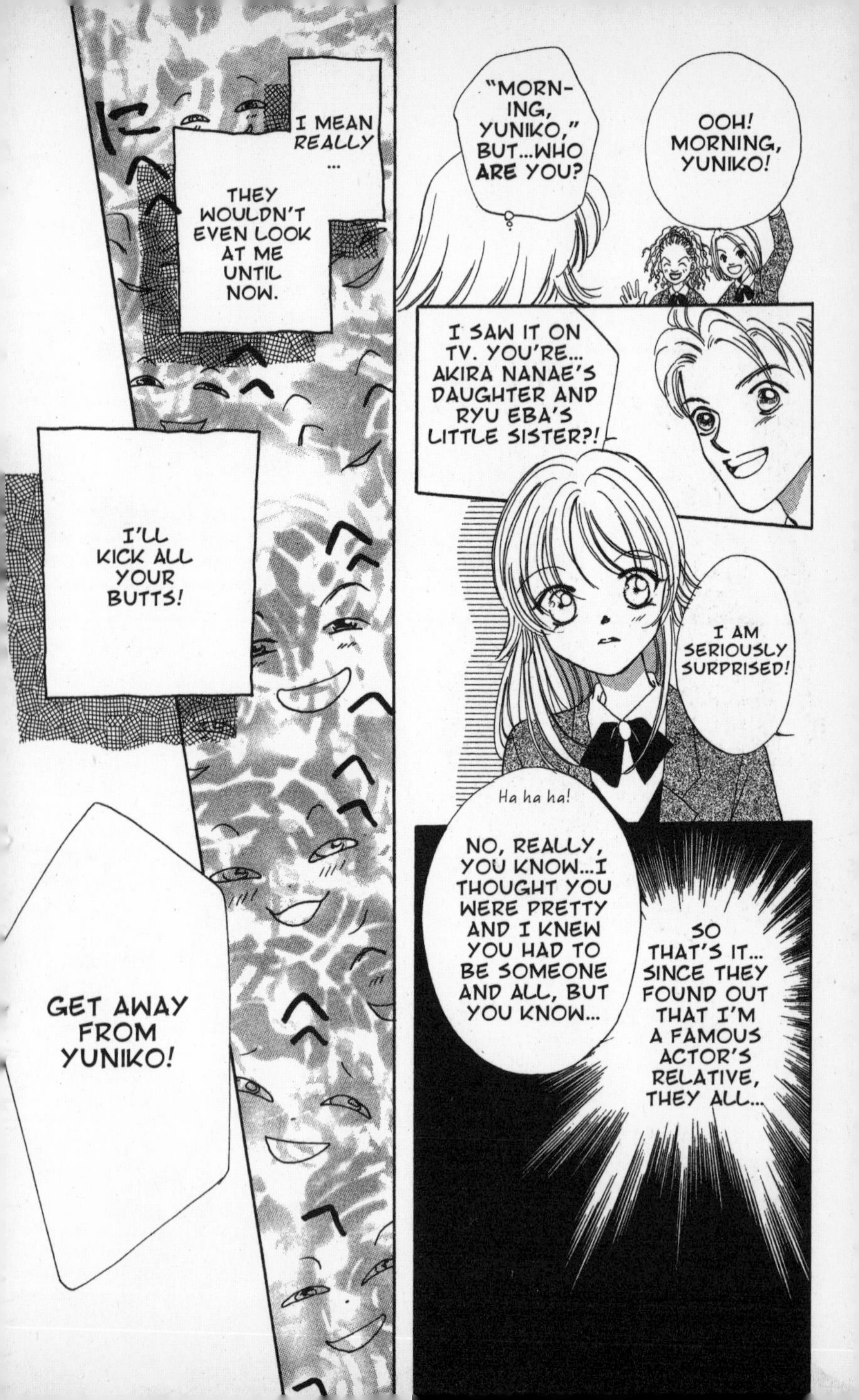
OOH! MORNING, YUNIKO!
"MORNING, YUNIKO," BUT...WHO ARE YOU?
I SAW IT ON TV. YOU'RE... AKIRA NANAE'S DAUGHTER AND RYU EBA'S LITTLE SISTER?!
I AM SERIOUSLY SURPRISED!
Ha ha ha!
NO, REALLY, YOU KNOW...I THOUGHT YOU WERE PRETTY AND I KNEW YOU HAD TO BE SOMEONE AND ALL, BUT YOU KNOW...
SO THAT'S IT... SINCE THEY FOUND OUT THAT I'M A FAMOUS ACTOR'S RELATIVE, THEY ALL...
I MEAN REALLY ...
THEY WOULDN'T EVEN LOOK AT ME UNTIL NOW.
I'LL KICK ALL YOUR BUTTS!
GET AWAY FROM YUNIKO!

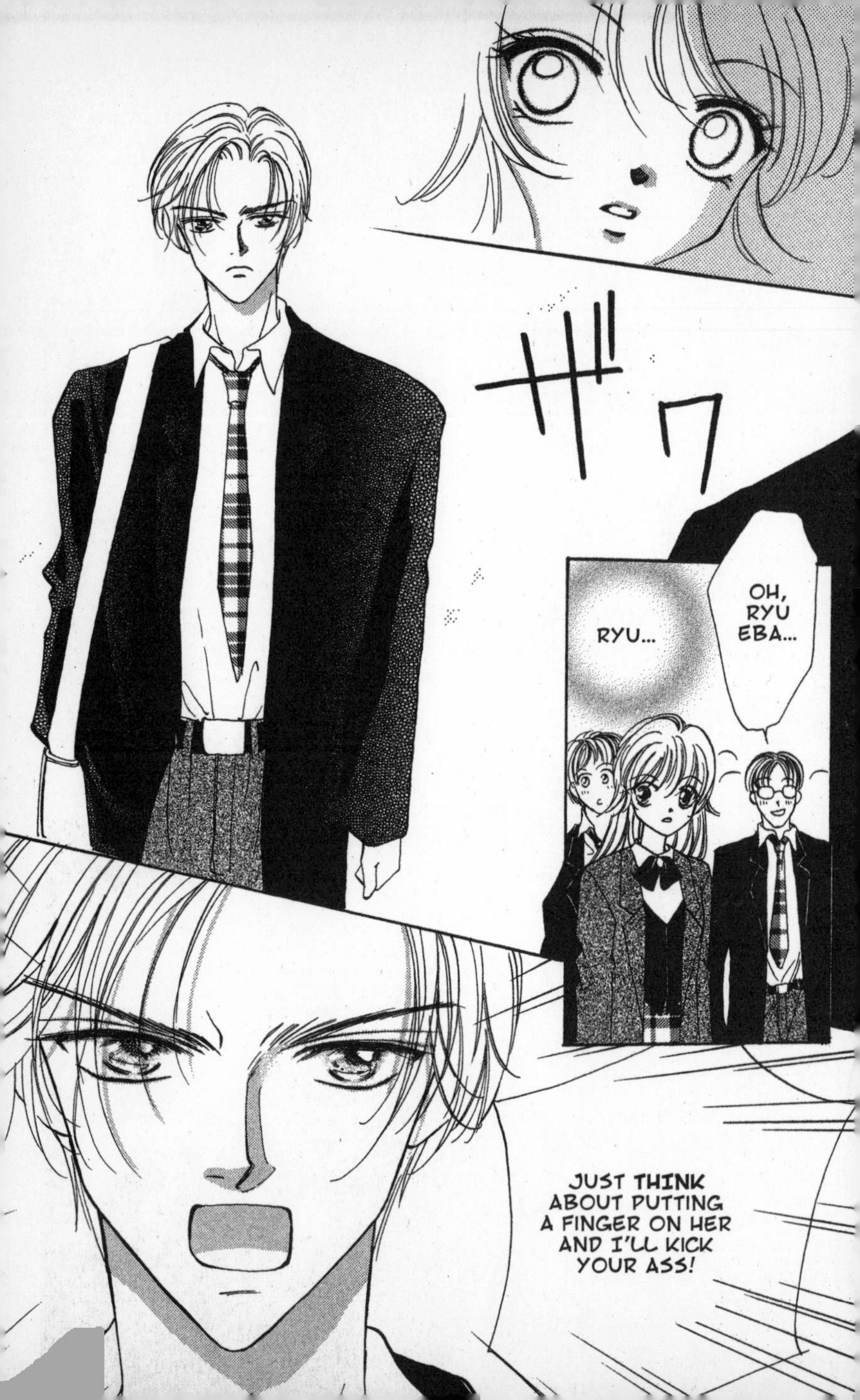
ザワ
OH, RYU EBA...
RYU...
JUST THINK ABOUT PUTTING A FINGER ON HER AND I'LL KICK YOUR ASS!

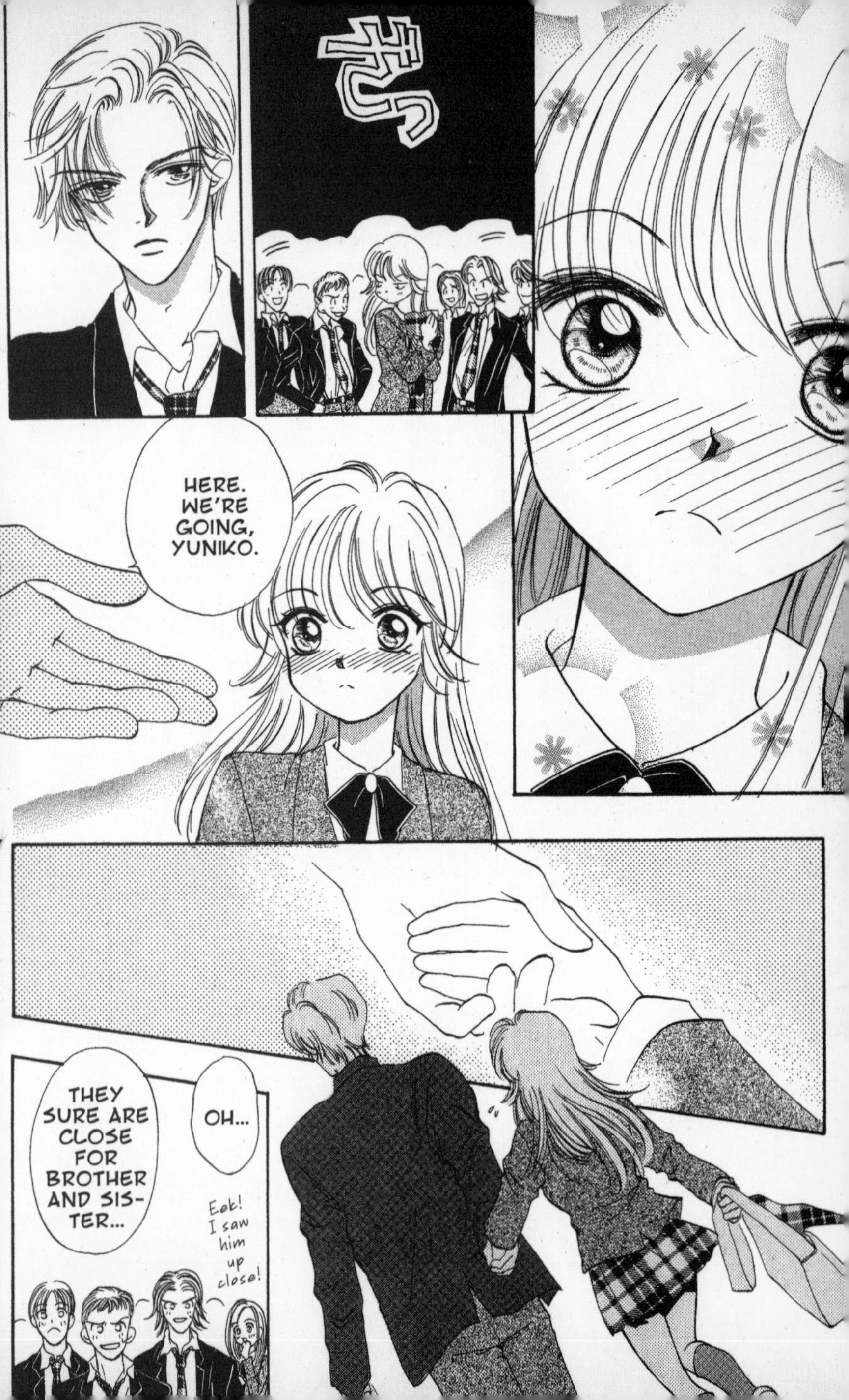

ざっ
HERE. WE'RE GOING, YUNIKO.
OH...
THEY SURE ARE CLOSE FOR BROTHER AND SIS-TER...
Eek! I saw him up close!

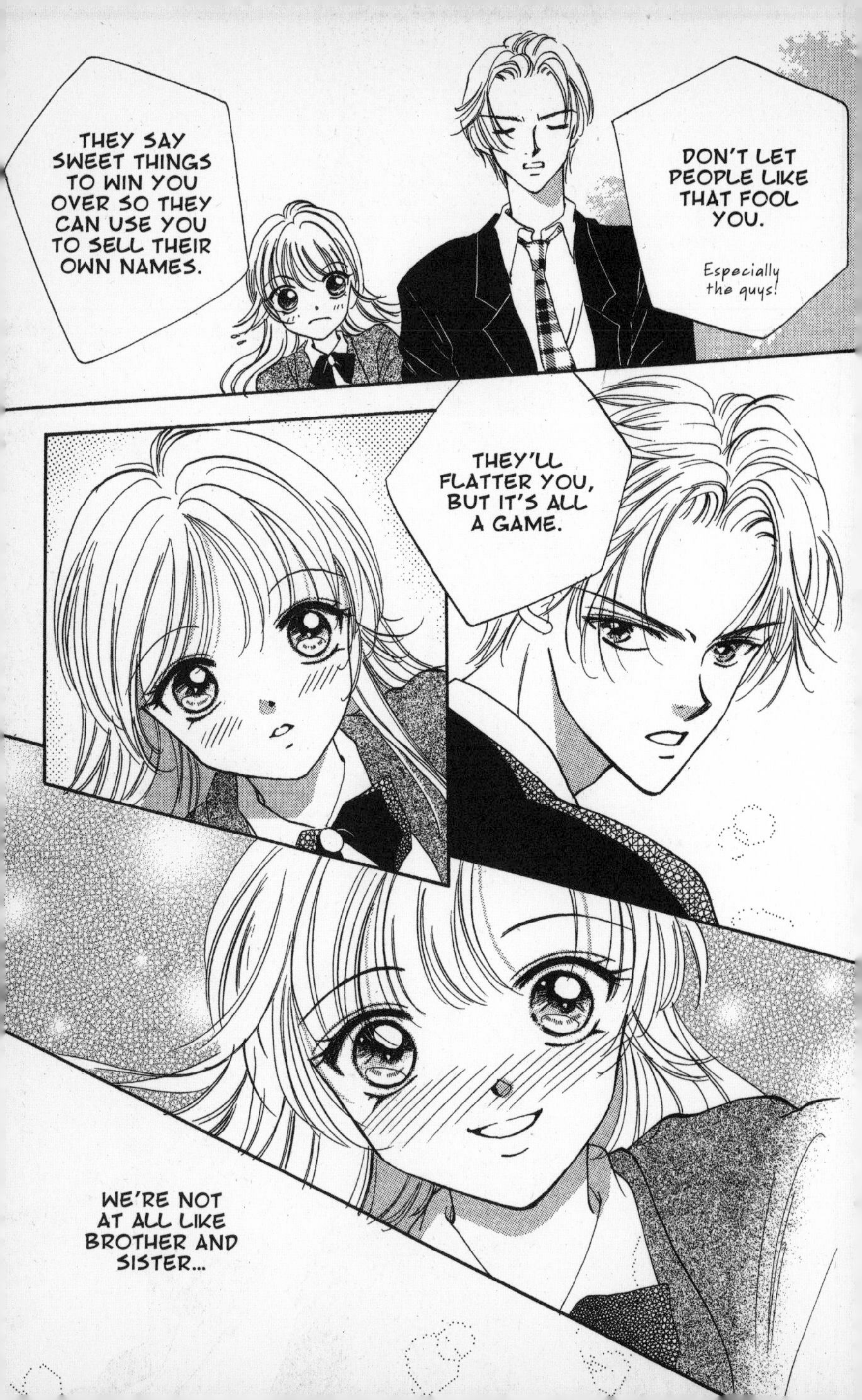
DON'T LET PEOPLE LIKE THAT FOOL YOU.
Especially the guys!
THEY SAY SWEET THINGS TO WIN YOU OVER SO THEY CAN USE YOU TO SELL THEIR OWN NAMES.
THEY'LL FLATTER YOU, BUT IT'S ALL A GAME.
WE'RE NOT AT ALL LIKE BROTHER AND SISTER...

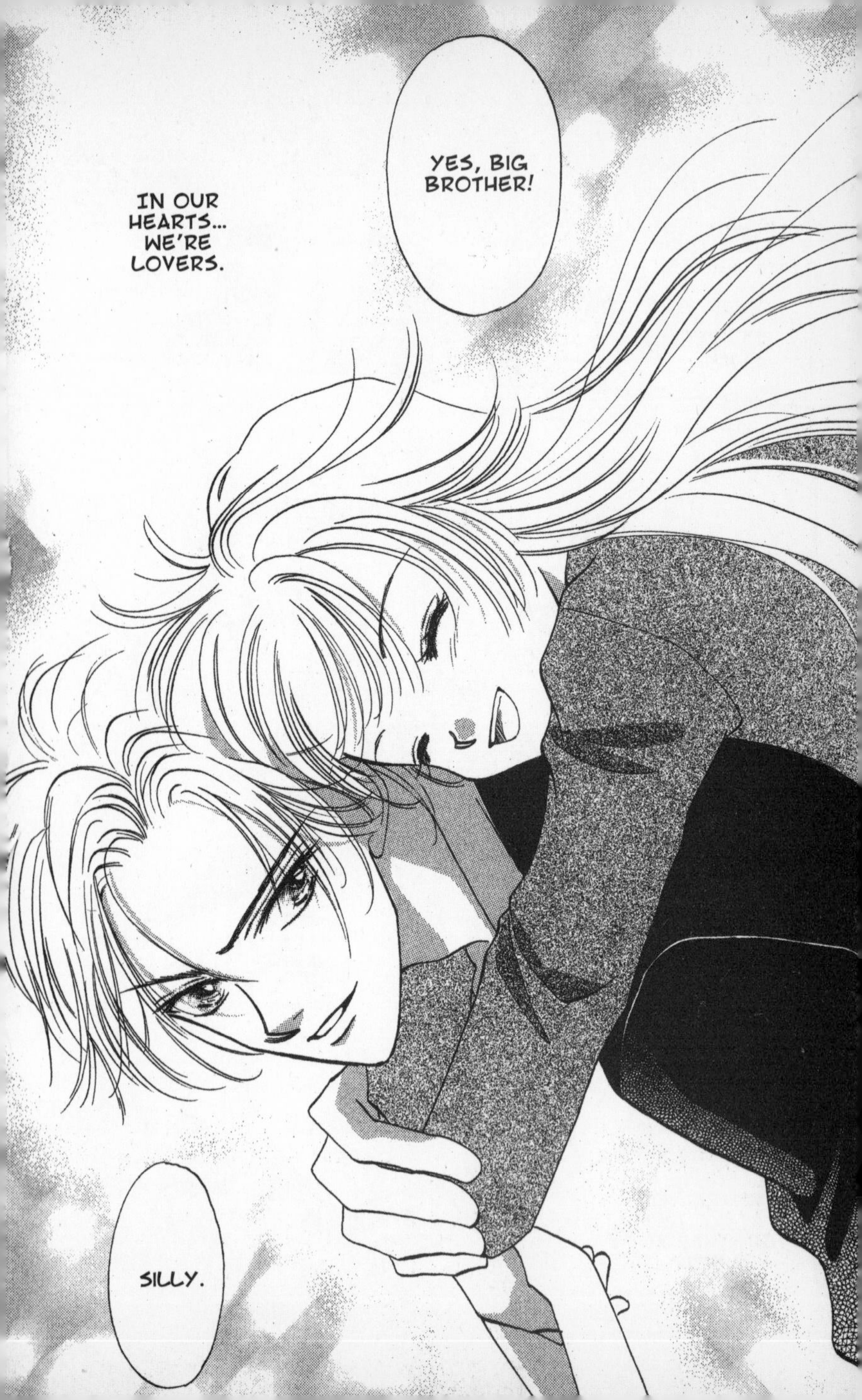
YES, BIG BROTHER!
IN OUR HEARTS... WE'RE LOVERS.
SILLY.

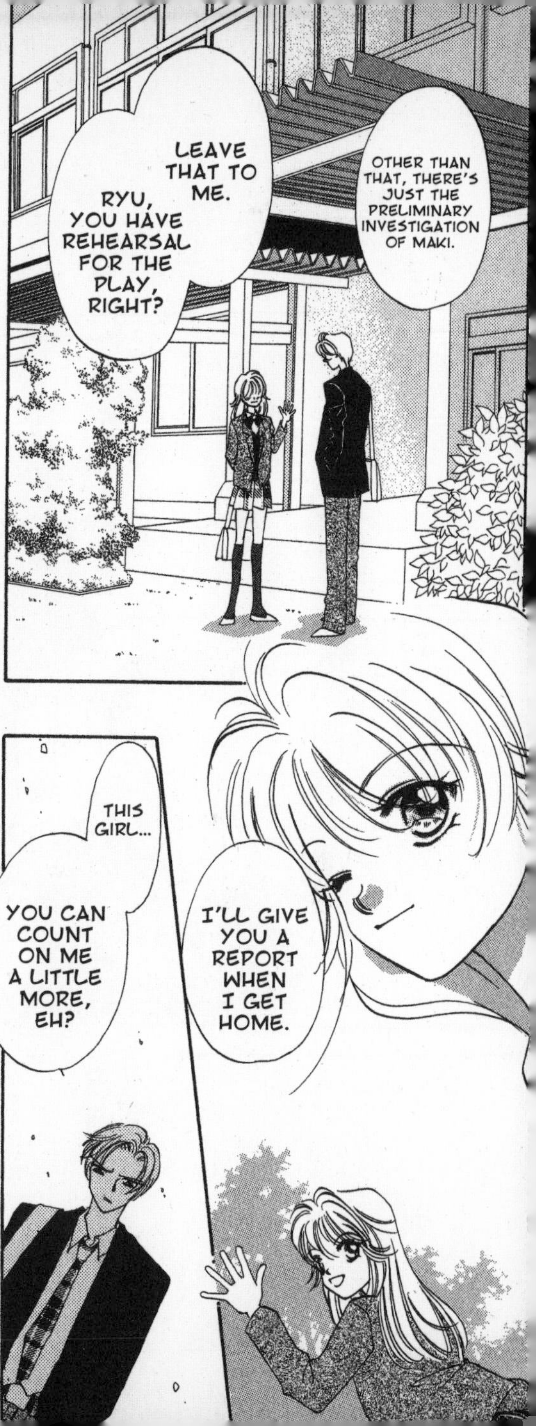
OTHER THAN THAT, THERE'S JUST THE PRELIMINARY INVESTIGATION OF MAKI.
LEAVE THAT TO ME.
RYU, YOU HAVE REHEARSAL FOR THE PLAY, RIGHT?
I'LL GIVE YOU A REPORT WHEN I GET HOME.
YOU CAN COUNT ON ME A LITTLE MORE, EH?
THIS GIRL...

Ryu Eba Data

To Fans of Ryu

1. Please get some mochi rice ready.
2. Cook it and then pound some mochi.

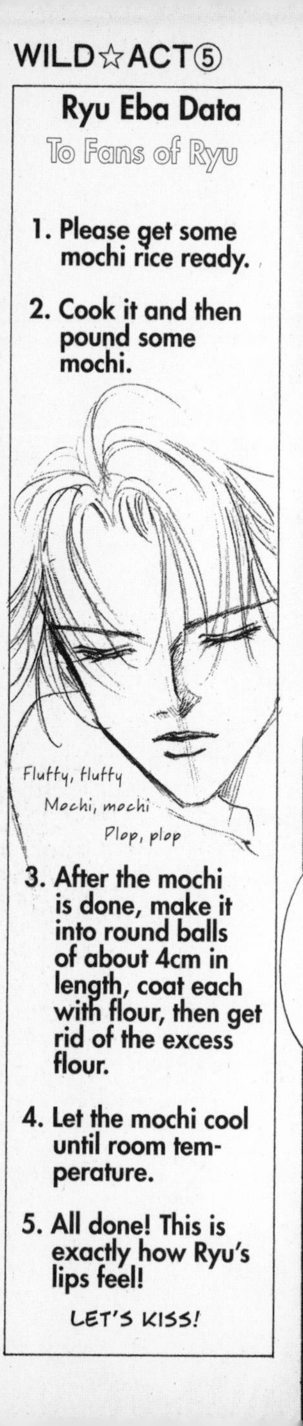
Fluffy, fluffy
Mochi, mochi
Plop, plop

3. After the mochi is done, make it into round balls of about 4cm in length, coat each with flour, then get rid of the excess flour.
4. Let the mochi cool until room temperature.
5. All done! This is exactly how Ryu's lips feel!

LET'S KISS!

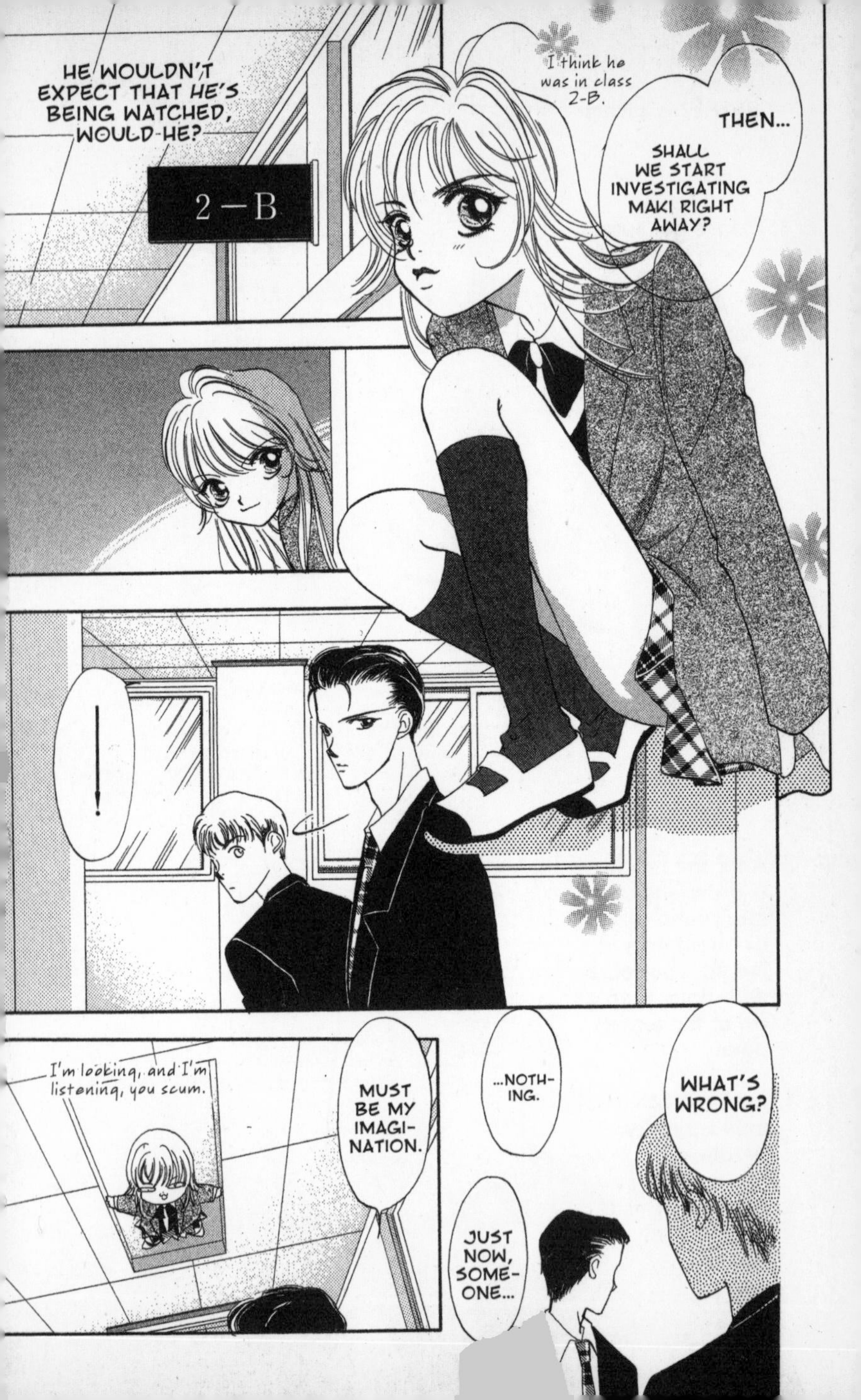

I think he was in class 2-B.
THEN...
SHALL WE START INVESTIGATING MAKI RIGHT AWAY?
2-B
HE WOULDN'T EXPECT THAT HE'S BEING WATCHED, WOULD HE?
!
WHAT'S WRONG?
...NOTH-ING.
JUST NOW, SOME-ONE...
MUST BE MY IMAGI-NATION.
I'm looking, and I'm listening, you scum.

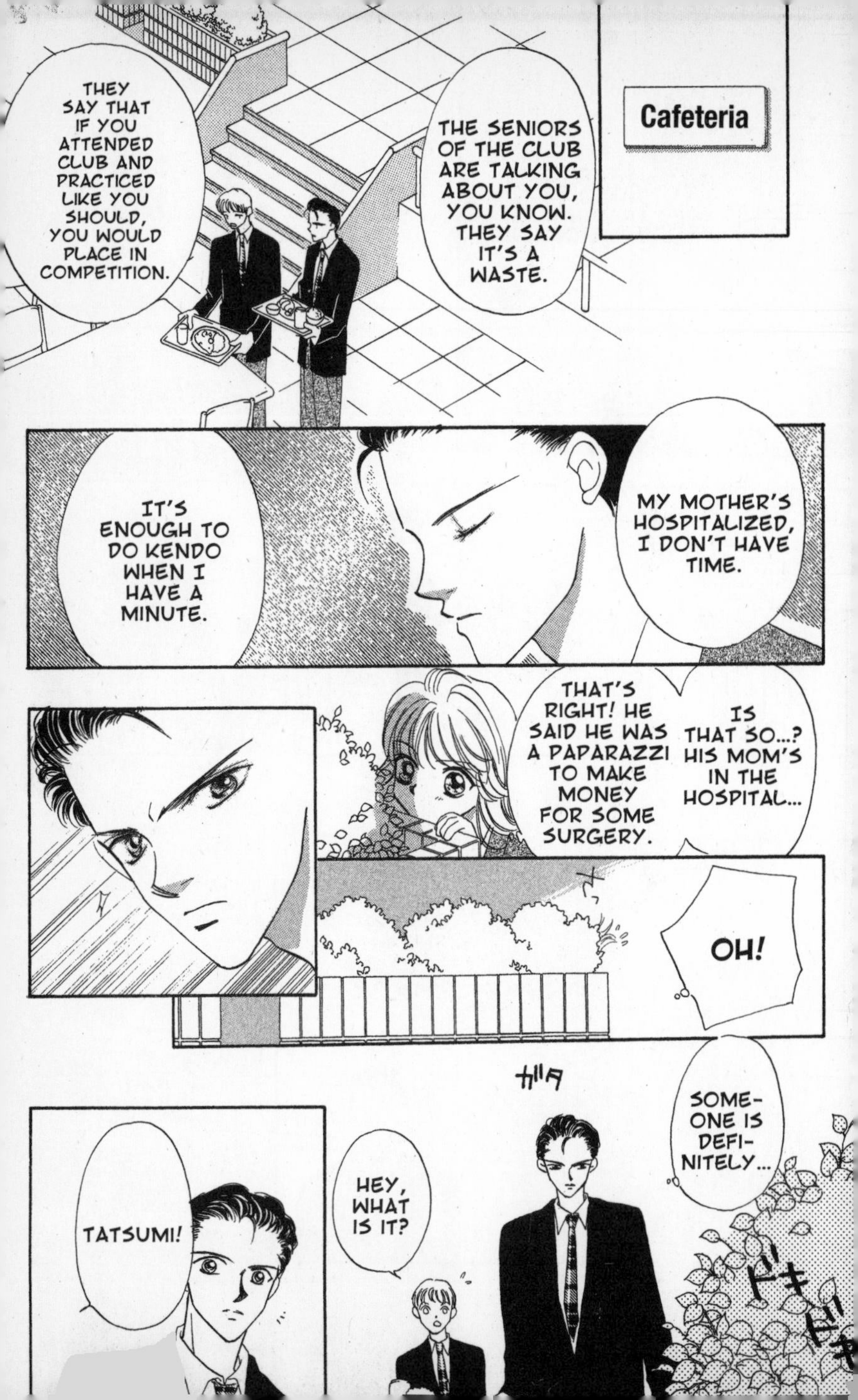
Cafeteria
THE SENIORS OF THE CLUB ARE TALKING ABOUT YOU, YOU KNOW. THEY SAY IT'S A WASTE.
THEY SAY THAT IF YOU ATTENDED CLUB AND PRACTICED LIKE YOU SHOULD, YOU WOULD PLACE IN COMPETITION.
MY MOTHER'S HOSPITALIZED, I DON'T HAVE TIME.
IT'S ENOUGH TO DO KENDO WHEN I HAVE A MINUTE.
IS THAT SO...? HIS MOM'S IN THE HOSPITAL...
THAT'S RIGHT! HE SAID HE WAS A PAPARAZZI TO MAKE MONEY FOR SOME SURGERY.
OH!
ガタ
SOME-ONE IS DEFI-NITELY...
ドキドキ
HEY, WHAT IS IT?
TATSUMI!

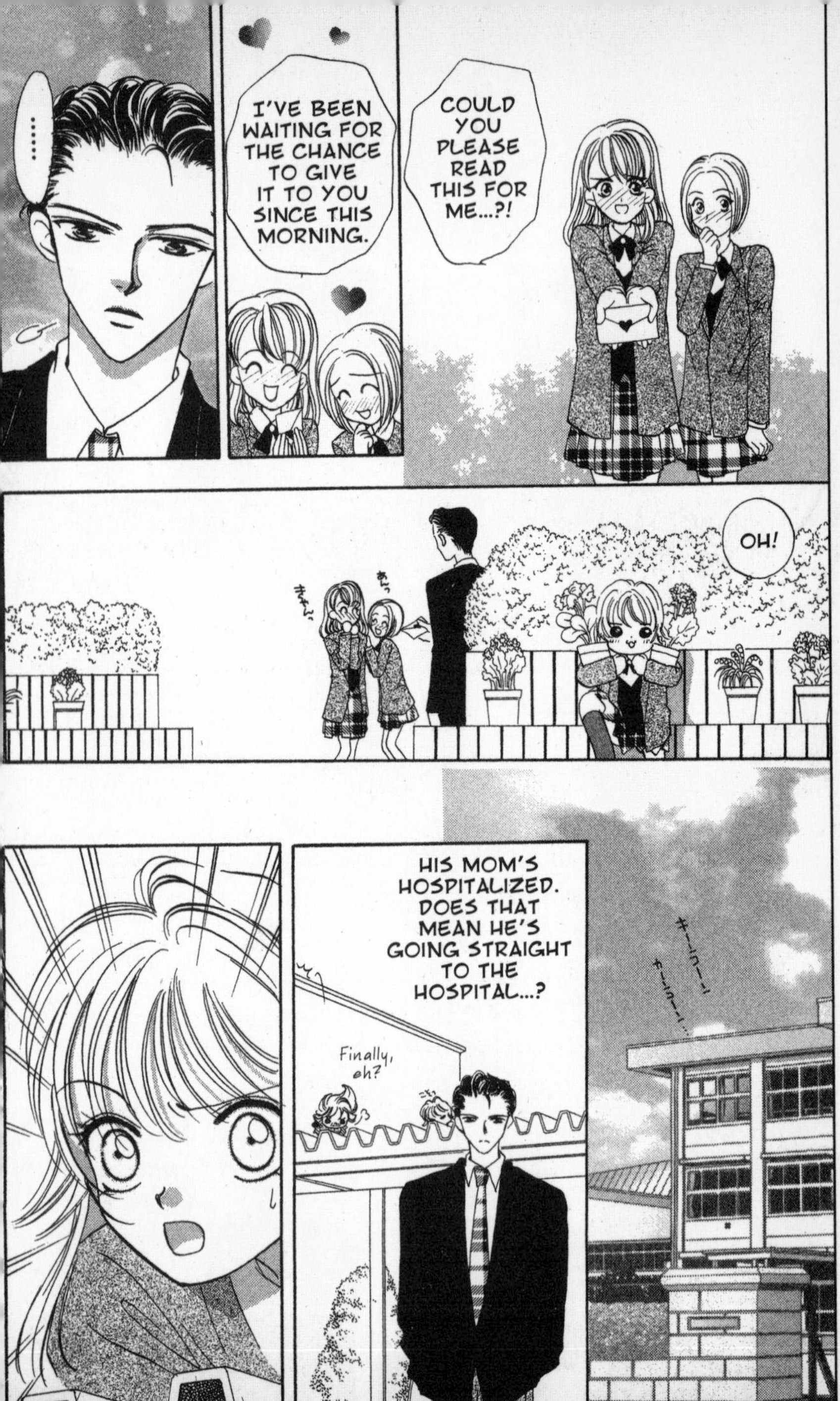
COULD YOU PLEASE READ THIS FOR ME...?!
I'VE BEEN WAITING FOR THE CHANCE TO GIVE IT TO YOU SINCE THIS MORNING.
......
OH!
HIS MOM'S HOSPITALIZED. DOES THAT MEAN HE'S GOING STRAIGHT TO THE HOSPITAL...?
Finally, eh?

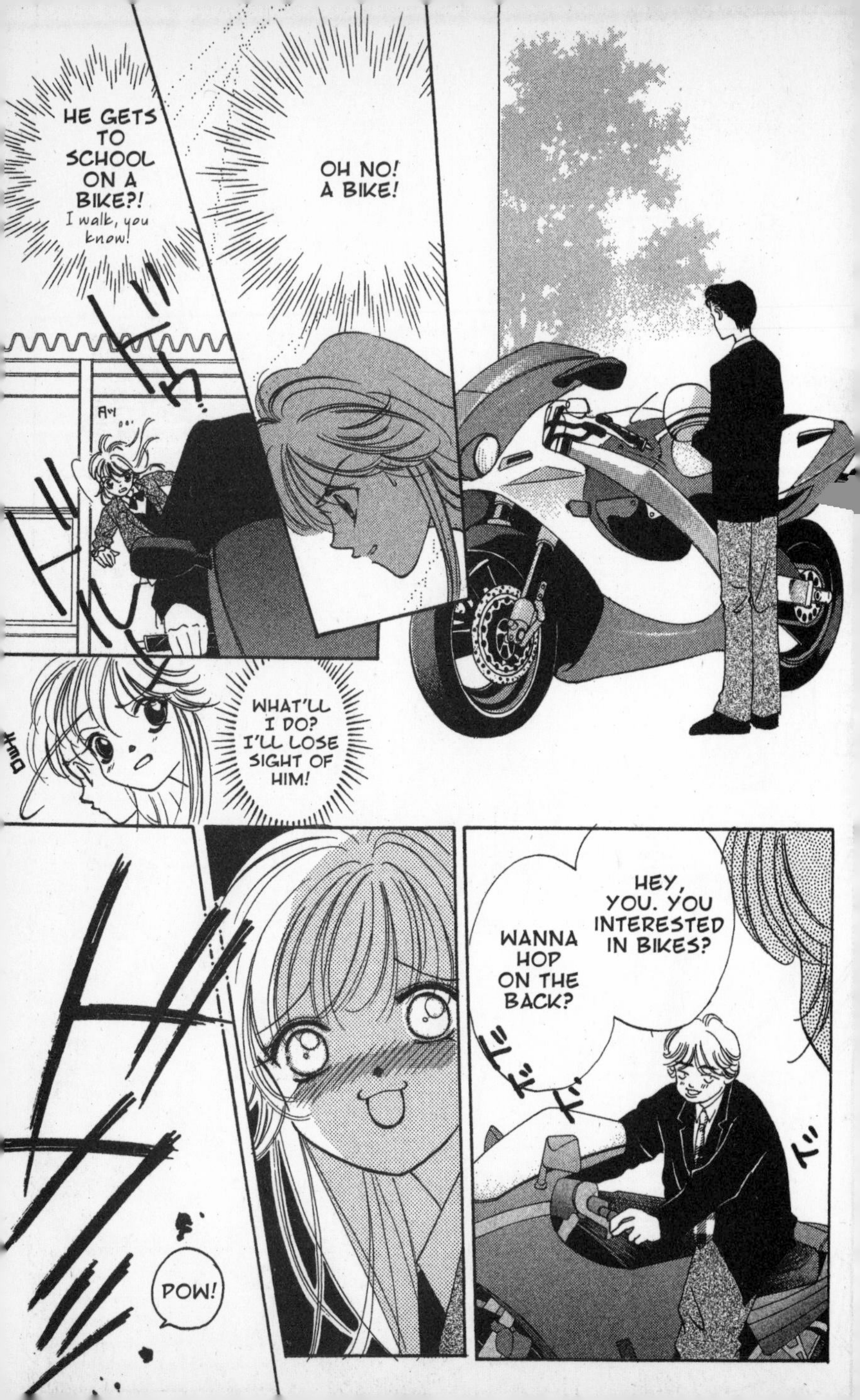
OH NO! A BIKE!
HE GETS TO SCHOOL ON A BIKE?!
I walk, you know!
WHAT'LL I DO? I'LL LOSE SIGHT OF HIM!
HEY, YOU. YOU INTERESTED IN BIKES?
WANNA HOP ON THE BACK?
POW!

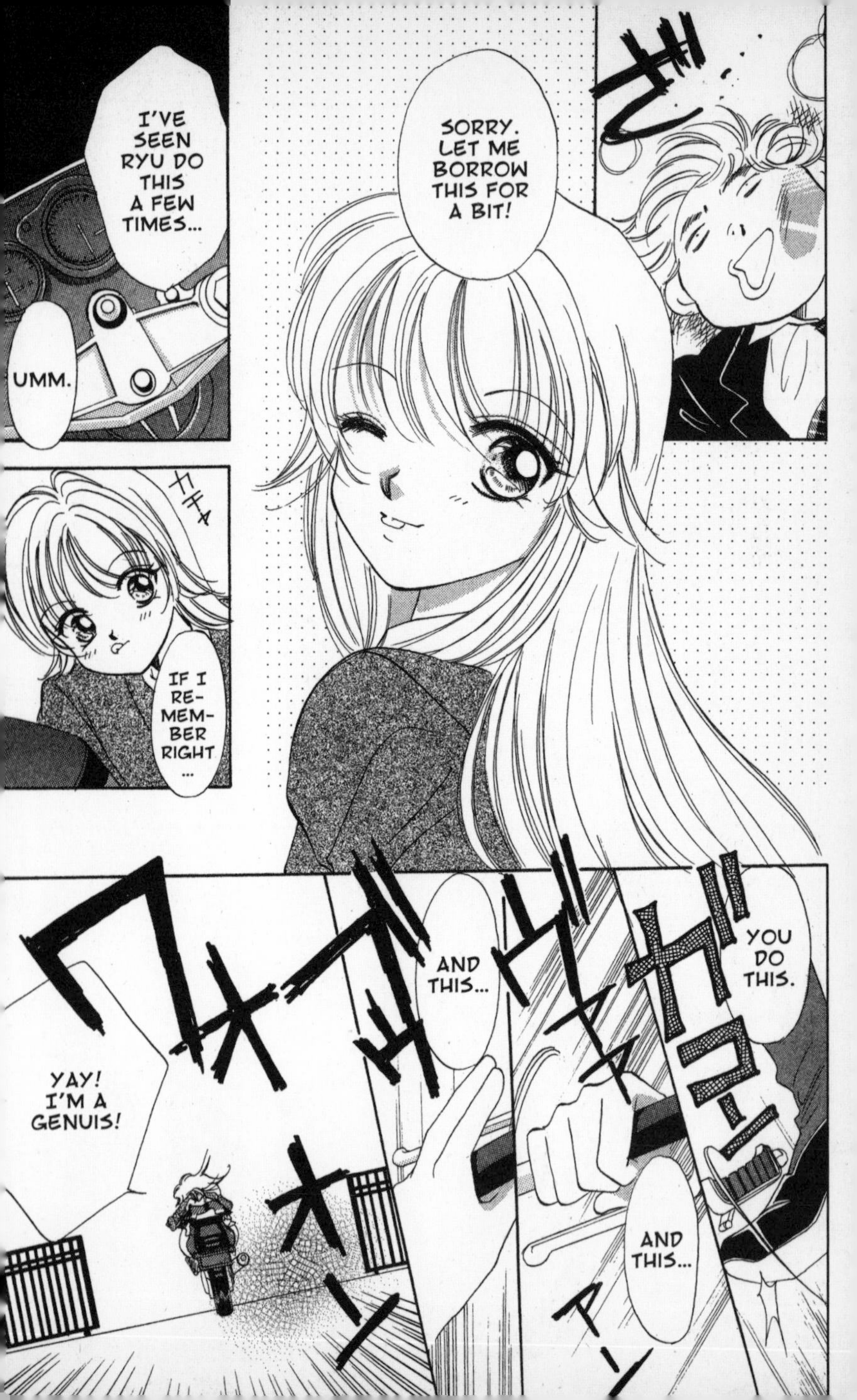
SORRY. LET ME BORROW THIS FOR A BIT!
I'VE SEEN RYU DO THIS A FEW TIMES...
UMM.
IF I RE-MEM-BER RIGHT...
YOU DO THIS.
AND THIS...
AND THIS...
YAY! I'M A GENUIS!

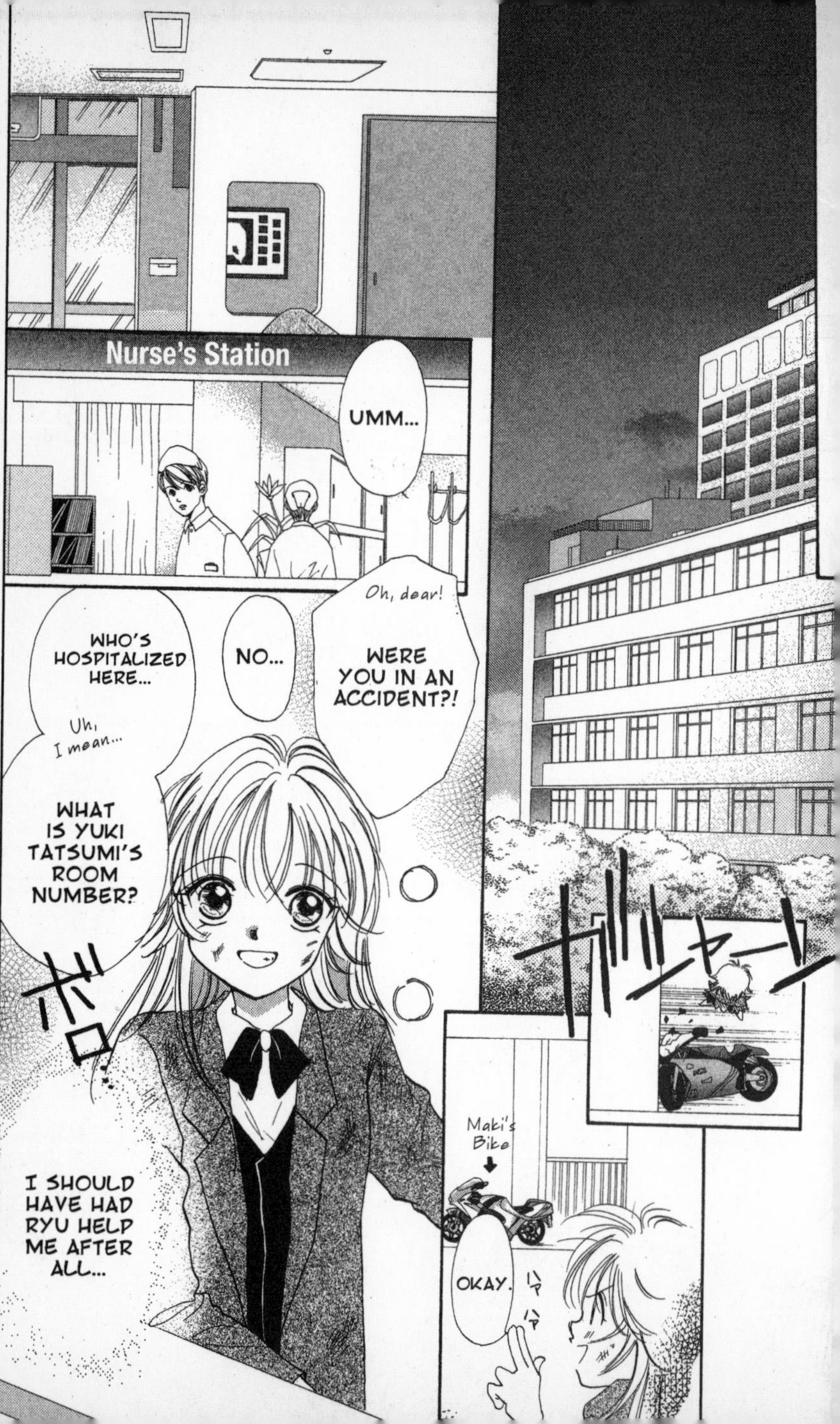
Maki's Bike
OKAY.
Nurse's Station
UMM...
Oh, dear!
WERE YOU IN AN ACCIDENT?!
NO...
WHO'S HOSPITALIZED HERE...
Uh, I mean...
WHAT IS YUKI TATSUMI'S ROOM NUMBER?
I SHOULD HAVE HAD RYU HELP ME AFTER ALL...

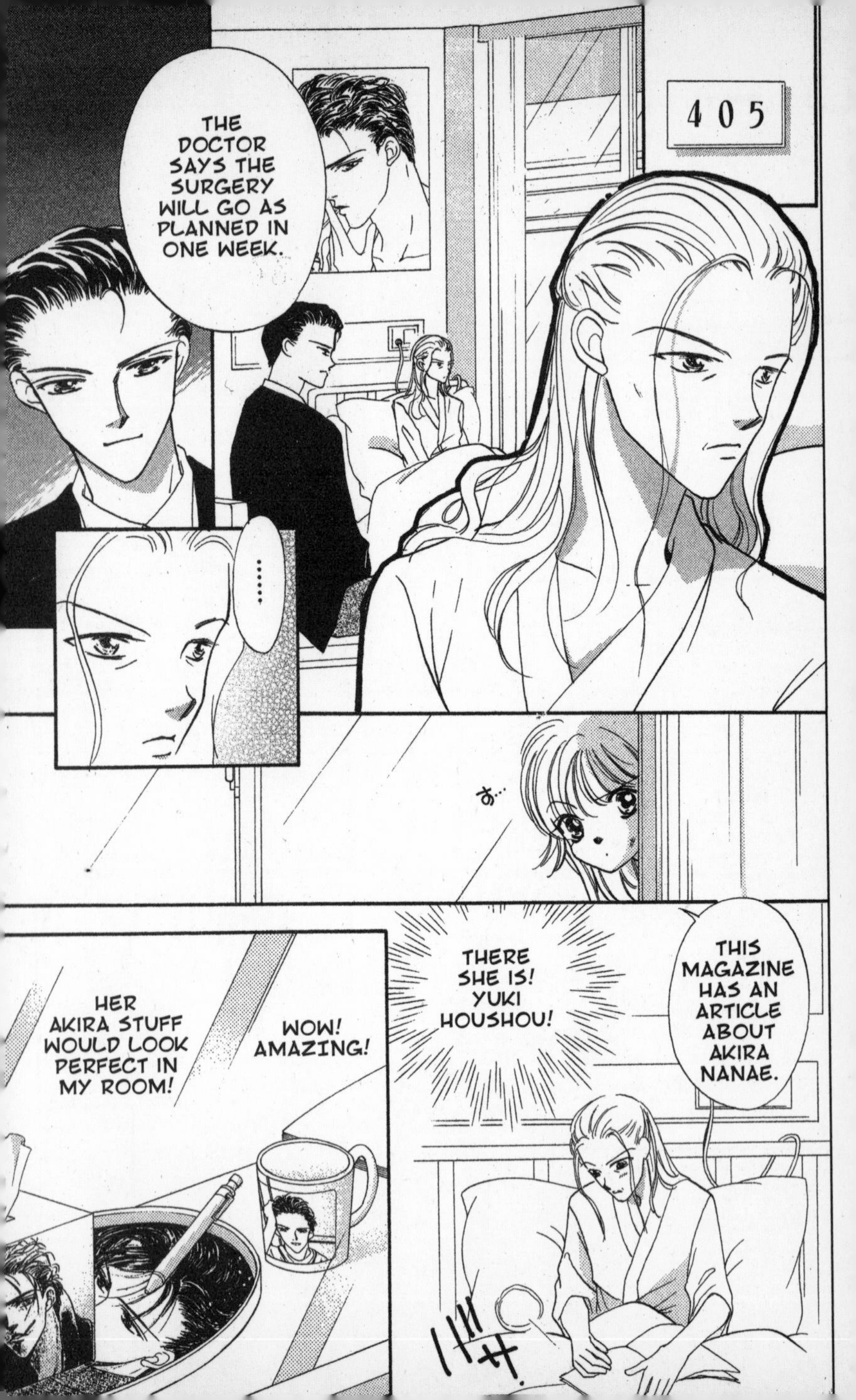
THE DOCTOR SAYS THE SURGERY WILL GO AS PLANNED IN ONE WEEK.
......
す…
THIS MAGAZINE HAS AN ARTICLE ABOUT AKIRA NANAE.
THERE SHE IS! YUKI HOUSHOU!
WOW! AMAZING!
HER AKIRA STUFF WOULD LOOK PERFECT IN MY ROOM!

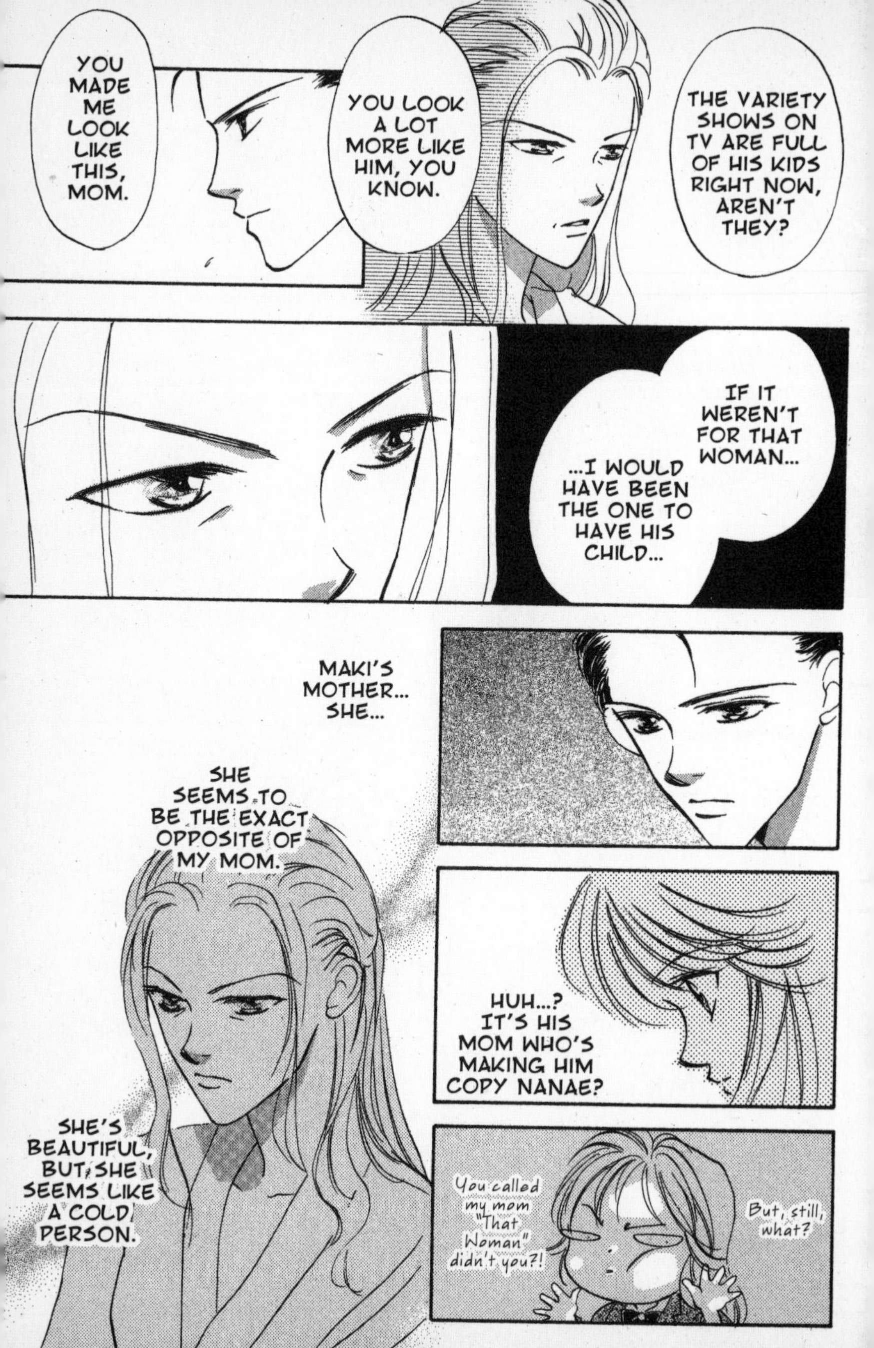
THE VARIETY SHOWS ON TV ARE FULL OF HIS KIDS RIGHT NOW, AREN'T THEY?
YOU LOOK A LOT MORE LIKE HIM, YOU KNOW.
YOU MADE ME LOOK LIKE THIS, MOM.
IF IT WEREN'T FOR THAT WOMAN...
...I WOULD HAVE BEEN THE ONE TO HAVE HIS CHILD...
MAKI'S MOTHER... SHE...
SHE SEEMS TO BE THE EXACT OPPOSITE OF MY MOM.
SHE'S BEAUTIFUL, BUT SHE SEEMS LIKE A COLD PERSON.
HUH...? IT'S HIS MOM WHO'S MAKING HIM COPY NANAE?
You called my mom "That Woman" didn't you?!
But, still, what?

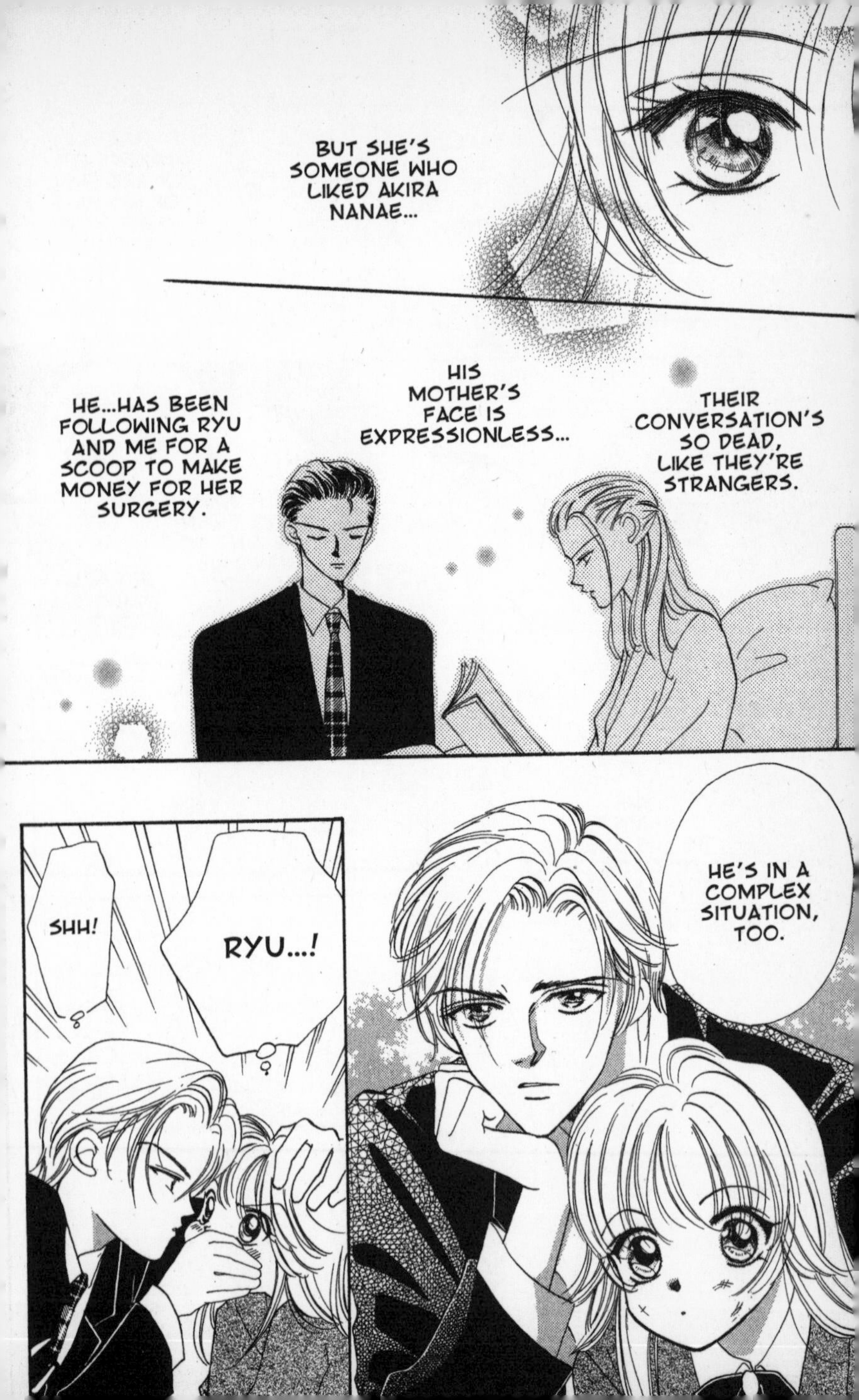
BUT SHE'S SOMEONE WHO LIKED AKIRA NANAE...
THEIR CONVERSATION'S SO DEAD, LIKE THEY'RE STRANGERS.
HIS MOTHER'S FACE IS EXPRESSIONLESS...
HE...HAS BEEN FOLLOWING RYU AND ME FOR A SCOOP TO MAKE MONEY FOR HER SURGERY.
HE'S IN A COMPLEX SITUATION, TOO.
RYU...!
SHH!

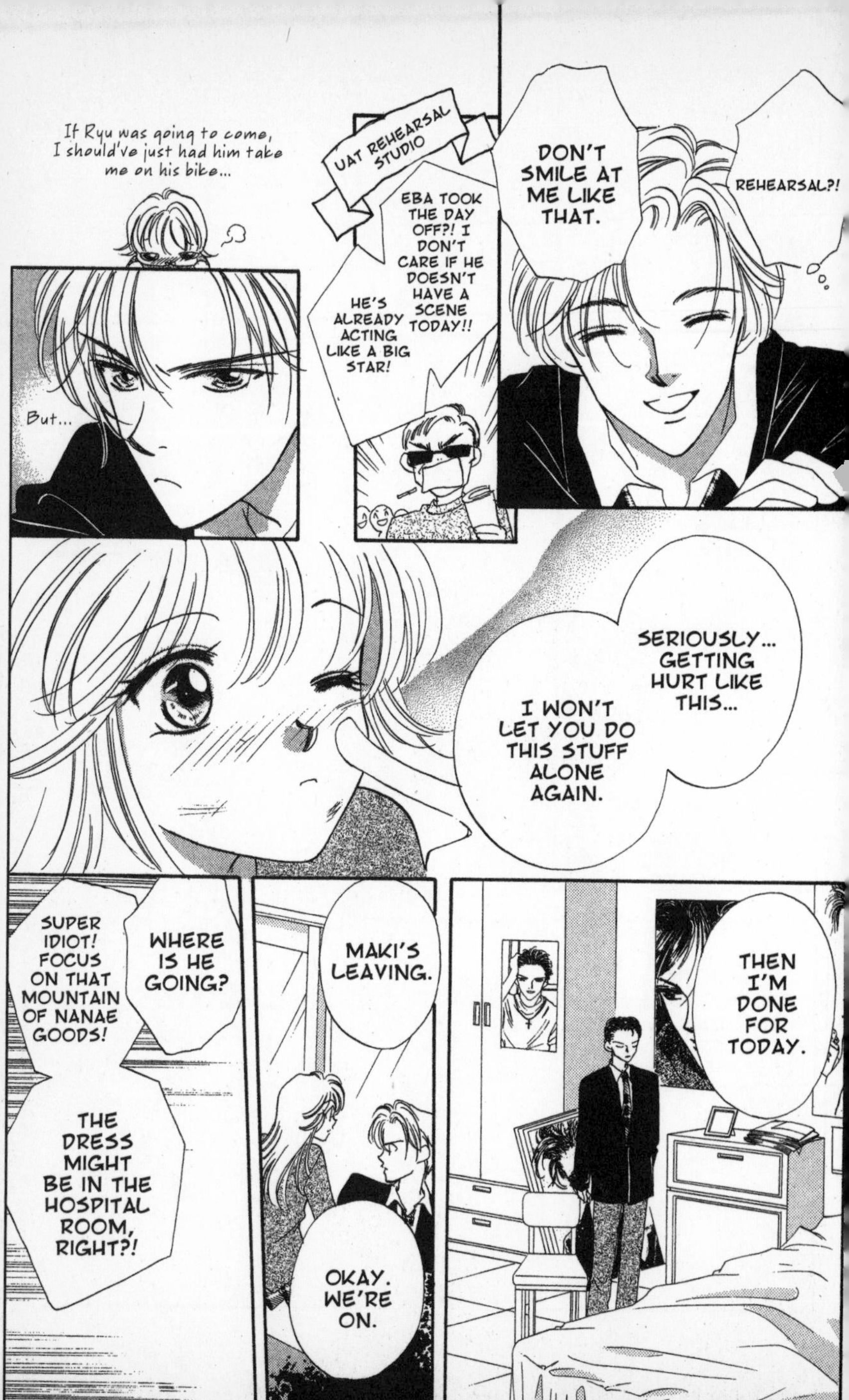
DON'T SMILE AT ME LIKE THAT.
REHEARSAL?!
UAT REHEARSAL STUDIO
EBA TOOK THE DAY OFF?! I DON'T CARE IF HE DOESN'T HAVE A SCENE TODAY!!
HE'S ALREADY ACTING LIKE A BIG STAR!
If Ryu was going to come, I should've just had him take me on his bike...
But...
SERIOUSLY... GETTING HURT LIKE THIS...
I WON'T LET YOU DO THIS STUFF ALONE AGAIN.
THEN I'M DONE FOR TODAY.
MAKI'S LEAVING.
OKAY. WE'RE ON.
WHERE IS HE GOING?
SUPER IDIOT! FOCUS ON THAT MOUNTAIN OF NANAE GOODS!
THE DRESS MIGHT BE IN THE HOSPITAL ROOM, RIGHT?!

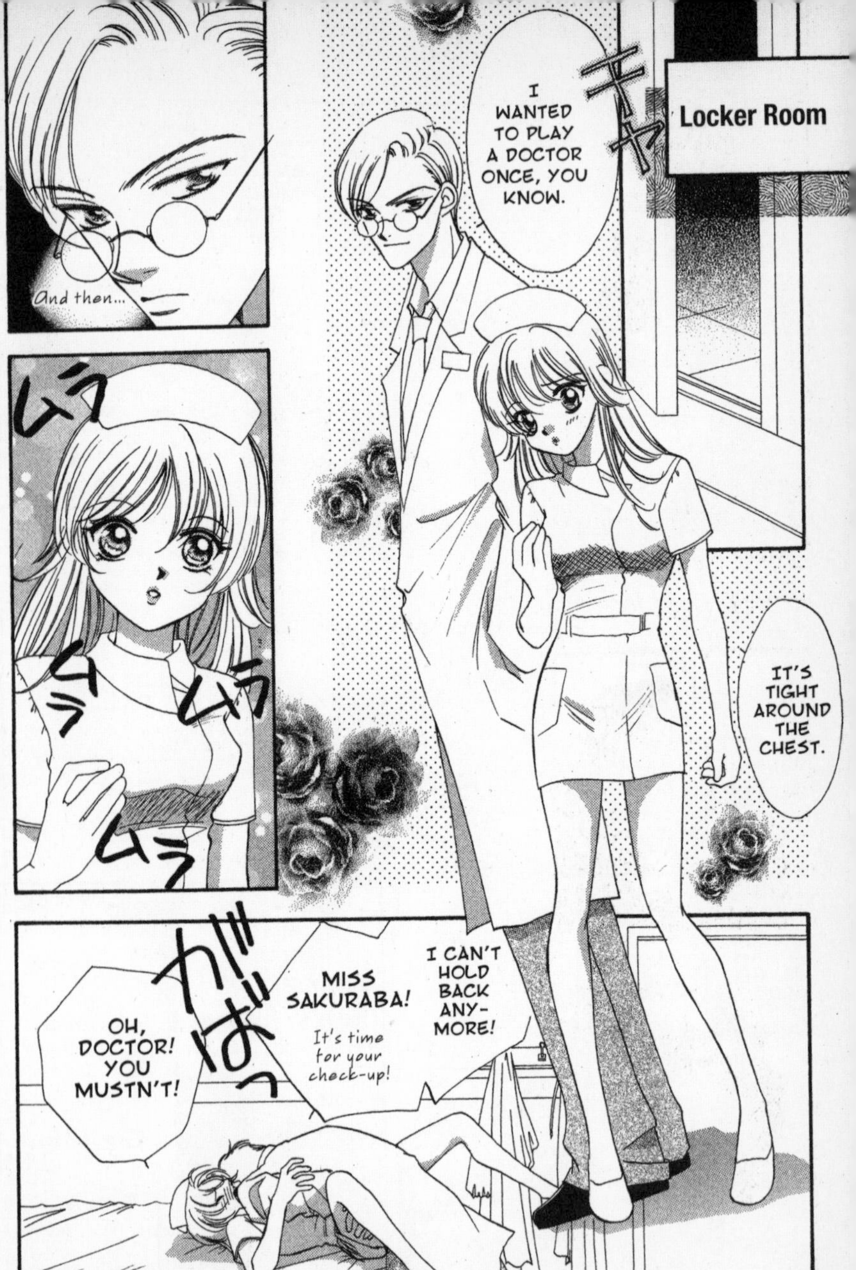
Locker Room
キャ
I WANTED TO PLAY A DOCTOR ONCE, YOU KNOW.
IT'S TIGHT AROUND THE CHEST.
And then...
がばっ
I CAN'T HOLD BACK ANY-MORE!
MISS SAKURABA!
It's time for your check-up!
OH, DOCTOR! YOU MUSTN'T!

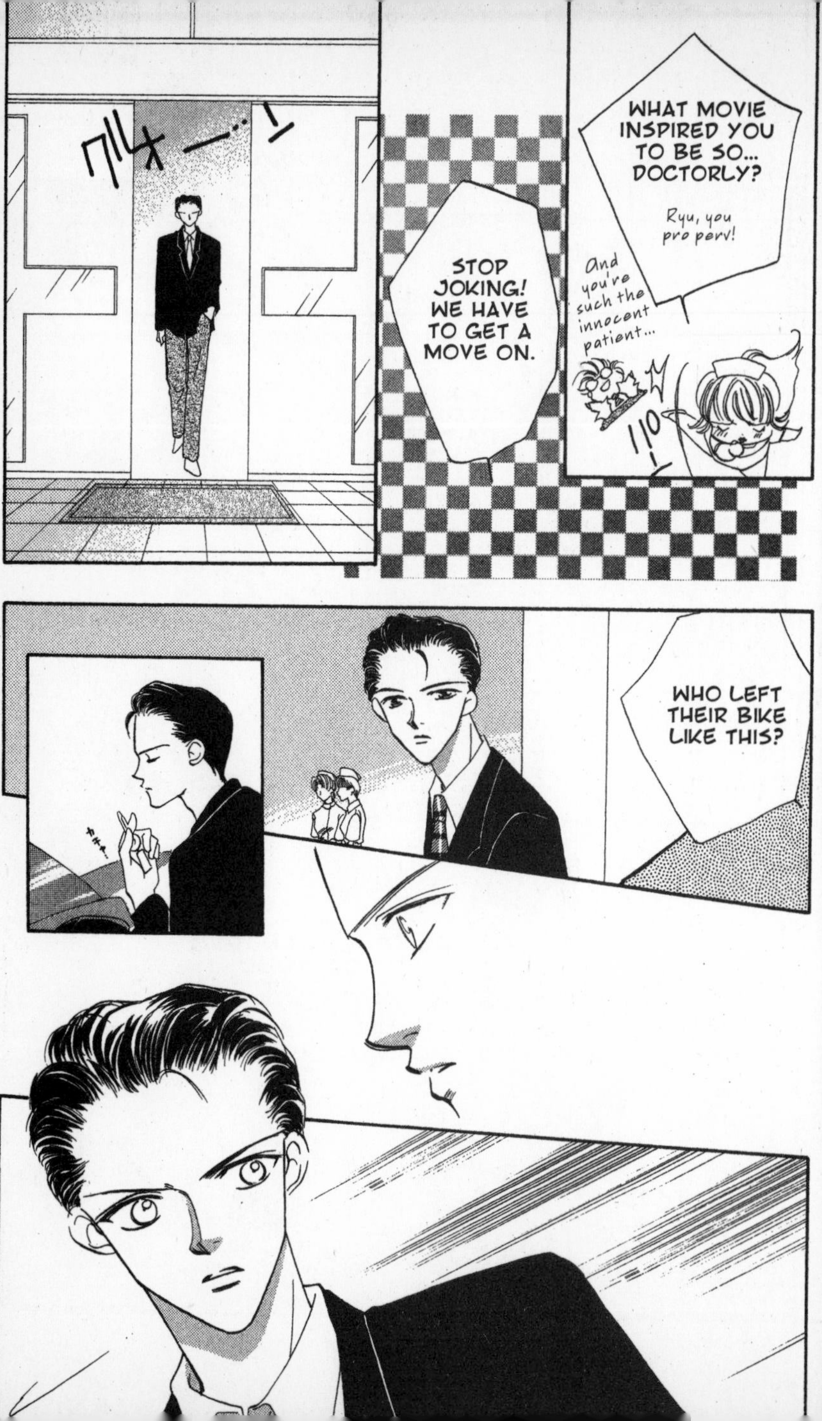
WHAT MOVIE INSPIRED YOU TO BE SO... DOCTORLY?
Ryu, you pro perv!
And you're such the innocent patient...
STOP JOKING! WE HAVE TO GET A MOVE ON.
WHO LEFT THEIR BIKE LIKE THIS?
カチャ

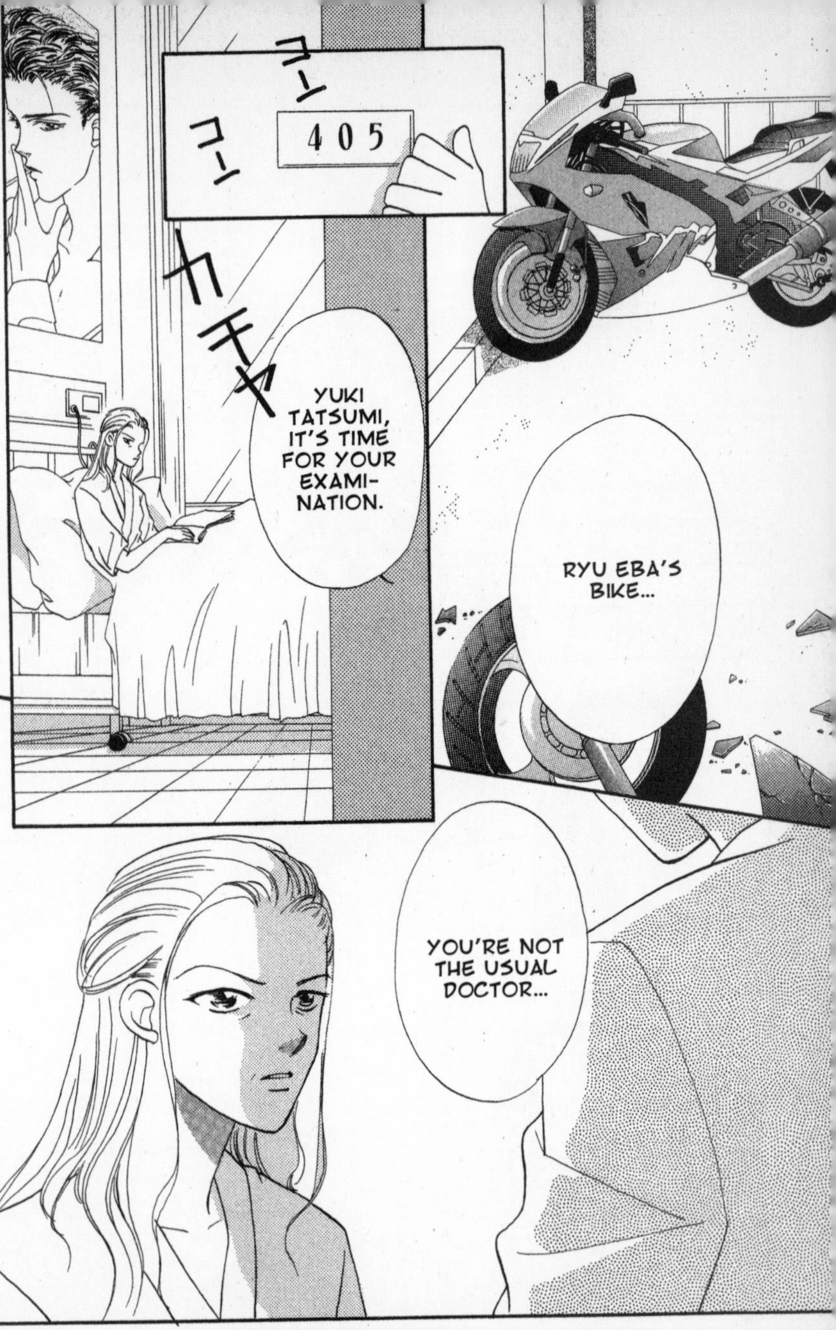
RYU EBA'S BIKE...
コン
コン
405
カチャ
YUKI TATSUMI, IT'S TIME FOR YOUR EXAMINATION.
YOU'RE NOT THE USUAL DOCTOR...

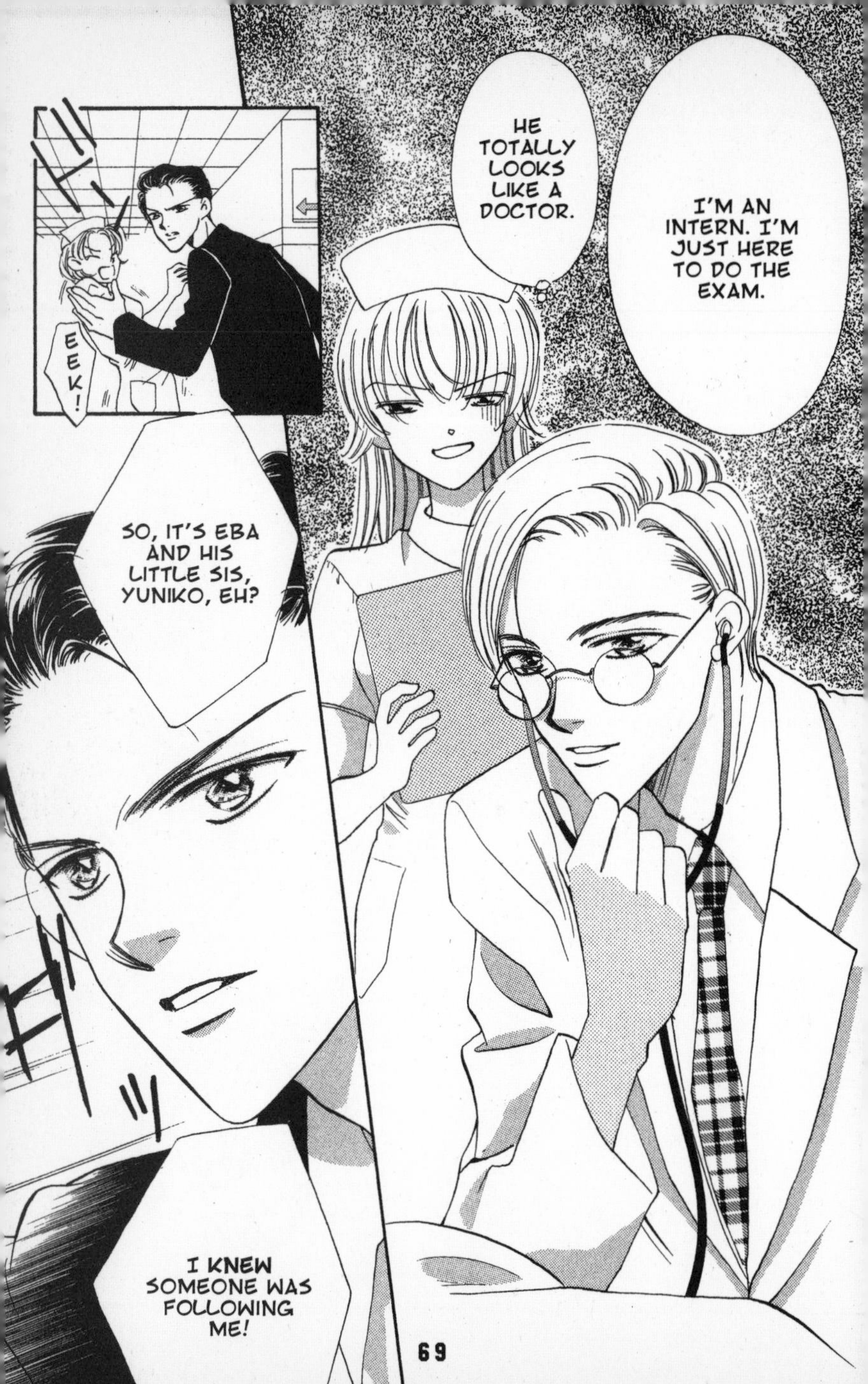
I'M AN INTERN. I'M JUST HERE TO DO THE EXAM.
HE TOTALLY LOOKS LIKE A DOCTOR.
EEK!
SO, IT'S EBA AND HIS LITTLE SIS, YUNIKO, EH?
I KNEW SOMEONE WAS FOLLOWING ME!

See, it
came out...

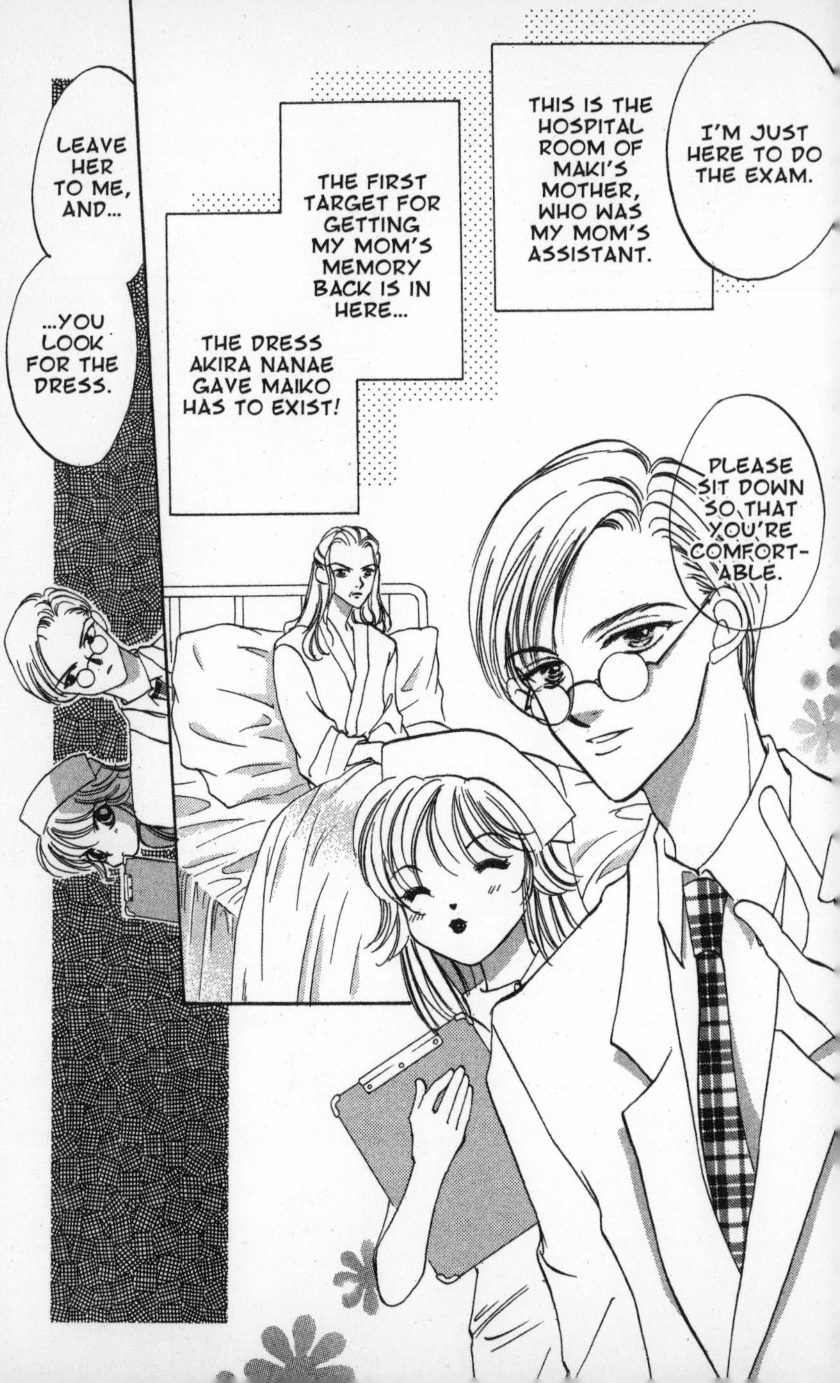
I'M JUST HERE TO DO THE EXAM.
THIS IS THE HOSPITAL ROOM OF MAKI'S MOTHER, WHO WAS MY MOM'S ASSISTANT.
THE FIRST TARGET FOR GETTING MY MOM'S MEMORY BACK IS IN HERE...
THE DRESS AKIRA NANAE GAVE MAIKO HAS TO EXIST!
PLEASE SIT DOWN SO THAT YOU'RE COMFORT-ABLE.
LEAVE HER TO ME, AND...
...YOU LOOK FOR THE DRESS.

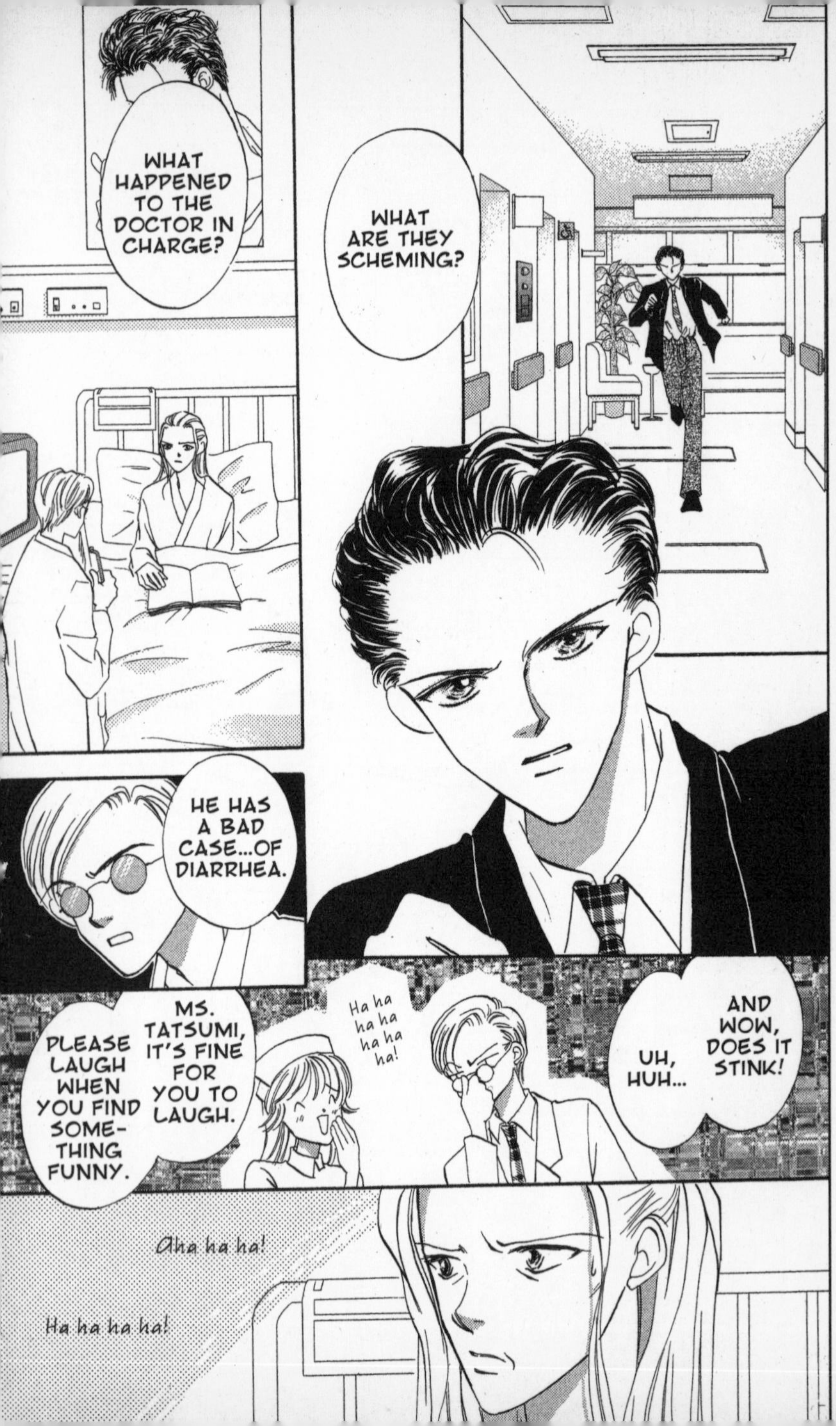
WHAT ARE THEY SCHEMING?
WHAT HAPPENED TO THE DOCTOR IN CHARGE?
HE HAS A BAD CASE...OF DIARRHEA.
AND WOW, DOES IT STINK!
UH, HUH...
Ha ha ha ha ha ha ha!
MS. TATSUMI, IT'S FINE FOR YOU TO LAUGH.
PLEASE LAUGH WHEN YOU FIND SOME-THING FUNNY.
Aha ha ha!
Ha ha ha ha!

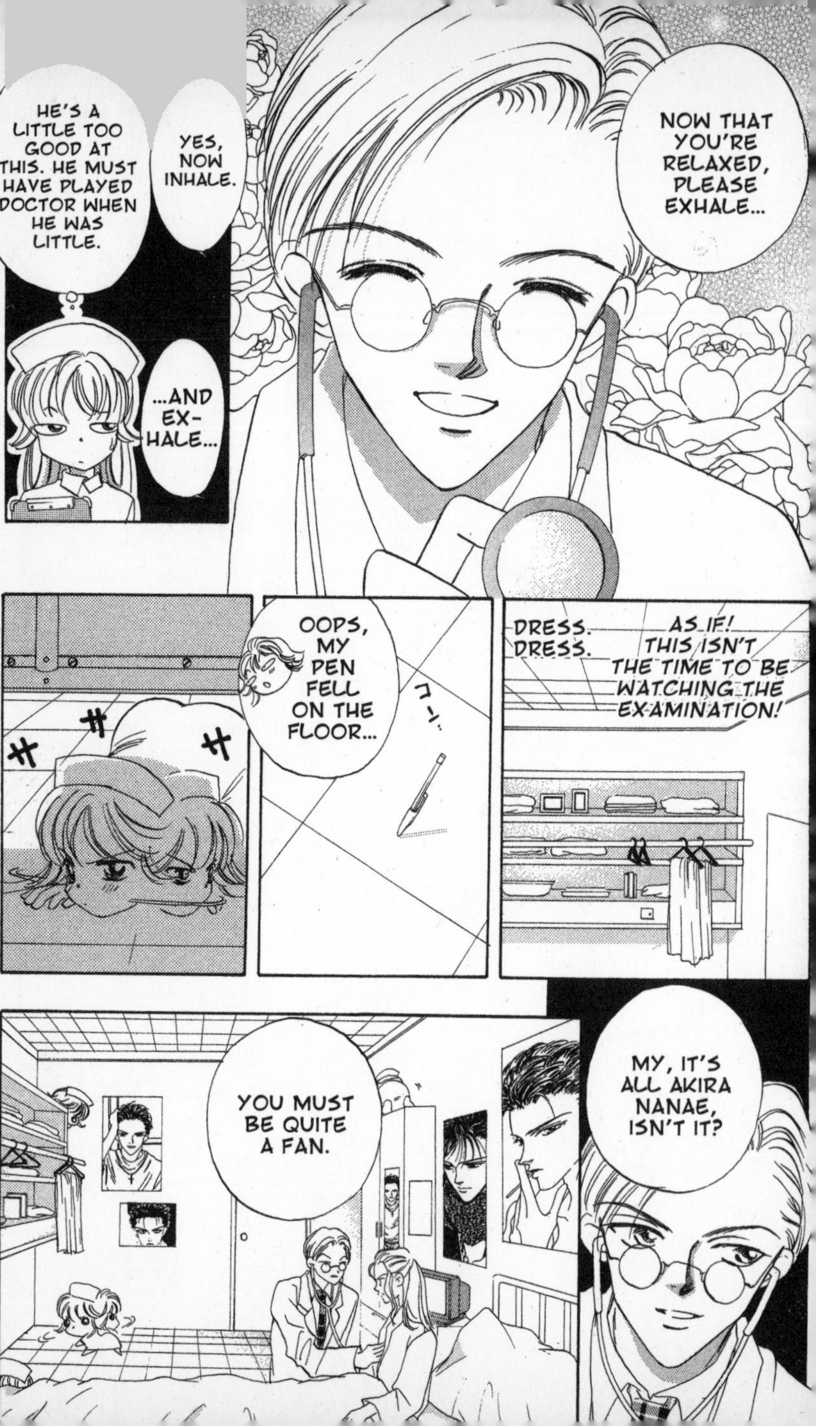
NOW THAT YOU'RE RELAXED, PLEASE EXHALE...
YES, NOW INHALE.
HE'S A LITTLE TOO GOOD AT THIS. HE MUST HAVE PLAYED DOCTOR WHEN HE WAS LITTLE.
...AND EX-HALE...
AS IF! THIS ISN'T THE TIME TO BE WATCHING THE EXAMINATION!
DRESS. DRESS.
OOPS, MY PEN FELL ON THE FLOOR...
MY, IT'S ALL AKIRA NANAE, ISN'T IT?
YOU MUST BE QUITE A FAN.

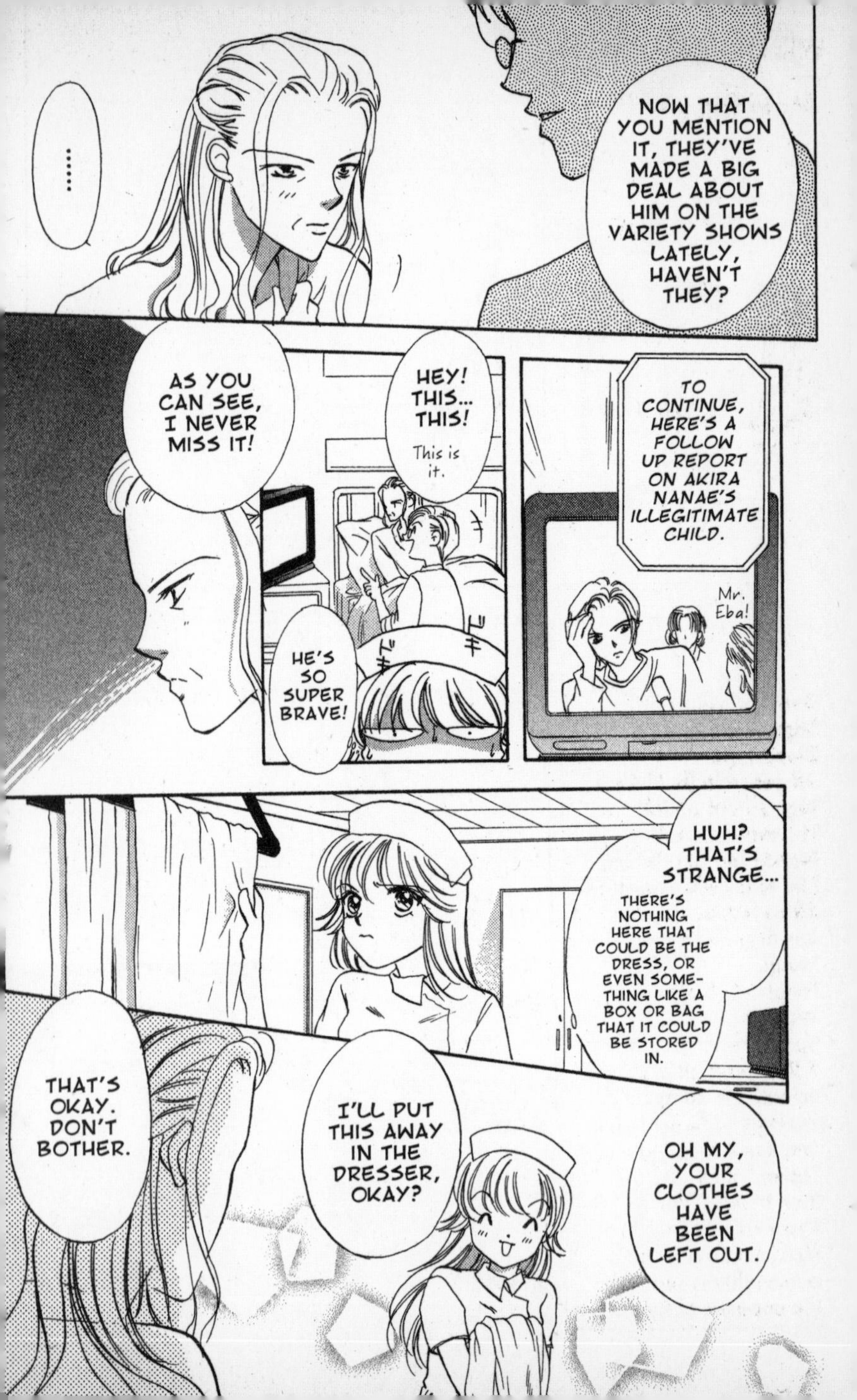
NOW THAT YOU MENTION IT, THEY'VE MADE A BIG DEAL ABOUT HIM ON THE VARIETY SHOWS LATELY, HAVEN'T THEY?
......
TO CONTINUE, HERE'S A FOLLOW UP REPORT ON AKIRA NANAE'S ILLEGITIMATE CHILD.
Mr. Eba!
HEY! THIS... THIS!
This is it.
HE'S SO SUPER BRAVE!
AS YOU CAN SEE, I NEVER MISS IT!
HUH? THAT'S STRANGE...
THERE'S NOTHING HERE THAT COULD BE THE DRESS, OR EVEN SOME-THING LIKE A BOX OR BAG THAT IT COULD BE STORED IN.
OH MY, YOUR CLOTHES HAVE BEEN LEFT OUT.
I'LL PUT THIS AWAY IN THE DRESSER, OKAY?
THAT'S OKAY. DON'T BOTHER.

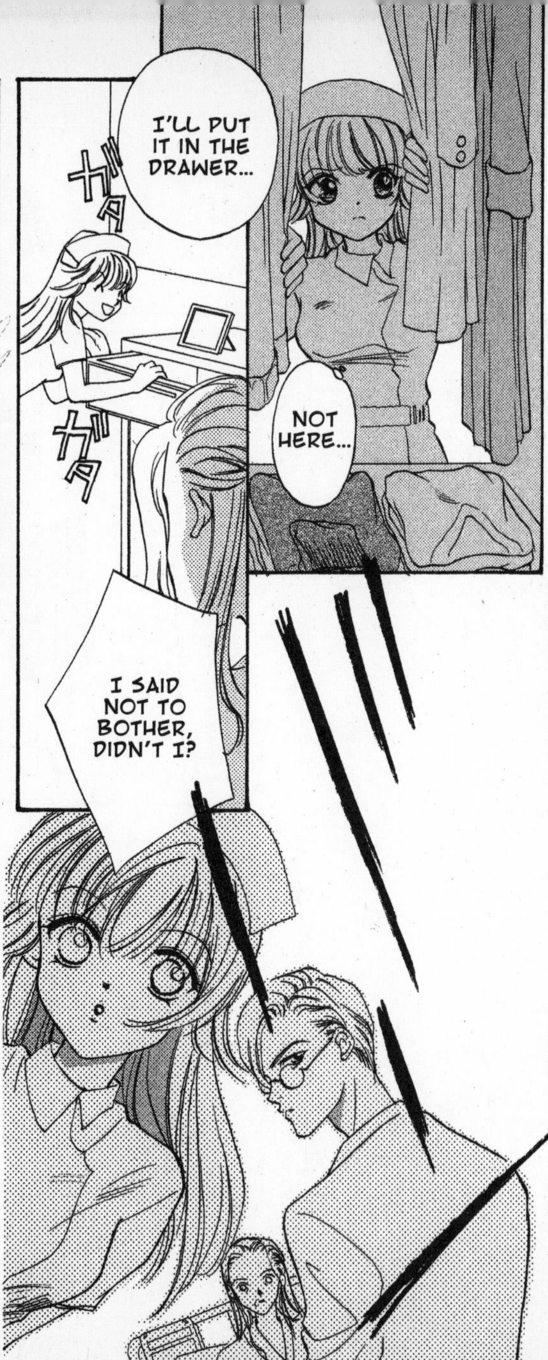
I'LL PUT IT IN THE DRAWER...
NOT HERE...
ガタ
ガタ
I SAID NOT TO BOTHER, DIDN'T I?

Maki Tatsumi Data

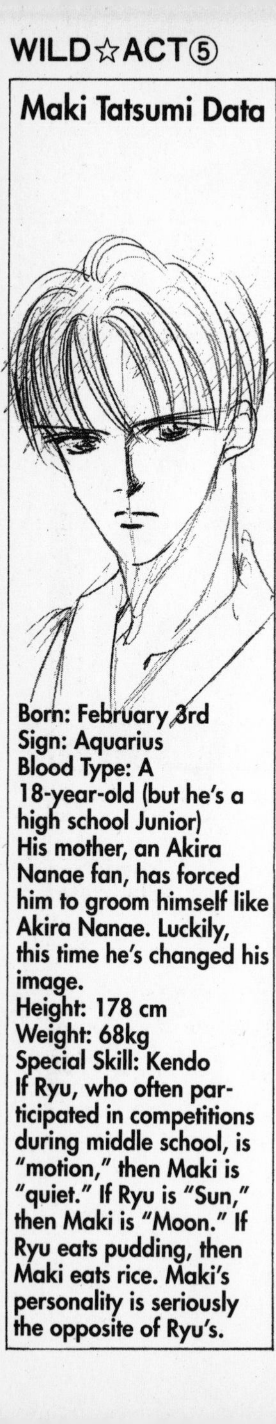

Born: February 3rd
Sign: Aquarius
Blood Type: A
18-year-old (but he's a high school Junior)
His mother, an Akira Nanae fan, has forced him to groom himself like Akira Nanae. Luckily, this time he's changed his image.
Height: 178 cm
Weight: 68kg
Special Skill: Kendo
If Ryu, who often participated in competitions during middle school, is "motion," then Maki is "quiet." If Ryu is "Sun," then Maki is "Moon." If Ryu eats pudding, then Maki eats rice. Maki's personality is seriously the opposite of Ryu's.

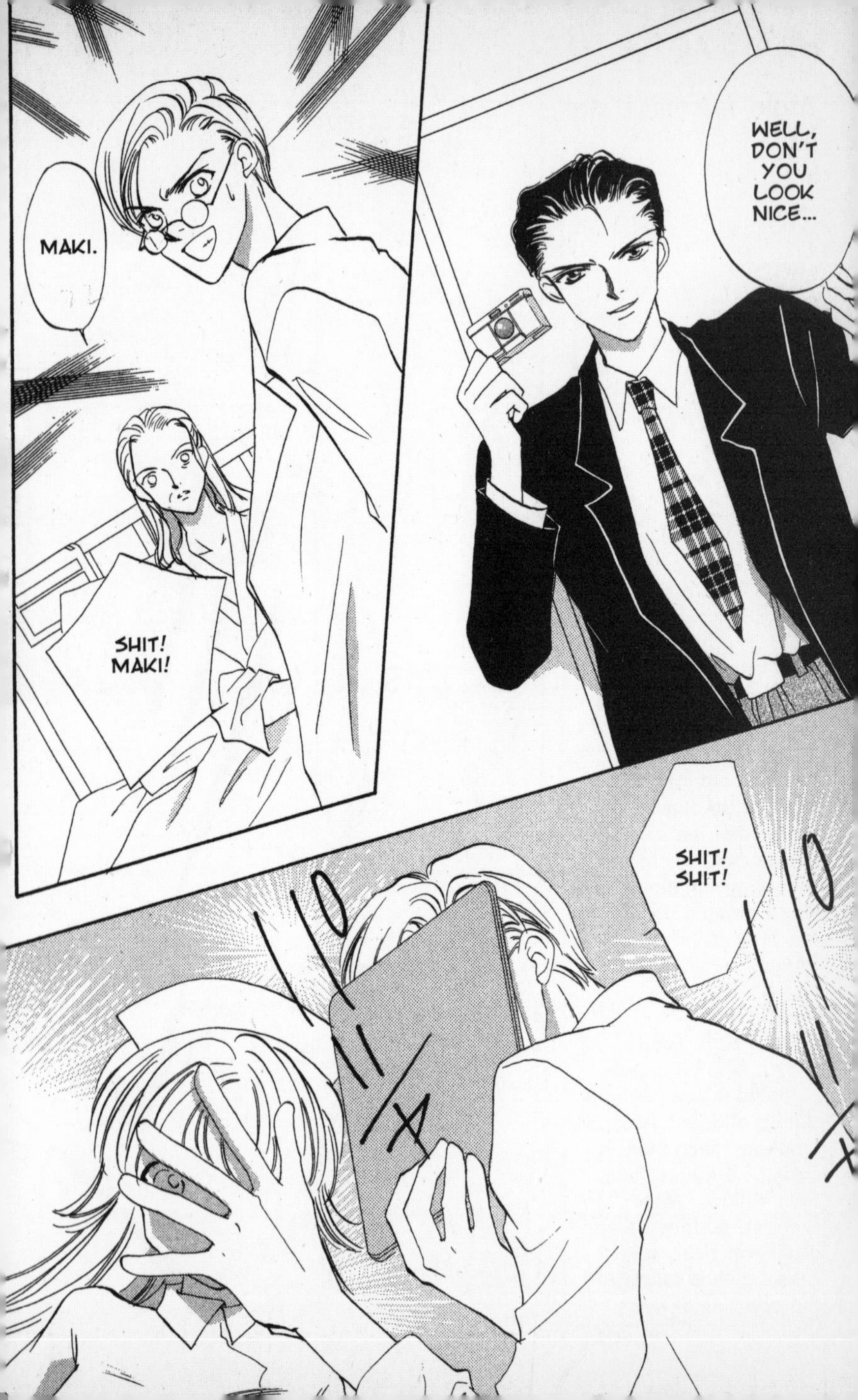
WELL, DON'T YOU LOOK NICE...
MAKI.
SHIT! MAKI!
SHIT! SHIT!

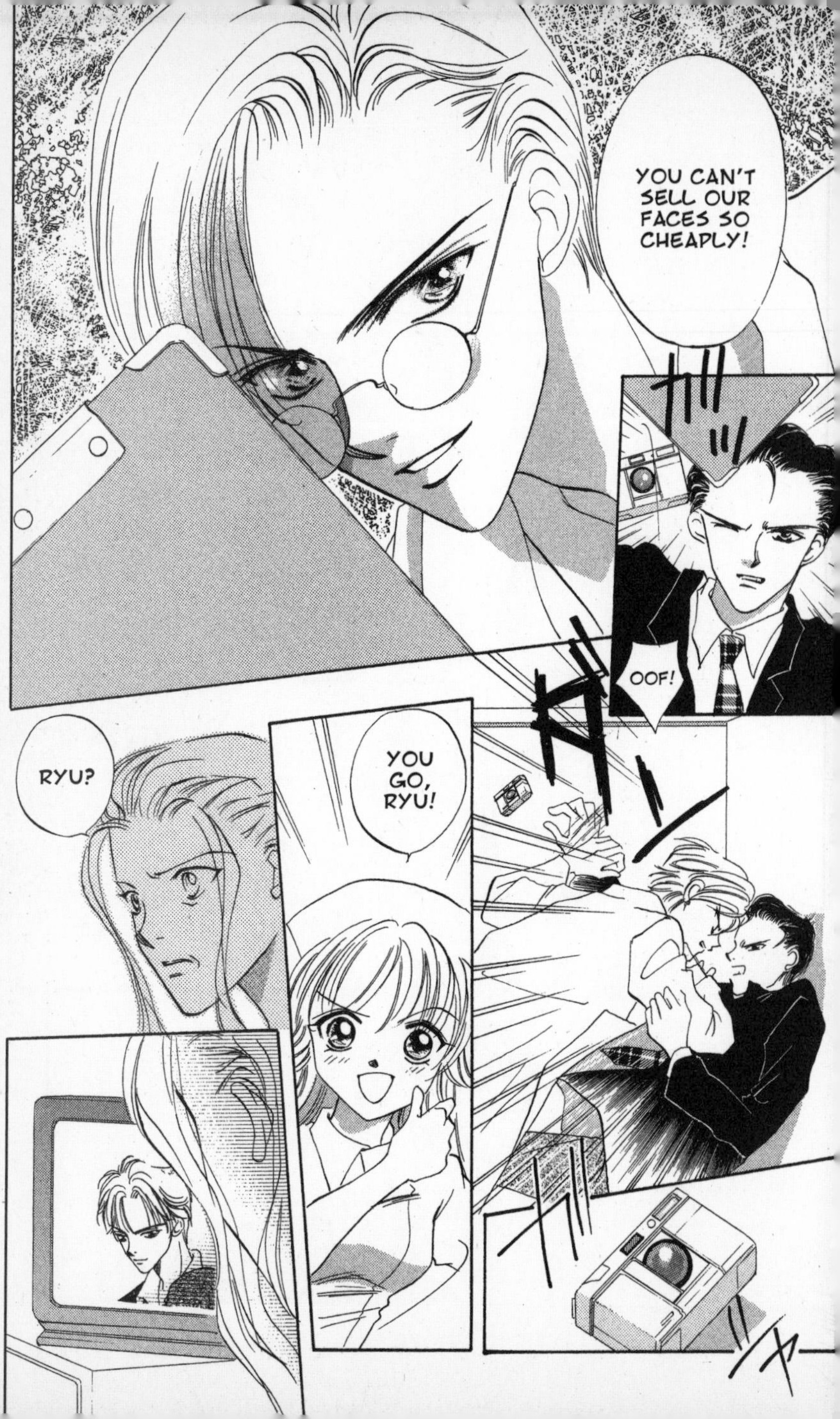
YOU CAN'T SELL OUR FACES SO CHEAPLY!
OOF!
YOU GO, RYU!
RYU?

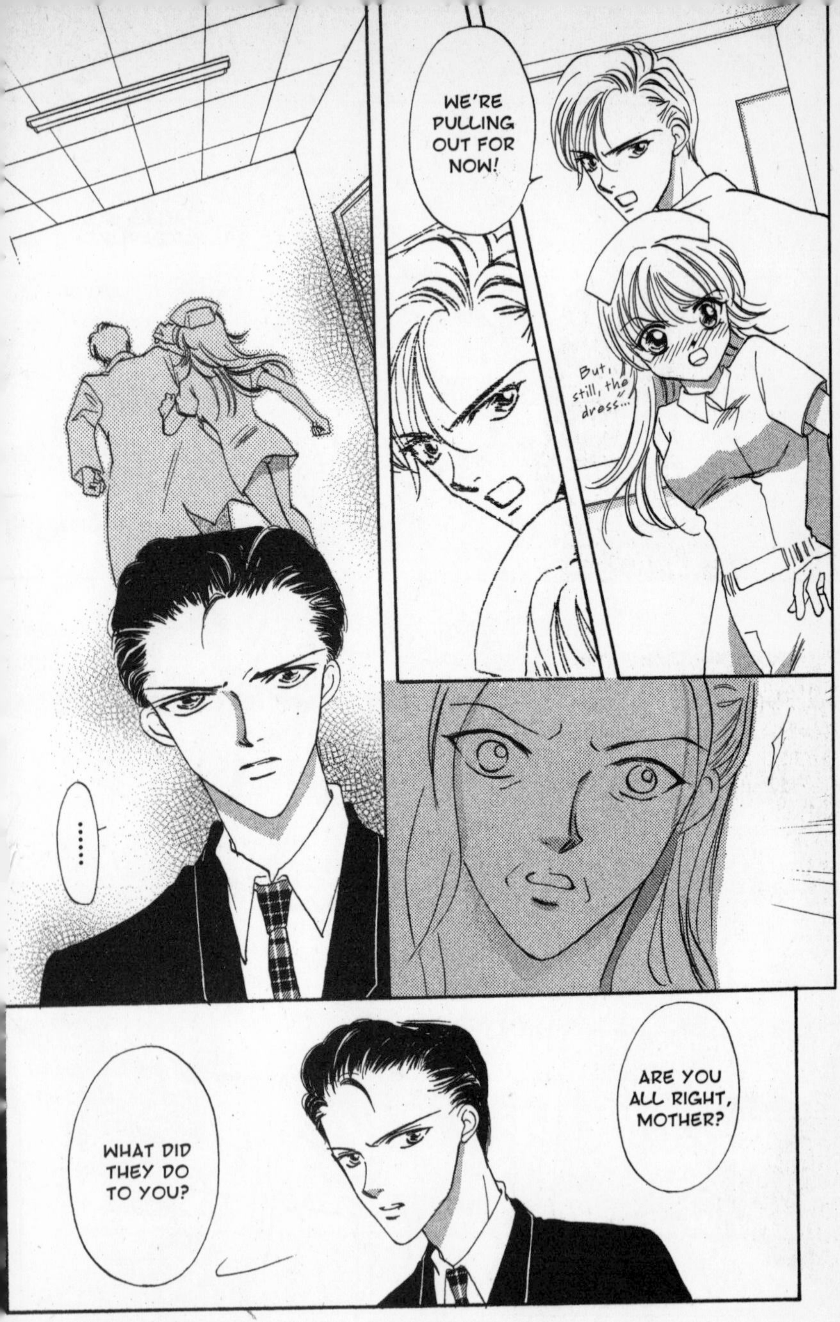

WE'RE PULLING OUT FOR NOW!
But, still, the dress...
......
ARE YOU ALL RIGHT, MOTHER?
WHAT DID THEY DO TO YOU?

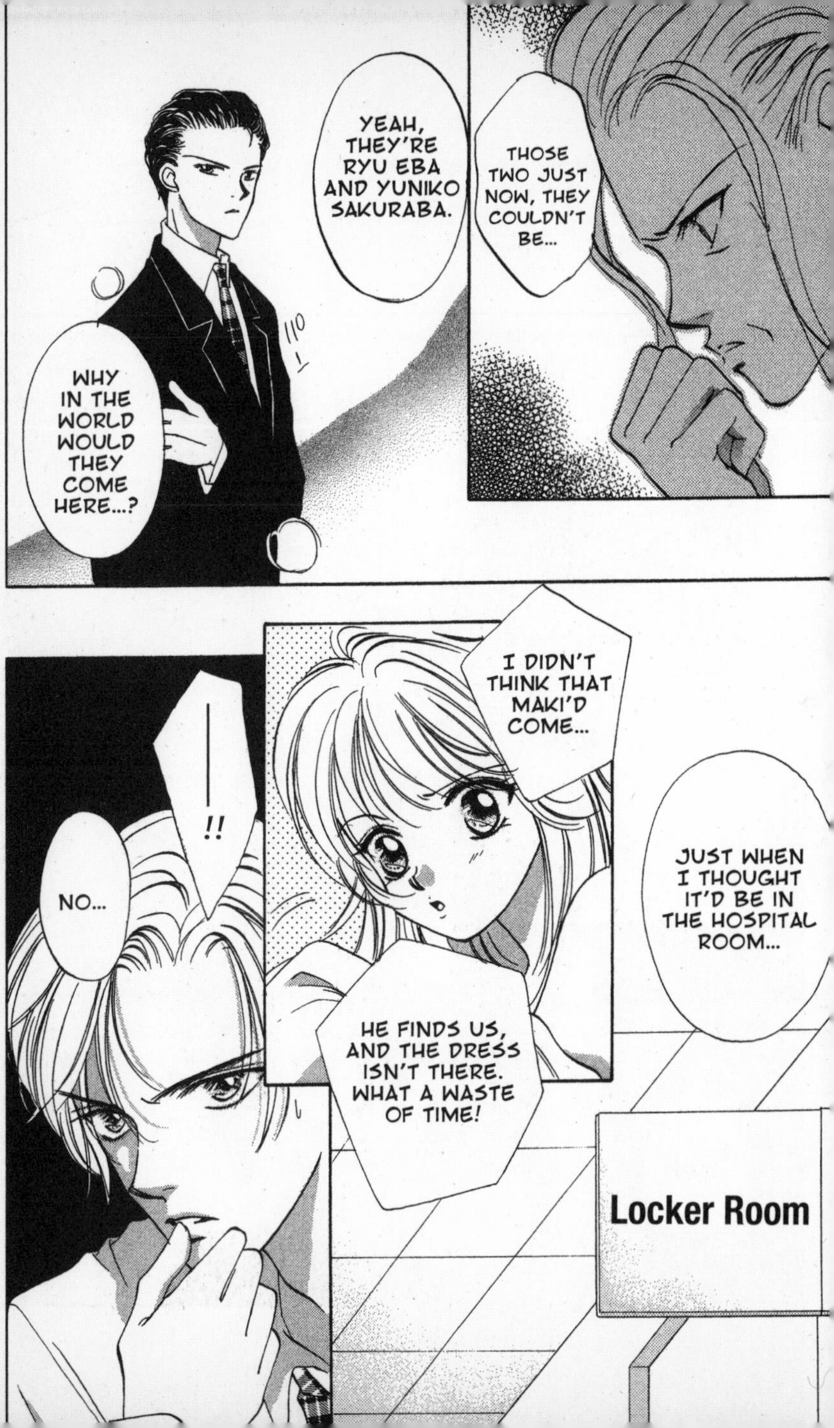
THOSE TWO JUST NOW, THEY COULDN'T BE...
YEAH, THEY'RE RYU EBA AND YUNIKO SAKURABA.
WHY IN THE WORLD WOULD THEY COME HERE...?
JUST WHEN I THOUGHT IT'D BE IN THE HOSPITAL ROOM...
Locker Room
I DIDN'T THINK THAT MAKI'D COME...
HE FINDS US, AND THE DRESS ISN'T THERE. WHAT A WASTE OF TIME!
—!!
NO...

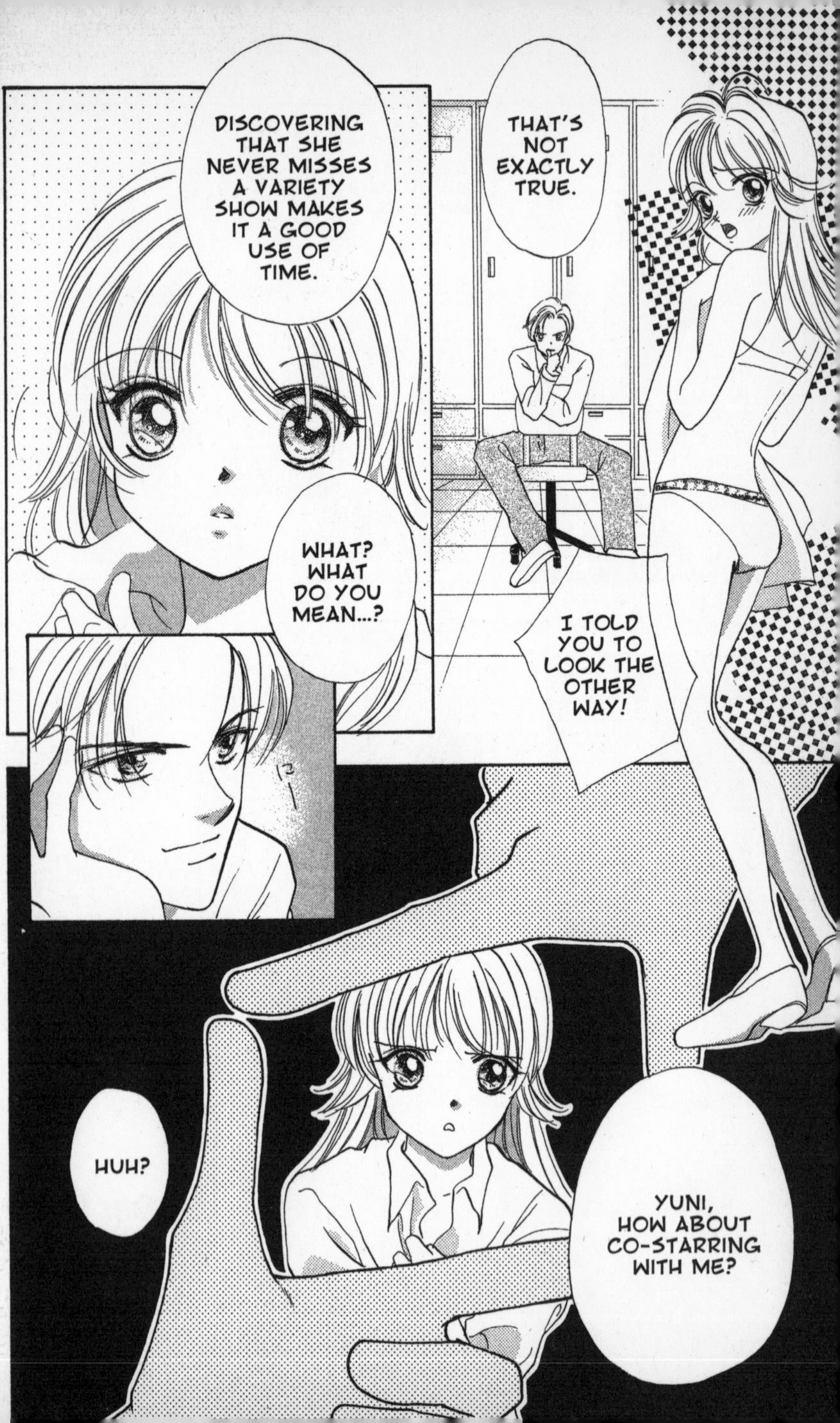
THAT'S NOT EXACTLY TRUE.
I TOLD YOU TO LOOK THE OTHER WAY!
DISCOVERING THAT SHE NEVER MISSES A VARIETY SHOW MAKES IT A GOOD USE OF TIME.
WHAT? WHAT DO YOU MEAN...?
YUNI, HOW ABOUT CO-STARRING WITH ME?
HUH?

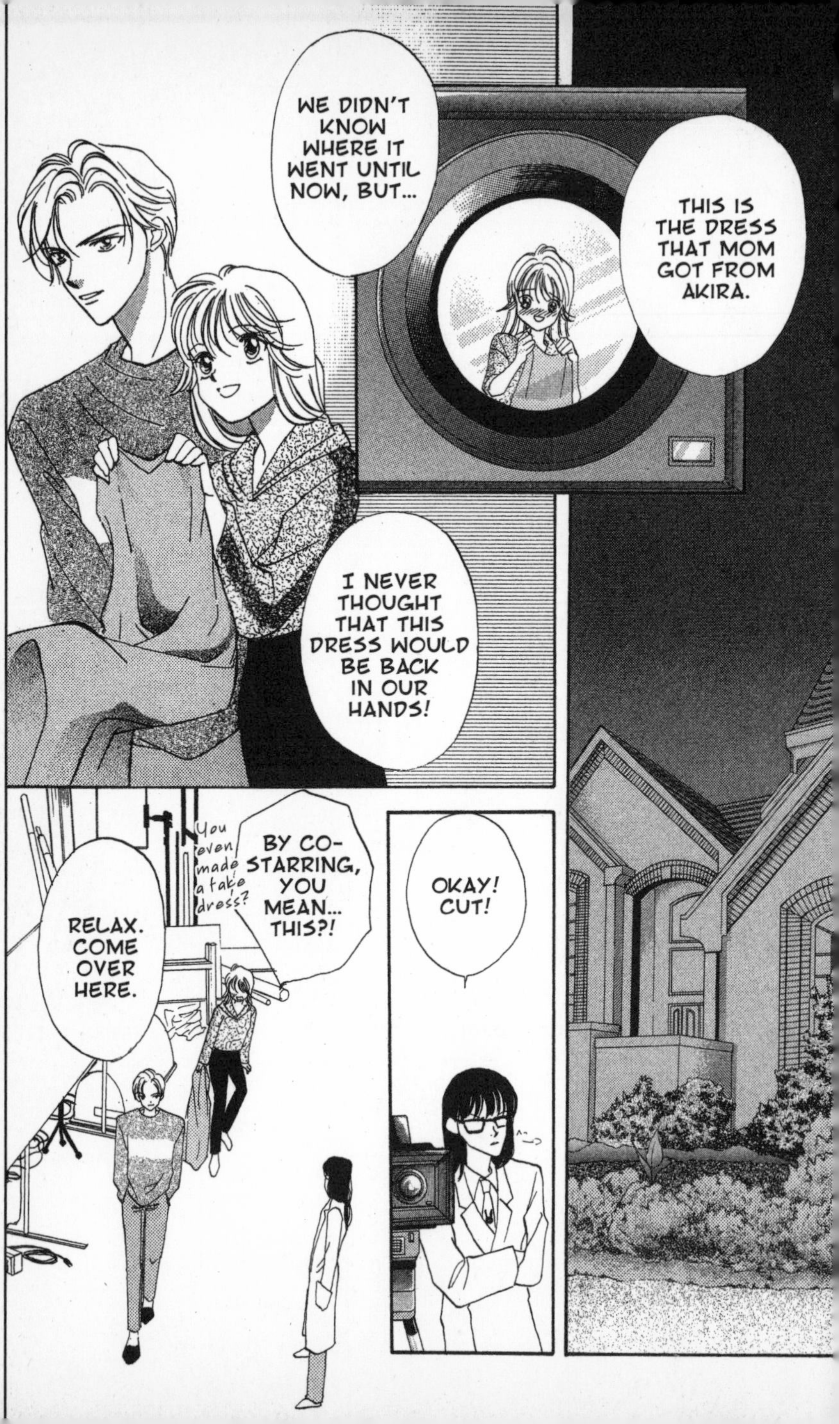
THIS IS THE DRESS THAT MOM GOT FROM AKIRA.
WE DIDN'T KNOW WHERE IT WENT UNTIL NOW, BUT...
I NEVER THOUGHT THAT THIS DRESS WOULD BE BACK IN OUR HANDS!
OKAY! CUT!
BY CO-STARRING, YOU MEAN... THIS?!
You even made a fake dress?
RELAX. COME OVER HERE.

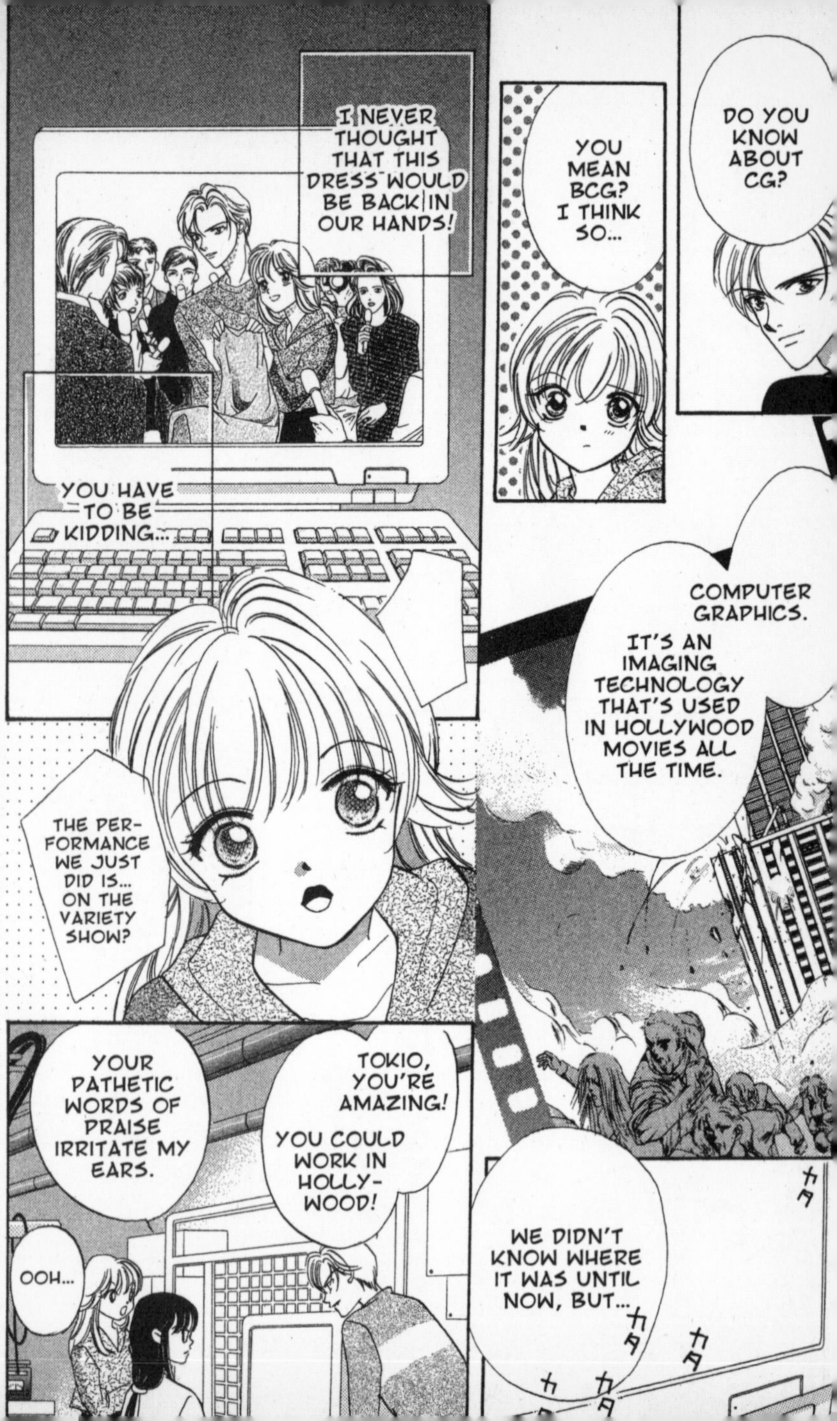

DO YOU KNOW ABOUT CG?
YOU MEAN BCG? I THINK SO...
COMPUTER GRAPHICS.
IT'S AN IMAGING TECHNOLOGY THAT'S USED IN HOLLYWOOD MOVIES ALL THE TIME.
I NEVER THOUGHT THAT THIS DRESS WOULD BE BACK IN OUR HANDS!
YOU HAVE TO BE KIDDING...
THE PERFORMANCE WE JUST DID IS... ON THE VARIETY SHOW?
カタ
WE DIDN'T KNOW WHERE IT WAS UNTIL NOW, BUT...
カタ
カタ
カタ
カタ
TOKIO, YOU'RE AMAZING!
YOU COULD WORK IN HOLLYWOOD!
YOUR PATHETIC WORDS OF PRAISE IRRITATE MY EARS.
OOH...

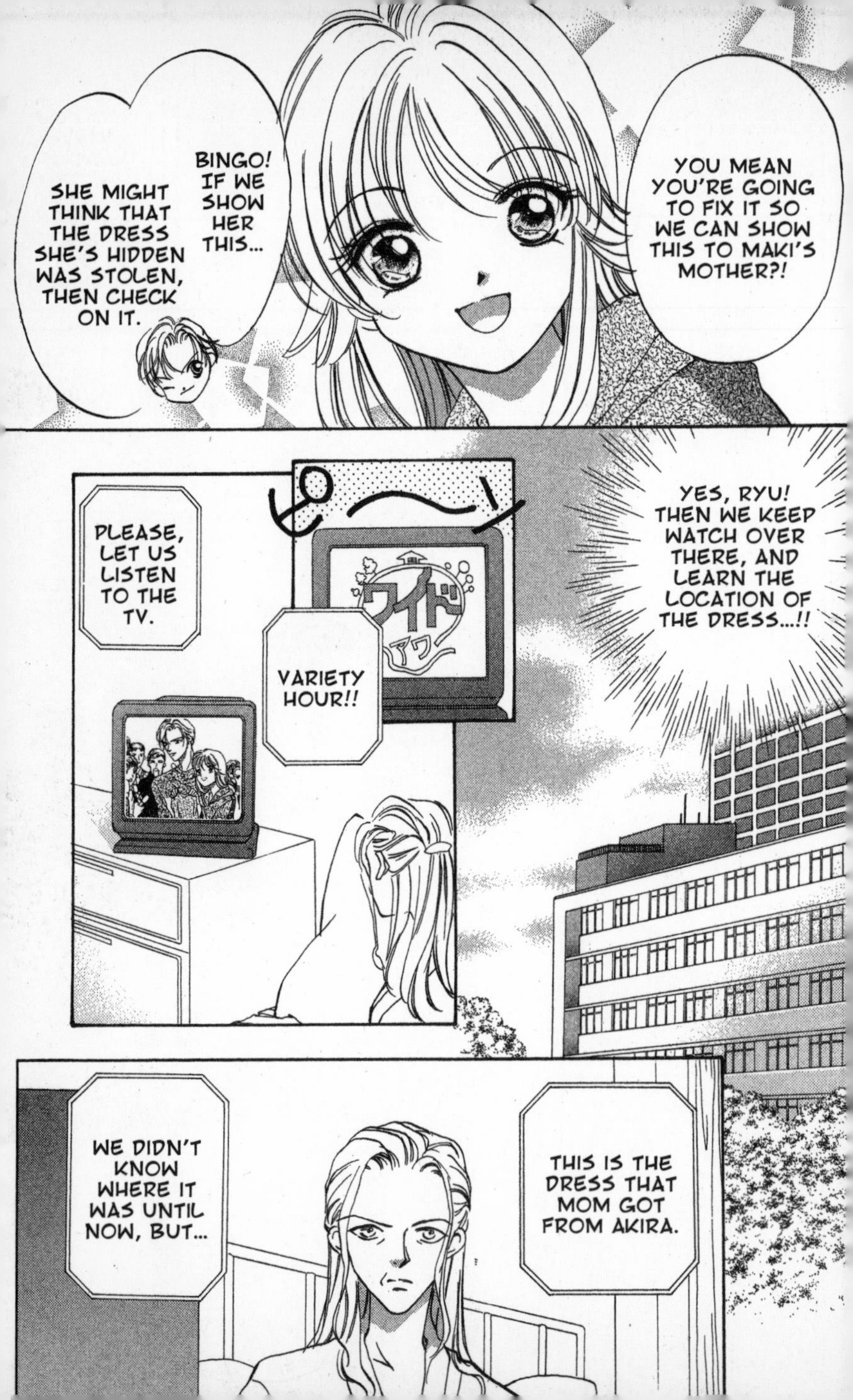
YOU MEAN YOU'RE GOING TO FIX IT SO WE CAN SHOW THIS TO MAKI'S MOTHER?!
BINGO! IF WE SHOW HER THIS...
SHE MIGHT THINK THAT THE DRESS SHE'S HIDDEN WAS STOLEN, THEN CHECK ON IT.
YES, RYU! THEN WE KEEP WATCH OVER THERE, AND LEARN THE LOCATION OF THE DRESS...!!
ピー―ッ
ワイド
アワー
VARIETY HOUR!!
PLEASE, LET US LISTEN TO THE TV.
THIS IS THE DRESS THAT MOM GOT FROM AKIRA.
WE DIDN'T KNOW WHERE IT WAS UNTIL NOW, BUT...

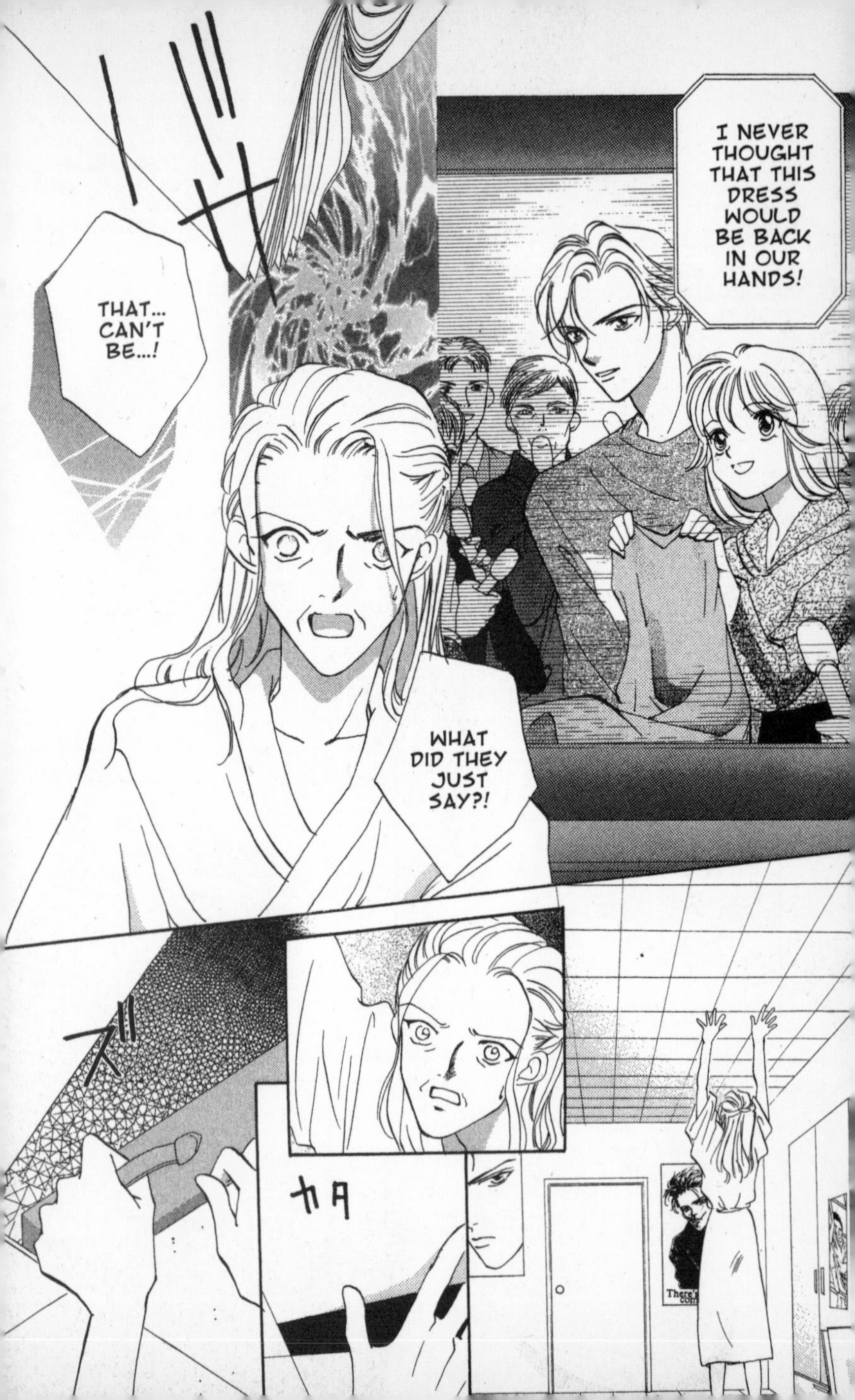
I NEVER THOUGHT THAT THIS DRESS WOULD BE BACK IN OUR HANDS!
THAT... CAN'T BE...!
WHAT DID THEY JUST SAY?!
カタ

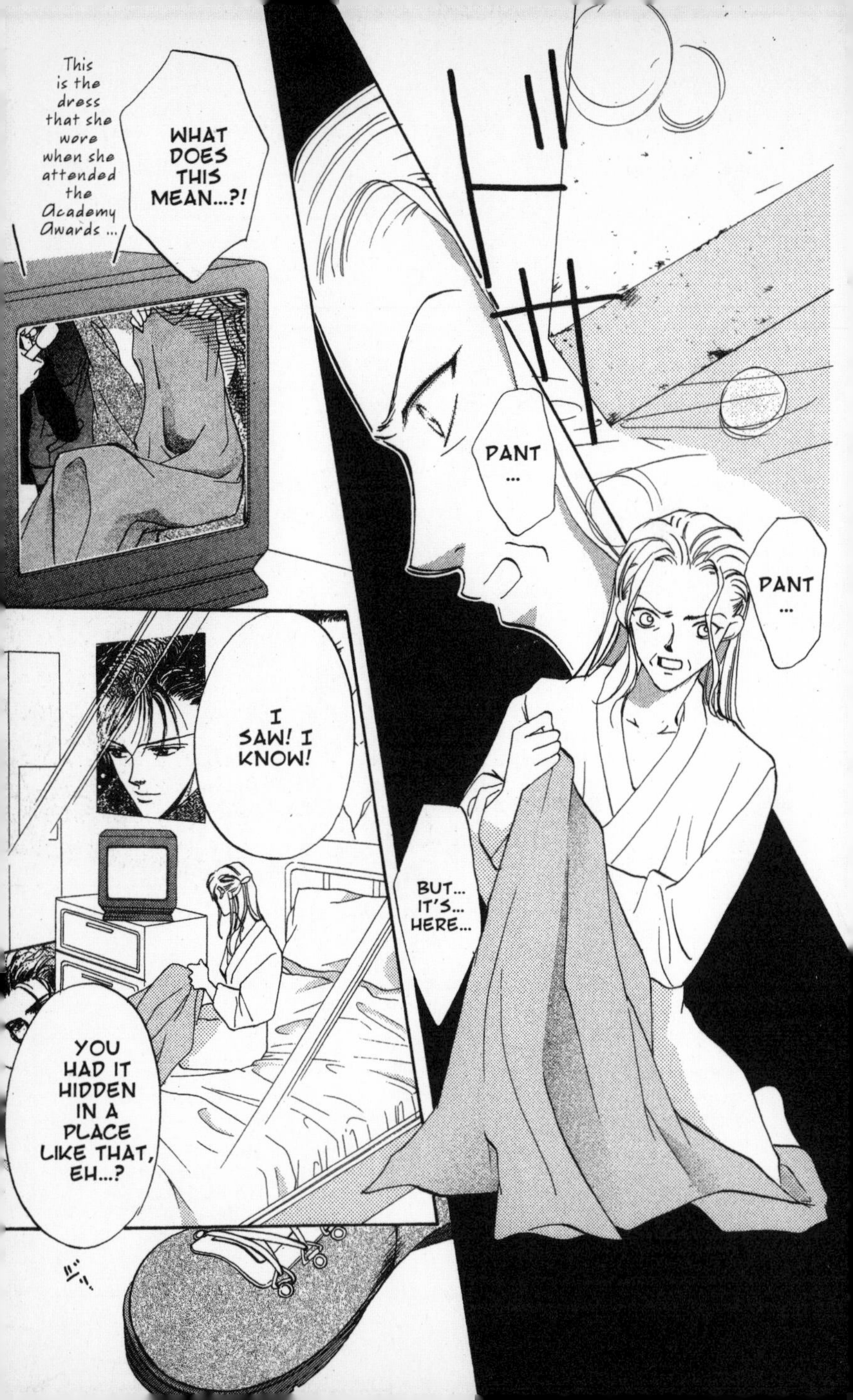

PANT...
PANT...
BUT... IT'S... HERE...
WHAT DOES THIS MEAN...?!
This is the dress that she wore when she attended the Academy Awards ...
I SAW! I KNOW!
YOU HAD IT HIDDEN IN A PLACE LIKE THAT, EH...?

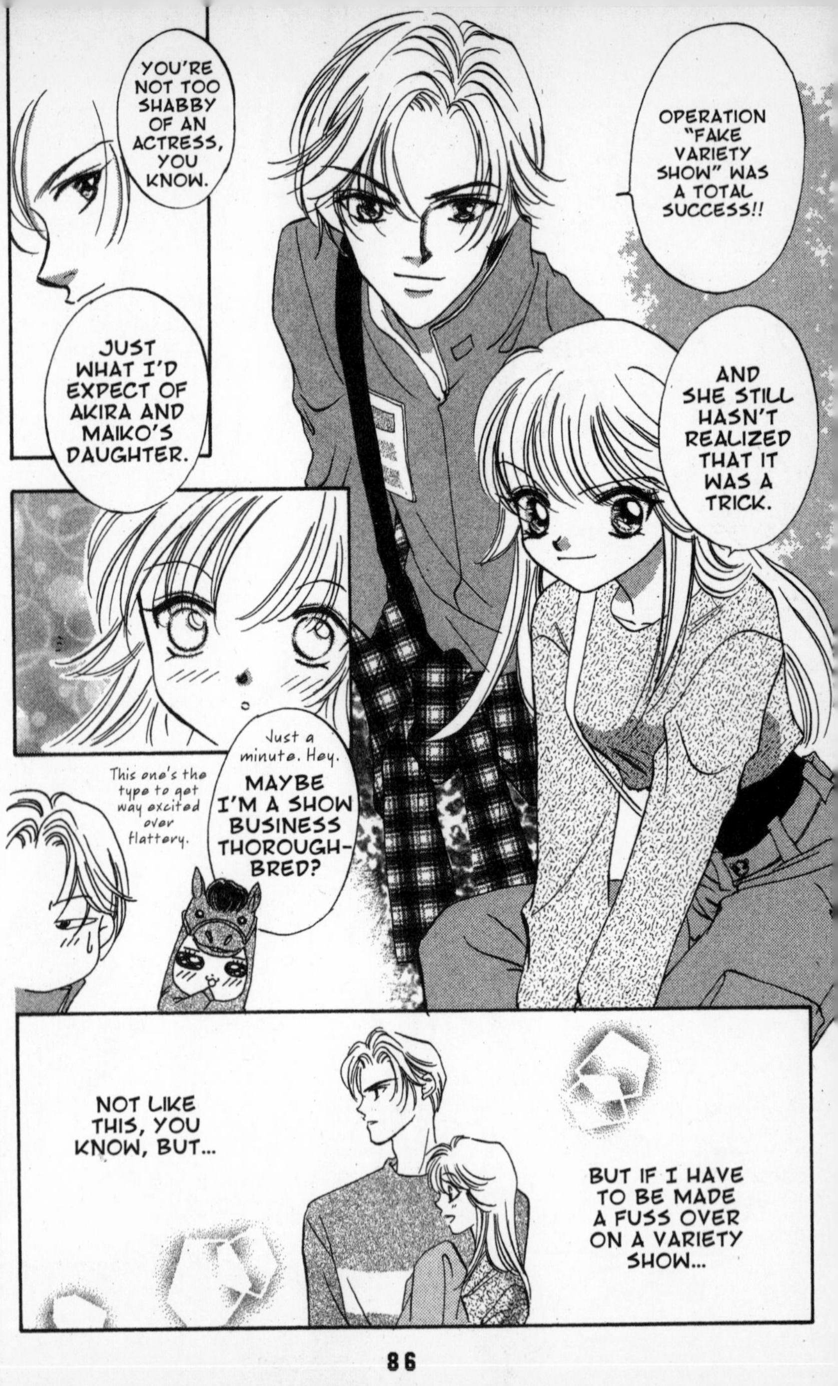
OPERATION "FAKE VARIETY SHOW" WAS A TOTAL SUCCESS!!
AND SHE STILL HASN'T REALIZED THAT IT WAS A TRICK.
YOU'RE NOT TOO SHABBY OF AN ACTRESS, YOU KNOW.
JUST WHAT I'D EXPECT OF AKIRA AND MAIKO'S DAUGHTER.
Just a minute. Hey. MAYBE I'M A SHOW BUSINESS THOROUGHBRED?
This one's the type to get way excited over flattery.
NOT LIKE THIS, YOU KNOW, BUT...
BUT IF I HAVE TO BE MADE A FUSS OVER ON A VARIETY SHOW...

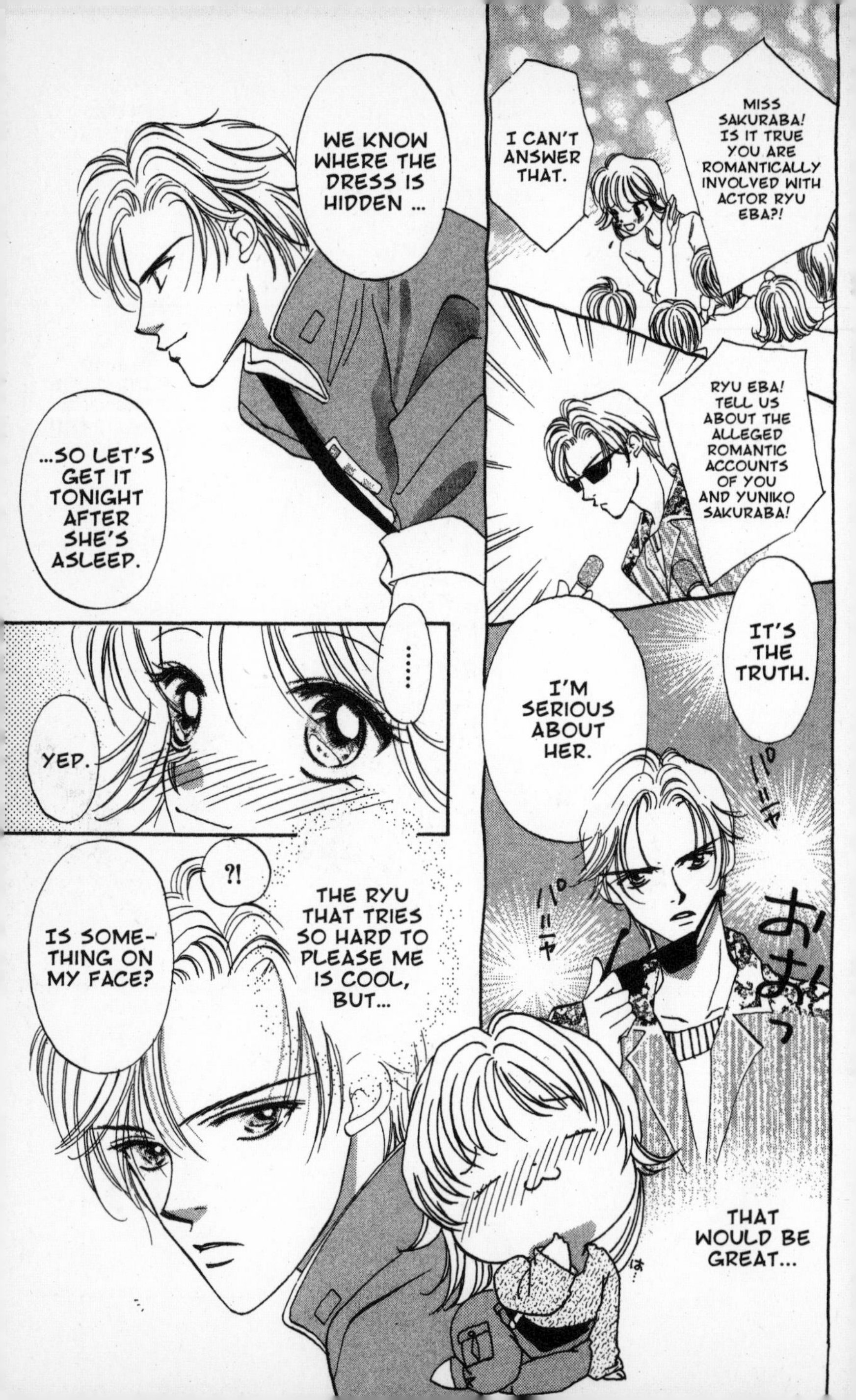
WE KNOW WHERE THE DRESS IS HIDDEN ...
...SO LET'S GET IT TONIGHT AFTER SHE'S ASLEEP.
......
YEP.
?!
IS SOME-THING ON MY FACE?
THE RYU THAT TRIES SO HARD TO PLEASE ME IS COOL, BUT...
MISS SAKURABA! IS IT TRUE YOU ARE ROMANTICALLY INVOLVED WITH ACTOR RYU EBA?!
I CAN'T ANSWER THAT.
RYU EBA! TELL US ABOUT THE ALLEGED ROMANTIC ACCOUNTS OF YOU AND YUNIKO SAKURABA!
IT'S THE TRUTH.
I'M SERIOUS ABOUT HER.
パシャ
パシャ
おおっ
THAT WOULD BE GREAT...
は…

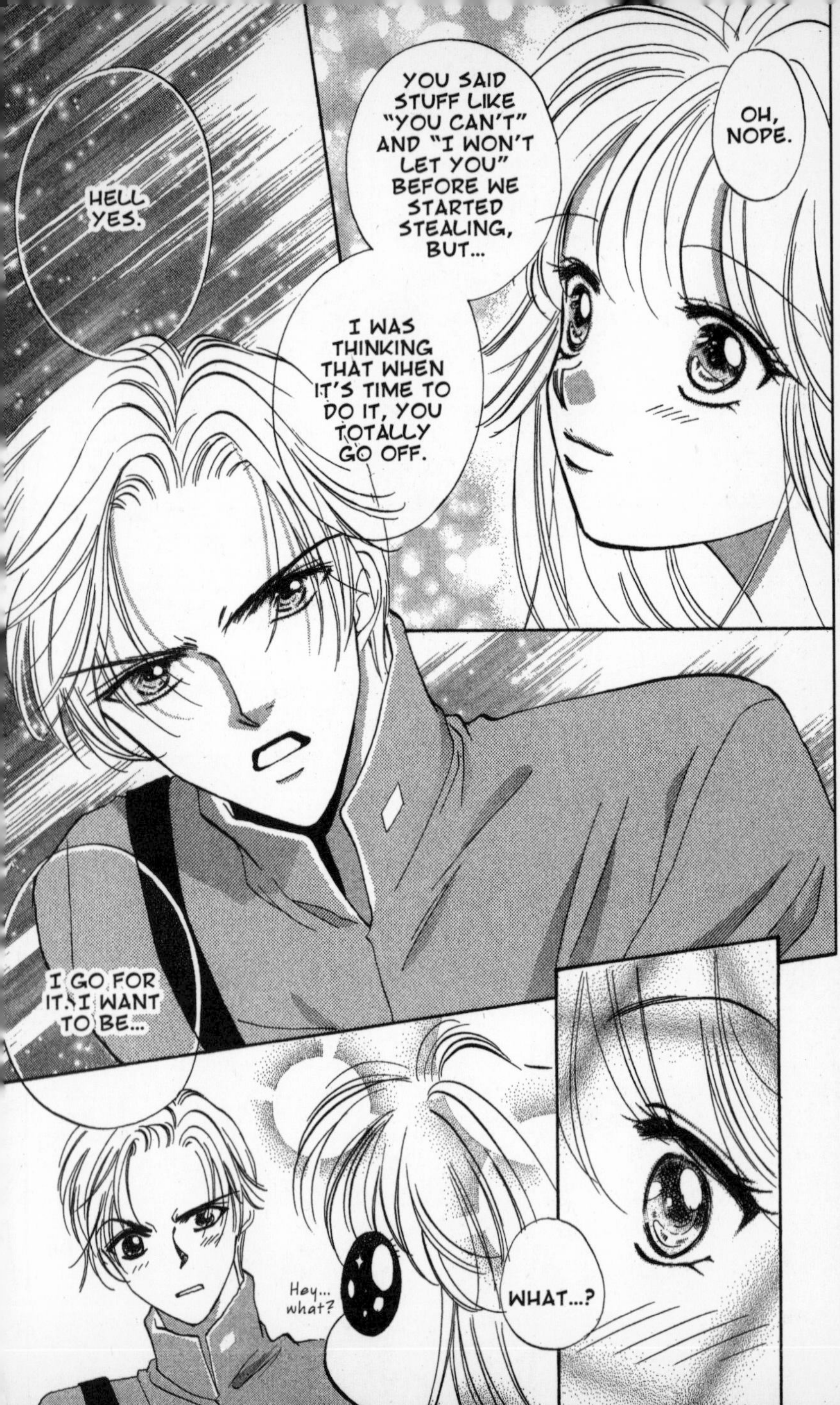
OH, NOPE.
YOU SAID STUFF LIKE "YOU CAN'T" AND "I WON'T LET YOU" BEFORE WE STARTED STEALING, BUT...
I WAS THINKING THAT WHEN IT'S TIME TO DO IT, YOU TOTALLY GO OFF.
HELL YES.
I GO FOR IT. I WANT TO BE...
WHAT...?
Hey... what?

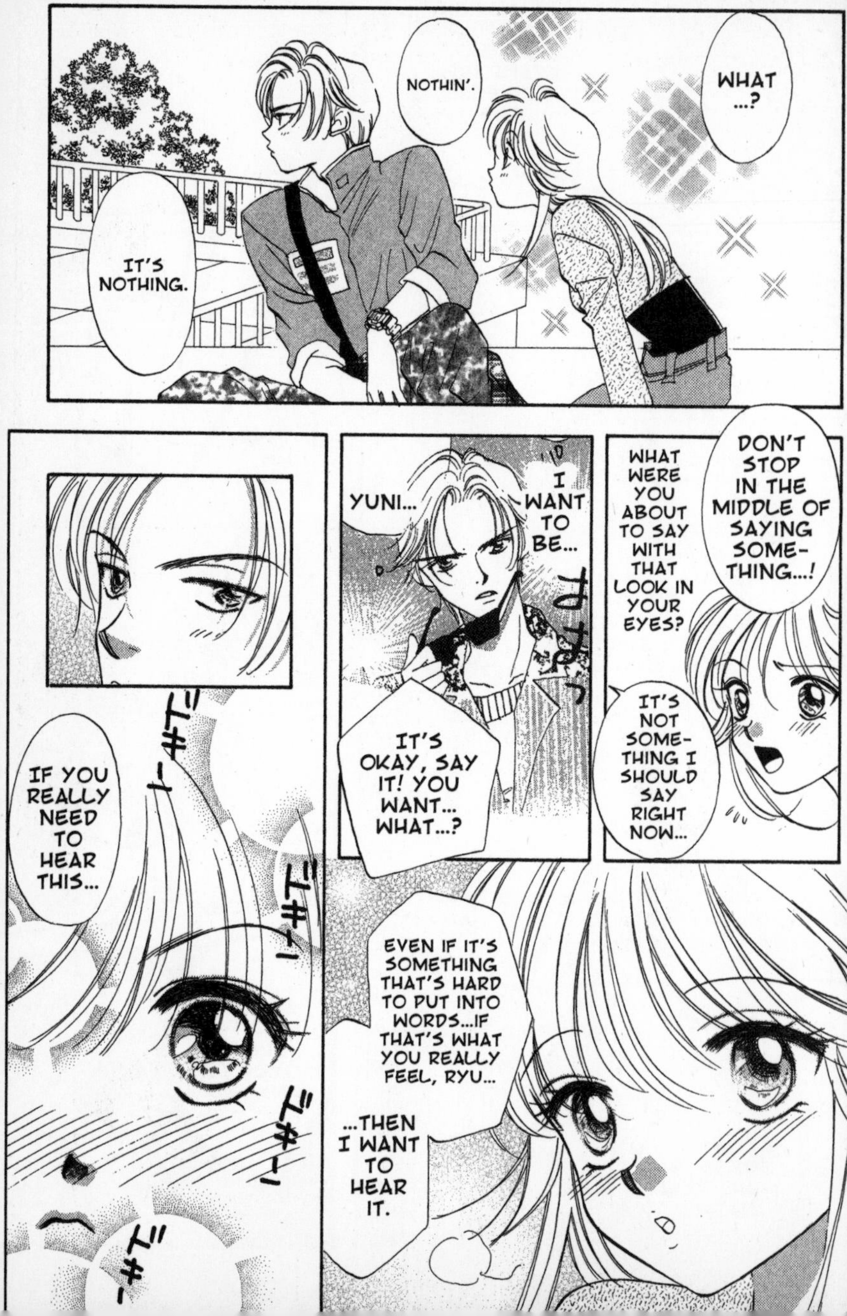
WHAT ...?
NOTHIN'.
IT'S NOTHING.
DON'T STOP IN THE MIDDLE OF SAYING SOME-THING...!
WHAT WERE YOU ABOUT TO SAY WITH THAT LOOK IN YOUR EYES?
IT'S NOT SOME-THING I SHOULD SAY RIGHT NOW...
I WANT TO BE...
YUNI...
IT'S OKAY, SAY IT! YOU WANT... WHAT...?
EVEN IF IT'S SOMETHING THAT'S HARD TO PUT INTO WORDS...IF THAT'S WHAT YOU REALLY FEEL, RYU...
...THEN I WANT TO HEAR IT.
IF YOU REALLY NEED TO HEAR THIS...

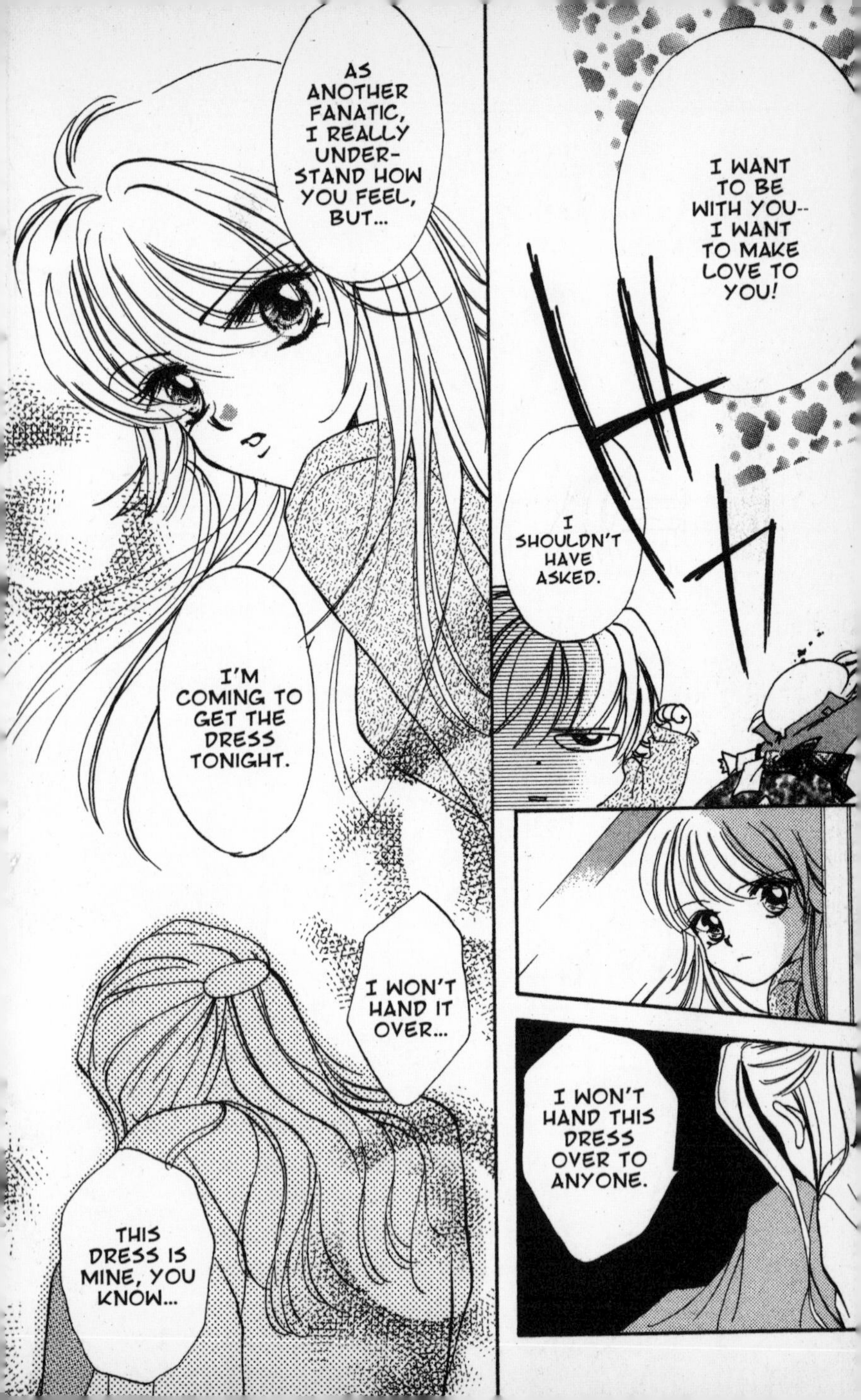
I WANT TO BE WITH YOU-- I WANT TO MAKE LOVE TO YOU!
I SHOULDN'T HAVE ASKED.
I WON'T HAND THIS DRESS OVER TO ANYONE.
AS ANOTHER FANATIC, I REALLY UNDER-STAND HOW YOU FEEL, BUT...
I'M COMING TO GET THE DRESS TONIGHT.
I WON'T HAND IT OVER...
THIS DRESS IS MINE, YOU KNOW...

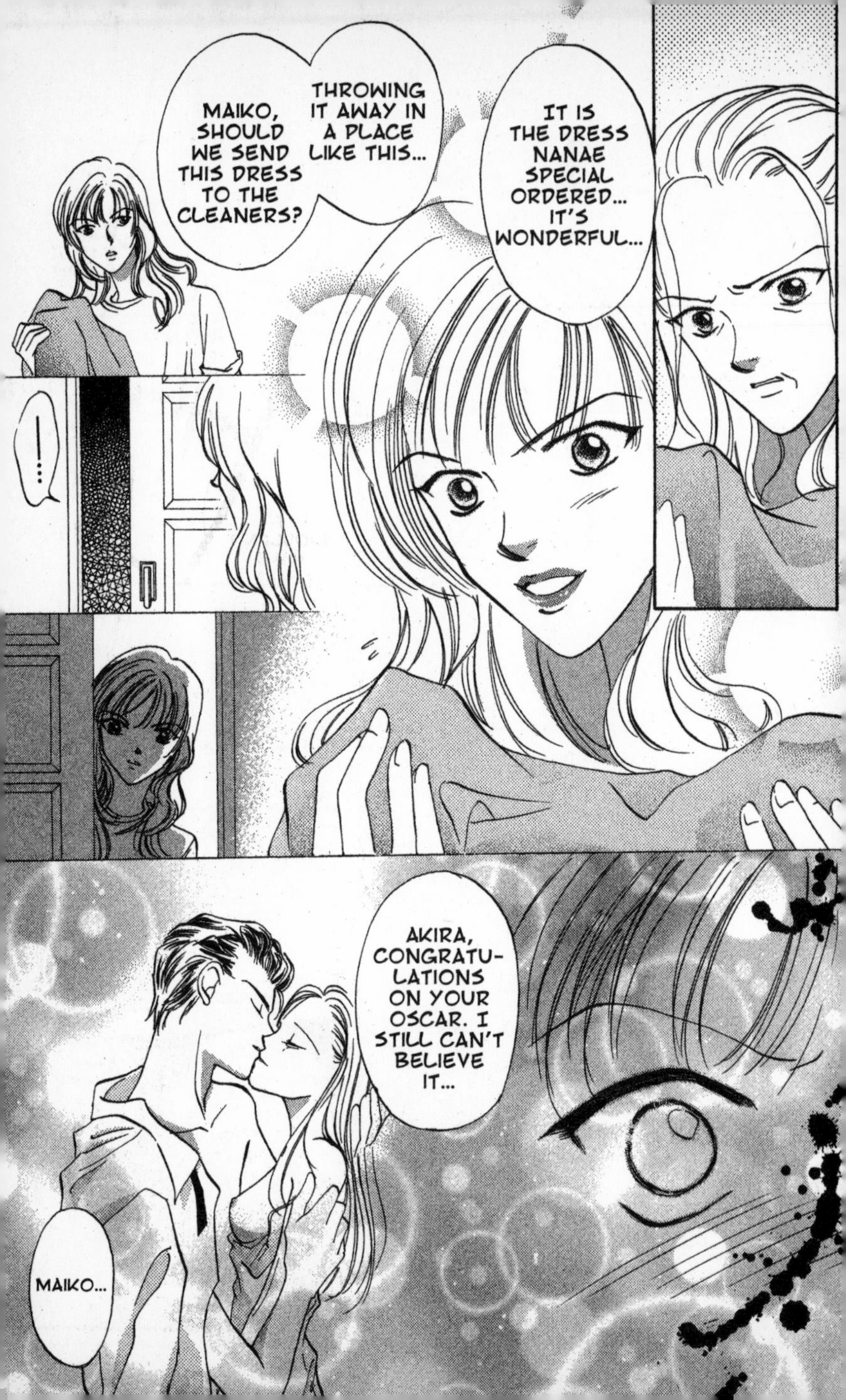
IT IS THE DRESS NANAE SPECIAL ORDERED... IT'S WONDERFUL...
MAIKO, SHOULD WE SEND THIS DRESS TO THE CLEANERS?
THROWING IT AWAY IN A PLACE LIKE THIS...
!...
AKIRA, CONGRATU-LATIONS ON YOUR OSCAR. I STILL CAN'T BELIEVE IT...
MAIKO...

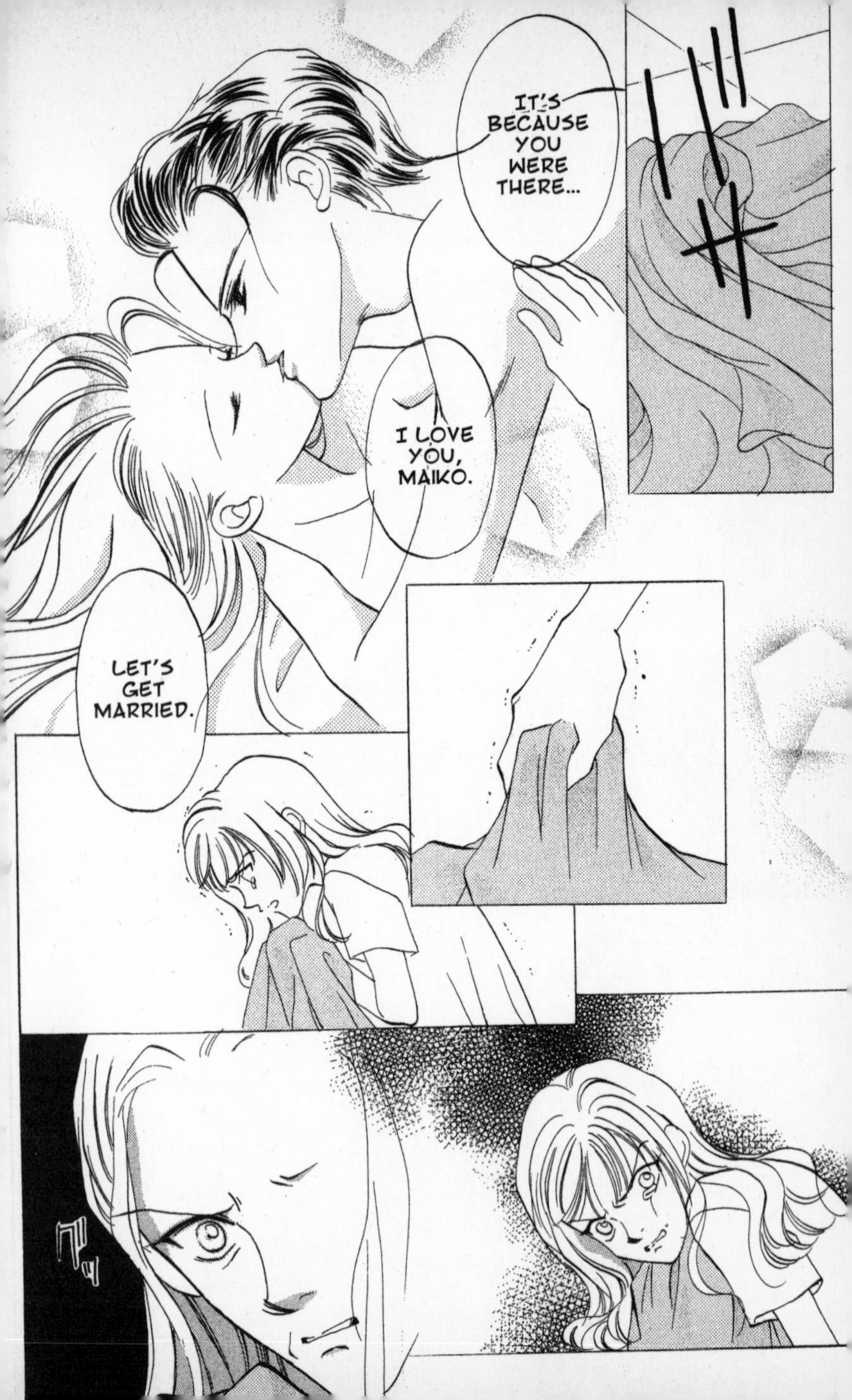
IT'S BECAUSE YOU WERE THERE...
I LOVE YOU, MAIKO.
LET'S GET MARRIED.

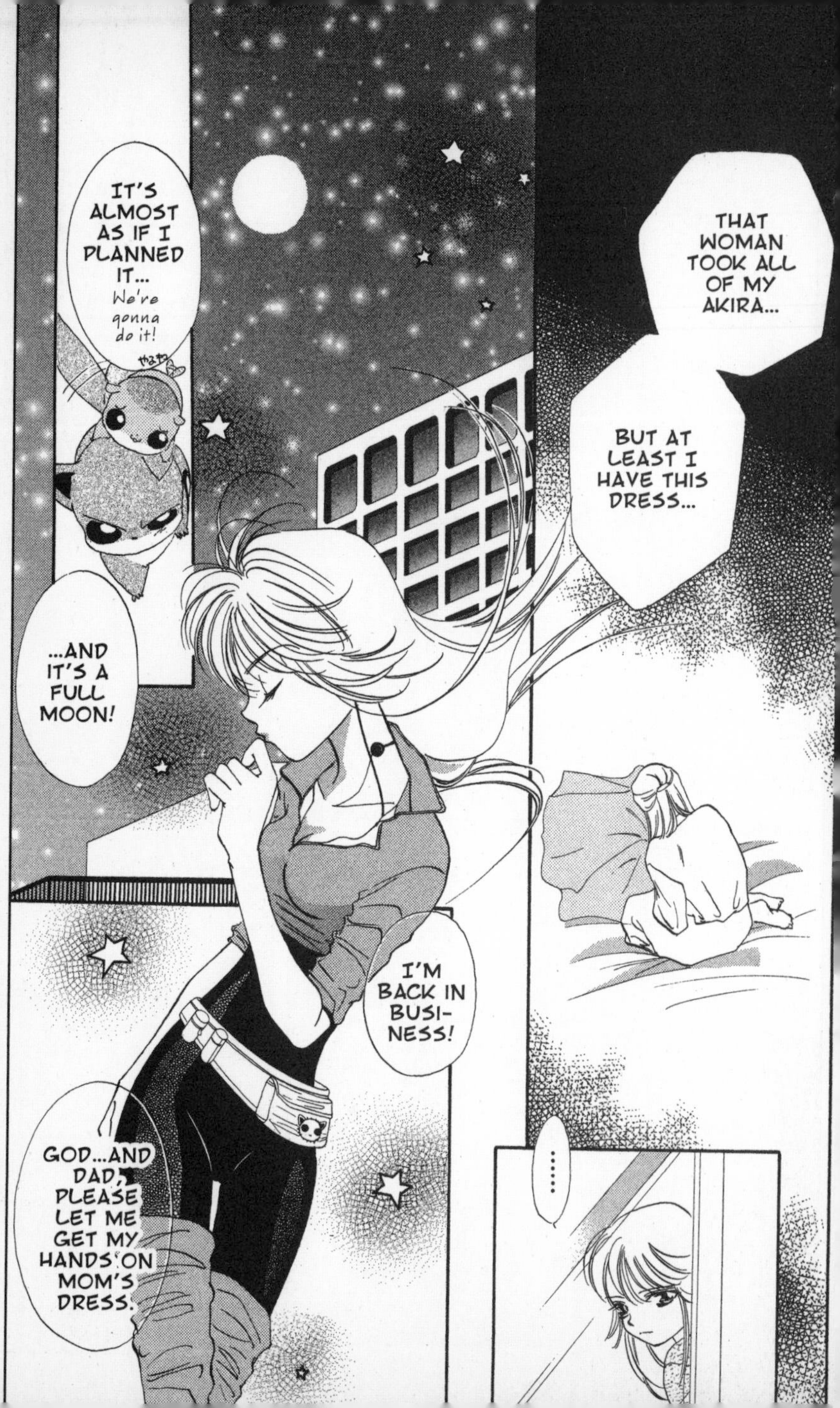
THAT WOMAN TOOK ALL OF MY AKIRA...
BUT AT LEAST I HAVE THIS DRESS...
......
IT'S ALMOST AS IF I PLANNED IT...
We're gonna do it!
...AND IT'S A FULL MOON!
I'M BACK IN BUSI-NESS!
GOD...AND DAD, PLEASE LET ME GET MY HANDS ON MOM'S DRESS.

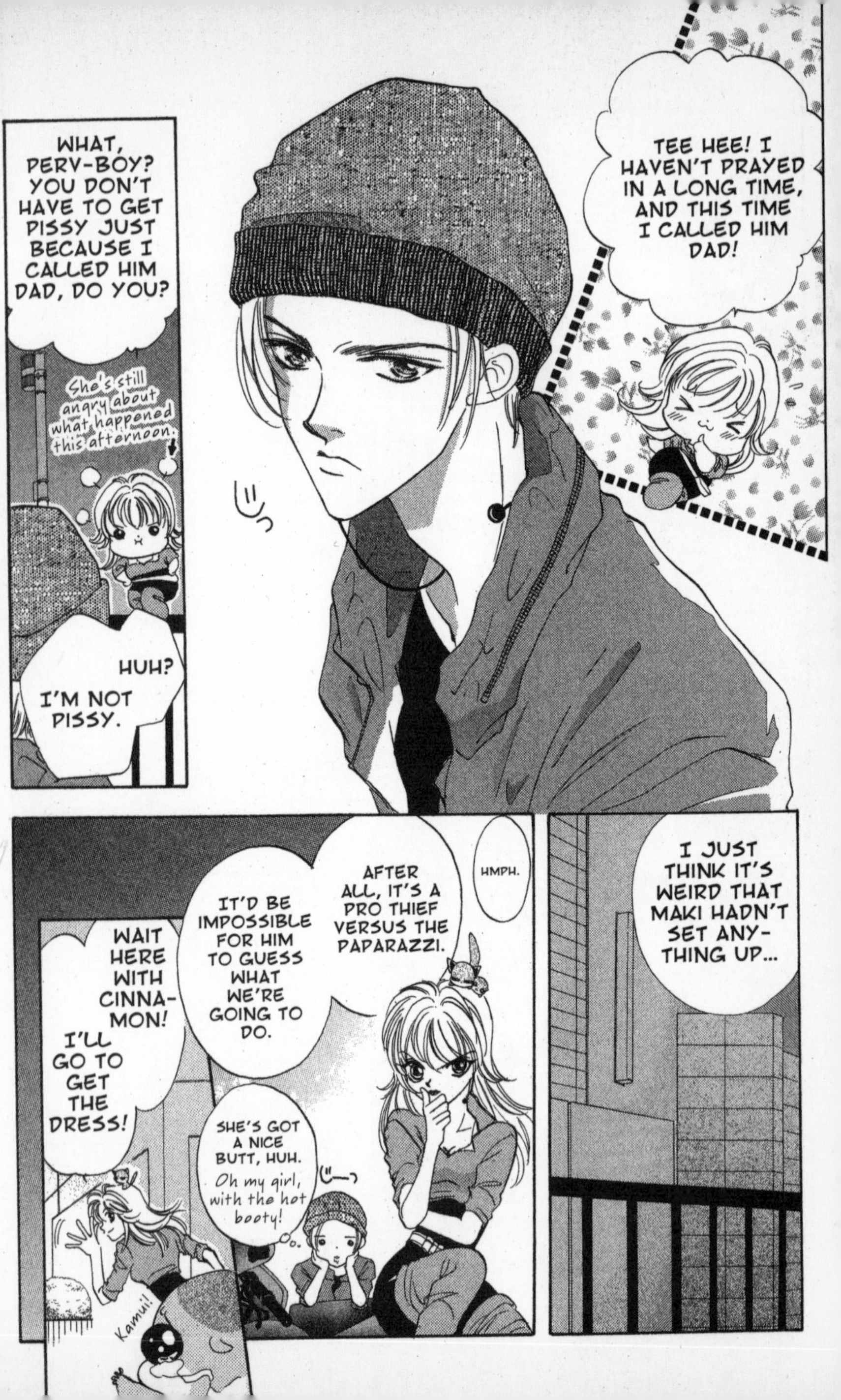
TEE HEE! I HAVEN'T PRAYED IN A LONG TIME, AND THIS TIME I CALLED HIM DAD!
WHAT, PERV-BOY? YOU DON'T HAVE TO GET PISSY JUST BECAUSE I CALLED HIM DAD, DO YOU?
She's still angry about what happened this afternoon.
HUH?
I'M NOT PISSY.
I JUST THINK IT'S WEIRD THAT MAKI HADN'T SET ANY-THING UP...
HMPH.
AFTER ALL, IT'S A PRO THIEF VERSUS THE PAPARAZZI.
IT'D BE IMPOSSIBLE FOR HIM TO GUESS WHAT WE'RE GOING TO DO.
WAIT HERE WITH CINNA-MON!
I'LL GO TO GET THE DRESS!
SHE'S GOT A NICE BUTT, HUH.
Oh my girl, with the hot booty!
Kamui!

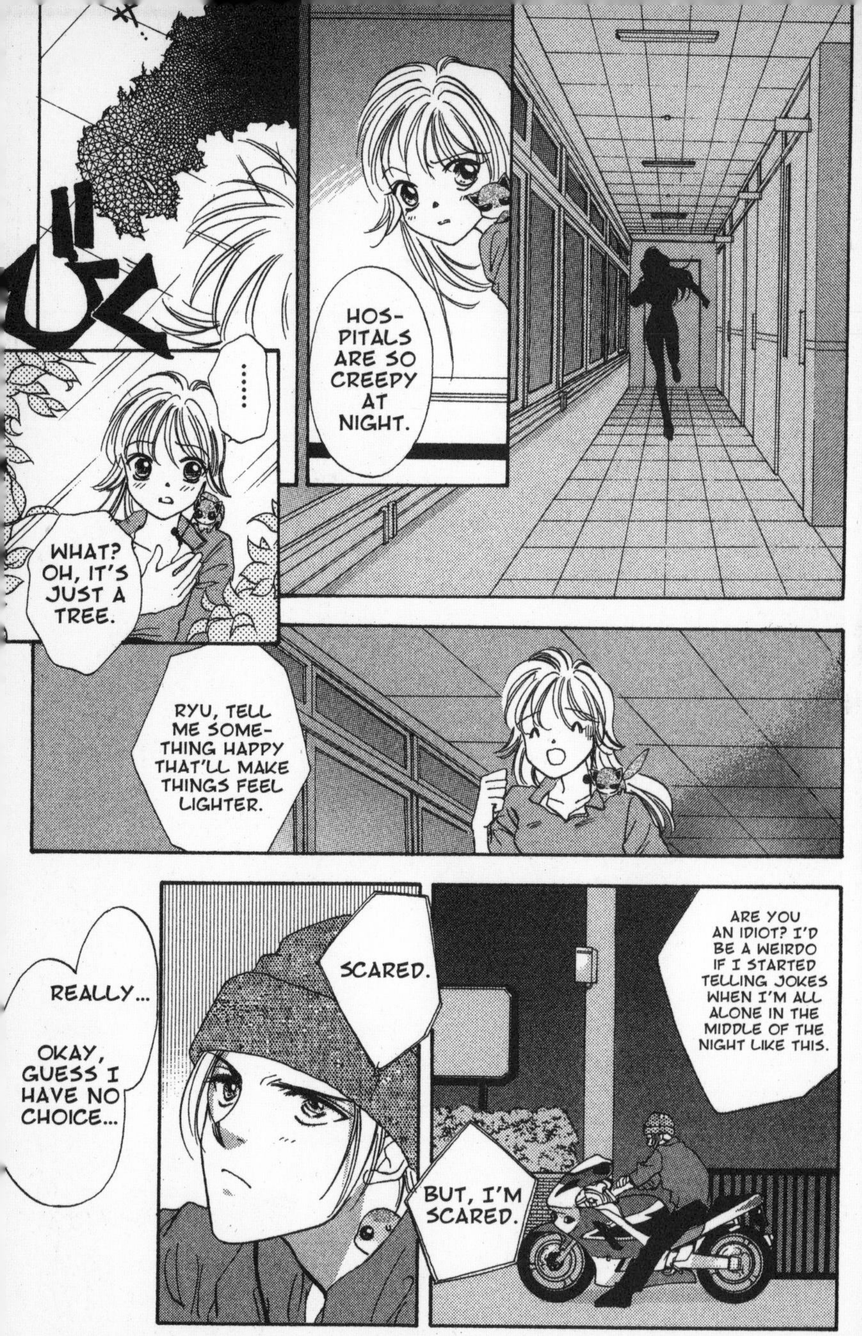
HOS-PITALS ARE SO CREEPY AT NIGHT.
びく
......
WHAT? OH, IT'S JUST A TREE.
RYU, TELL ME SOME-THING HAPPY THAT'LL MAKE THINGS FEEL LIGHTER.
ARE YOU AN IDIOT? I'D BE A WEIRDO IF I STARTED TELLING JOKES WHEN I'M ALL ALONE IN THE MIDDLE OF THE NIGHT LIKE THIS.
BUT, I'M SCARED.
SCARED.
REALLY...
OKAY, GUESS I HAVE NO CHOICE...

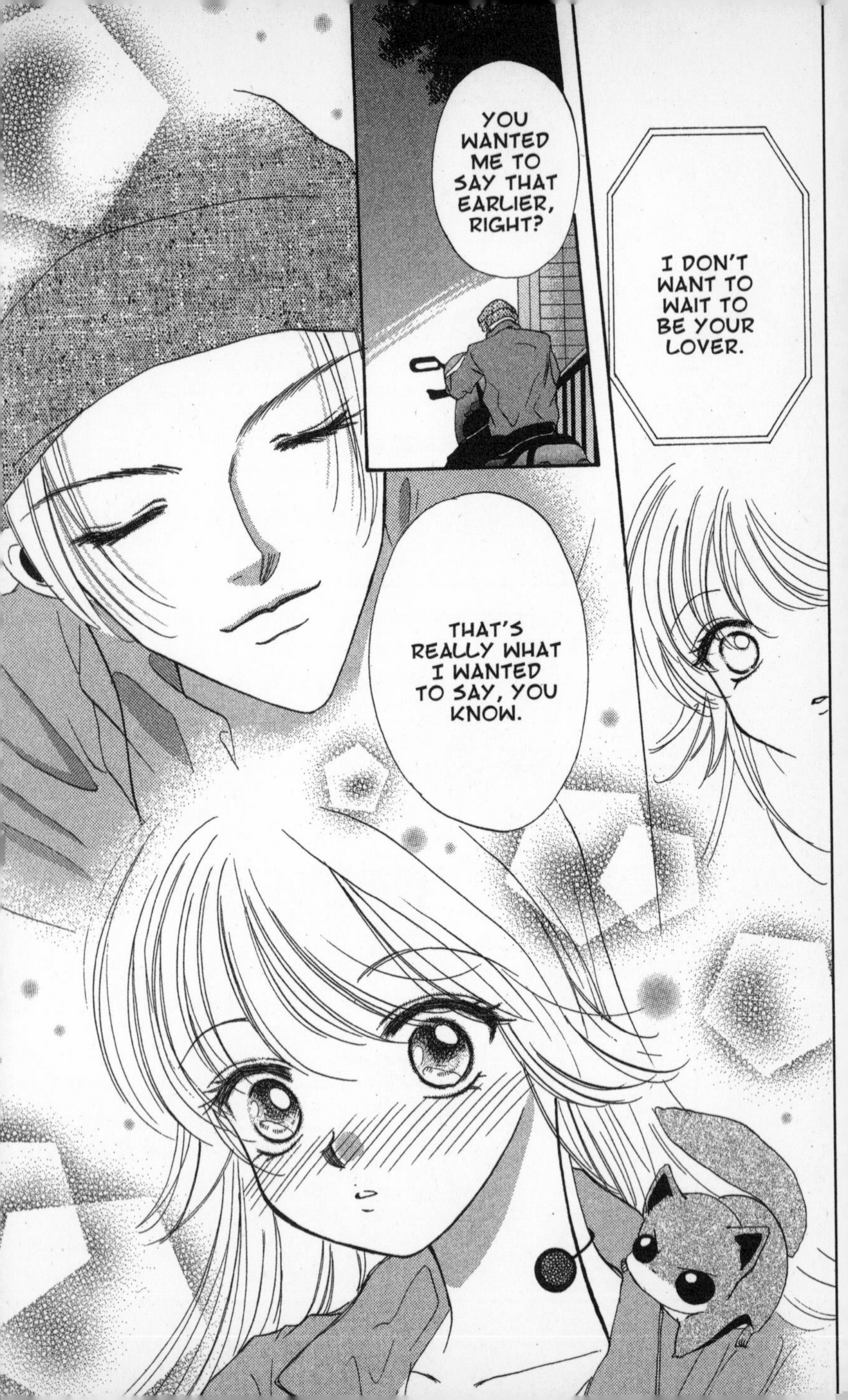
I DON'T WANT TO WAIT TO BE YOUR LOVER.
YOU WANTED ME TO SAY THAT EARLIER, RIGHT?
THAT'S REALLY WHAT I WANTED TO SAY, YOU KNOW.

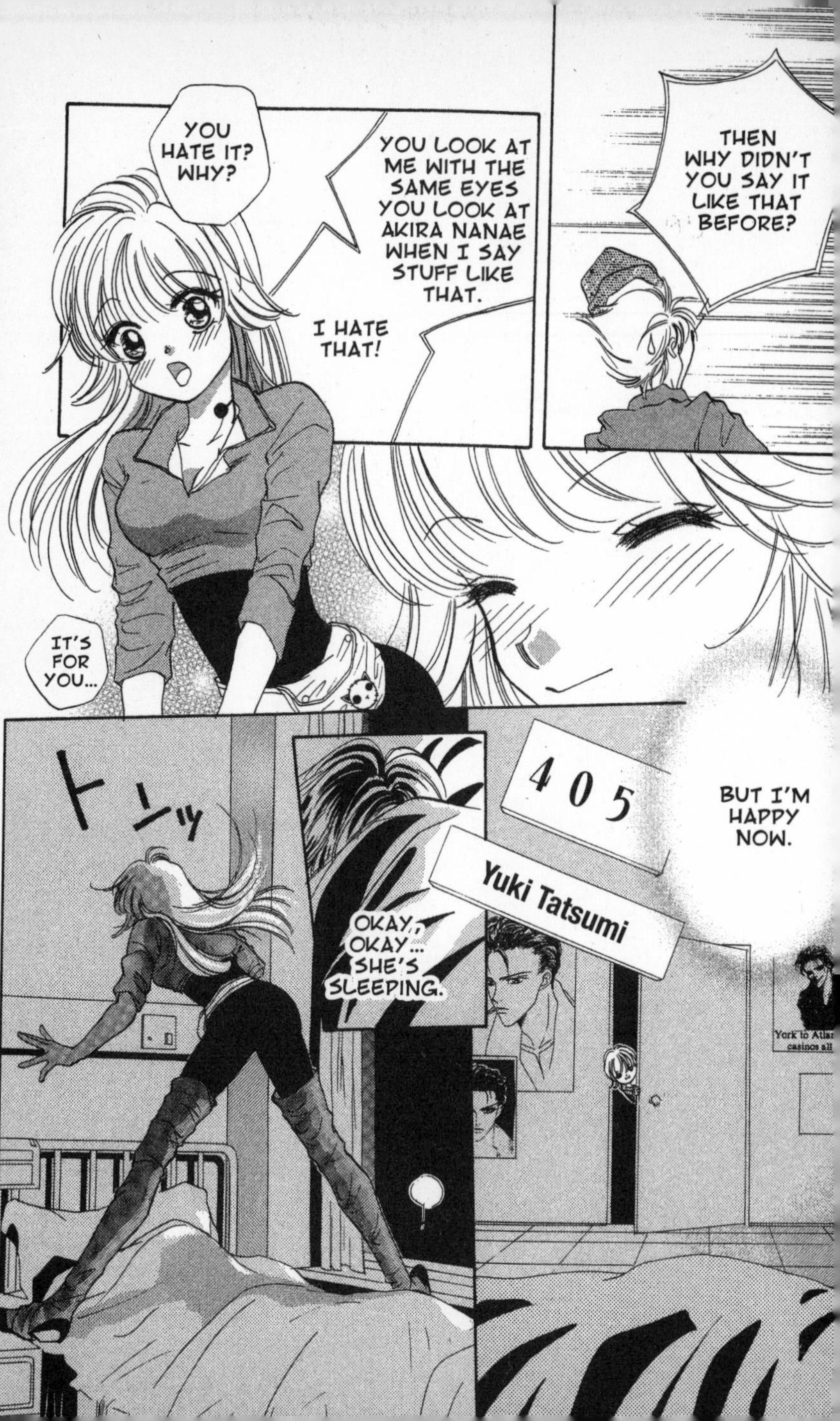
THEN WHY DIDN'T YOU SAY IT LIKE THAT BEFORE?
YOU LOOK AT ME WITH THE SAME EYES YOU LOOK AT AKIRA NANAE WHEN I SAY STUFF LIKE THAT.
I HATE THAT!
YOU HATE IT? WHY?
BUT I'M HAPPY NOW.
IT'S FOR YOU...
4 0 5
Yuki Tatsumi
OKAY, OKAY... SHE'S SLEEPING.
トンッ

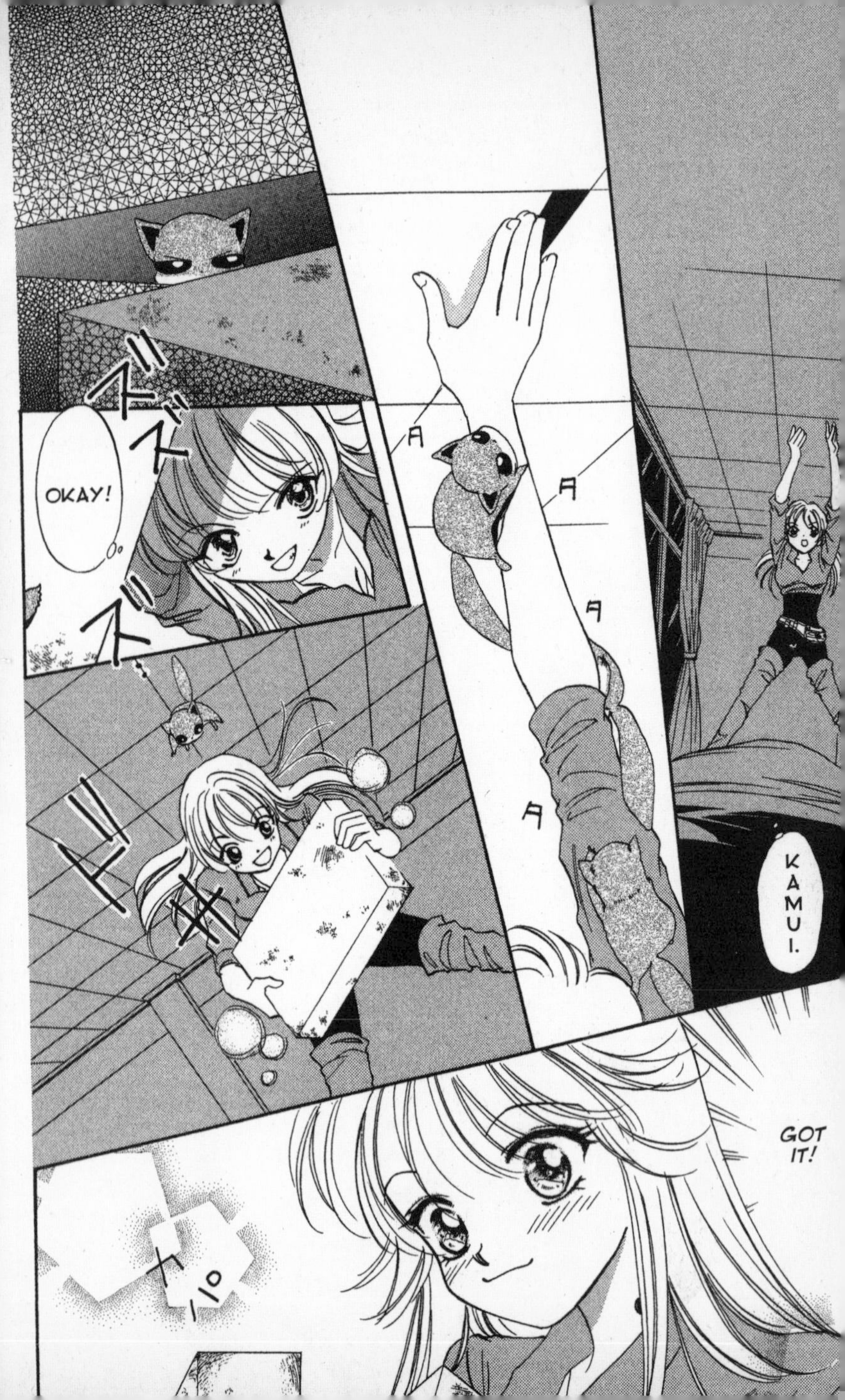
KAMUI.
OKAY!
GOT IT!

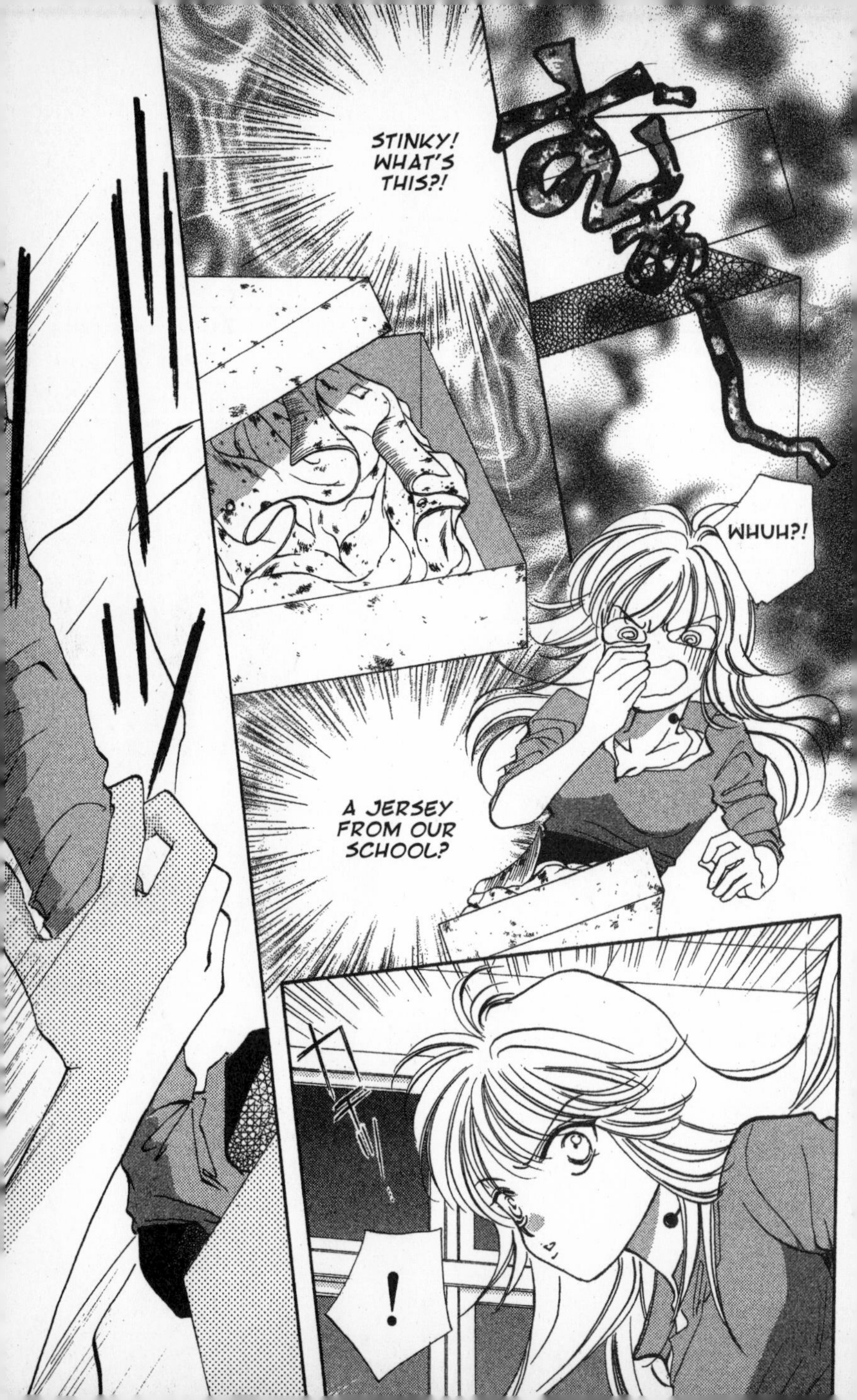
WHUH?!
STINKY! WHAT'S THIS?!
A JERSEY FROM OUR SCHOOL?
!

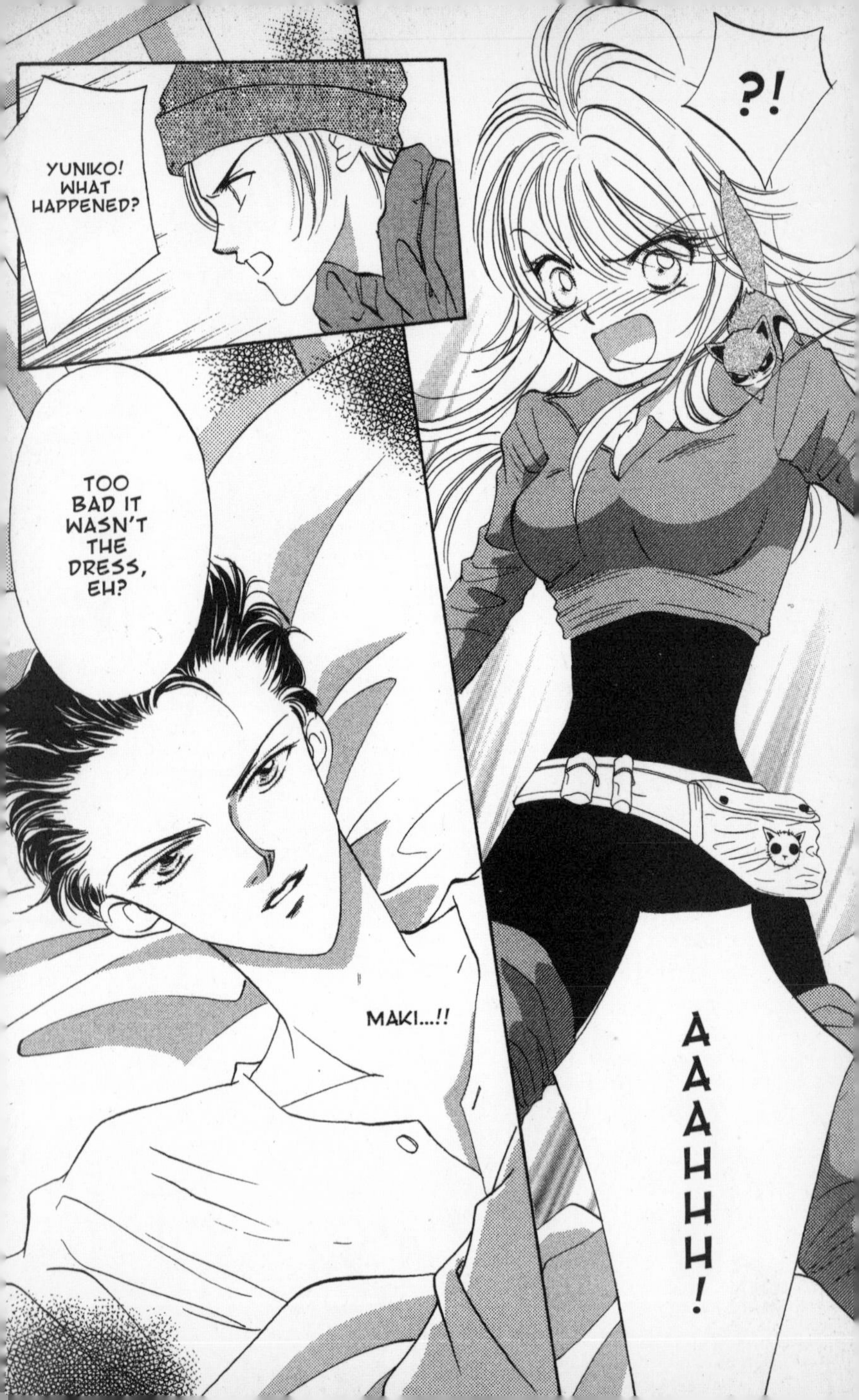
?!
AAAHHH!
YUNIKO! WHAT HAPPENED?
TOO BAD IT WASN'T THE DRESS, EH?
MAKI...!!

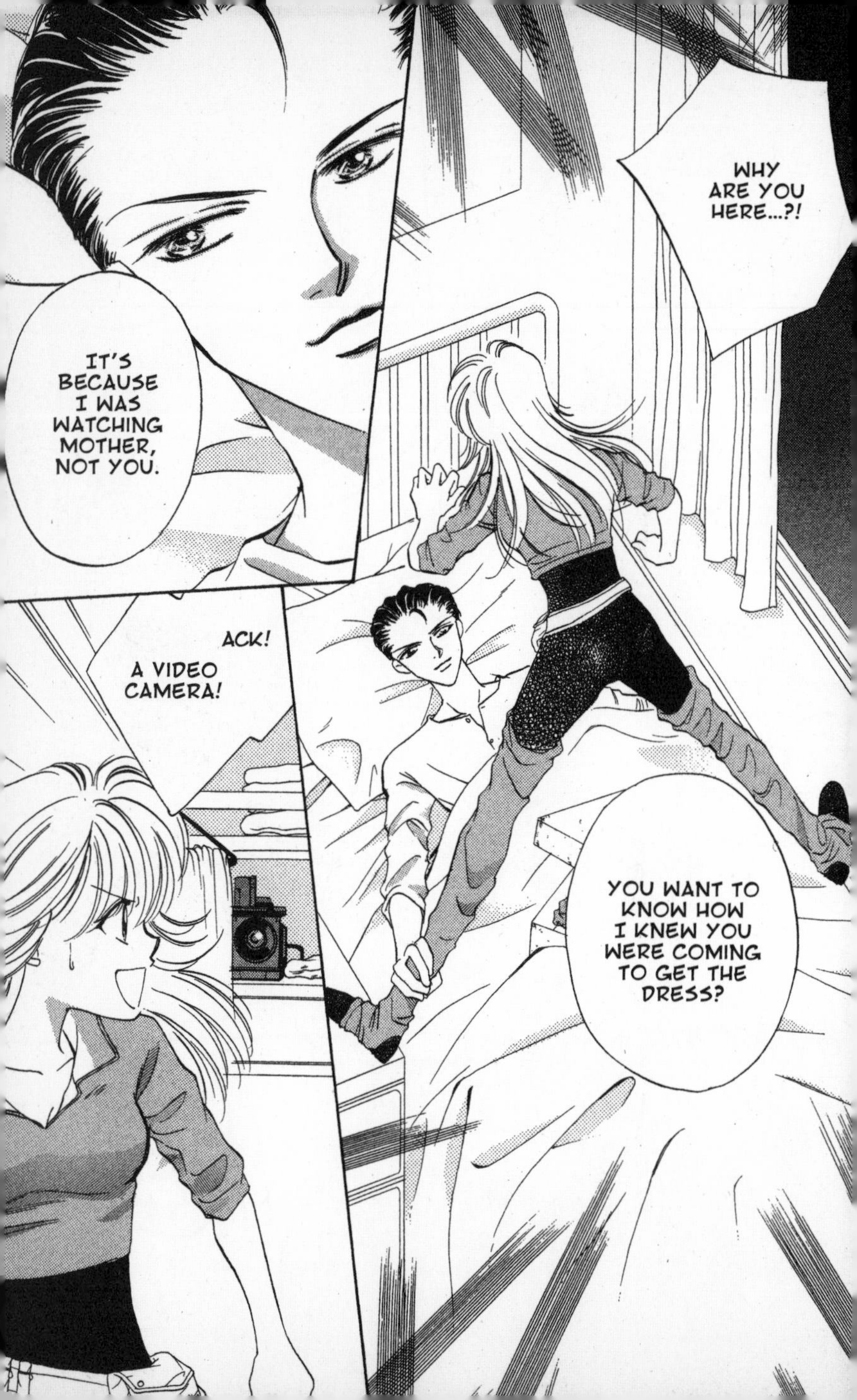
WHY ARE YOU HERE...?!
YOU WANT TO KNOW HOW I KNEW YOU WERE COMING TO GET THE DRESS?
IT'S BECAUSE I WAS WATCHING MOTHER, NOT YOU.
ACK! A VIDEO CAMERA!

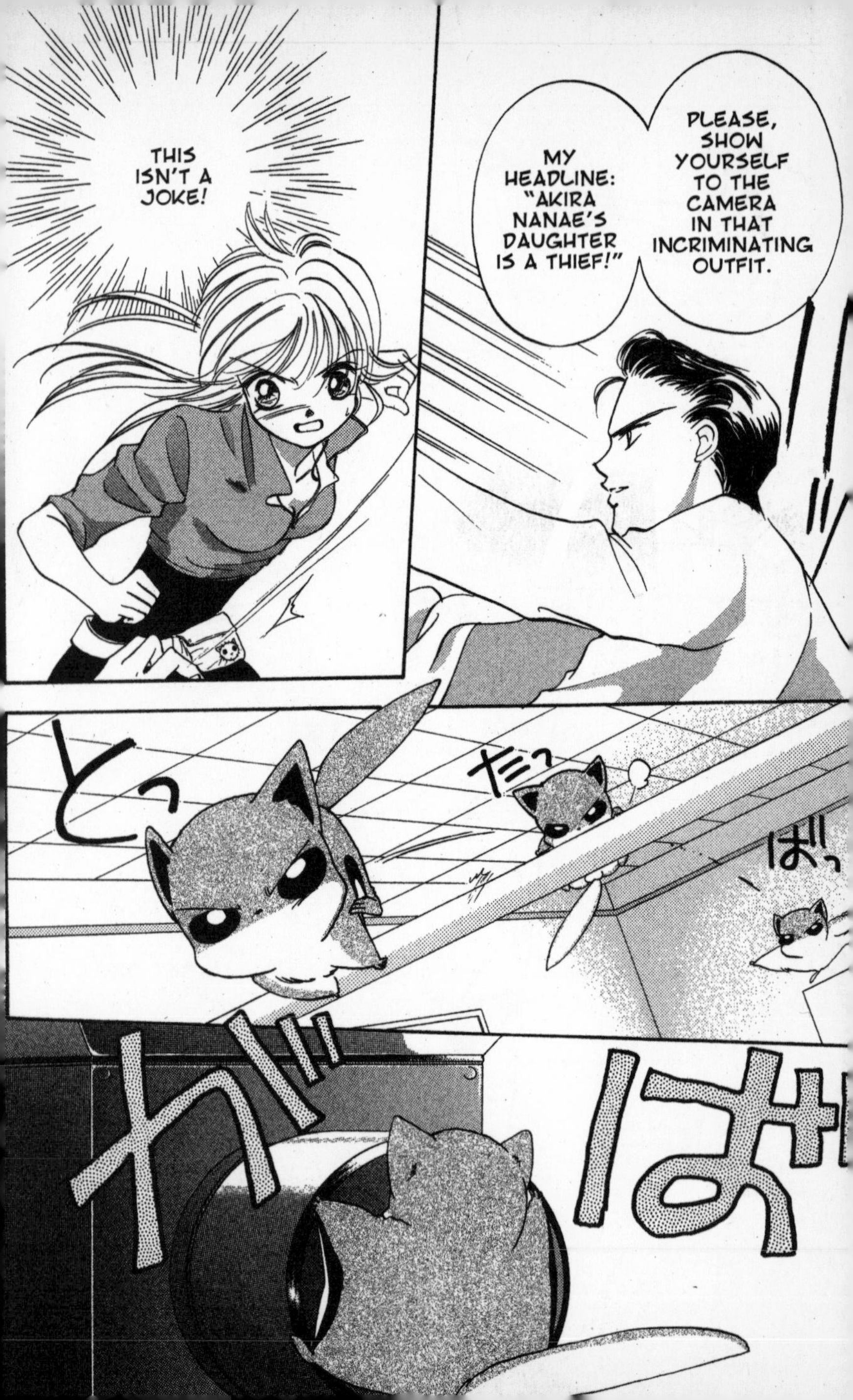
PLEASE, SHOW YOURSELF TO THE CAMERA IN THAT INCRIMINATING OUTFIT.
MY HEADLINE: "AKIRA NANAE'S DAUGHTER IS A THIEF!"
THIS ISN'T A JOKE!
とっ

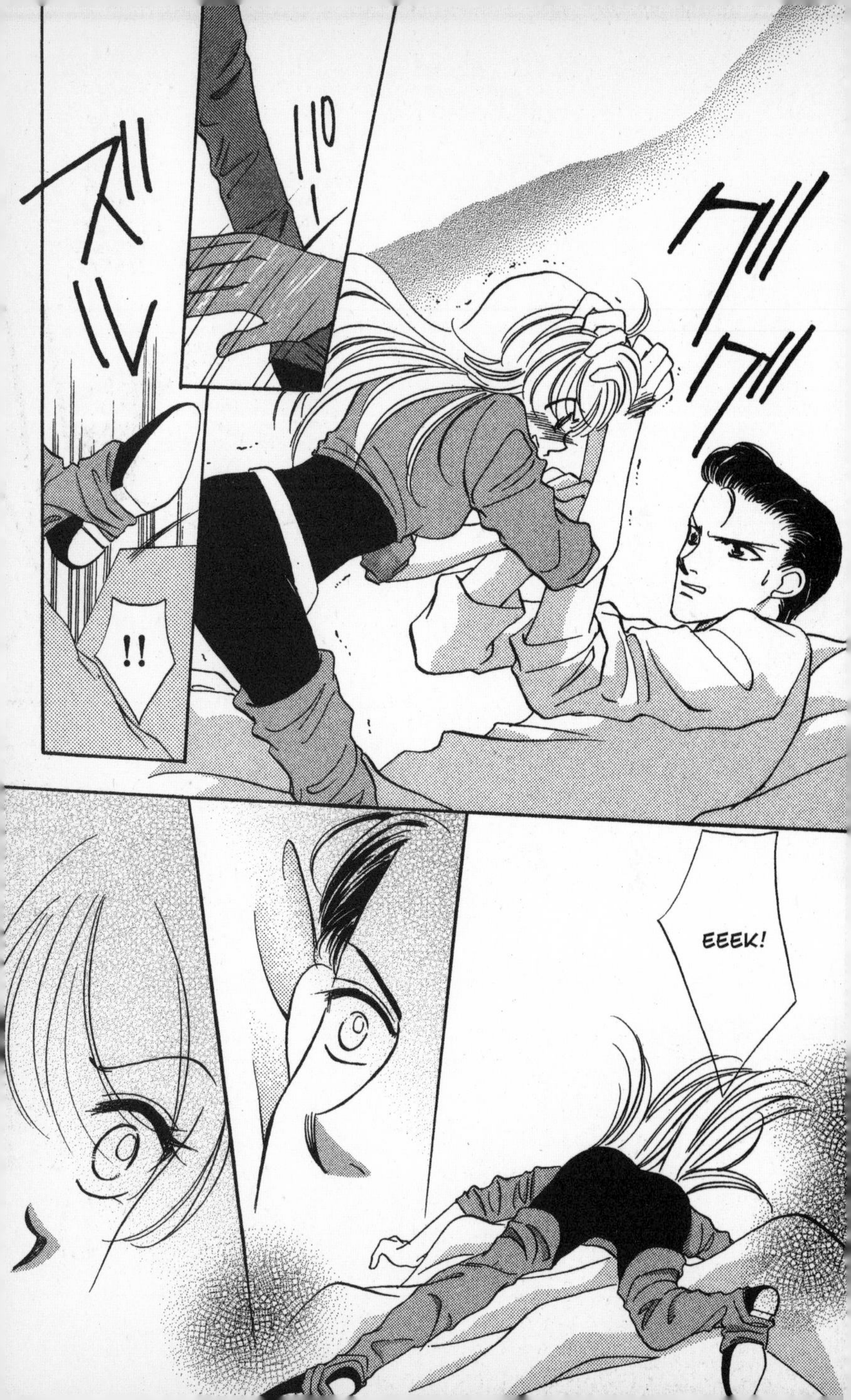
!!
EEEK!

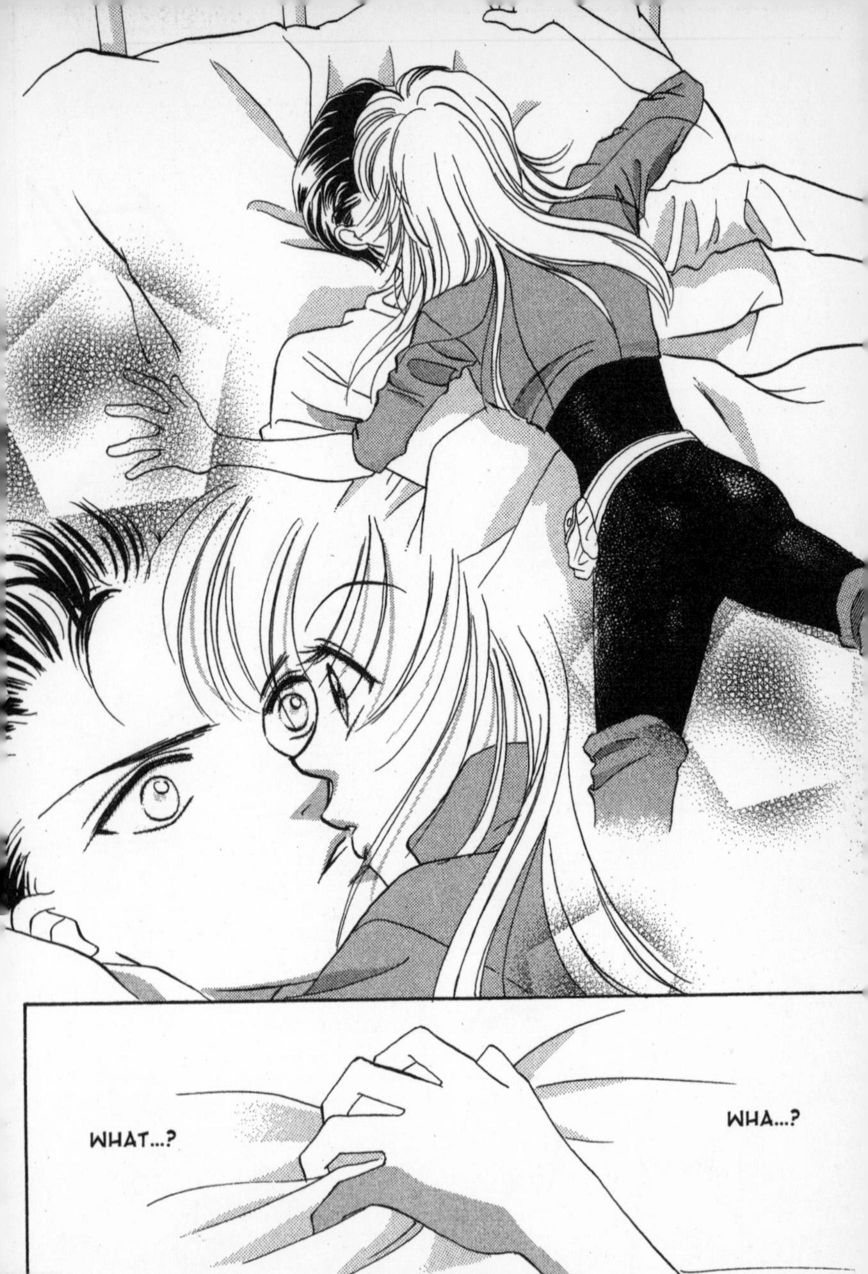
WHA...?
WHAT...?

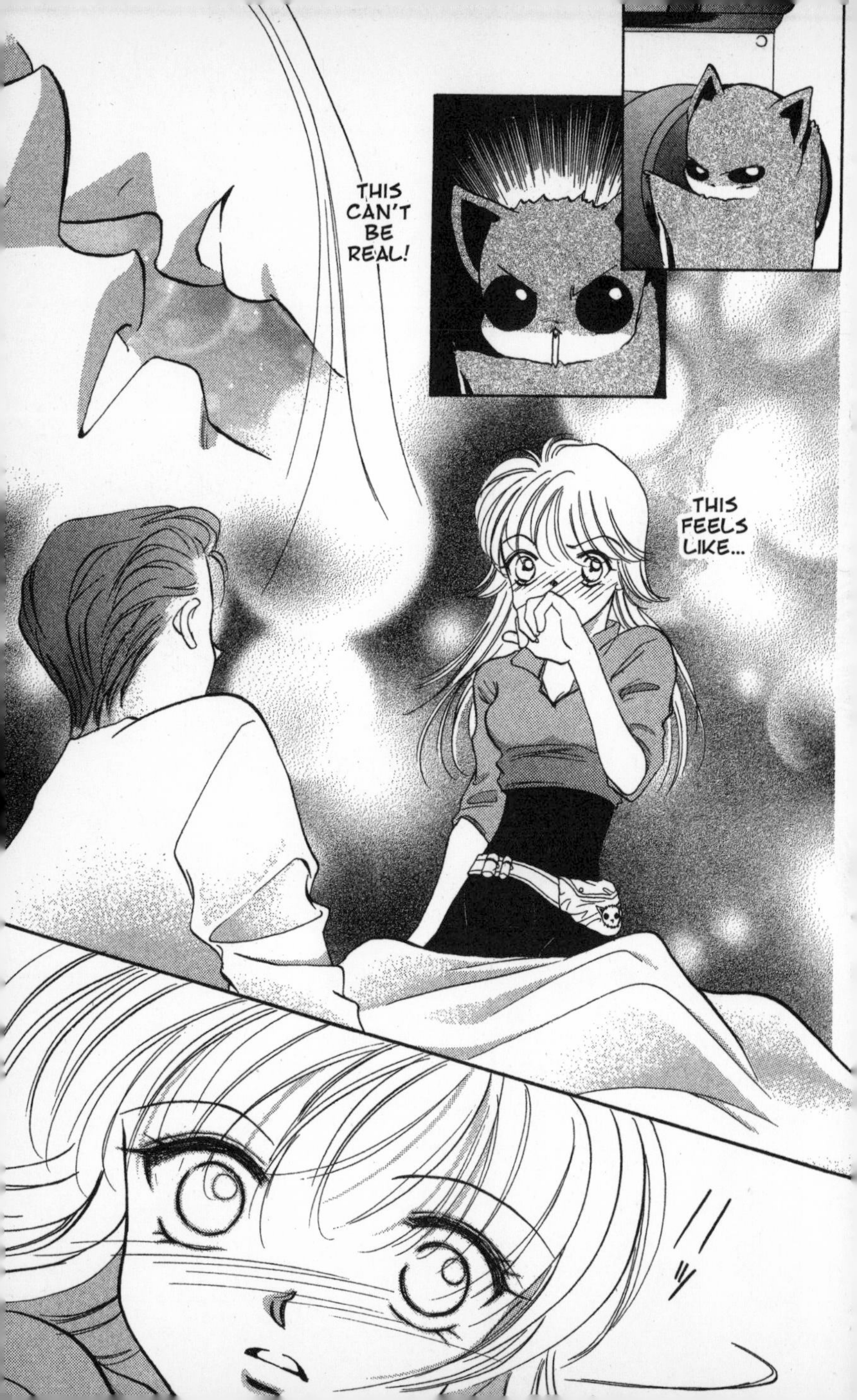
THIS CAN'T BE REAL!
THIS FEELS LIKE...

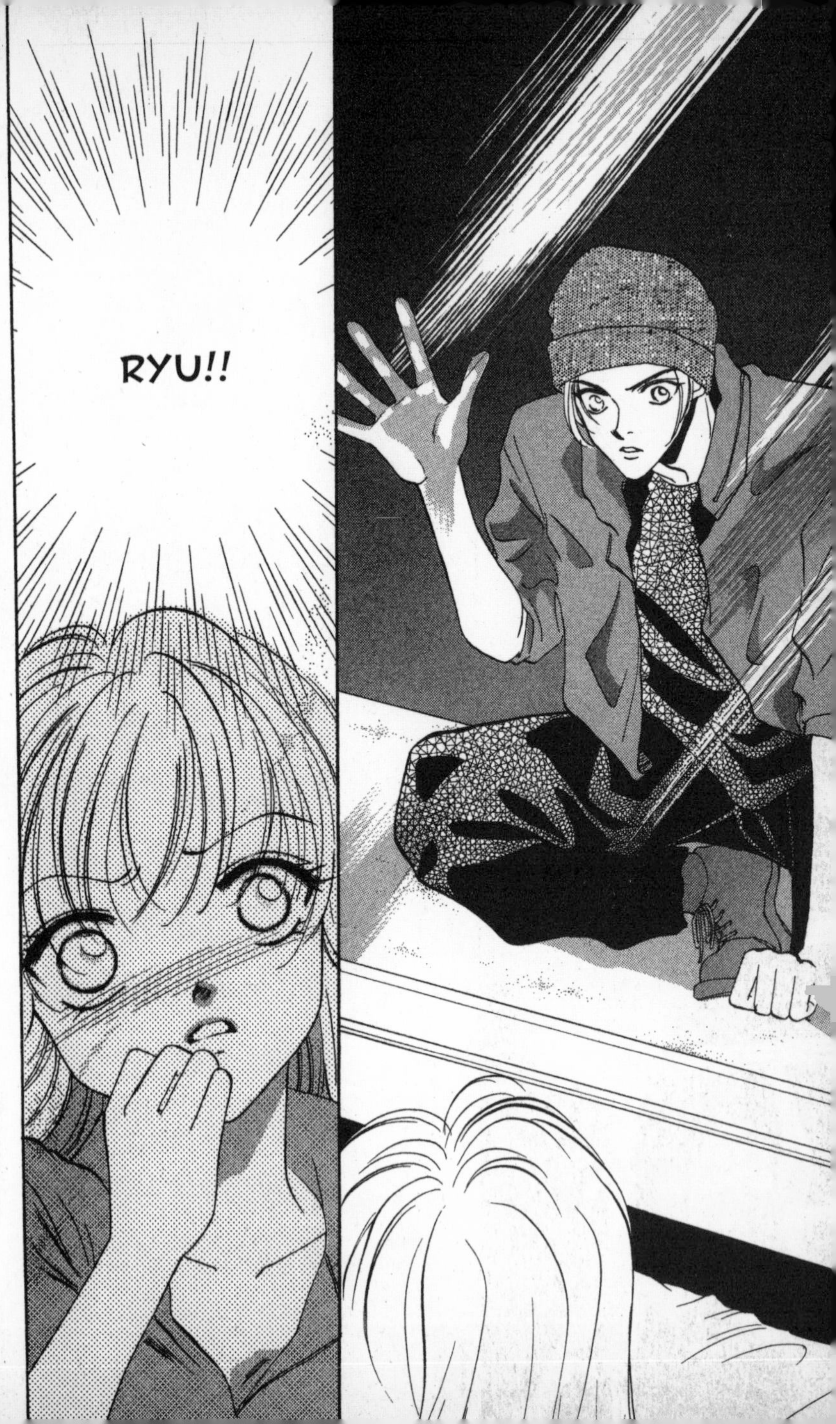
RYU!!

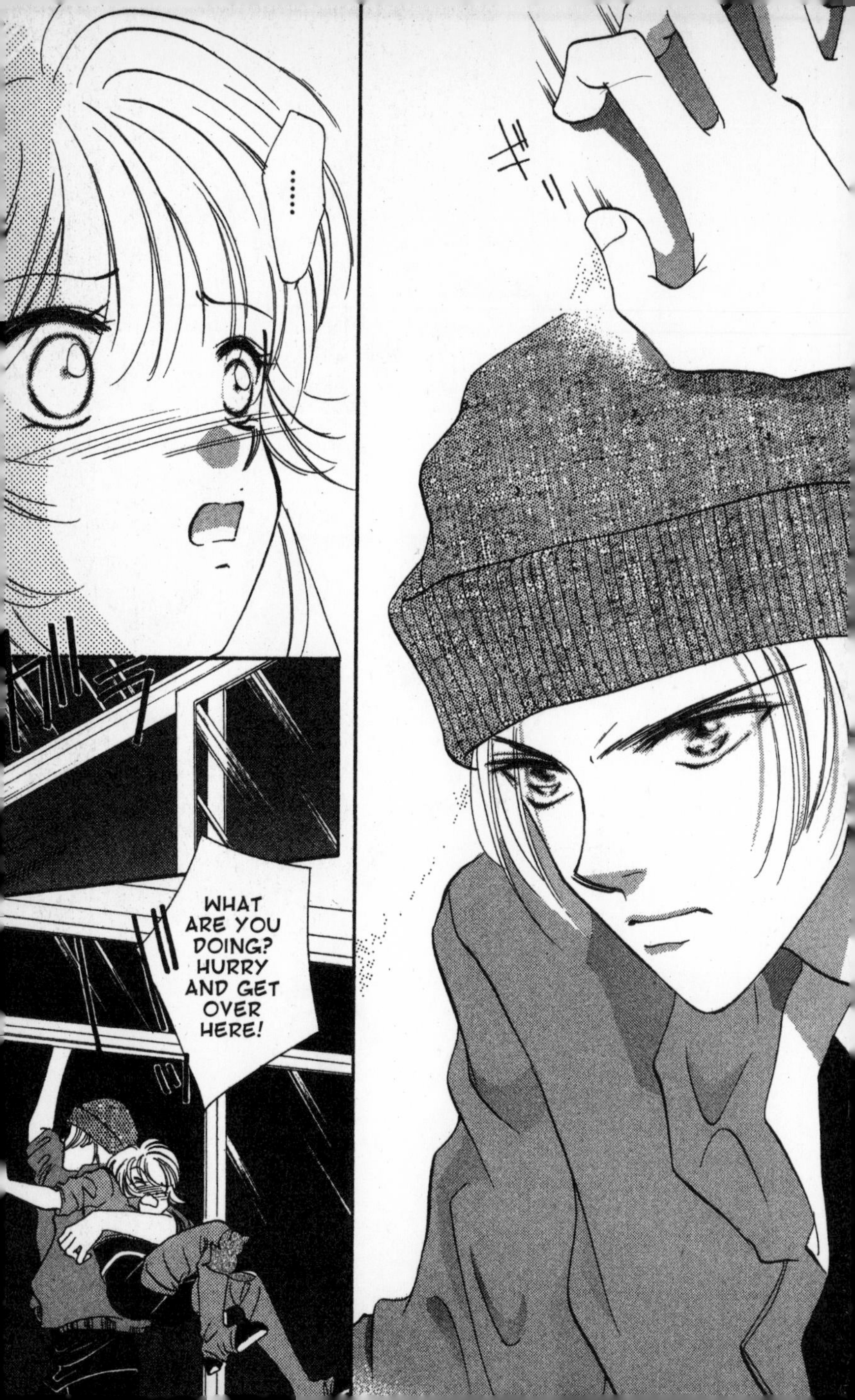

WHAT ARE YOU DOING? HURRY AND GET OVER HERE!

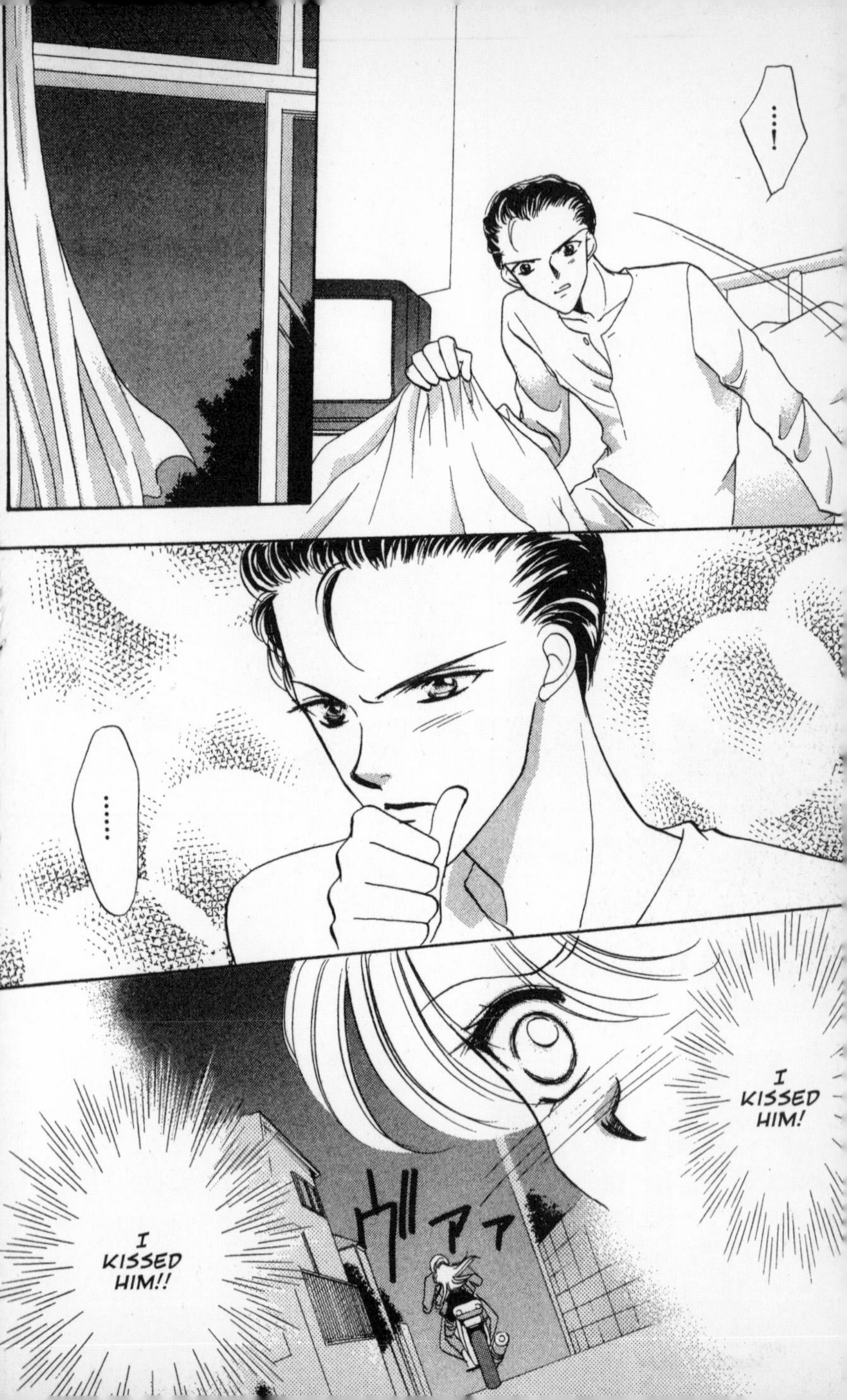
...!
......
I KISSED HIM!
ヴァァ
I KISSED HIM!!

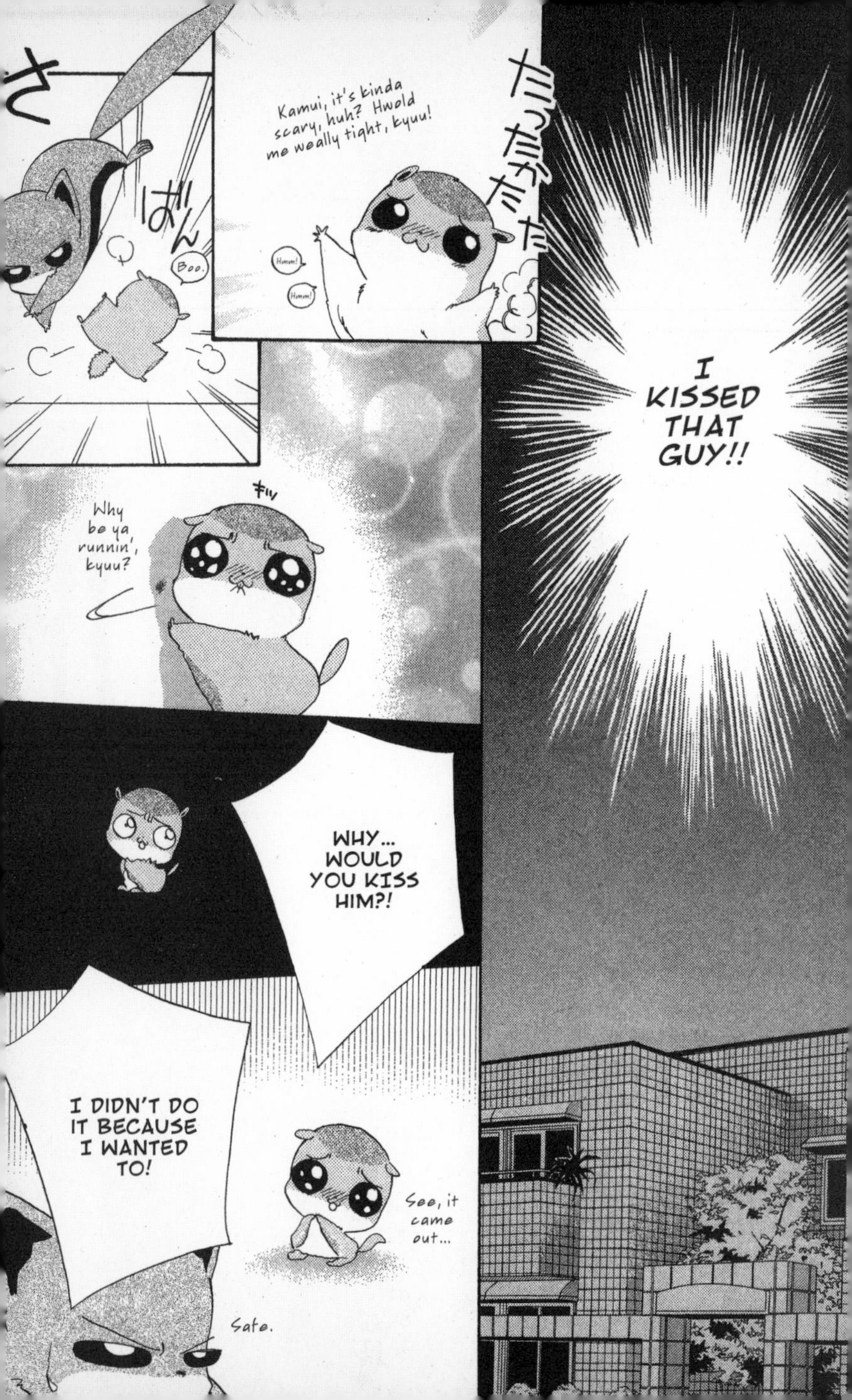

I KISSED THAT GUY!!
たったかたた
Kamui, it's kinda scary, huh? Hwold me weally tight, kyuu!
Hmm!
Hmm!
さ
ばん
Boo.
キッ
Why be ya runnin', kyuu?
WHY... WOULD YOU KISS HIM?!
I DIDN'T DO IT BECAUSE I WANTED TO!
See, it came out...
Safe.

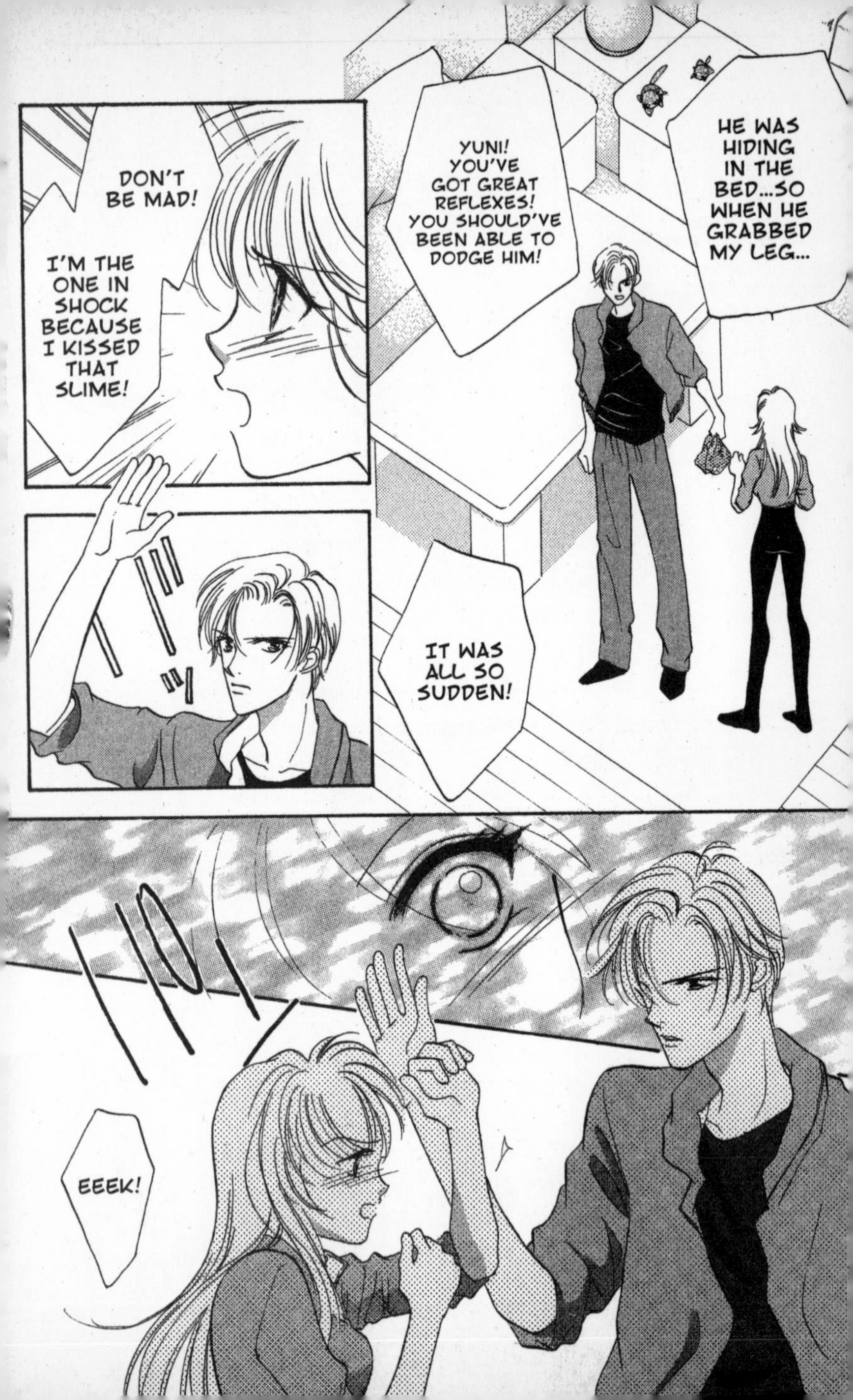
HE WAS HIDING IN THE BED...SO WHEN HE GRABBED MY LEG...
YUNI! YOU'VE GOT GREAT REFLEXES! YOU SHOULD'VE BEEN ABLE TO DODGE HIM!
IT WAS ALL SO SUDDEN!
DON'T BE MAD!
I'M THE ONE IN SHOCK BECAUSE I KISSED THAT SLIME!
EEEK!

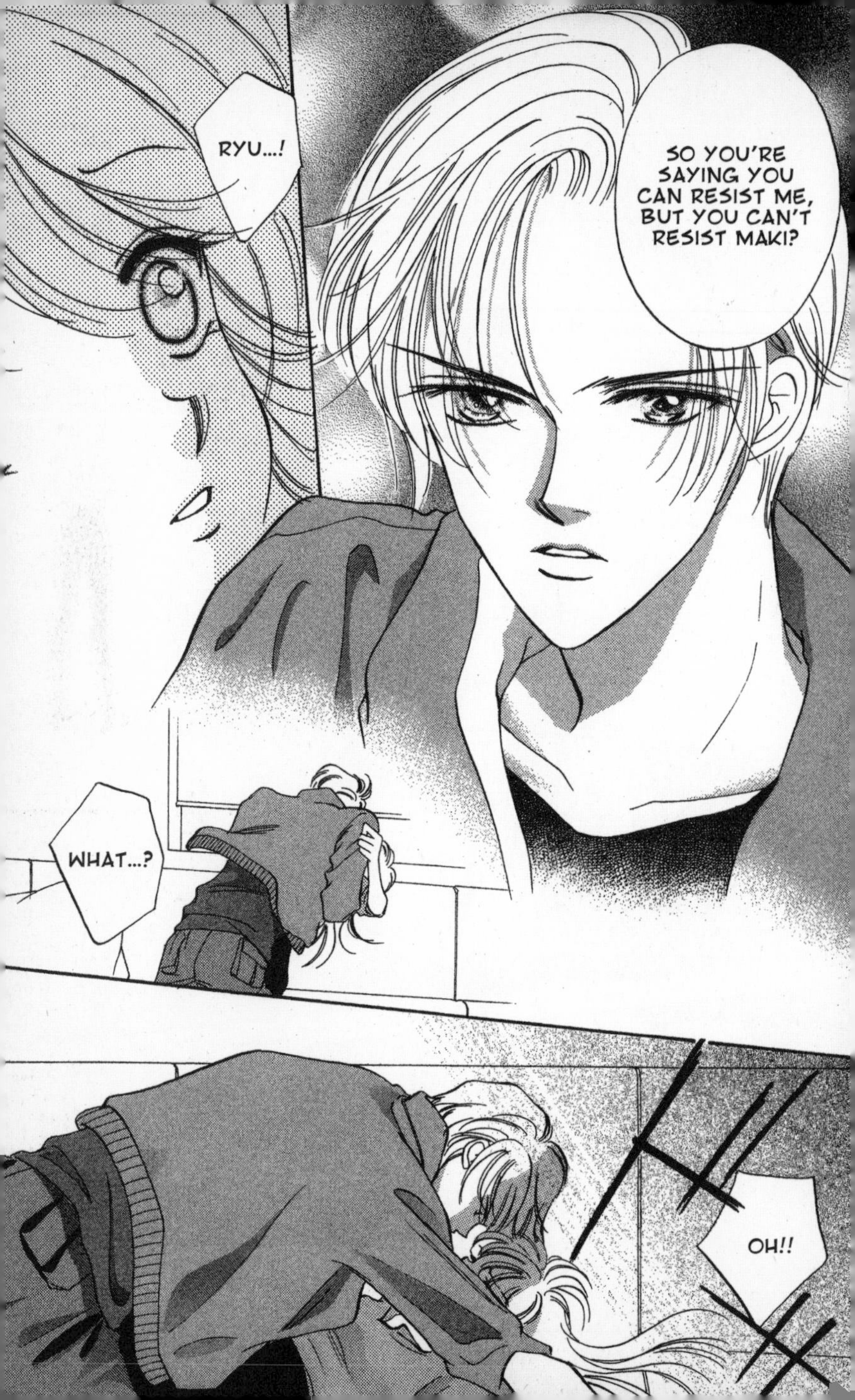
SO YOU'RE SAYING YOU CAN RESIST ME, BUT YOU CAN'T RESIST MAKI?
RYU...!
WHAT...?
OH!!

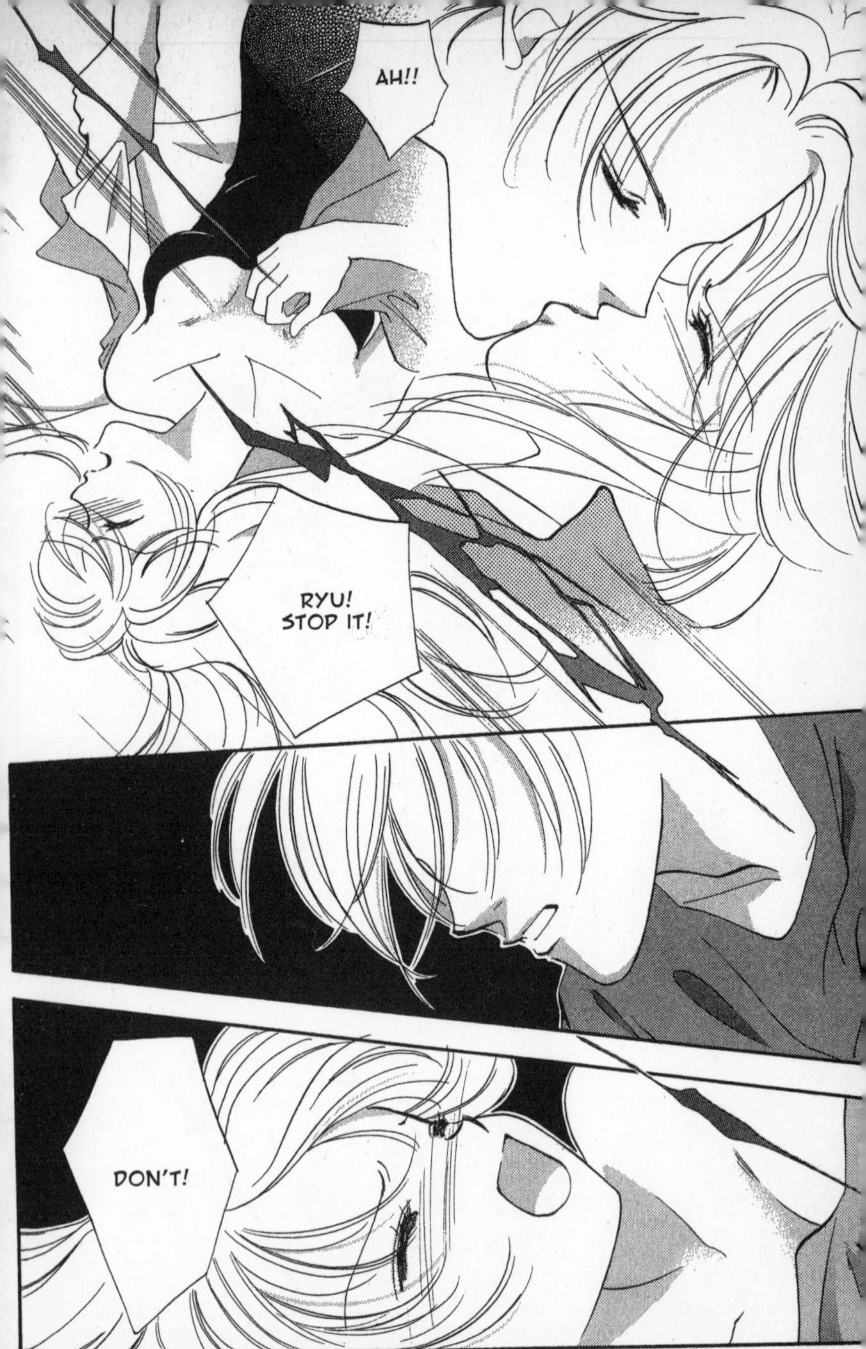
AH!!
RYU! STOP IT!
DON'T!

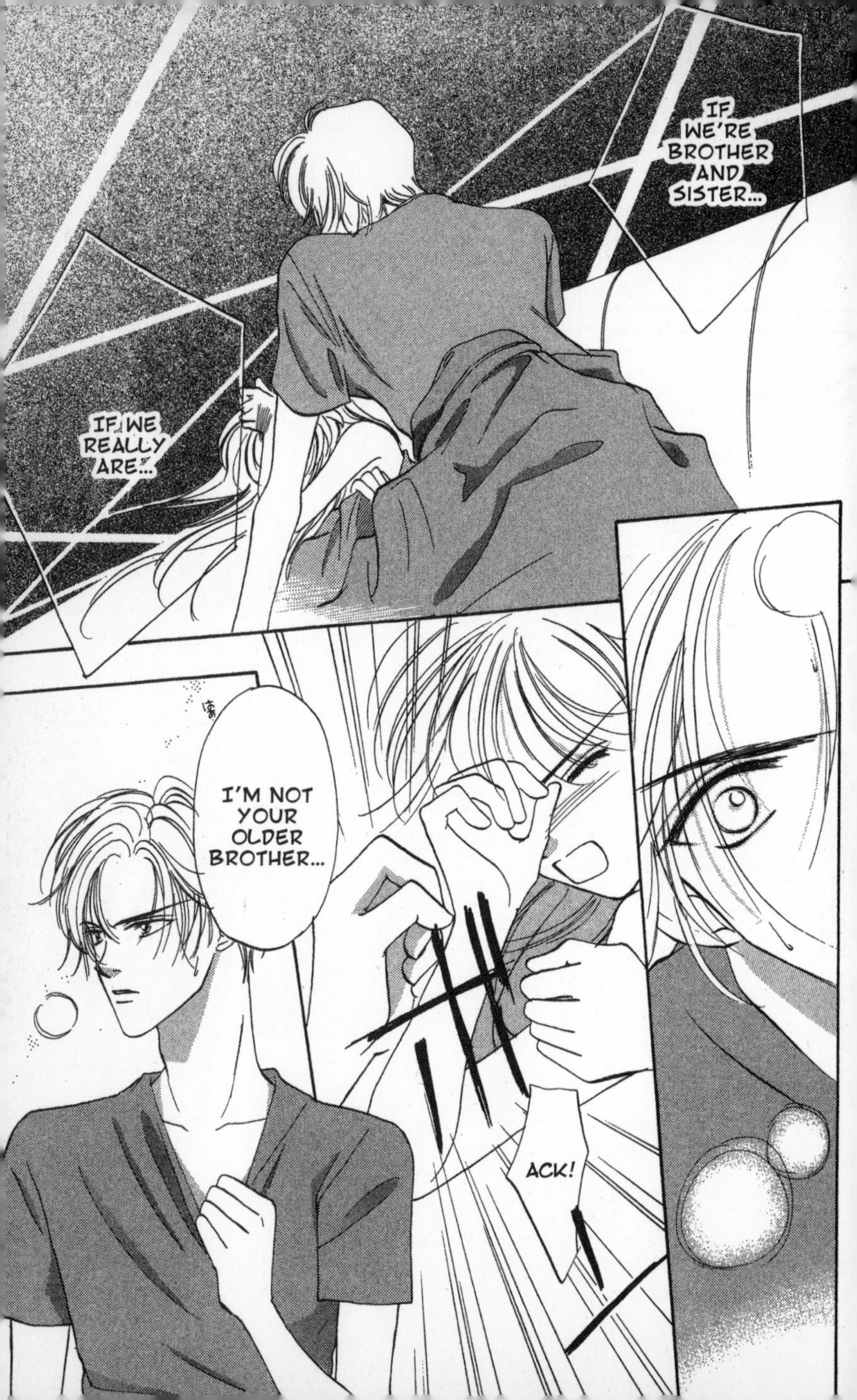
IF WE'RE BROTHER AND SISTER...
IF WE REALLY ARE...
ACK!
I'M NOT YOUR OLDER BROTHER...

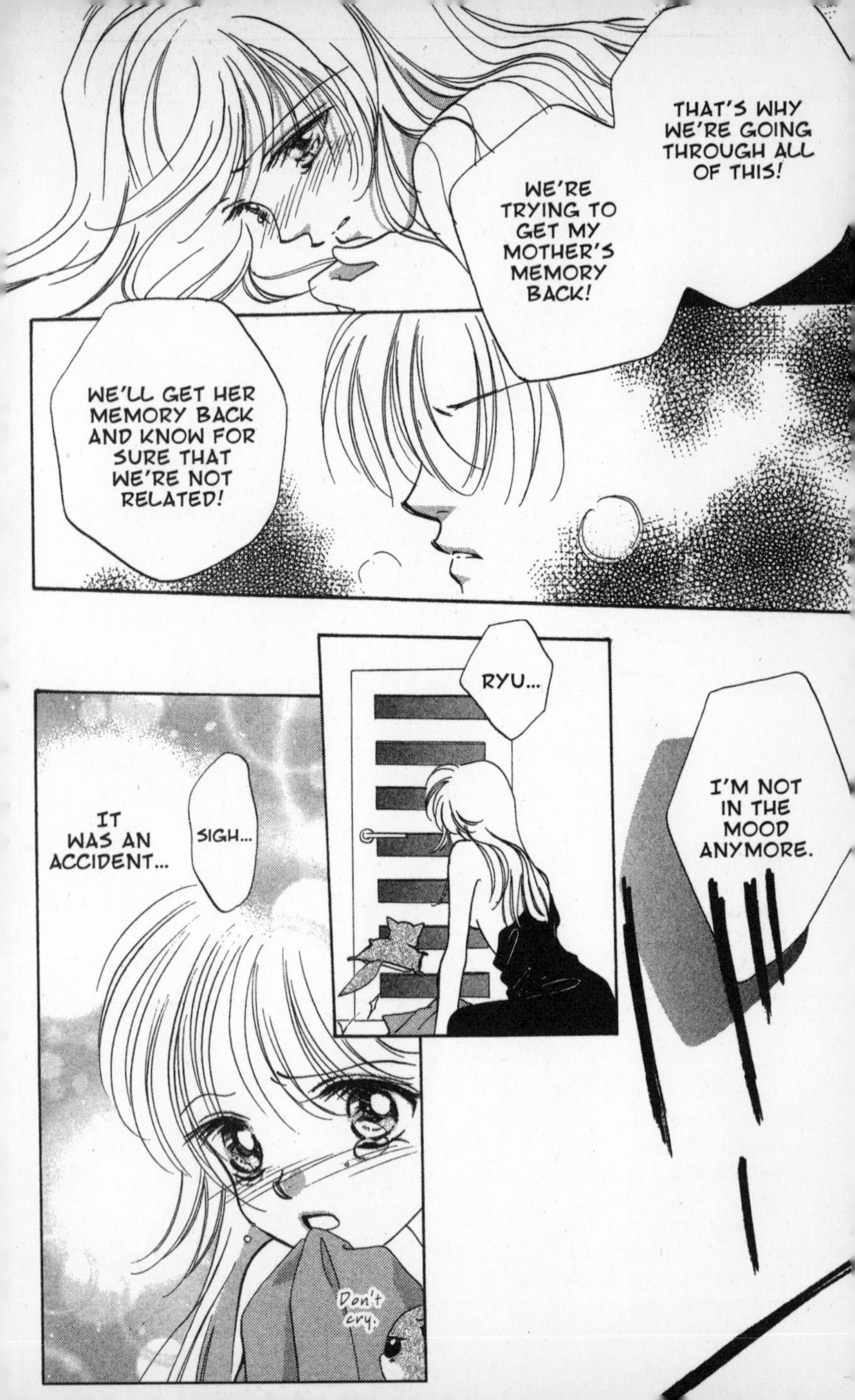
THAT'S WHY WE'RE GOING THROUGH ALL OF THIS!
WE'RE TRYING TO GET MY MOTHER'S MEMORY BACK!
WE'LL GET HER MEMORY BACK AND KNOW FOR SURE THAT WE'RE NOT RELATED!
I'M NOT IN THE MOOD ANYMORE.
RYU...
SIGH...
IT WAS AN ACCIDENT...
Don't cry.

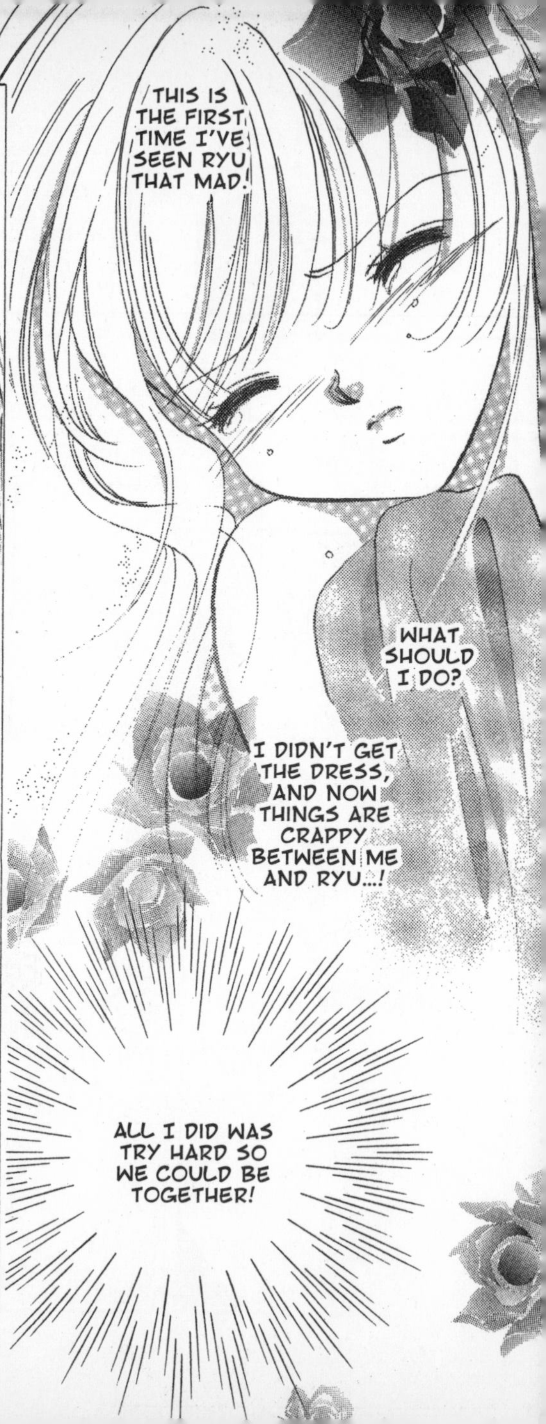
THIS IS THE FIRST TIME I'VE SEEN RYU THAT MAD!
WHAT SHOULD I DO?
I DIDN'T GET THE DRESS, AND NOW THINGS ARE CRAPPY BETWEEN ME AND RYU...!
ALL I DID WAS TRY HARD SO WE COULD BE TOGETHER!

Tokio's Data

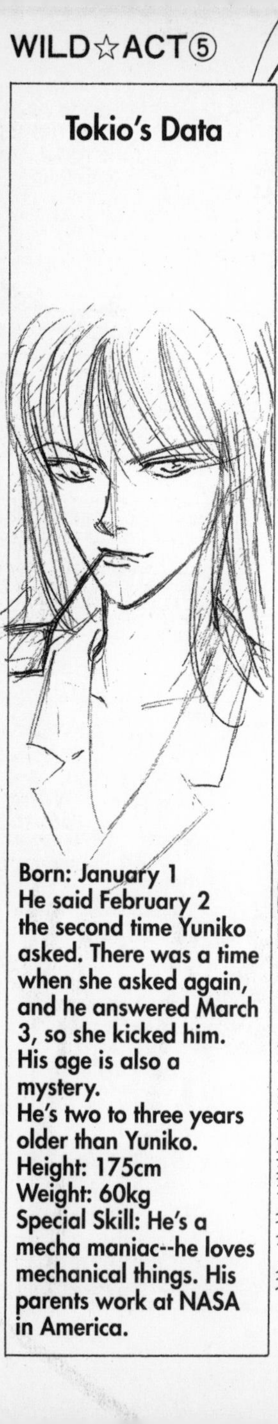

Born: January 1
He said February 2 the second time Yuniko asked. There was a time when she asked again, and he answered March 3, so she kicked him.
His age is also a mystery.
He's two to three years older than Yuniko.
Height: 175cm
Weight: 60kg
Special Skill: He's a mecha maniac--he loves mechanical things. His parents work at NASA in America.

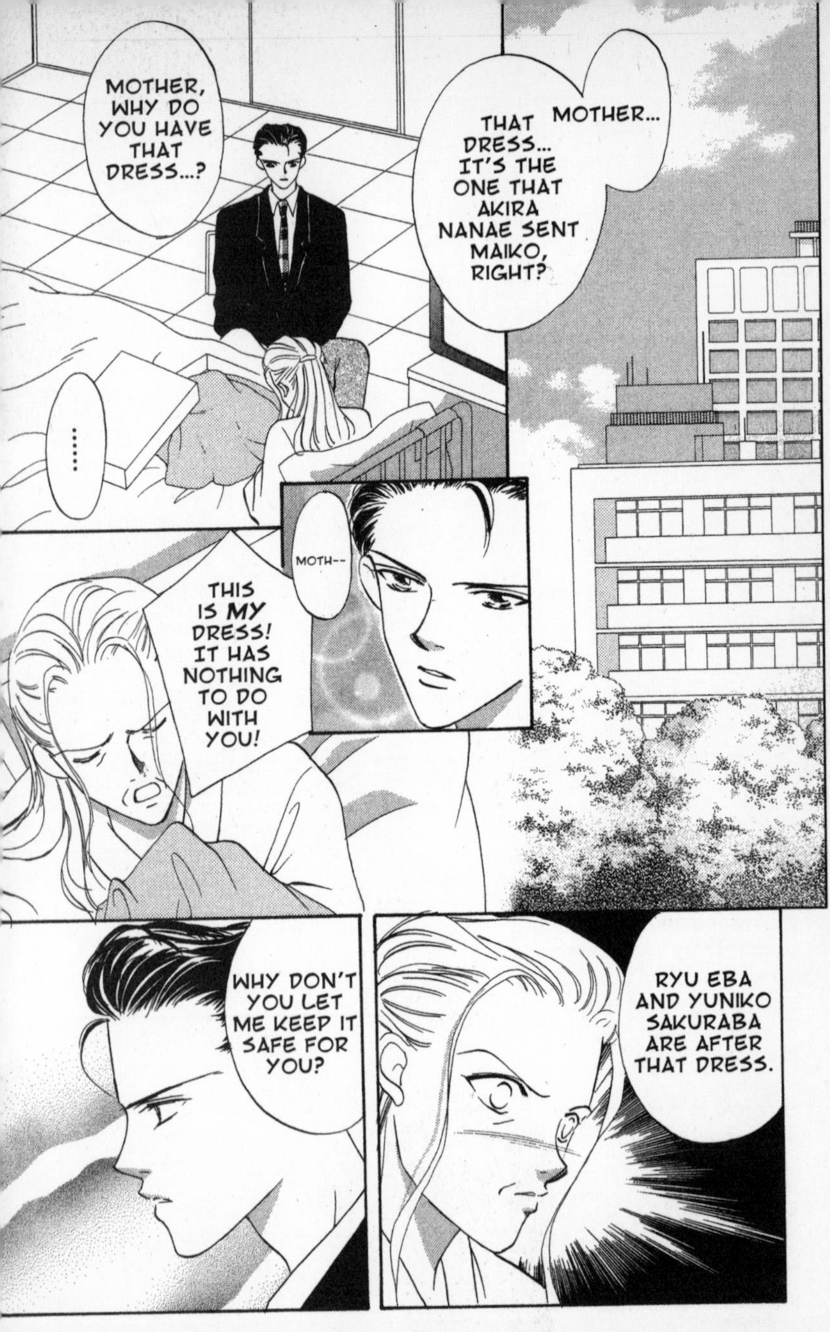
MOTHER...
THAT DRESS... IT'S THE ONE THAT AKIRA NANAE SENT MAIKO, RIGHT?
MOTHER, WHY DO YOU HAVE THAT DRESS...?
......
MOTH--
THIS IS MY DRESS! IT HAS NOTHING TO DO WITH YOU!
RYU EBA AND YUNIKO SAKURABA ARE AFTER THAT DRESS.
WHY DON'T YOU LET ME KEEP IT SAFE FOR YOU?

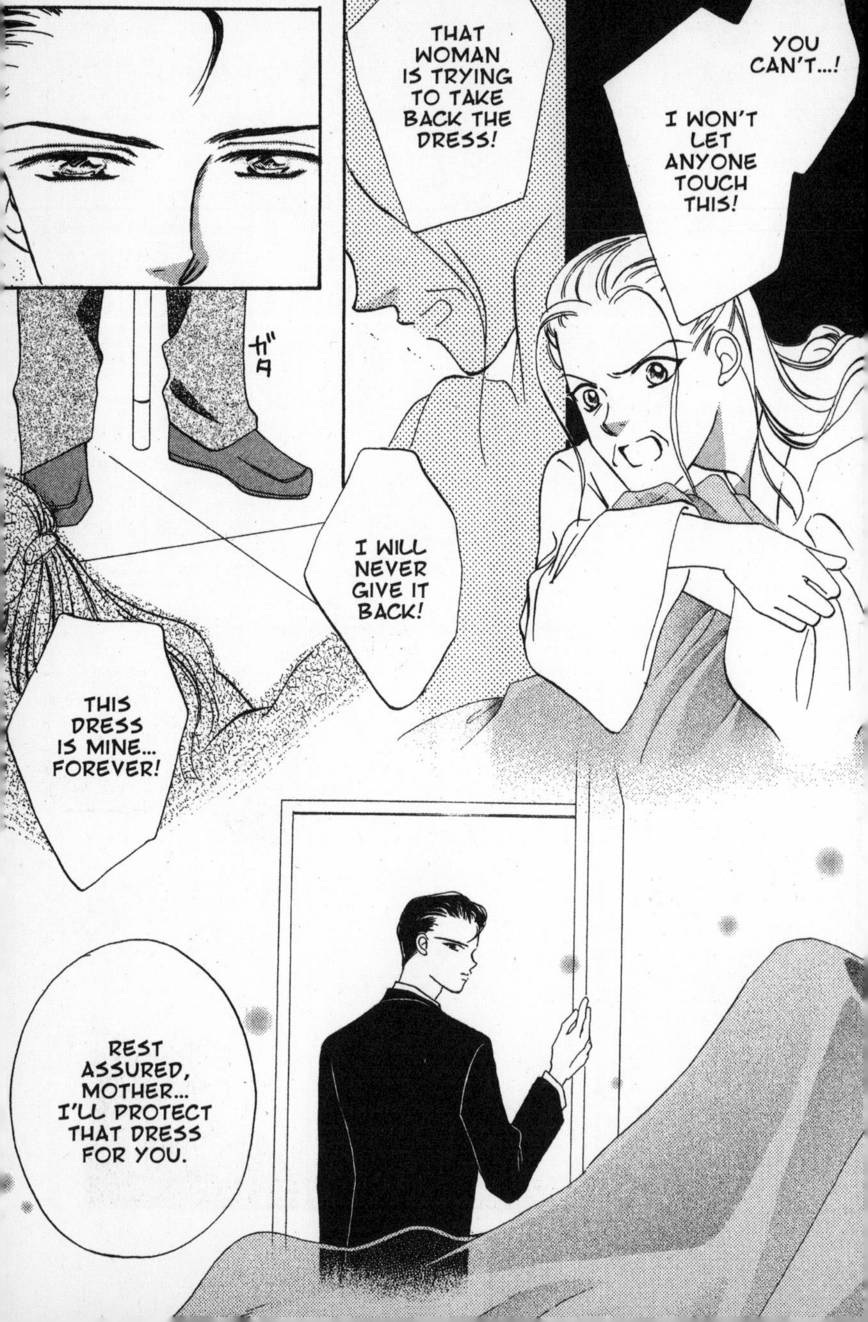
YOU CAN'T...!
I WON'T LET ANYONE TOUCH THIS!
THAT WOMAN IS TRYING TO TAKE BACK THE DRESS!
I WILL NEVER GIVE IT BACK!
ガタ
THIS DRESS IS MINE... FOREVER!
REST ASSURED, MOTHER... I'LL PROTECT THAT DRESS FOR YOU.

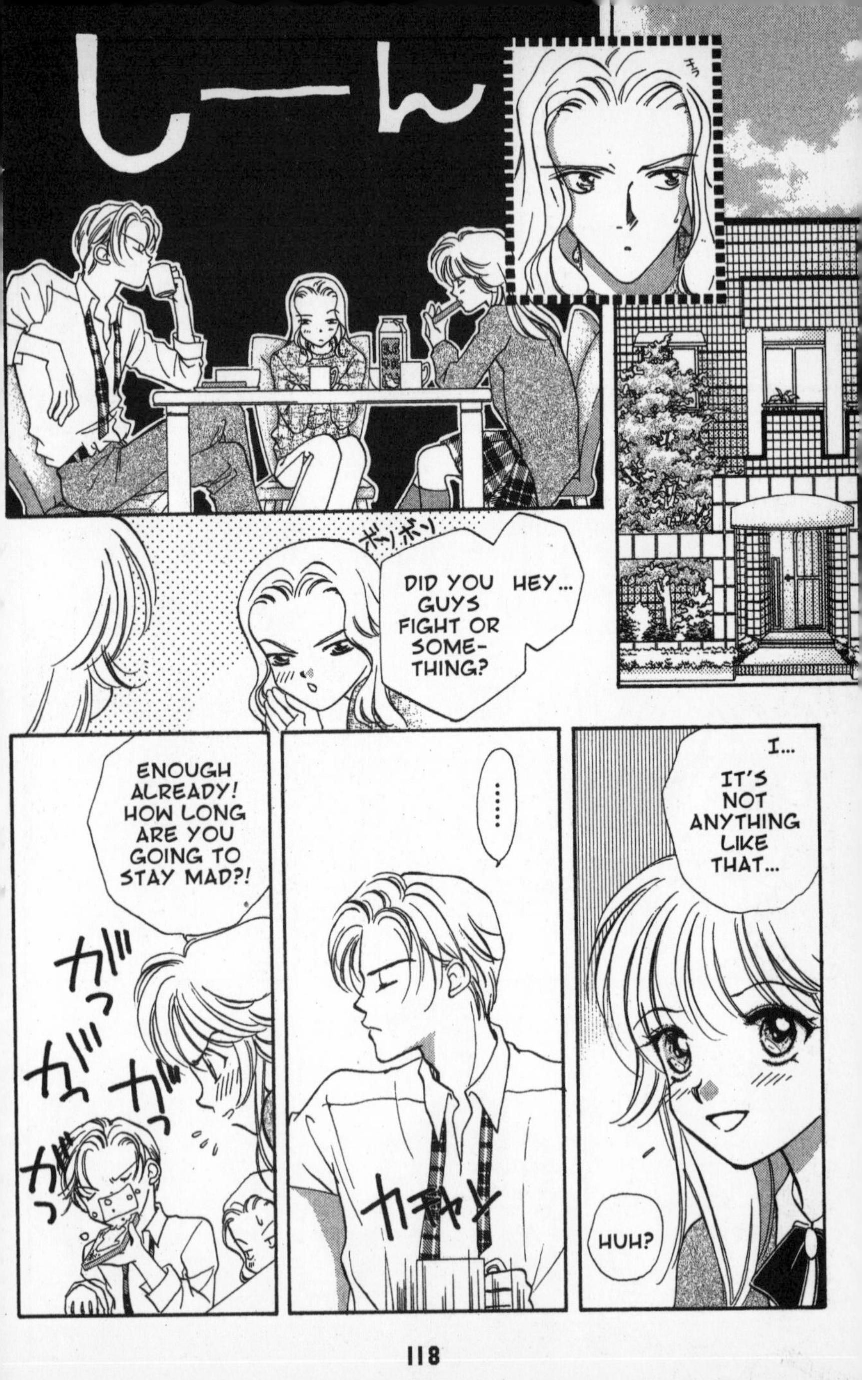

しーん
ボリボリ
HEY... DID YOU GUYS FIGHT OR SOMETHING?
I...
IT'S NOT ANYTHING LIKE THAT...
HUH?
......
カチャン
ENOUGH ALREADY! HOW LONG ARE YOU GOING TO STAY MAD?!
ガッ ガッ ガッ ガッ

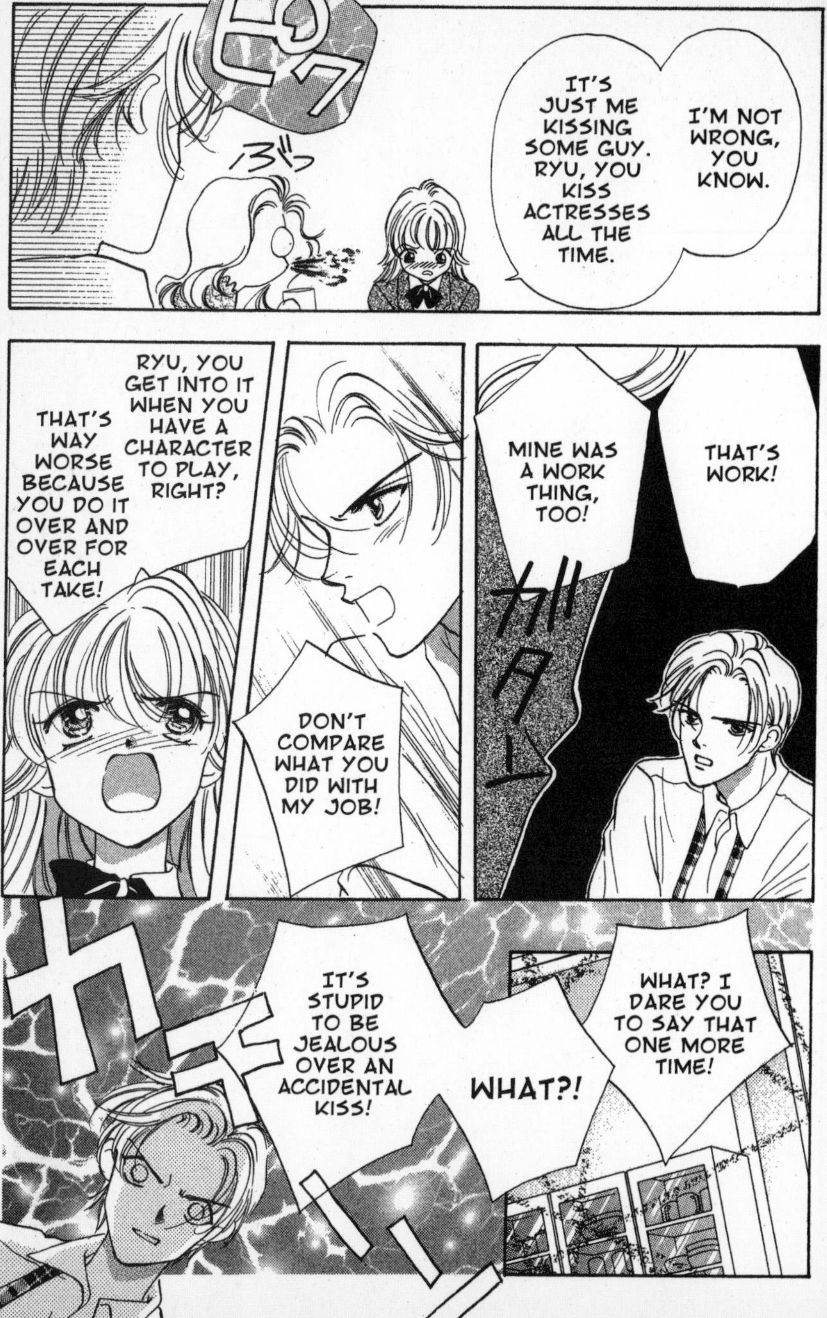
ピク
ぶっ
I'M NOT WRONG, YOU KNOW.
IT'S JUST ME KISSING SOME GUY. RYU, YOU KISS ACTRESSES ALL THE TIME.
THAT'S WORK!
MINE WAS A WORK THING, TOO!
ガタ
DON'T COMPARE WHAT YOU DID WITH MY JOB!
RYU, YOU GET INTO IT WHEN YOU HAVE A CHARACTER TO PLAY, RIGHT?
THAT'S WAY WORSE BECAUSE YOU DO IT OVER AND OVER FOR EACH TAKE!
WHAT? I DARE YOU TO SAY THAT ONE MORE TIME!
WHAT?!
IT'S STUPID TO BE JEALOUS OVER AN ACCIDENTAL KISS!

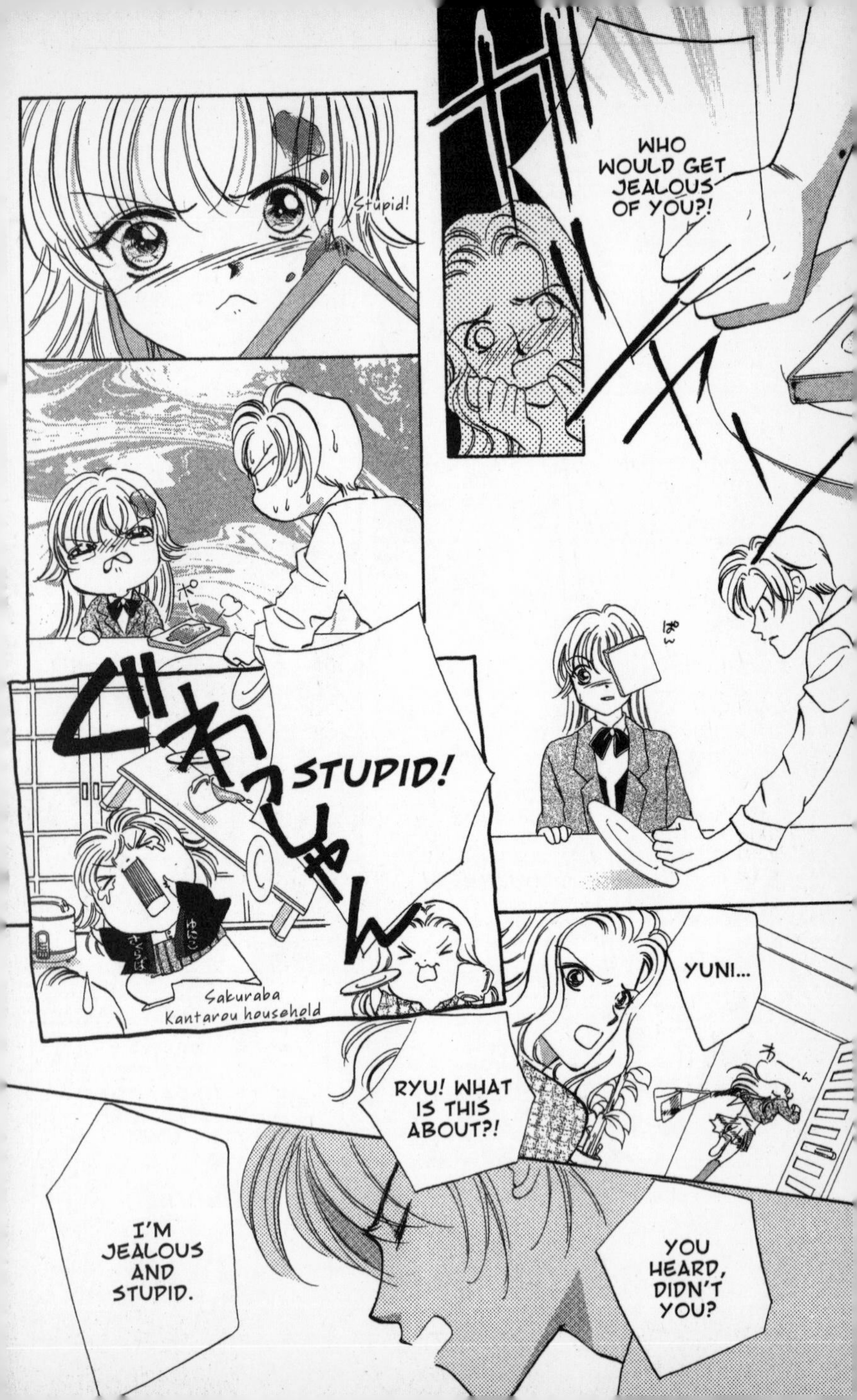
WHO WOULD GET JEALOUS OF YOU?!
Stupid!
STUPID!
ぐわっしゃん
Sakuraba Kantarou household
YUNI...
RYU! WHAT IS THIS ABOUT?!
YOU HEARD, DIDN'T YOU?
I'M JEALOUS AND STUPID.

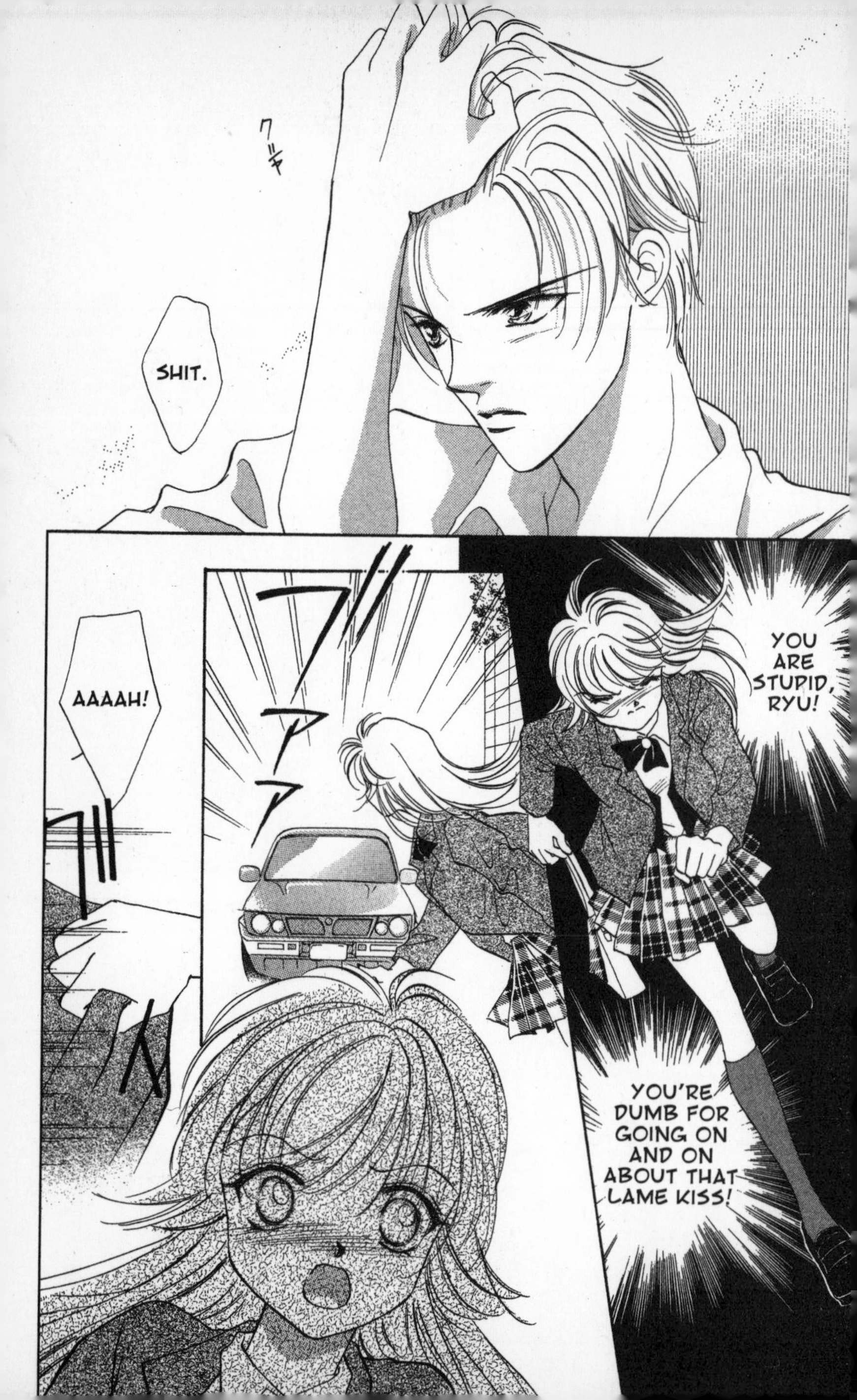
クシャ
SHIT.
YOU ARE STUPID, RYU!
YOU'RE DUMB FOR GOING ON AND ON ABOUT THAT LAME KISS!
AAAAH!

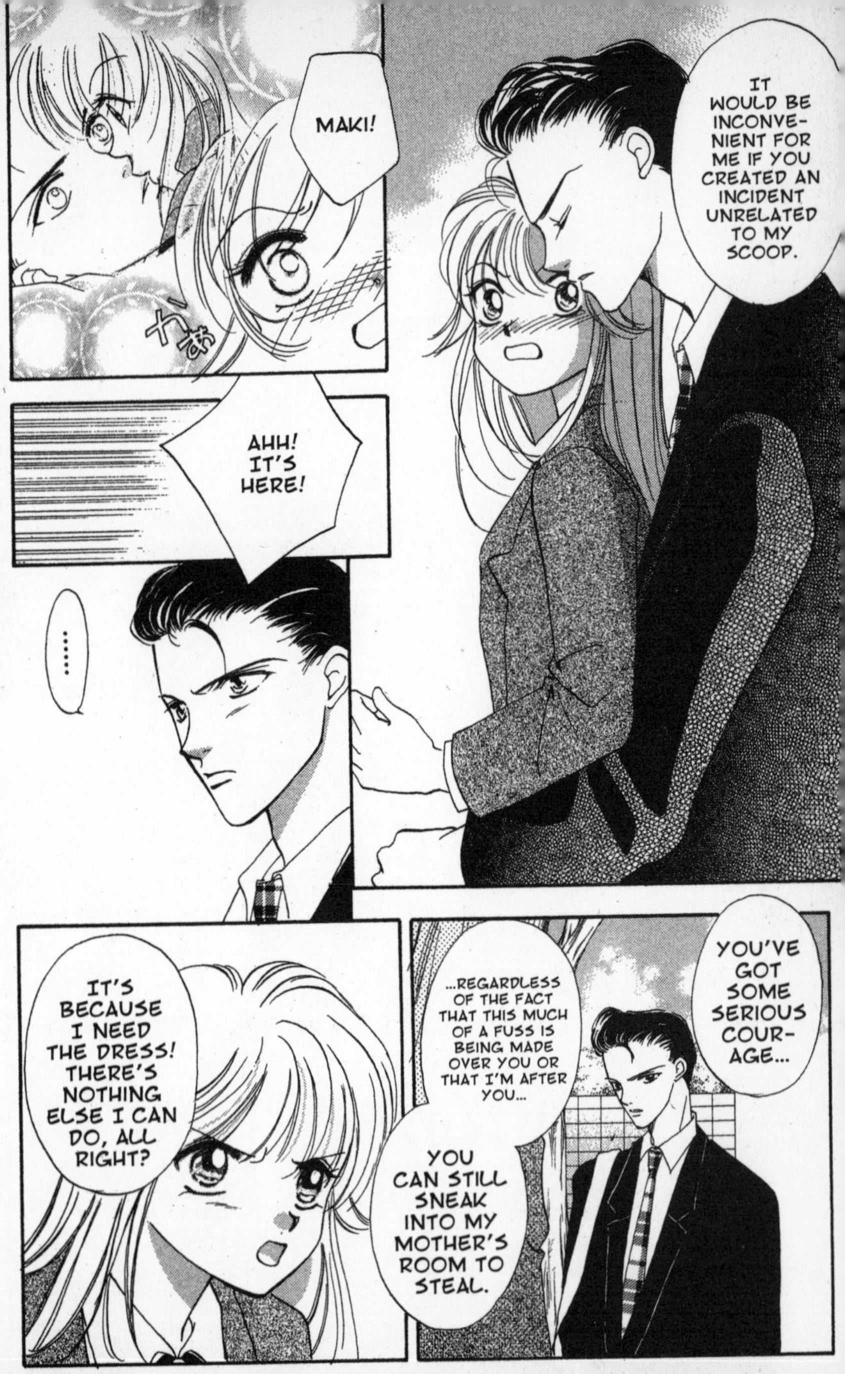
IT WOULD BE INCONVENIENT FOR ME IF YOU CREATED AN INCIDENT UNRELATED TO MY SCOOP.
MAKI!
AHH! IT'S HERE!
......
YOU'VE GOT SOME SERIOUS COURAGE...
...REGARDLESS OF THE FACT THAT THIS MUCH OF A FUSS IS BEING MADE OVER YOU OR THAT I'M AFTER YOU...
YOU CAN STILL SNEAK INTO MY MOTHER'S ROOM TO STEAL.
IT'S BECAUSE I NEED THE DRESS! THERE'S NOTHING ELSE I CAN DO, ALL RIGHT?

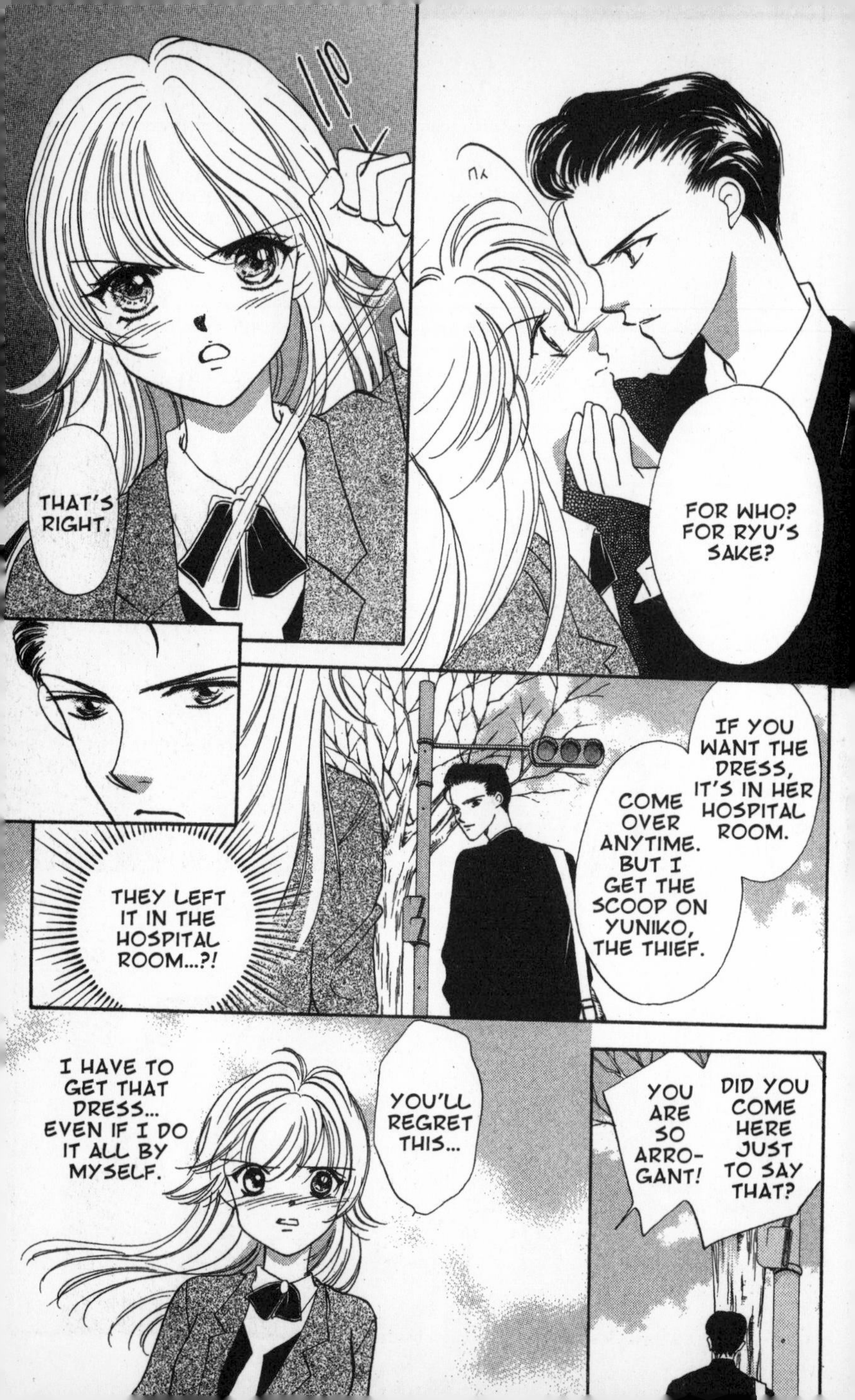
FOR WHO? FOR RYU'S SAKE?
THAT'S RIGHT.
IF YOU WANT THE DRESS, IT'S IN HER HOSPITAL ROOM.
COME OVER ANYTIME. BUT I GET THE SCOOP ON YUNIKO, THE THIEF.
THEY LEFT IT IN THE HOSPITAL ROOM...?!
DID YOU COME HERE JUST TO SAY THAT?
YOU ARE SO ARRO-GANT!
YOU'LL REGRET THIS...
I HAVE TO GET THAT DRESS... EVEN IF I DO IT ALL BY MYSELF.

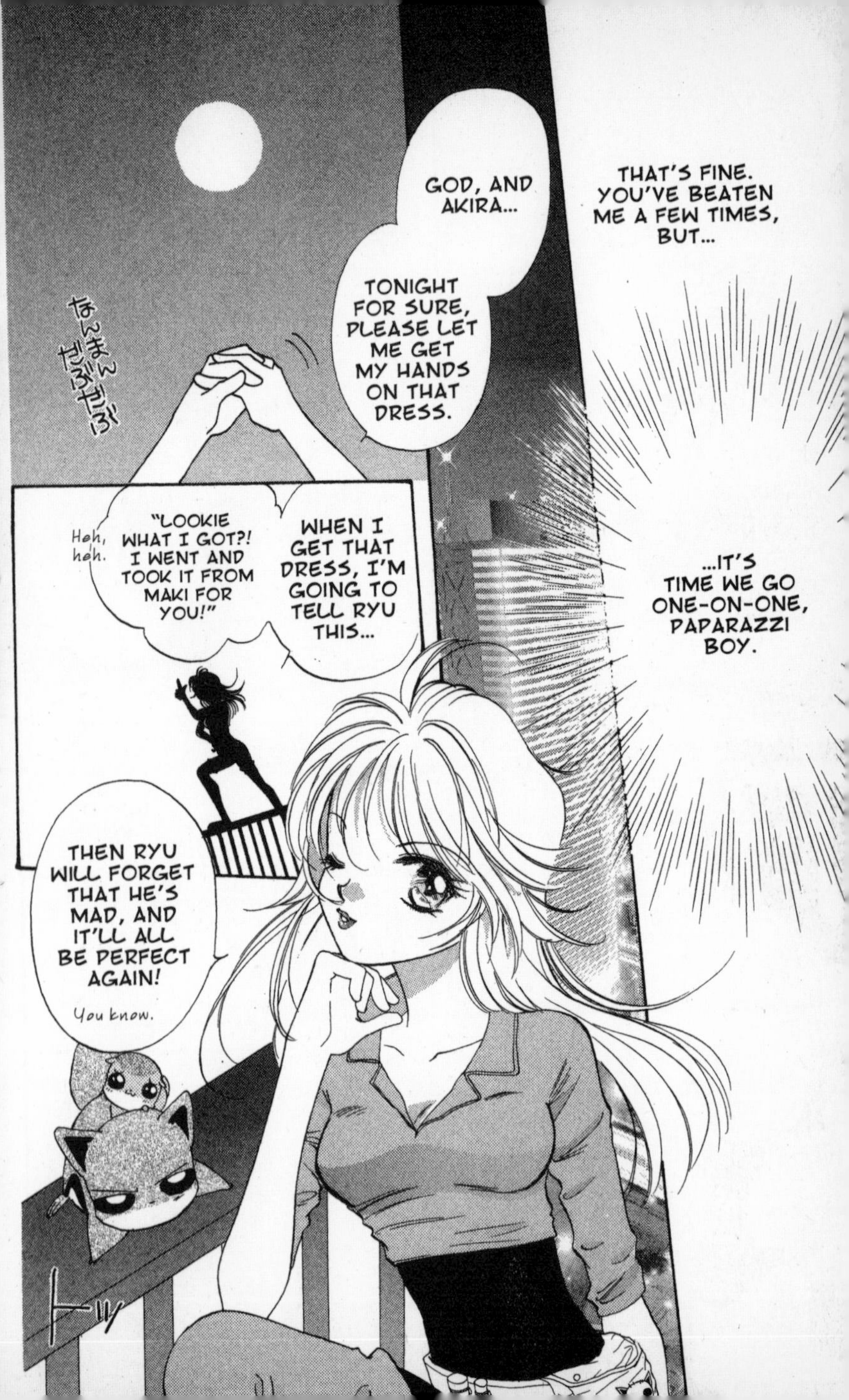
THAT'S FINE. YOU'VE BEATEN ME A FEW TIMES, BUT...
...IT'S TIME WE GO ONE-ON-ONE, PAPARAZZI BOY.
GOD, AND AKIRA...
TONIGHT FOR SURE, PLEASE LET ME GET MY HANDS ON THAT DRESS.
なんまんだぶだぶ
WHEN I GET THAT DRESS, I'M GOING TO TELL RYU THIS...
"LOOKIE WHAT I GOT?! I WENT AND TOOK IT FROM MAKI FOR YOU!"
Heh, heh.
THEN RYU WILL FORGET THAT HE'S MAD, AND IT'LL ALL BE PERFECT AGAIN!
You know.
トッ

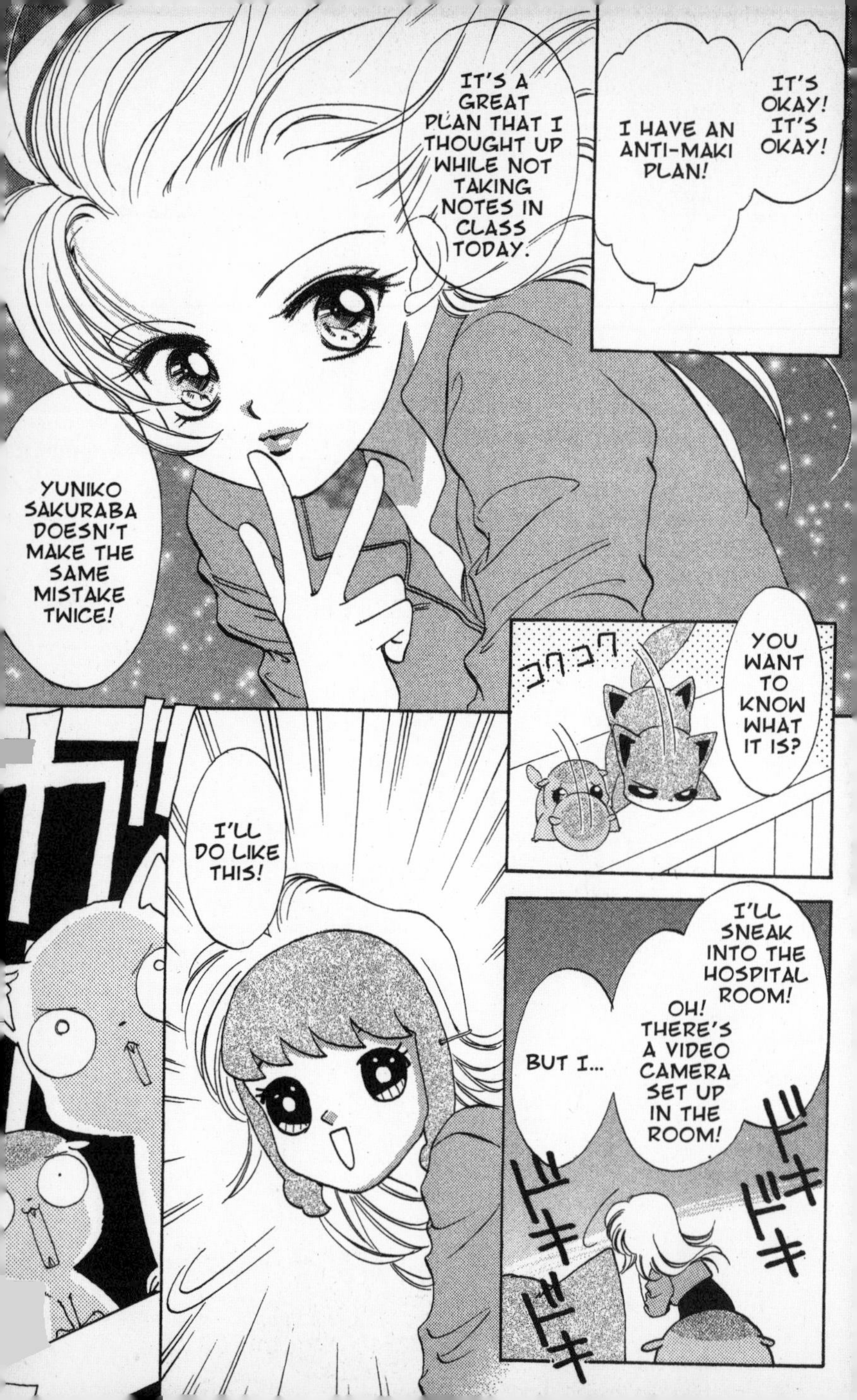
IT'S OKAY! IT'S OKAY!
I HAVE AN ANTI-MAKI PLAN!
IT'S A GREAT PLAN THAT I THOUGHT UP WHILE NOT TAKING NOTES IN CLASS TODAY.
YUNIKO SAKURABA DOESN'T MAKE THE SAME MISTAKE TWICE!
YOU WANT TO KNOW WHAT IT IS?
I'LL DO LIKE THIS!
I'LL SNEAK INTO THE HOSPITAL ROOM!
OH! THERE'S A VIDEO CAMERA SET UP IN THE ROOM!
BUT I...

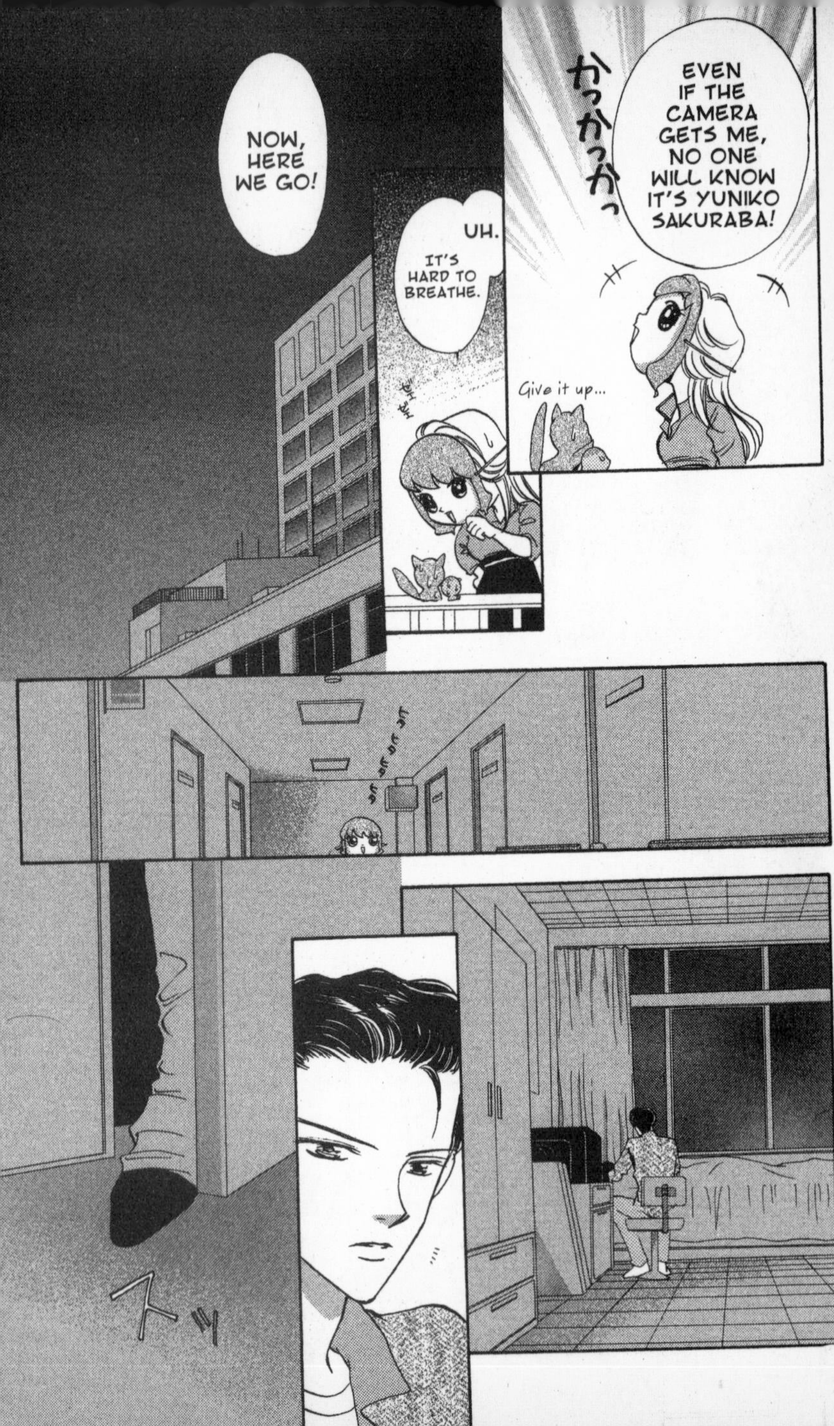
EVEN IF THE CAMERA GETS ME, NO ONE WILL KNOW IT'S YUNIKO SAKURABA!
かっかっかっ
Give it up...
UH.
IT'S HARD TO BREATHE.
NOW, HERE WE GO!

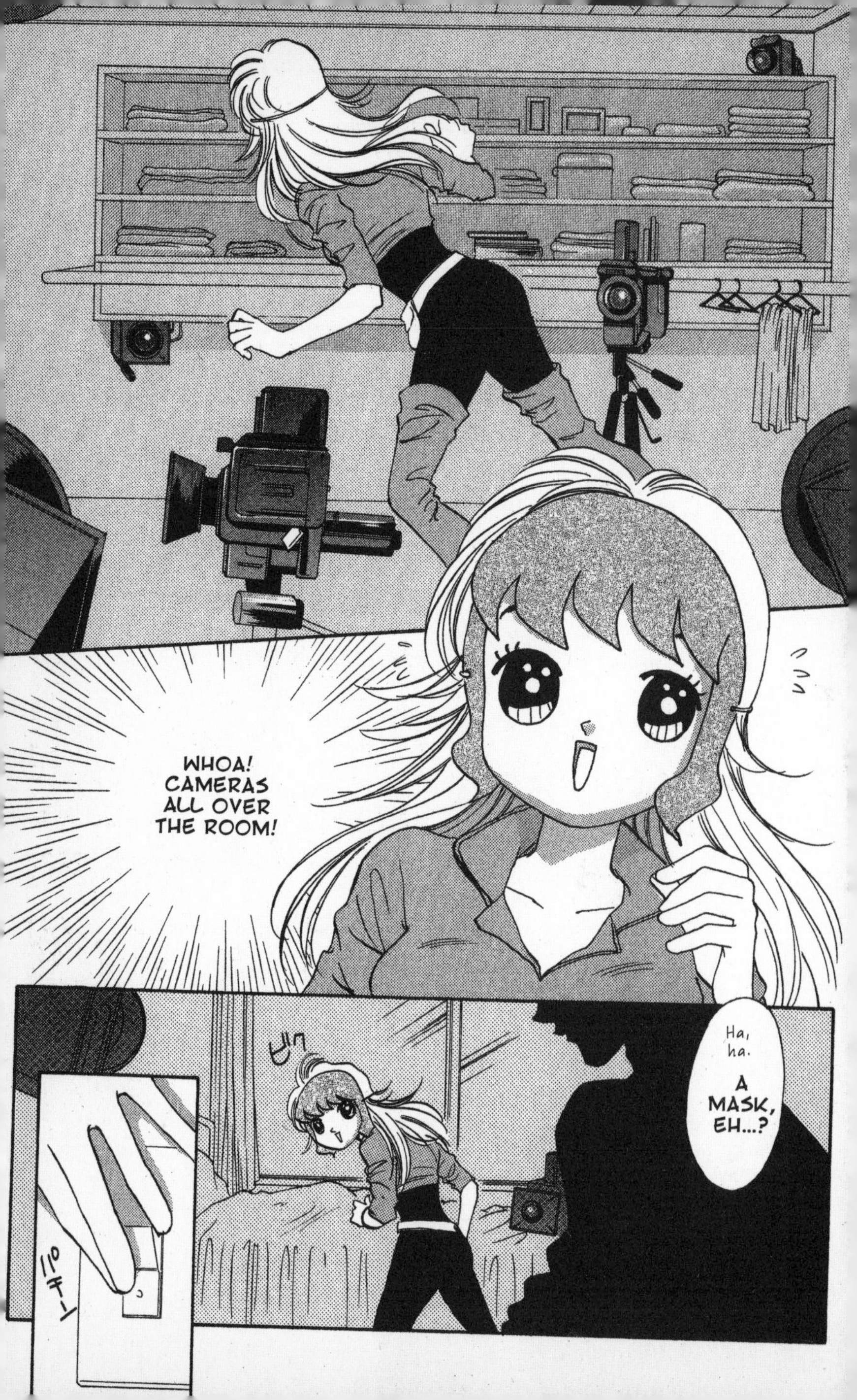
WHOA! CAMERAS ALL OVER THE ROOM!
Ha, ha.
A MASK, EH...?

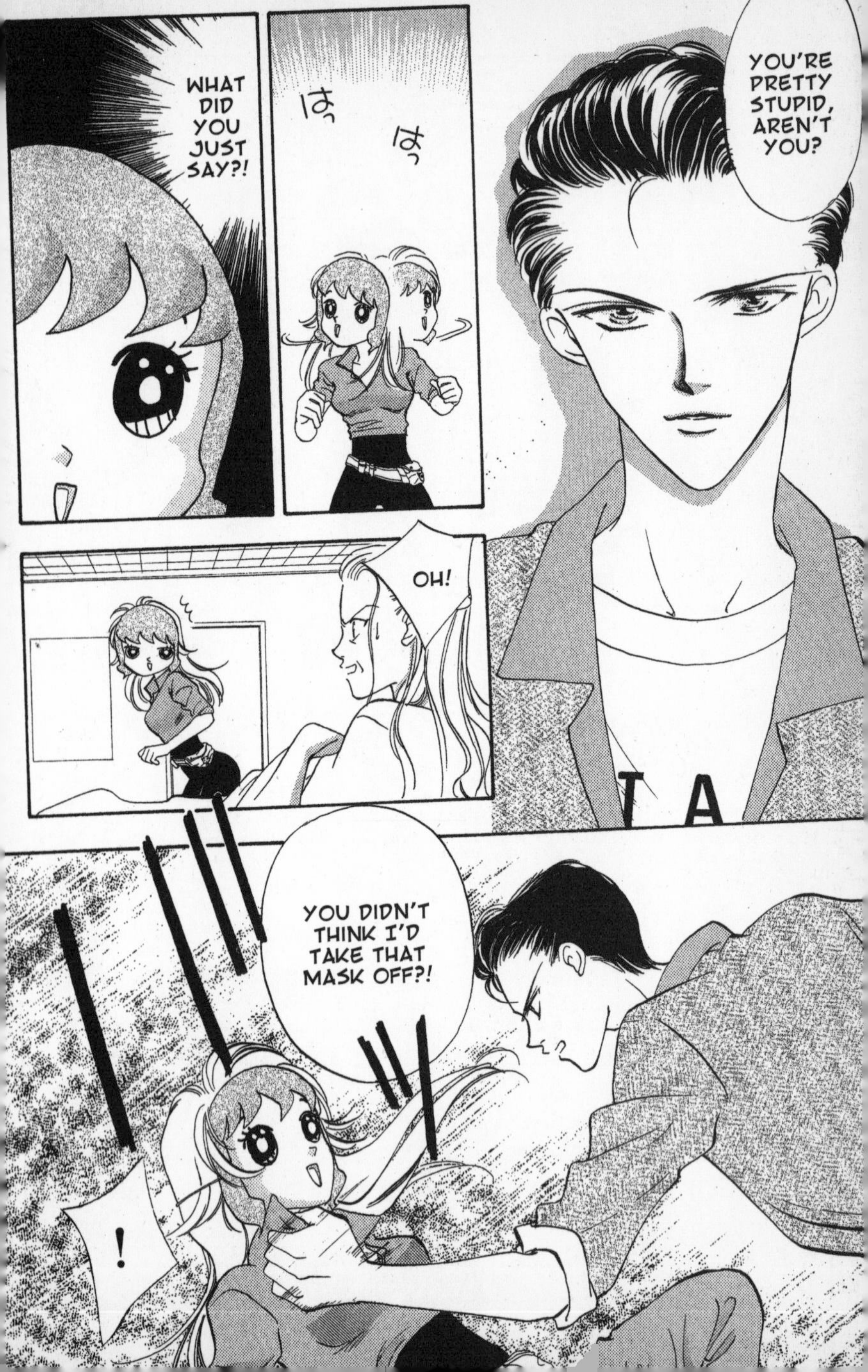
YOU'RE PRETTY STUPID, AREN'T YOU?
はっ
はっ
WHAT DID YOU JUST SAY?!
OH!
YOU DIDN'T THINK I'D TAKE THAT MASK OFF?!
!

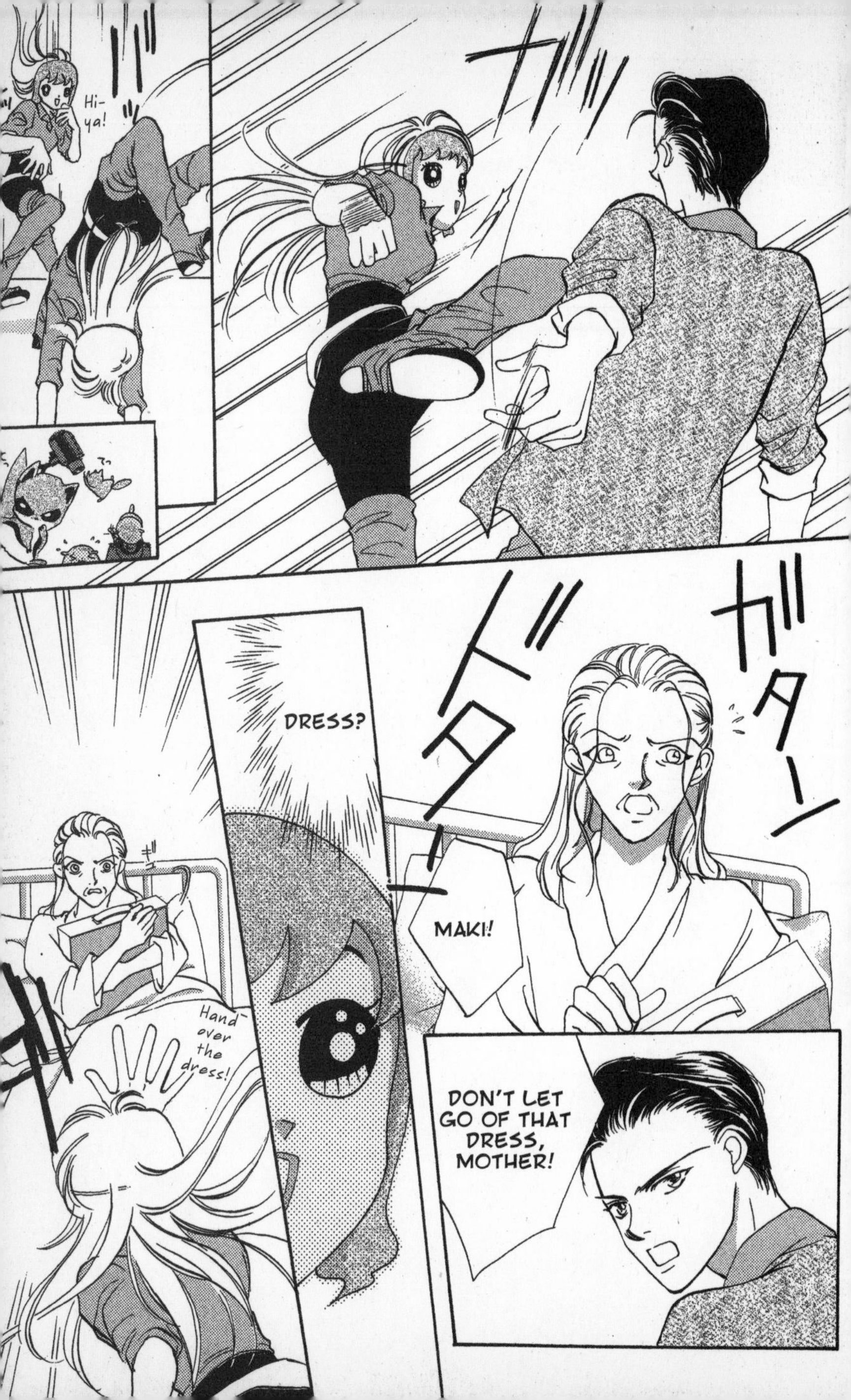
Hi-ya!
ガターン
MAKI!
DON'T LET GO OF THAT DRESS, MOTHER!
DRESS?
Hand over the dress!

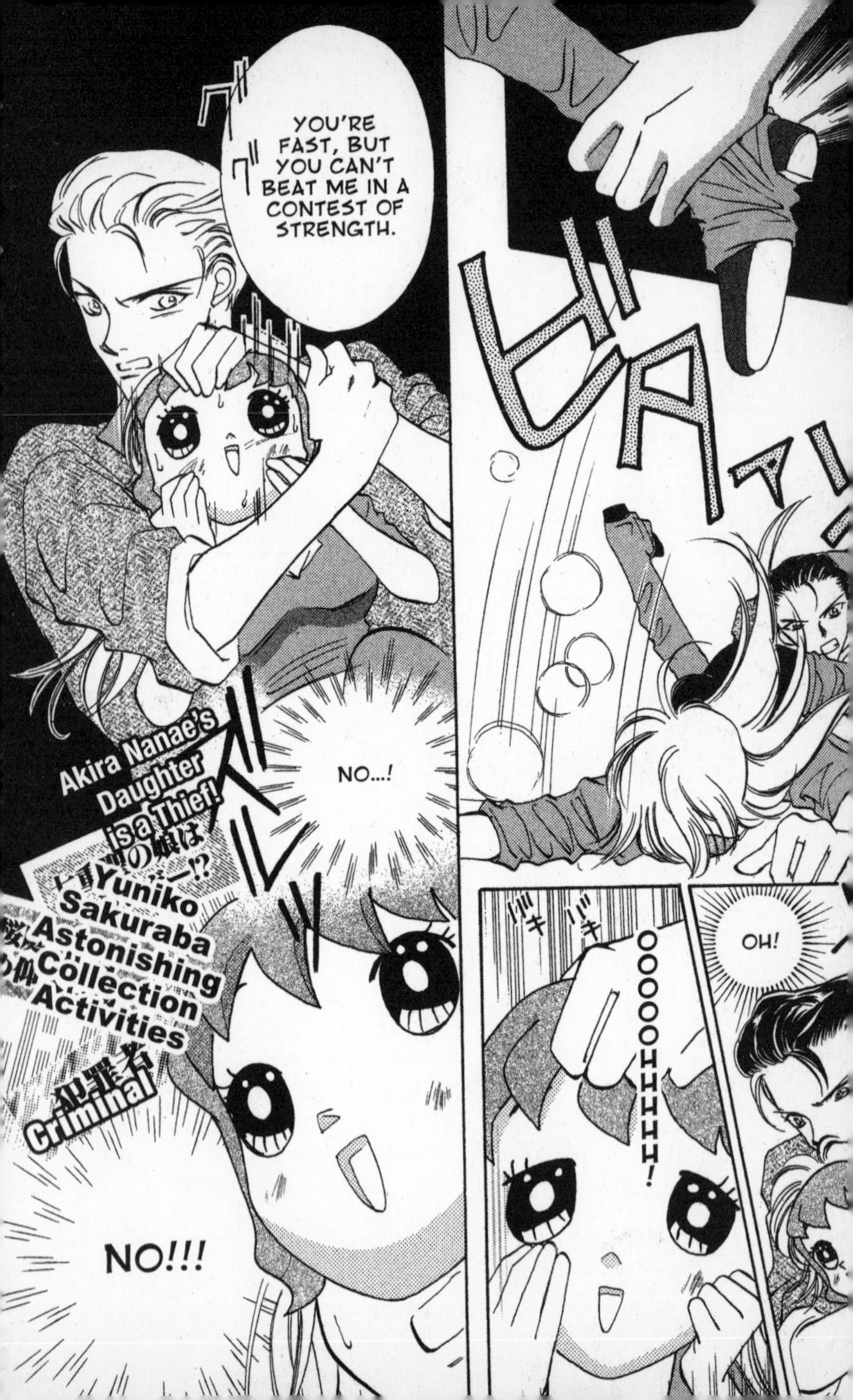
OH!
OOOOOHHHHHH!
YOU'RE FAST, BUT YOU CAN'T BEAT ME IN A CONTEST OF STRENGTH.
Akira Nanae's Daughter is a Thief!
Yuniko Sakuraba
Astonishing Collection Activities
Criminal
NO...!
NO!!!

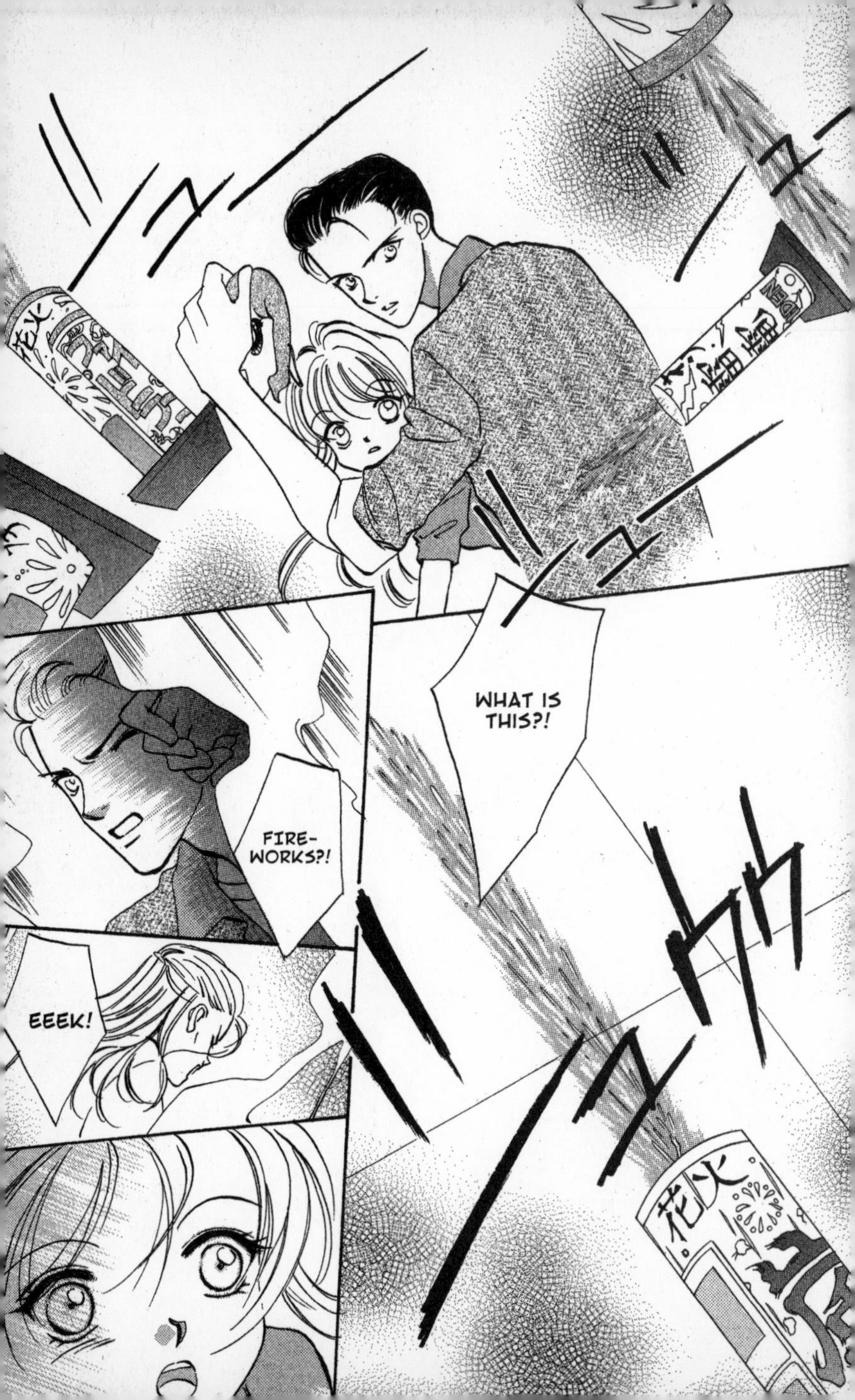
WHAT IS THIS?!
FIRE-WORKS?!
EEEK!

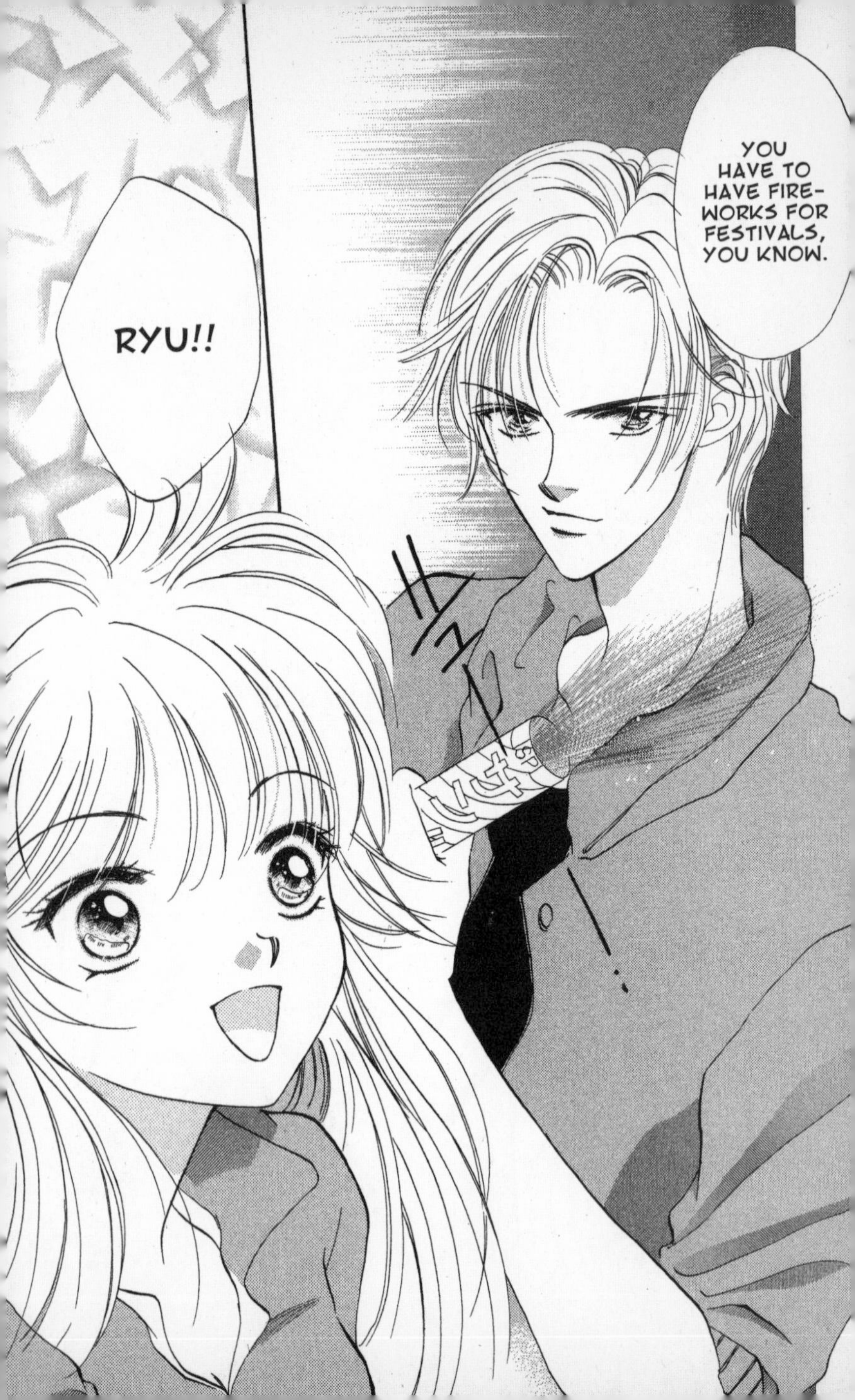
YOU HAVE TO HAVE FIRE-WORKS FOR FESTIVALS, YOU KNOW.
RYU!!

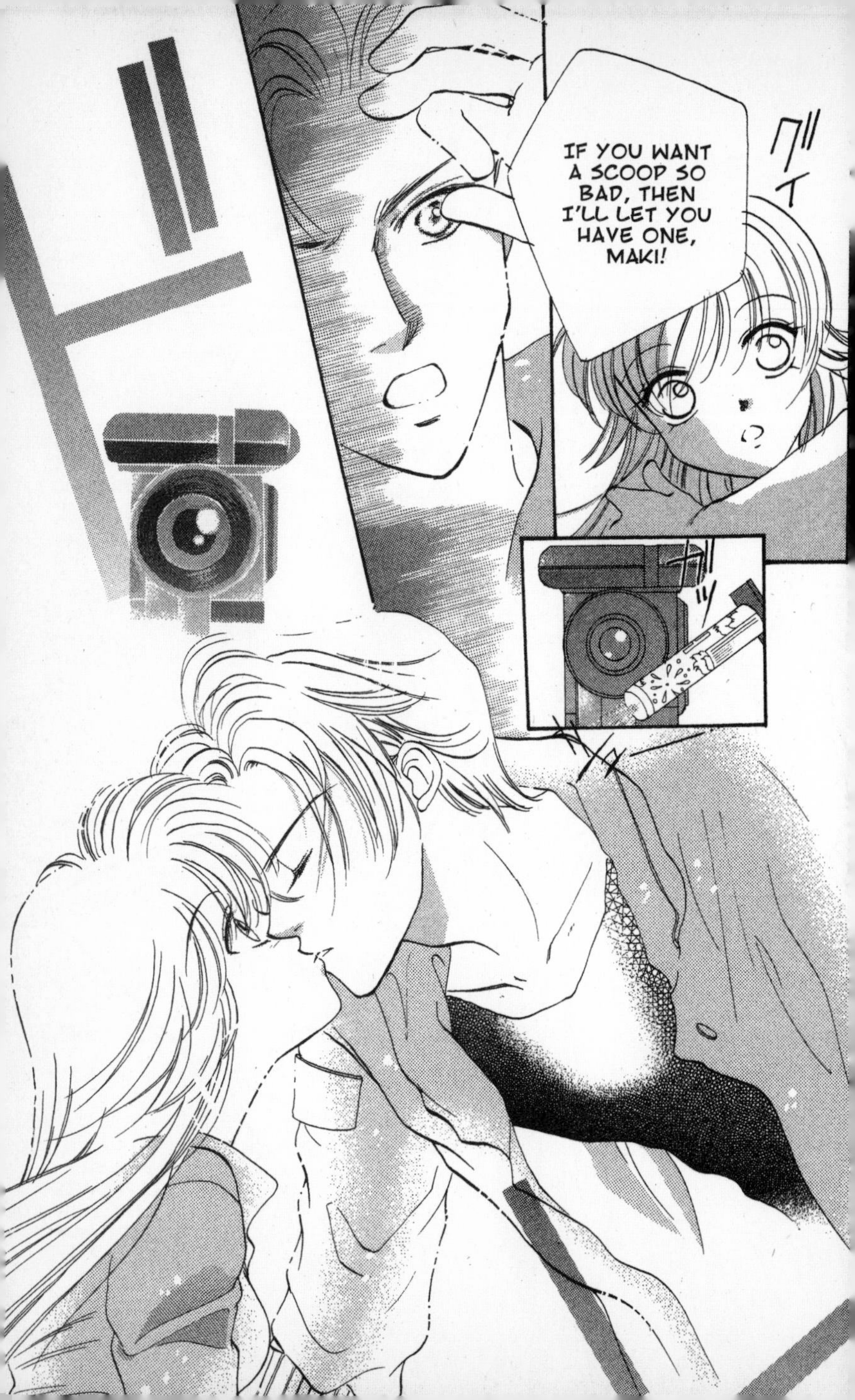
IF YOU WANT A SCOOP SO BAD, THEN I'LL LET YOU HAVE ONE, MAKI!

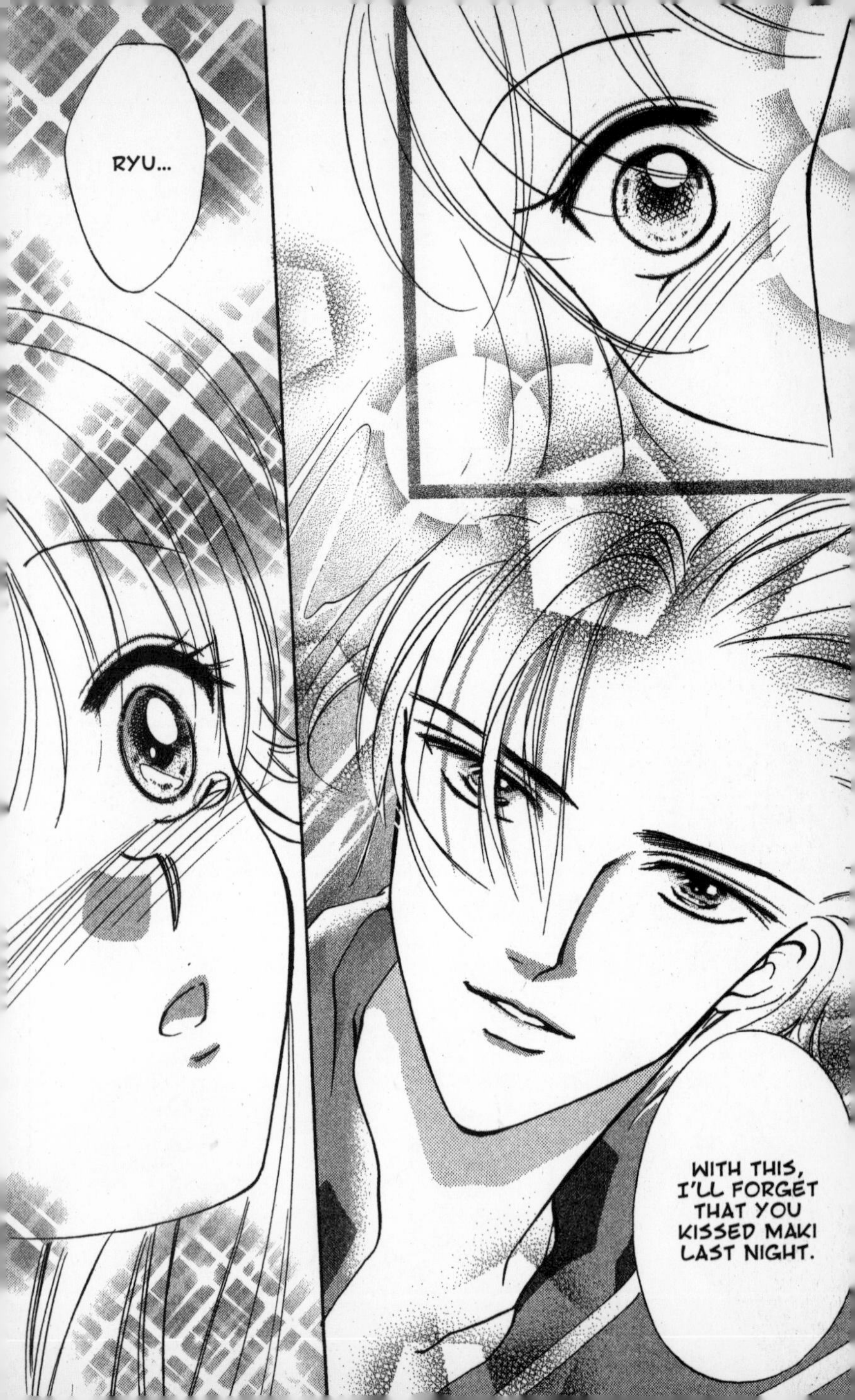
WITH THIS, I'LL FORGET THAT YOU KISSED MAKI LAST NIGHT.
RYU...

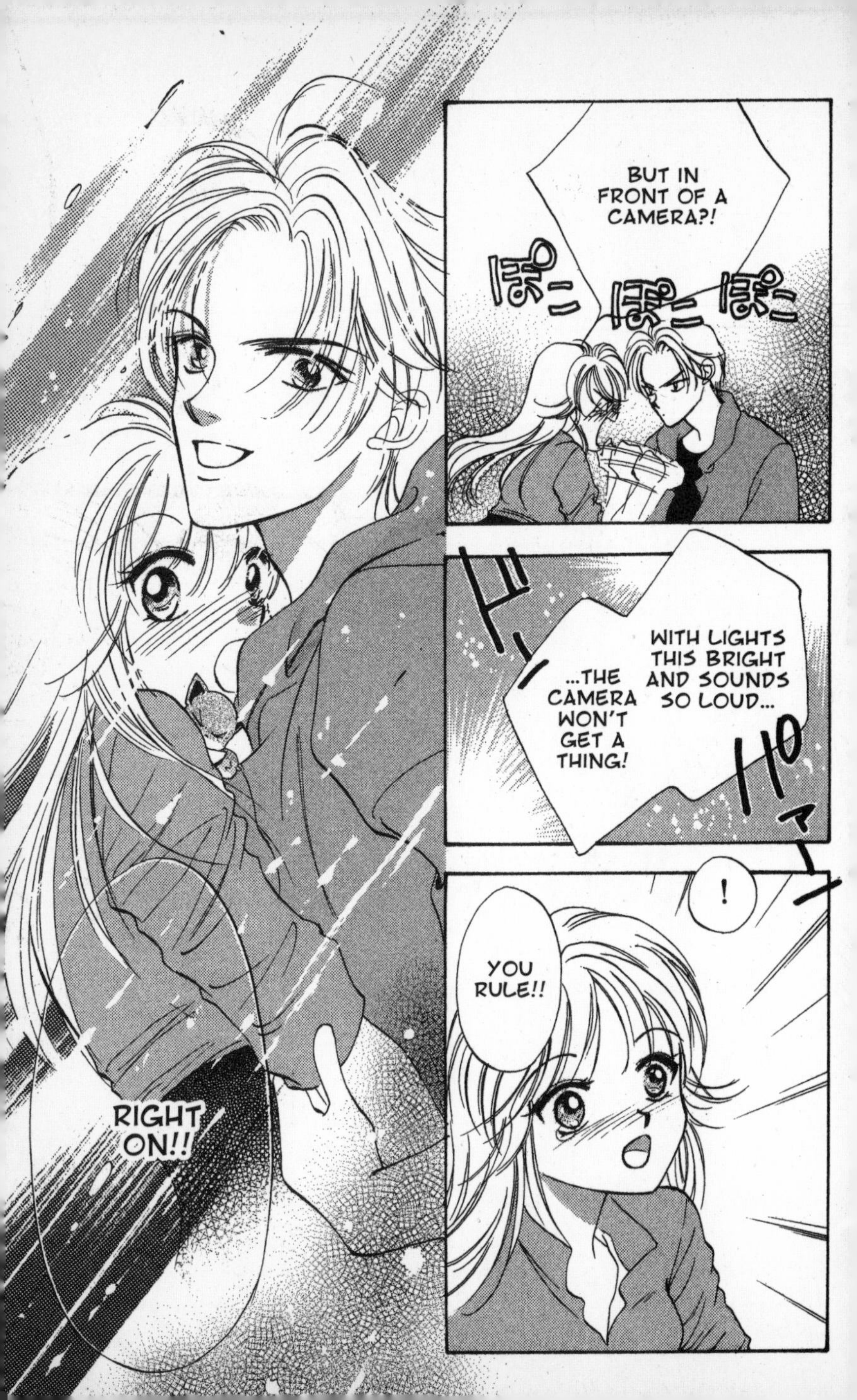
BUT IN FRONT OF A CAMERA?!
ぽこ ぽこ ぽこ
ジー
WITH LIGHTS THIS BRIGHT AND SOUNDS SO LOUD...
...THE CAMERA WON'T GET A THING!
パァー
!
YOU RULE!!
RIGHT ON!!

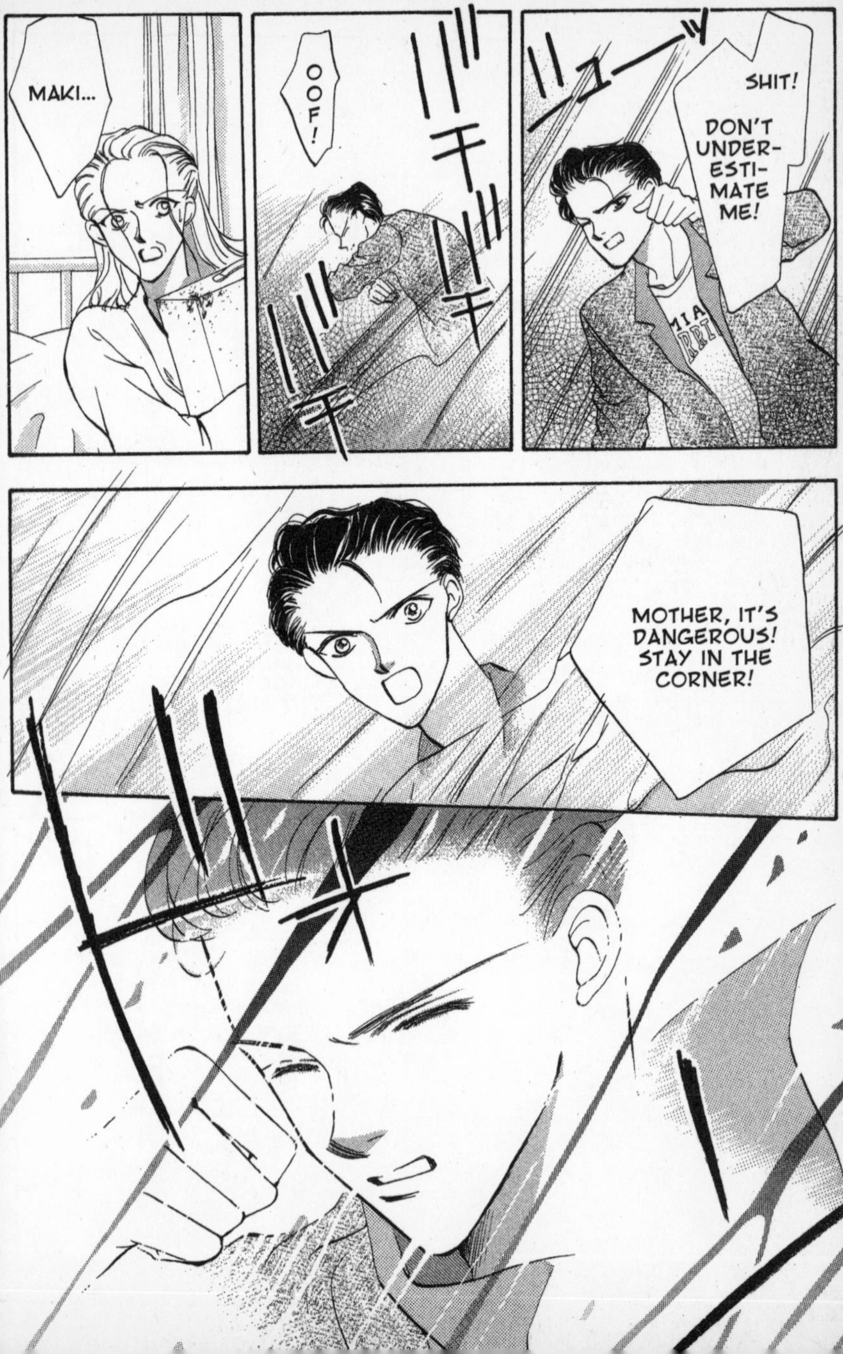
SHIT!
DON'T UNDER-ESTI-MATE ME!
OOF!
MAKI...
MOTHER, IT'S DANGEROUS! STAY IN THE CORNER!

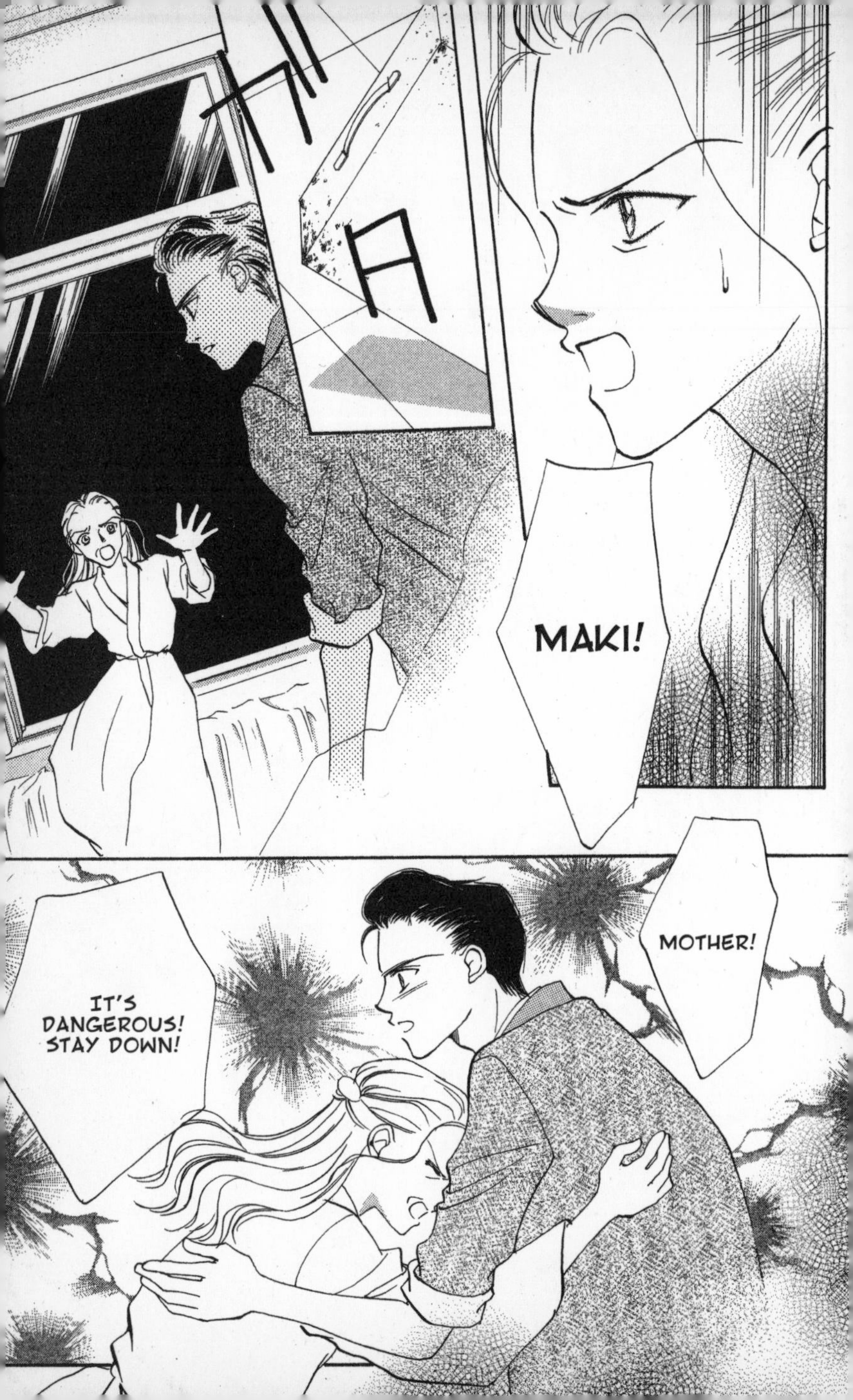
MAKI!
MOTHER!
IT'S DANGEROUS! STAY DOWN!

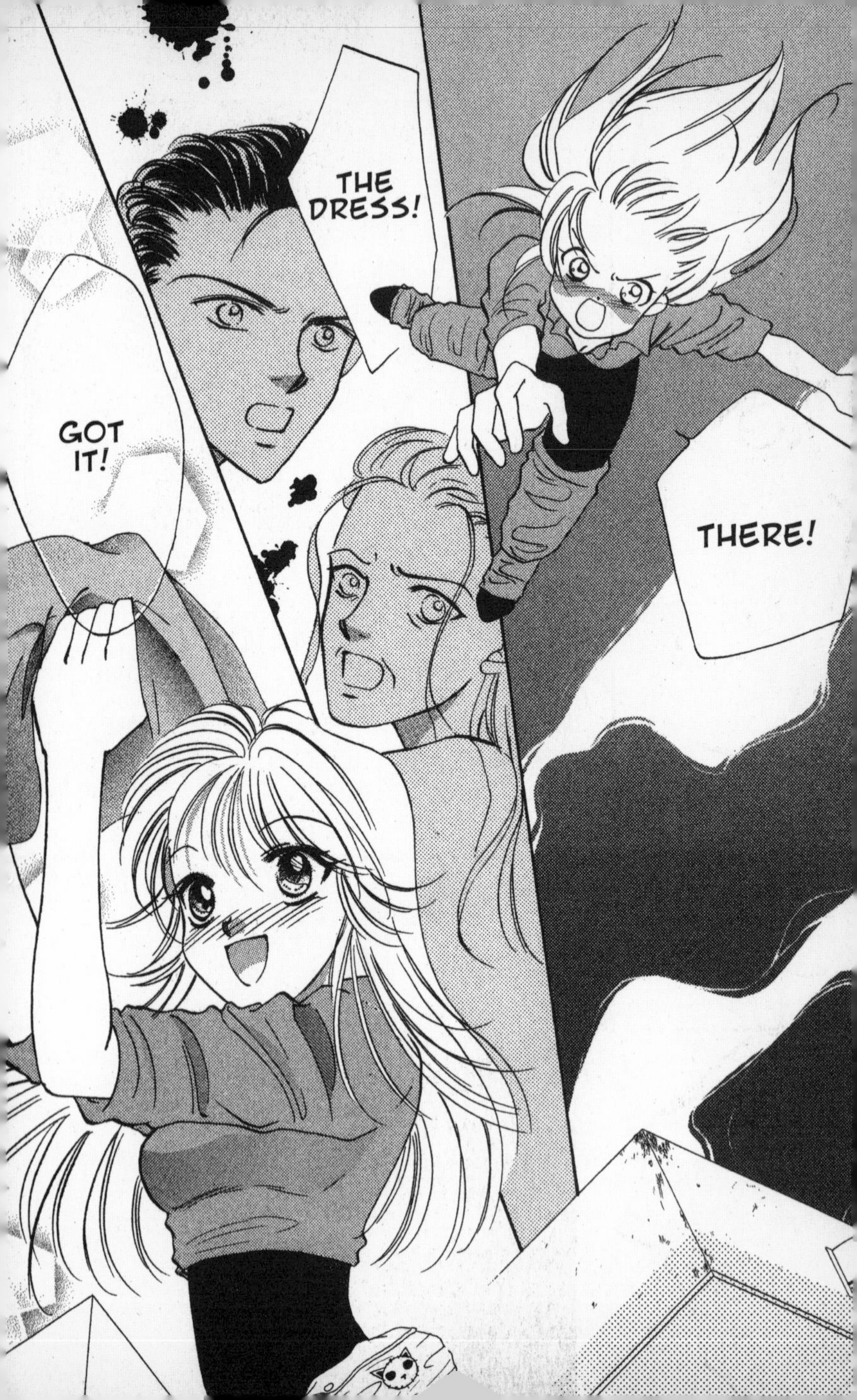
THERE!
THE DRESS!
GOT IT!

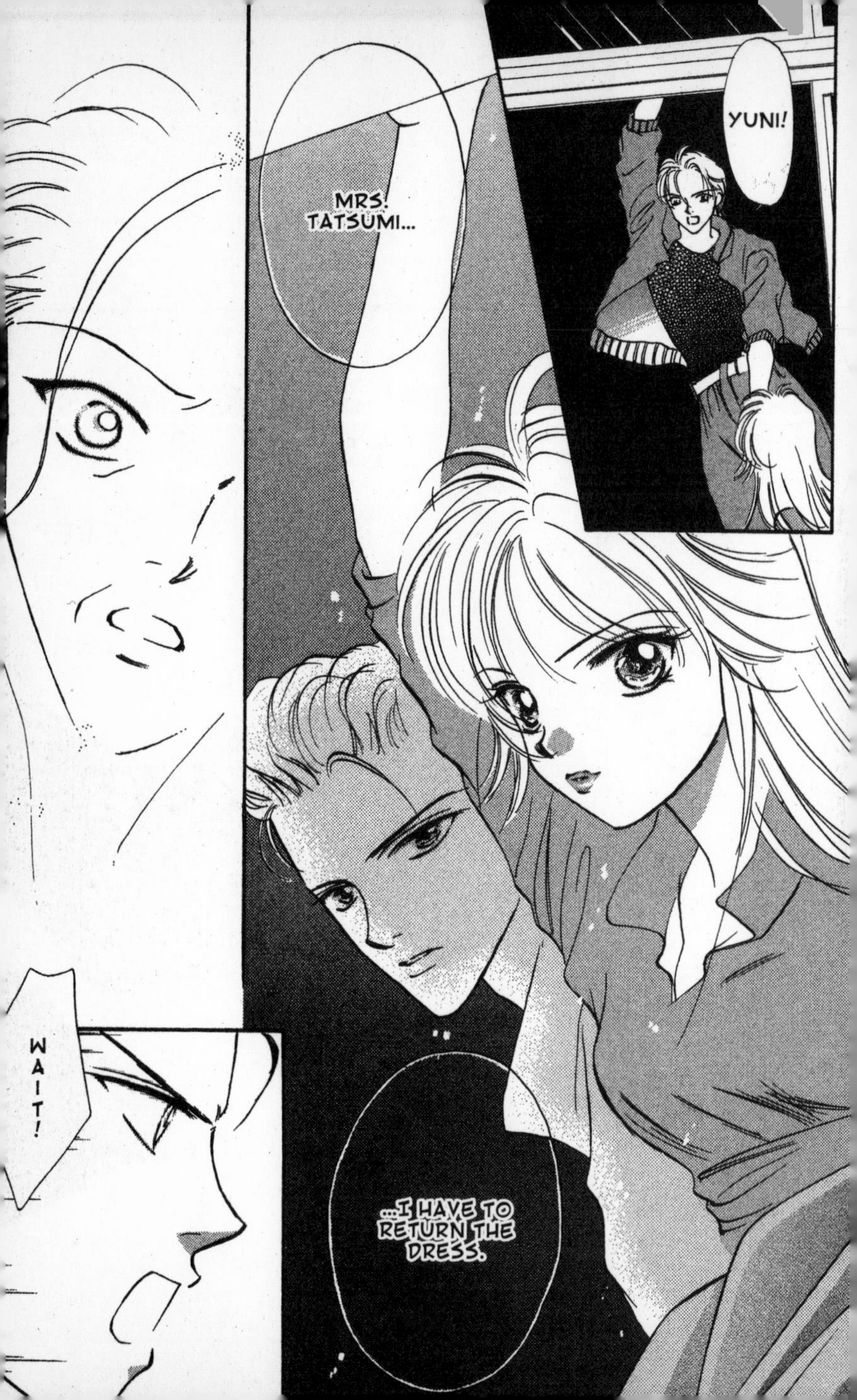
YUNI!
MRS. TATSUMI...
...I HAVE TO RETURN THE DRESS.
WAIT!

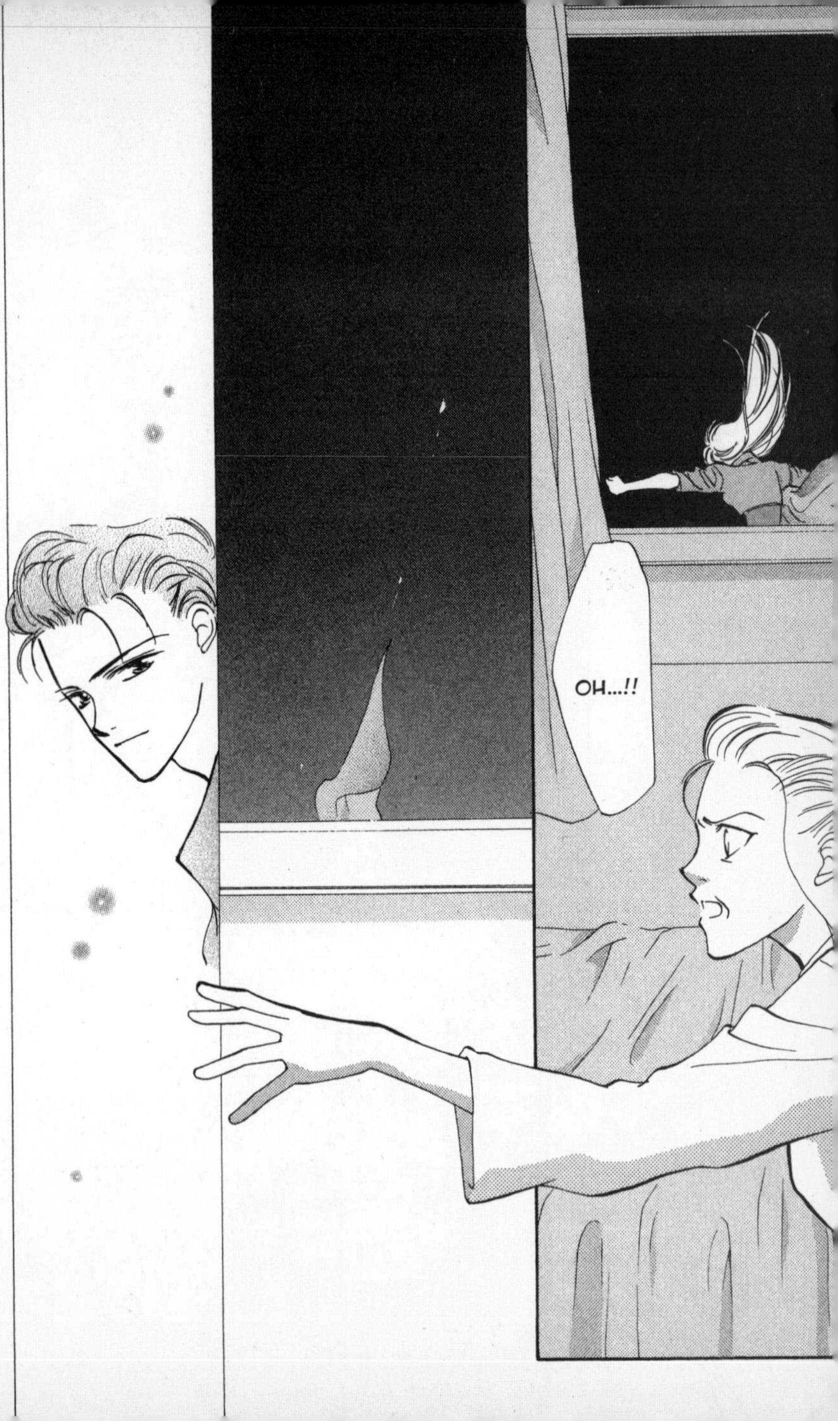
OH...!!

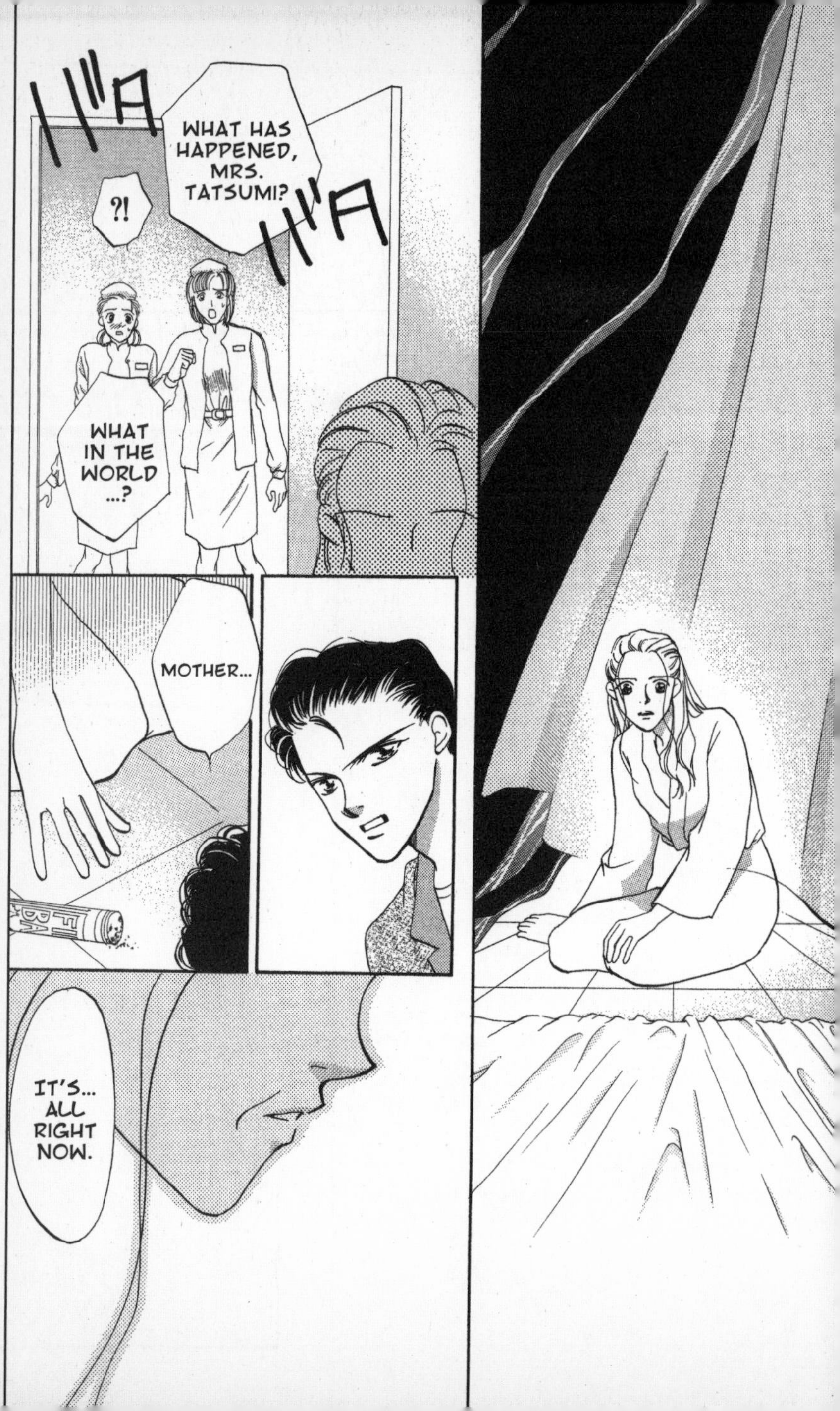
バタ
WHAT HAS HAPPENED, MRS. TATSUMI?
バタ
?!
WHAT IN THE WORLD ...?
MOTHER...
IT'S... ALL RIGHT NOW.

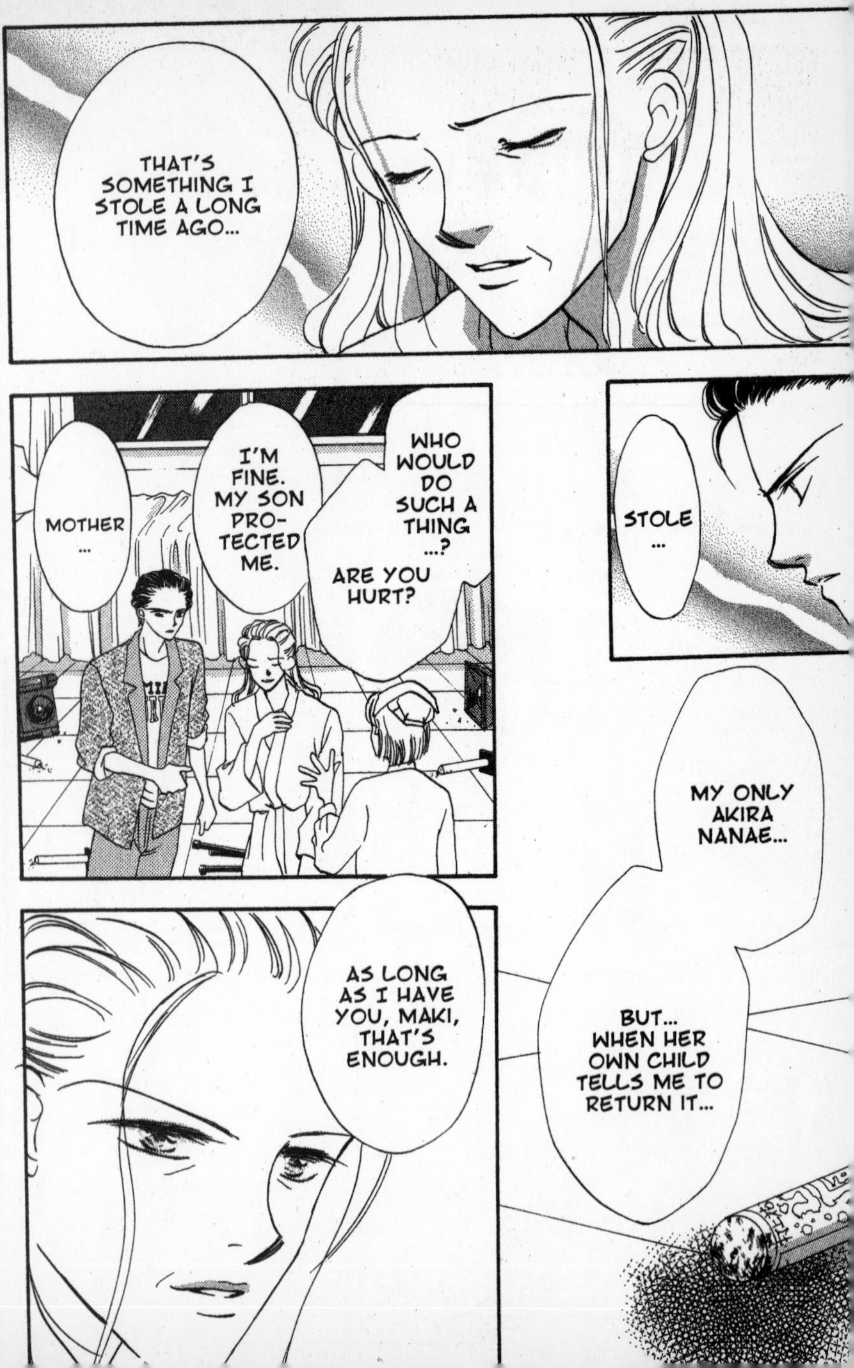
THAT'S SOMETHING I STOLE A LONG TIME AGO...
STOLE ...
WHO WOULD DO SUCH A THING ...?
ARE YOU HURT?
I'M FINE. MY SON PROTECTED ME.
MOTHER ...
MY ONLY AKIRA NANAE...
BUT... WHEN HER OWN CHILD TELLS ME TO RETURN IT...
AS LONG AS I HAVE YOU, MAKI, THAT'S ENOUGH.

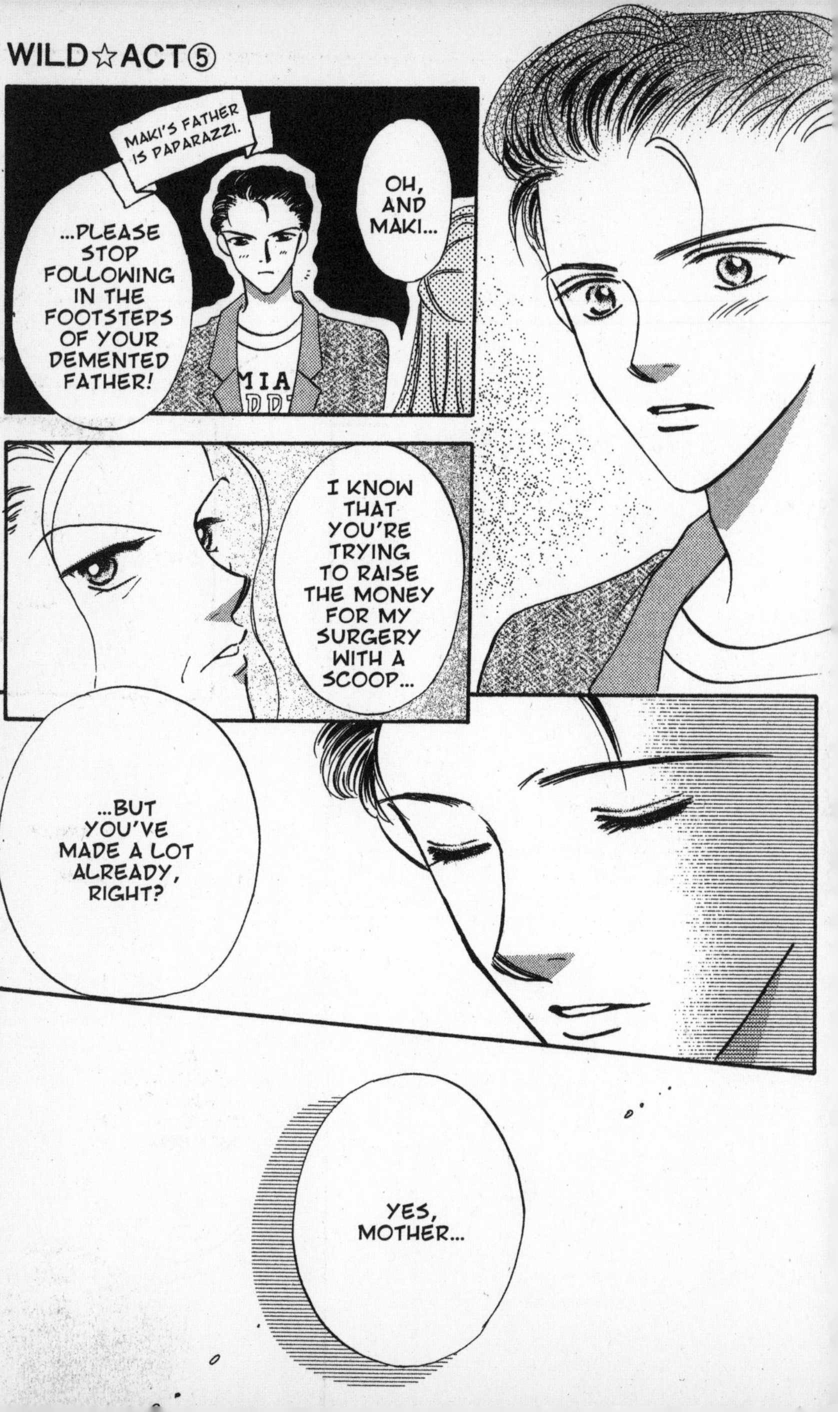
OH, AND MAKI...
MAKI'S FATHER IS PAPARAZZI.
...PLEASE STOP FOLLOWING IN THE FOOTSTEPS OF YOUR DEMENTED FATHER!
I KNOW THAT YOU'RE TRYING TO RAISE THE MONEY FOR MY SURGERY WITH A SCOOP...
...BUT YOU'VE MADE A LOT ALREADY, RIGHT?
YES, MOTHER...

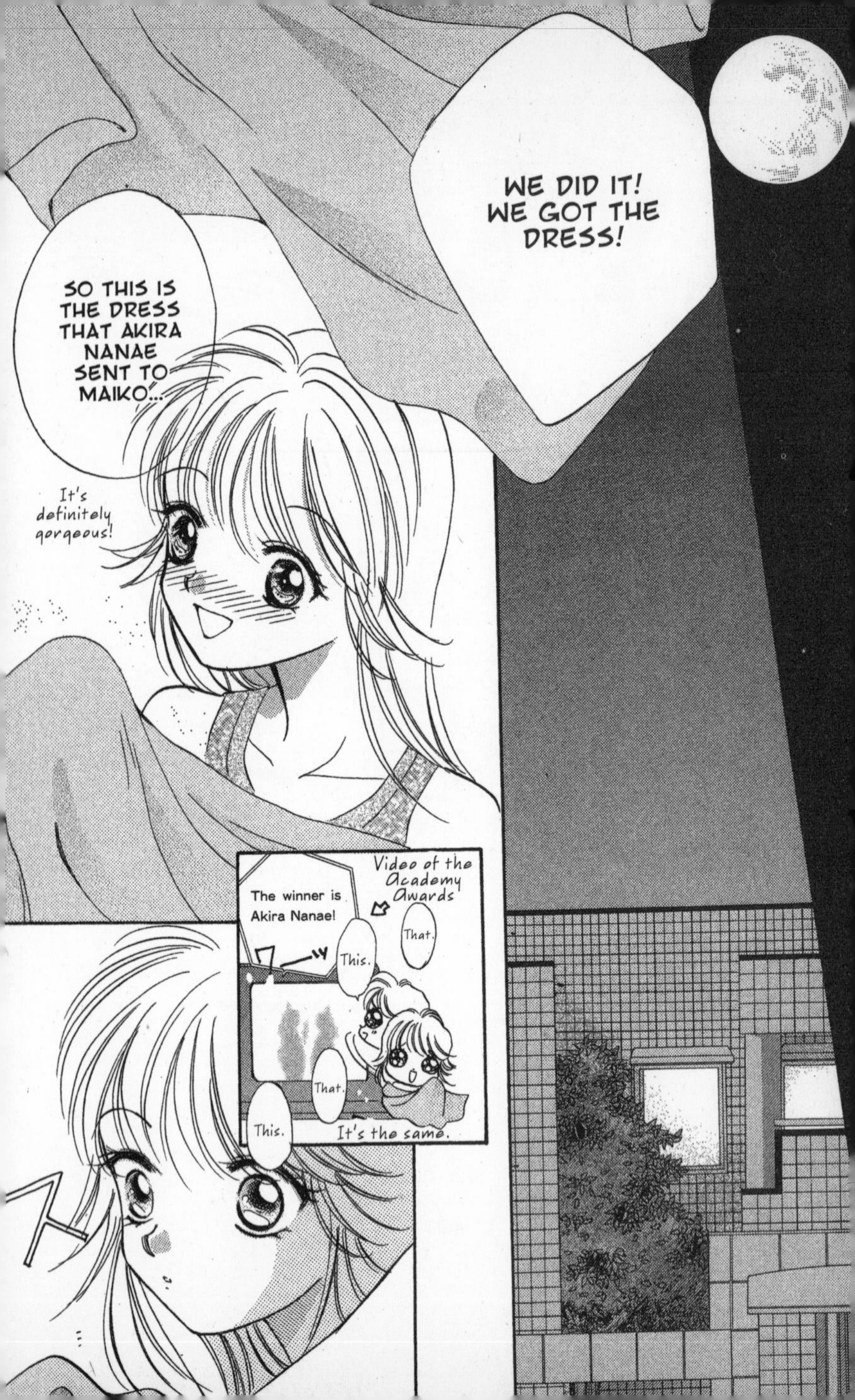
WE DID IT! WE GOT THE DRESS!
SO THIS IS THE DRESS THAT AKIRA NANAE SENT TO MAIKO...
It's definitely gorgeous!
Video of the Academy Awards
The winner is Akira Nanae!
That.
This.
That.
This.
It's the same.

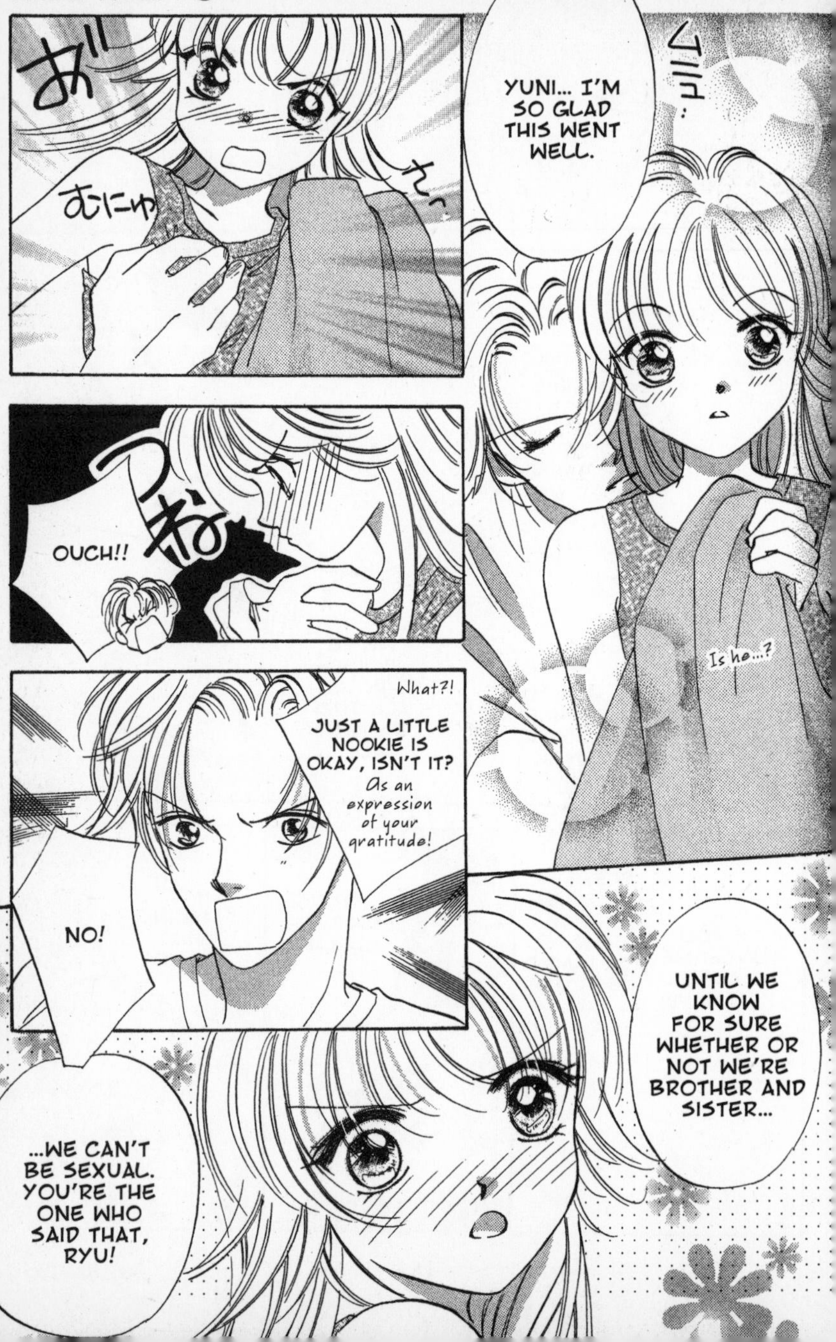
ムニュ
YUNI... I'M SO GLAD THIS WENT WELL.
Is he...?
あ゛
さっ
むにゅ
つね
OUCH!!
What?!
JUST A LITTLE NOOKIE IS OKAY, ISN'T IT?
As an expression of your gratitude!
NO!
UNTIL WE KNOW FOR SURE WHETHER OR NOT WE'RE BROTHER AND SISTER...
...WE CAN'T BE SEXUAL. YOU'RE THE ONE WHO SAID THAT, RYU!

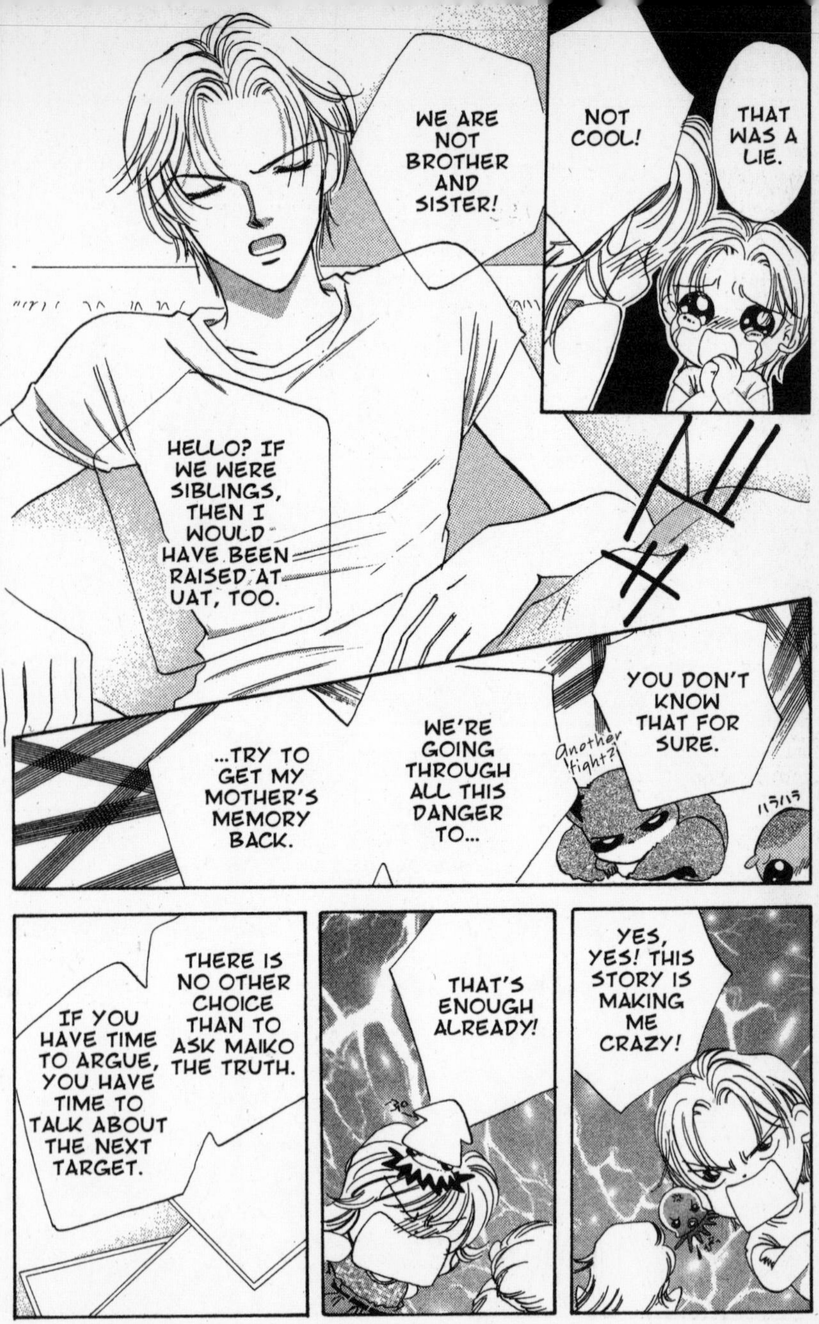
THAT WAS A LIE.
NOT COOL!
WE ARE NOT BROTHER AND SISTER!
HELLO? IF WE WERE SIBLINGS, THEN I WOULD HAVE BEEN RAISED AT UAT, TOO.
YOU DON'T KNOW THAT FOR SURE.
Another fight?
ハラハラ
WE'RE GOING THROUGH ALL THIS DANGER TO...
...TRY TO GET MY MOTHER'S MEMORY BACK.
YES, YES! THIS STORY IS MAKING ME CRAZY!
THAT'S ENOUGH ALREADY!
THERE IS NO OTHER CHOICE THAN TO ASK MAIKO THE TRUTH.
IF YOU HAVE TIME TO ARGUE, YOU HAVE TIME TO TALK ABOUT THE NEXT TARGET.

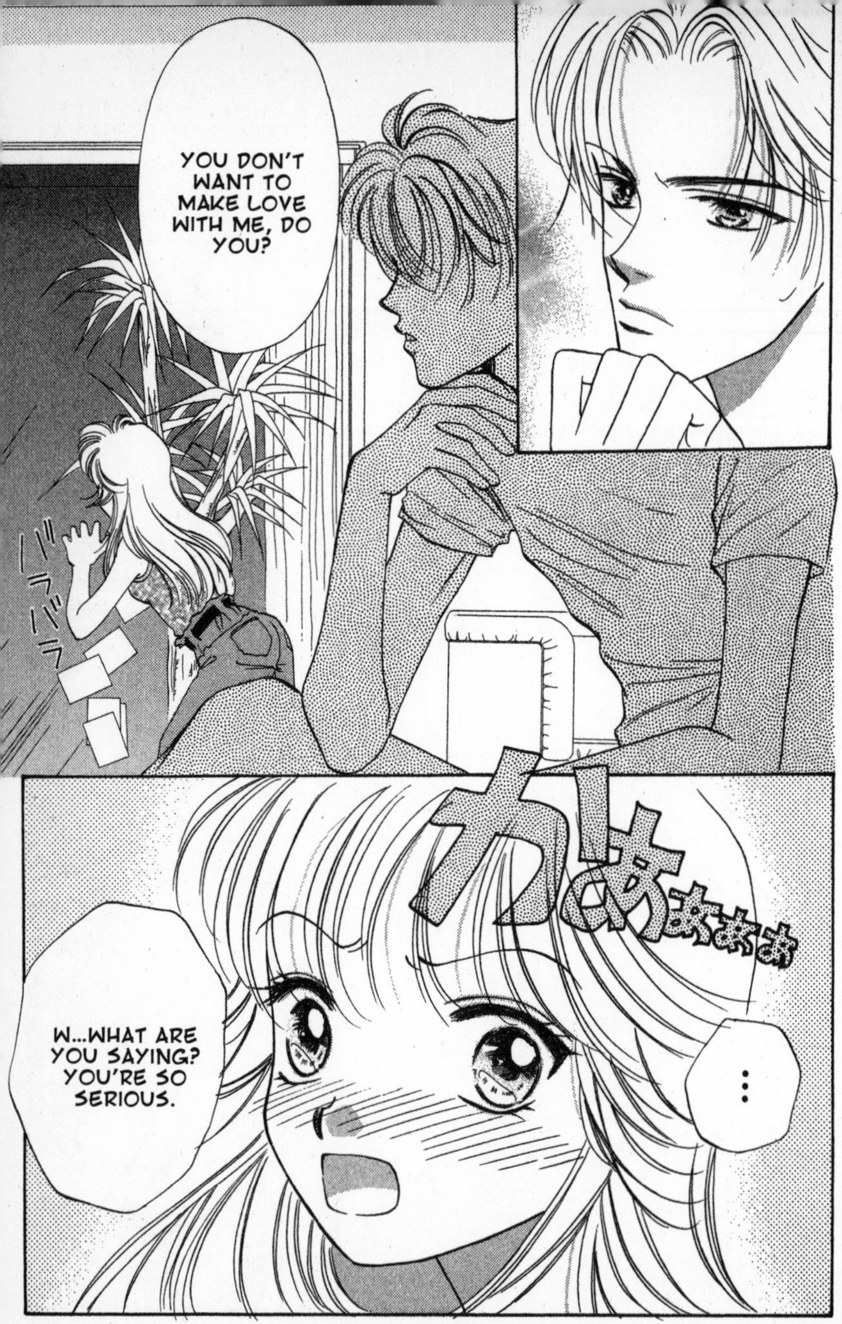
YOU DON'T WANT TO MAKE LOVE WITH ME, DO YOU?
バラバラ
わあああああ
...
W...WHAT ARE YOU SAYING? YOU'RE SO SERIOUS.

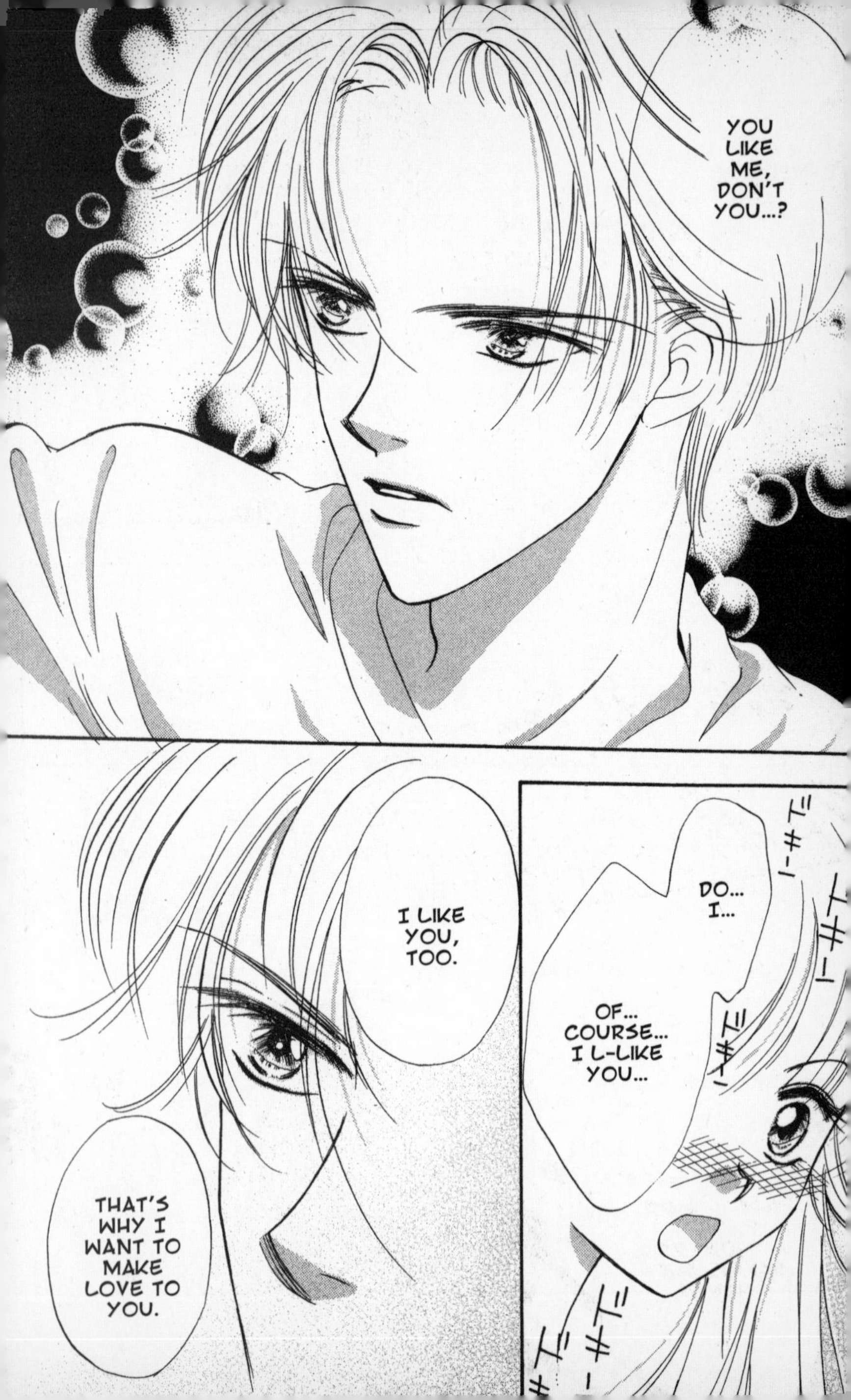
YOU LIKE ME, DON'T YOU...?
ドキー ドキー
DO... I...
OF... COURSE... I L-LIKE YOU...
ドキー ドキー
I LIKE YOU, TOO.
THAT'S WHY I WANT TO MAKE LOVE TO YOU.

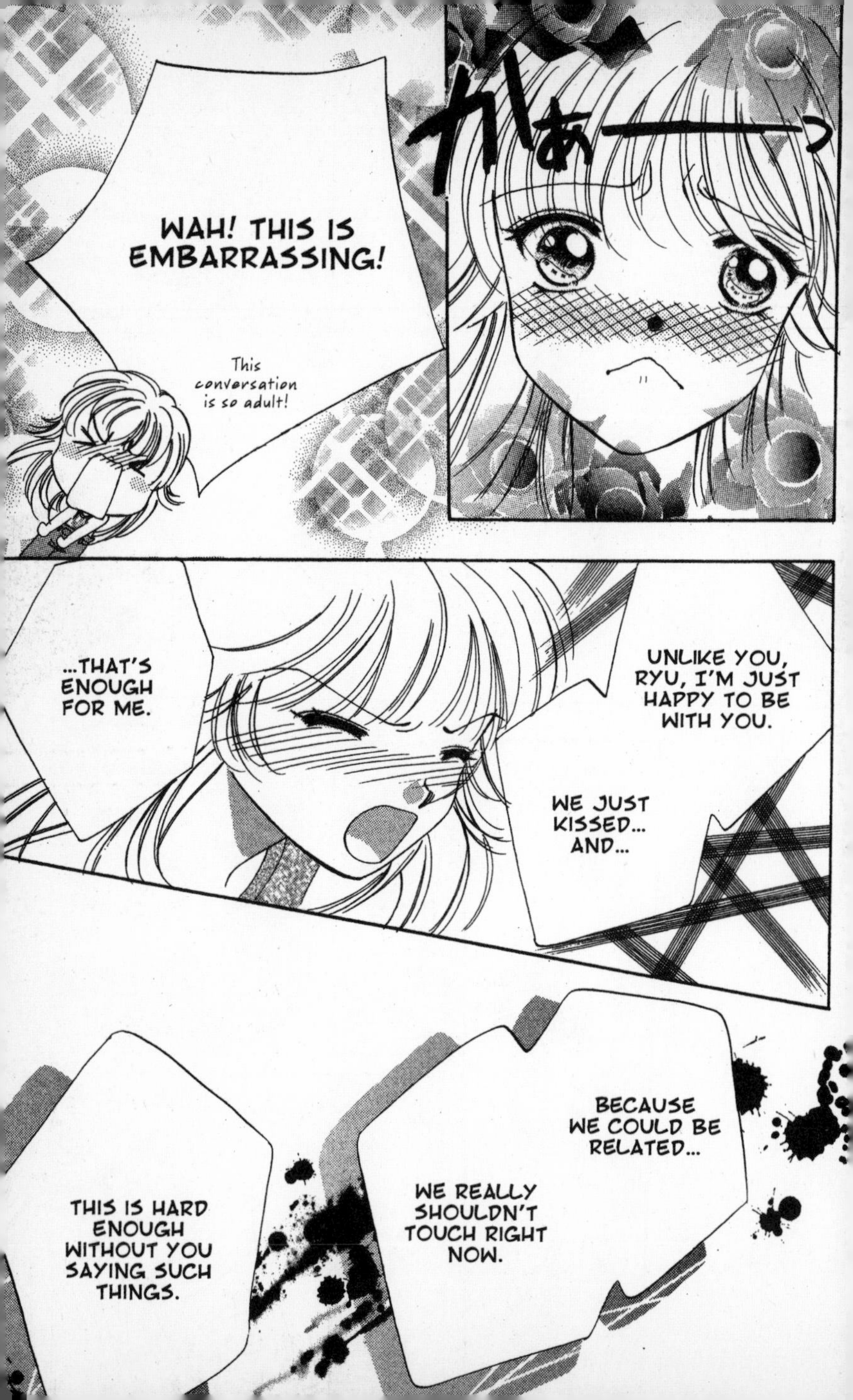
かぁーーっ
WAH! THIS IS EMBARRASSING!
This conversation is so adult!
UNLIKE YOU, RYU, I'M JUST HAPPY TO BE WITH YOU.
WE JUST KISSED... AND...
...THAT'S ENOUGH FOR ME.
BECAUSE WE COULD BE RELATED...
WE REALLY SHOULDN'T TOUCH RIGHT NOW.
THIS IS HARD ENOUGH WITHOUT YOU SAYING SUCH THINGS.

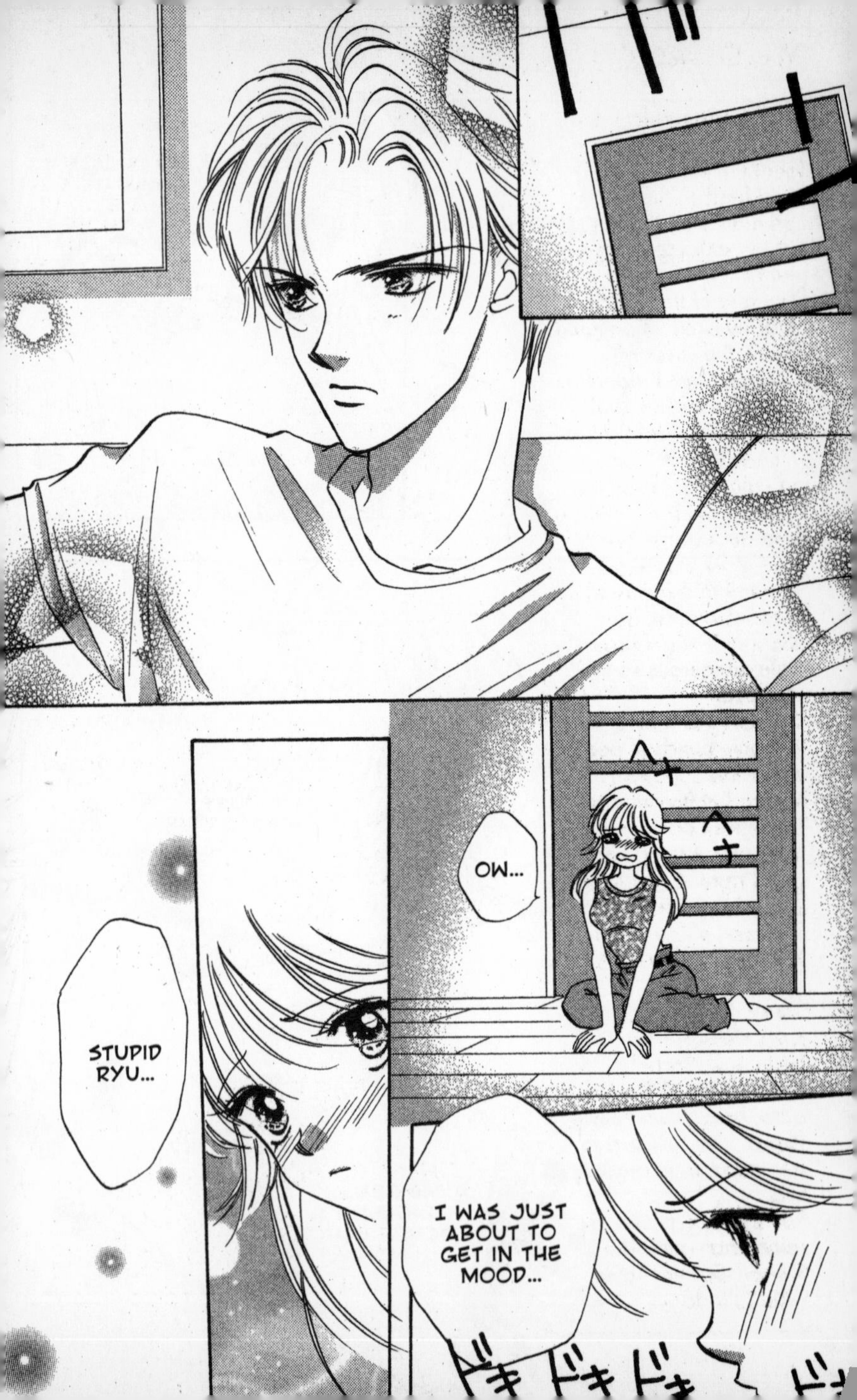
OW...
I WAS JUST ABOUT TO GET IN THE MOOD...
STUPID RYU...

WILD☆ACT⑤

Hello, WA readers and especially those who sent me letters. Thank you for the stuffed animals and pictures (they're displayed, you know) all the time!
Did any of the people that guessed who would be on the cover of volume 5 get it right? This time it's Ryu and Maki! That's right. Akira Nanae is on the cover of volume 3. I read the letters from everyone and decided on Ryu and Maki. As for me, I wanted to draw Yuniko and Tokio once, but I thought it might be a little dangerous so I stopped.
Speaking of letters, well, a whole bunch of people ask if Ryu's model is Akira! But it's amazing! There isn't one person who was wrong. You all got it right! Every once in a while, someone is wrong about Akira Nanae, but most of you get it right.
That's right. WA's story definitely won't be leaked. Probably.
I'm thinking of a super, ultra, background setup. Please look forward to it in addition to reading WA.
You know, Kamui is the reincarnation of Akira Nanae. See you later!
--Rie Takada

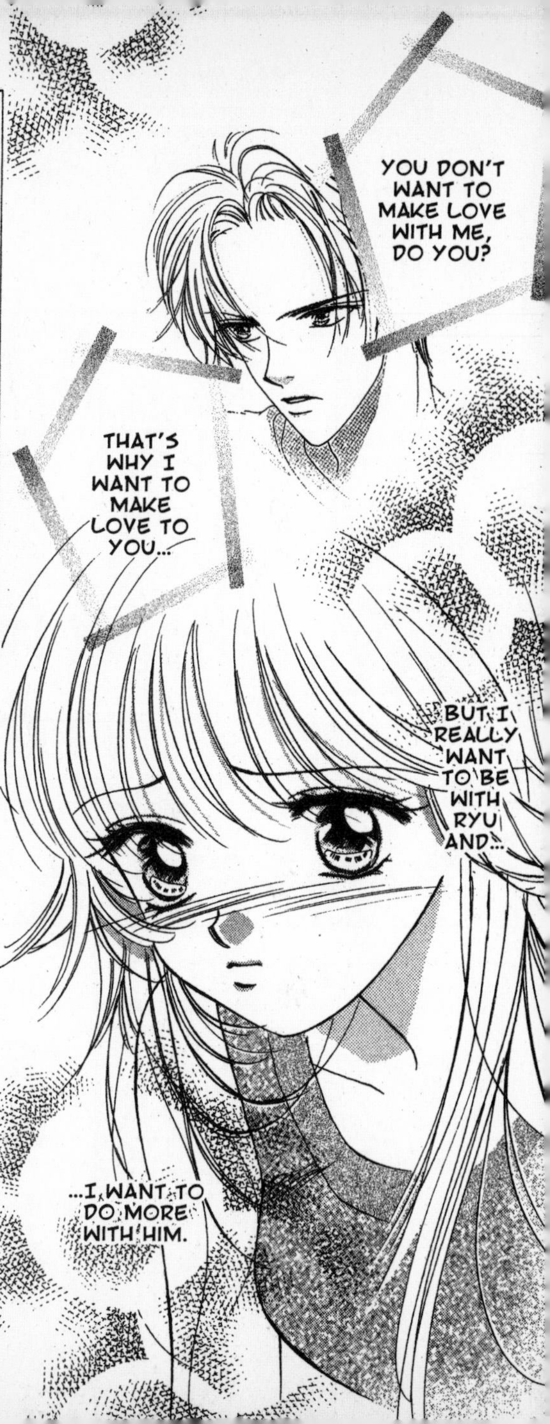
YOU DON'T WANT TO MAKE LOVE WITH ME, DO YOU?
THAT'S WHY I WANT TO MAKE LOVE TO YOU...
BUT I REALLY WANT TO BE WITH RYU AND...
...I WANT TO DO MORE WITH HIM.

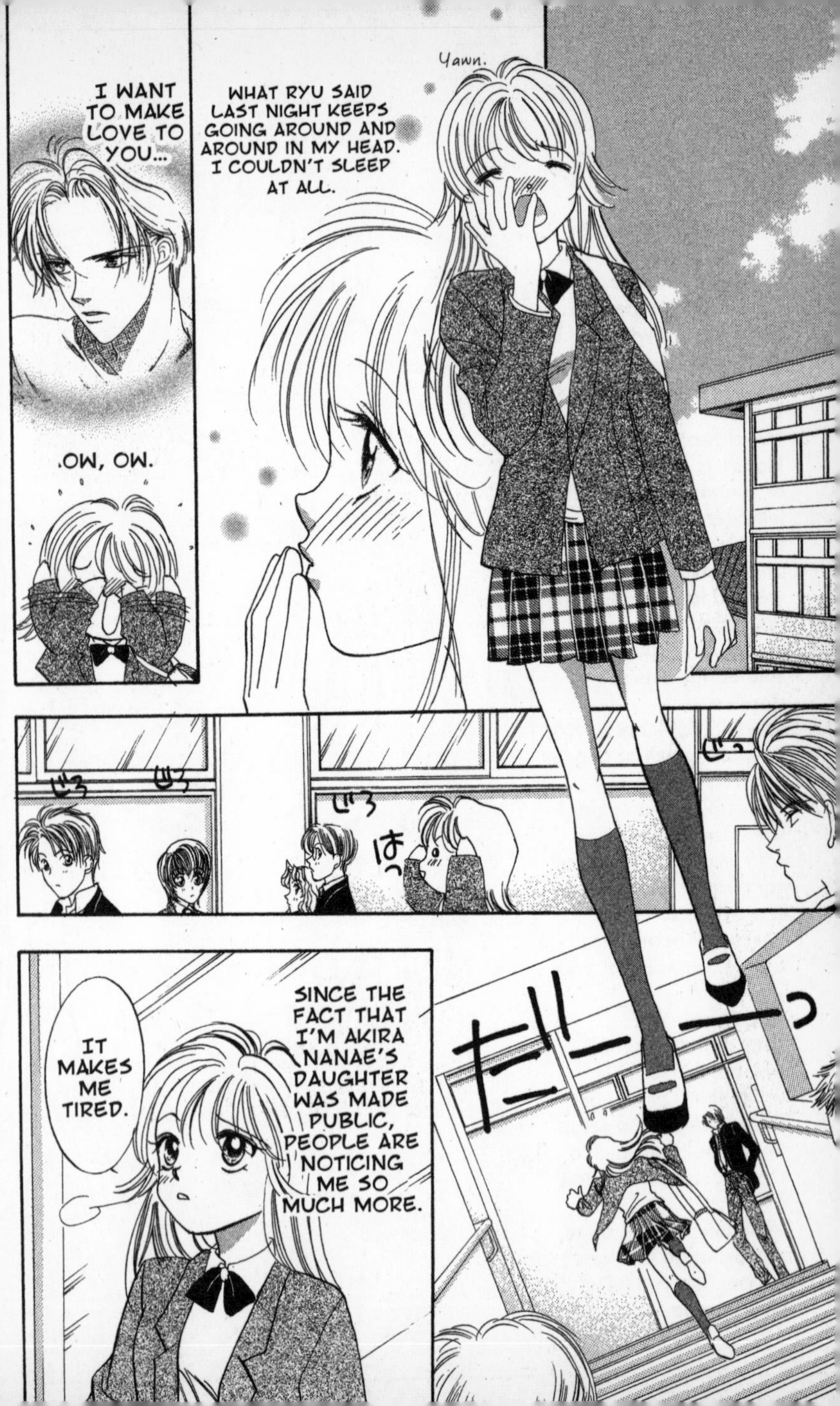
Yawn.
WHAT RYU SAID LAST NIGHT KEEPS GOING AROUND AND AROUND IN MY HEAD. I COULDN'T SLEEP AT ALL.
I WANT TO MAKE LOVE TO YOU...
OW, OW.
じっ
はっ
じろ
じろ
じろ
だーーっ
SINCE THE FACT THAT I'M AKIRA NANAE'S DAUGHTER WAS MADE PUBLIC, PEOPLE ARE NOTICING ME SO MUCH MORE.
IT MAKES ME TIRED.

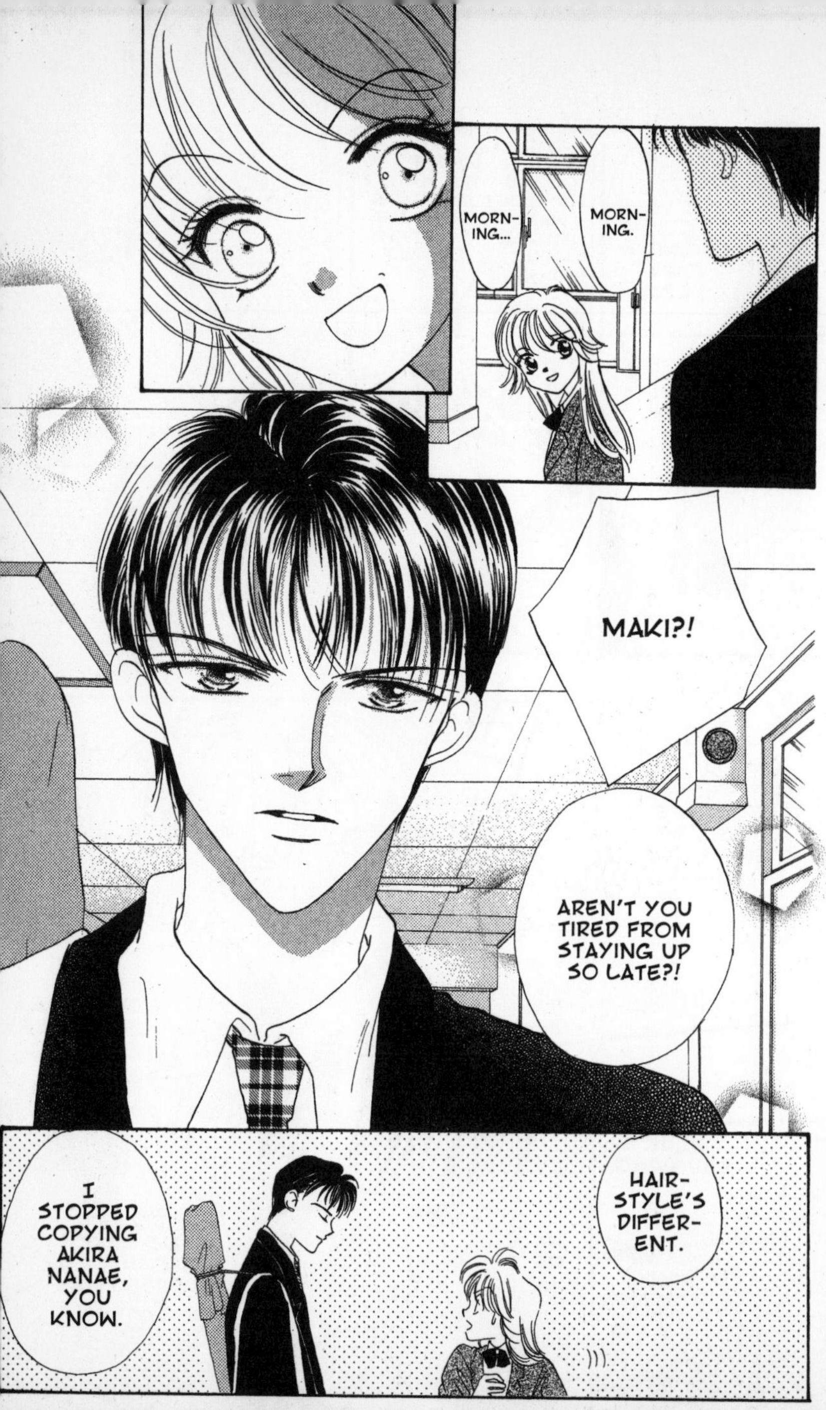
MORN-
ING.
MORN-
ING...
MAKI?!
AREN'T YOU
TIRED FROM
STAYING UP
SO LATE?!
HAIR-
STYLE'S
DIFFER-
ENT.
I
STOPPED
COPYING
AKIRA
NANAE,
YOU
KNOW.

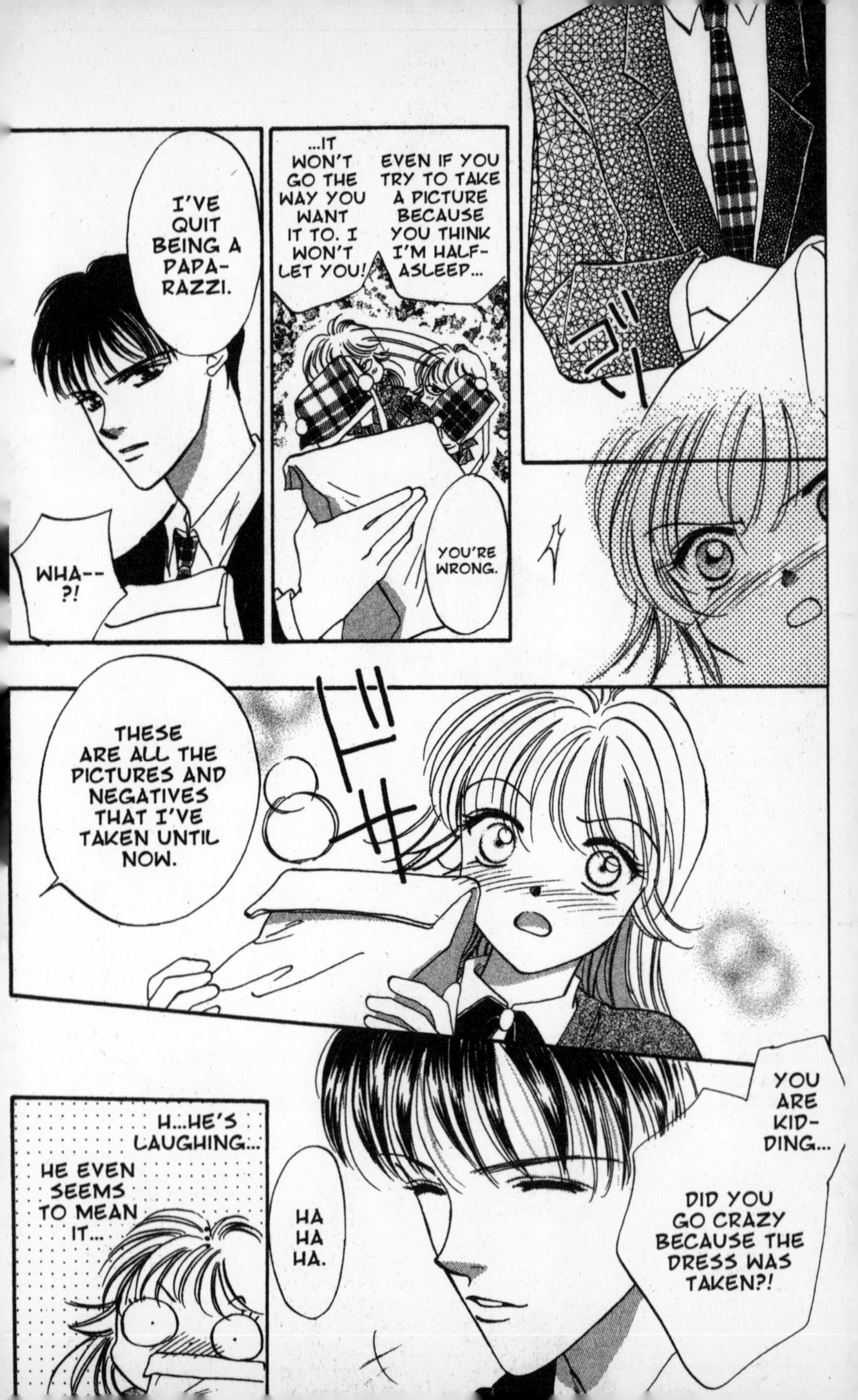
EVEN IF YOU TRY TO TAKE A PICTURE BECAUSE YOU THINK I'M HALF-ASLEEP...
...IT WON'T GO THE WAY YOU WANT IT TO. I WON'T LET YOU!
YOU'RE WRONG.
I'VE QUIT BEING A PAPARAZZI.
WHA-- ?!
THESE ARE ALL THE PICTURES AND NEGATIVES THAT I'VE TAKEN UNTIL NOW.
YOU ARE KIDDING...
DID YOU GO CRAZY BECAUSE THE DRESS WAS TAKEN?!
HA HA HA.
H...HE'S LAUGHING...
HE EVEN SEEMS TO MEAN IT...

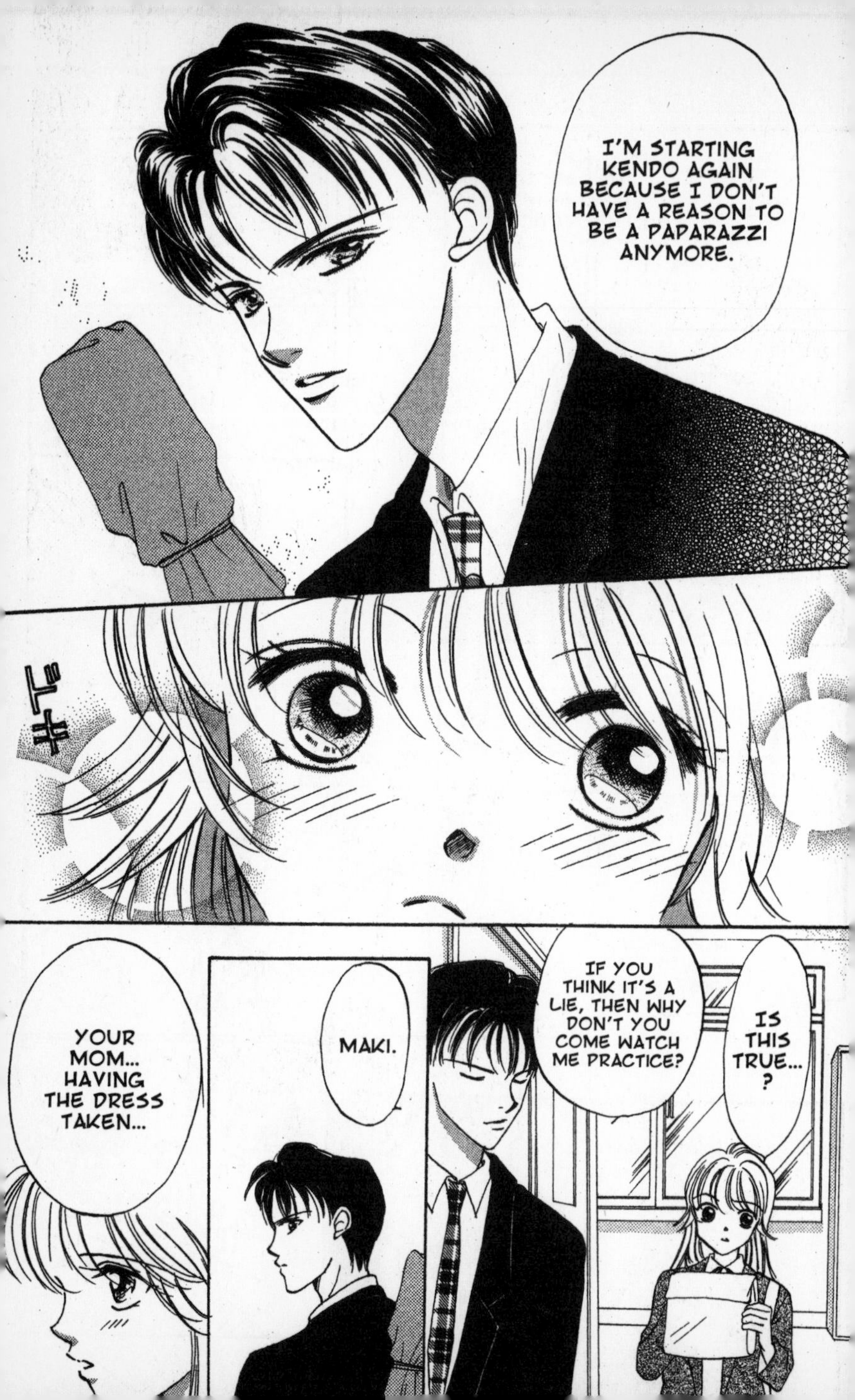
I'M STARTING KENDO AGAIN BECAUSE I DON'T HAVE A REASON TO BE A PAPARAZZI ANYMORE.
IS THIS TRUE...?
IF YOU THINK IT'S A LIE, THEN WHY DON'T YOU COME WATCH ME PRACTICE?
MAKI.
YOUR MOM... HAVING THE DRESS TAKEN...

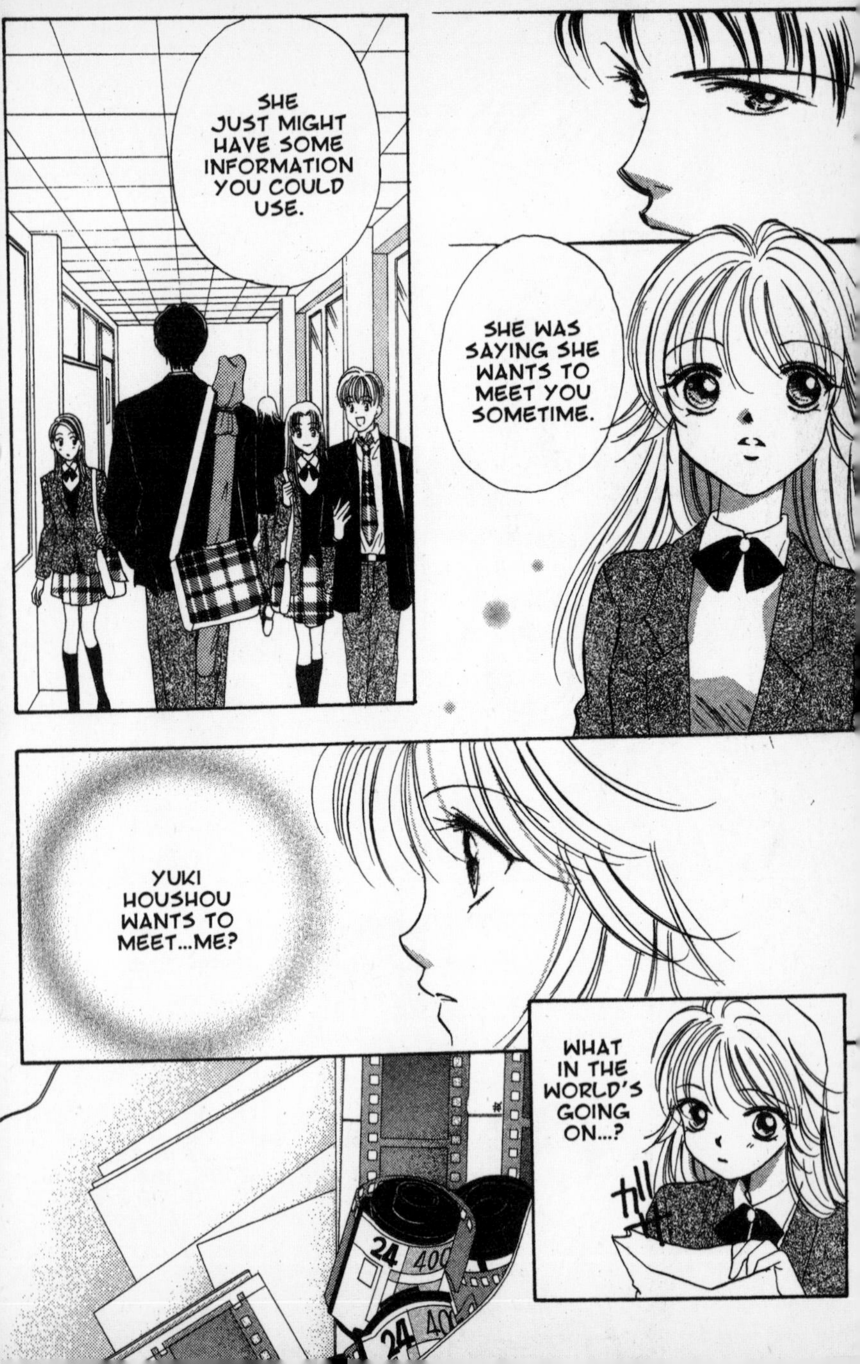
SHE WAS SAYING SHE WANTS TO MEET YOU SOMETIME.
SHE JUST MIGHT HAVE SOME INFORMATION YOU COULD USE.
YUKI HOUSHOU WANTS TO MEET...ME?
WHAT IN THE WORLD'S GOING ON...?

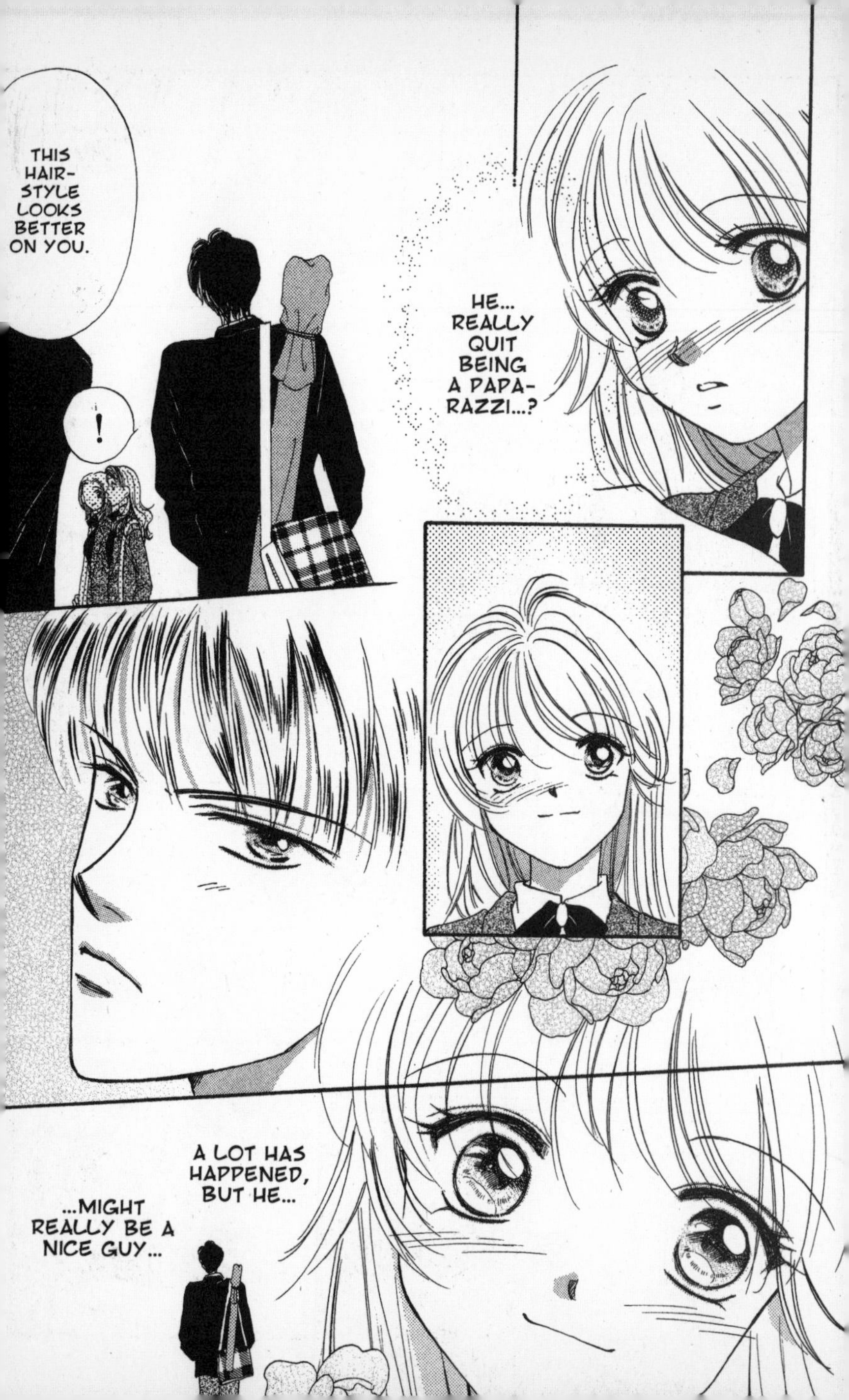
HE... REALLY QUIT BEING A PAPA-RAZZI...?
THIS HAIR-STYLE LOOKS BETTER ON YOU.
!
A LOT HAS HAPPENED, BUT HE...
...MIGHT REALLY BE A NICE GUY...

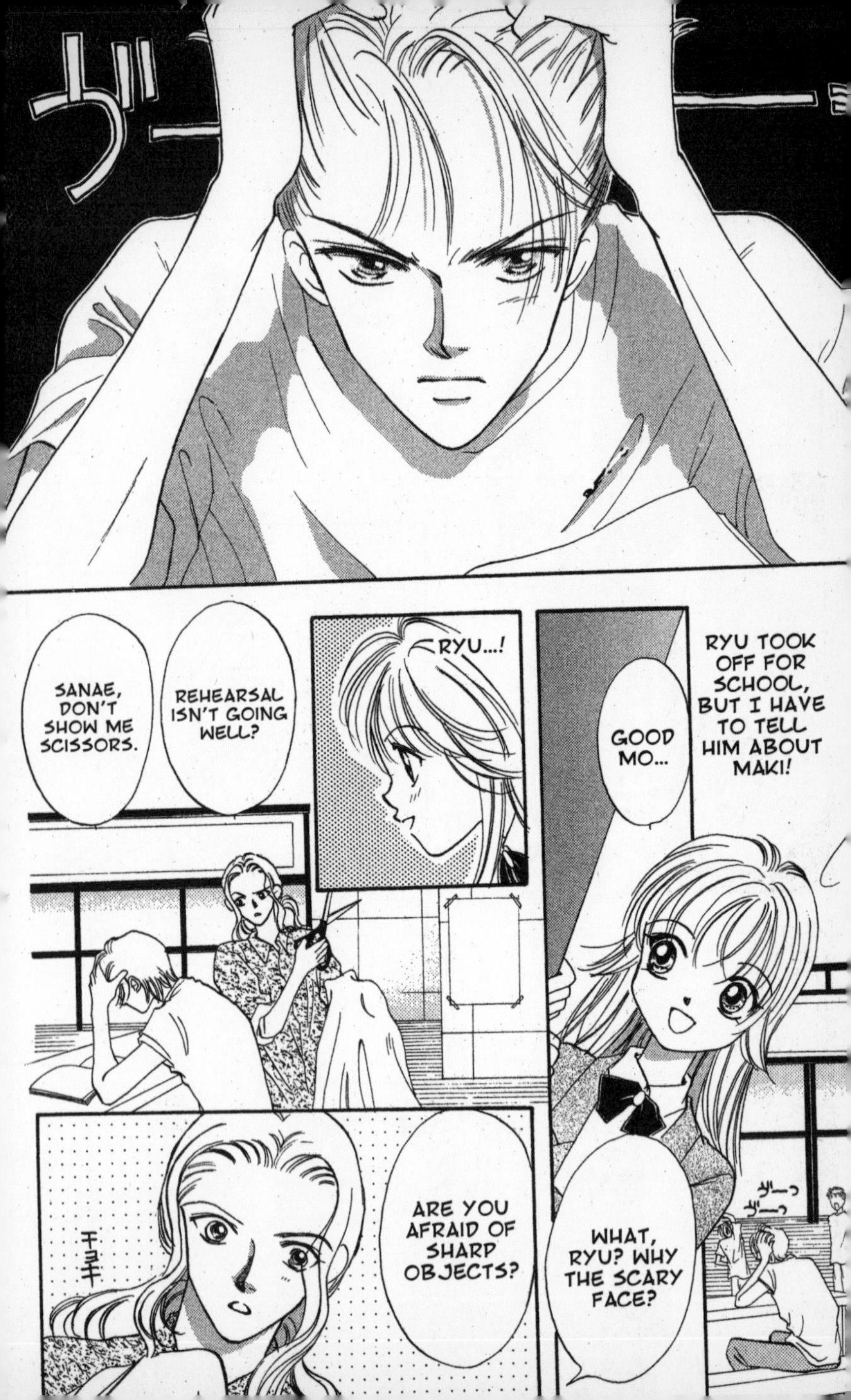
RYU TOOK OFF FOR SCHOOL, BUT I HAVE TO TELL HIM ABOUT MAKI!
GOOD MO...
RYU...!
REHEARSAL ISN'T GOING WELL?
SANAE, DON'T SHOW ME SCISSORS.
WHAT, RYU? WHY THE SCARY FACE?
ARE YOU AFRAID OF SHARP OBJECTS?
チョキ

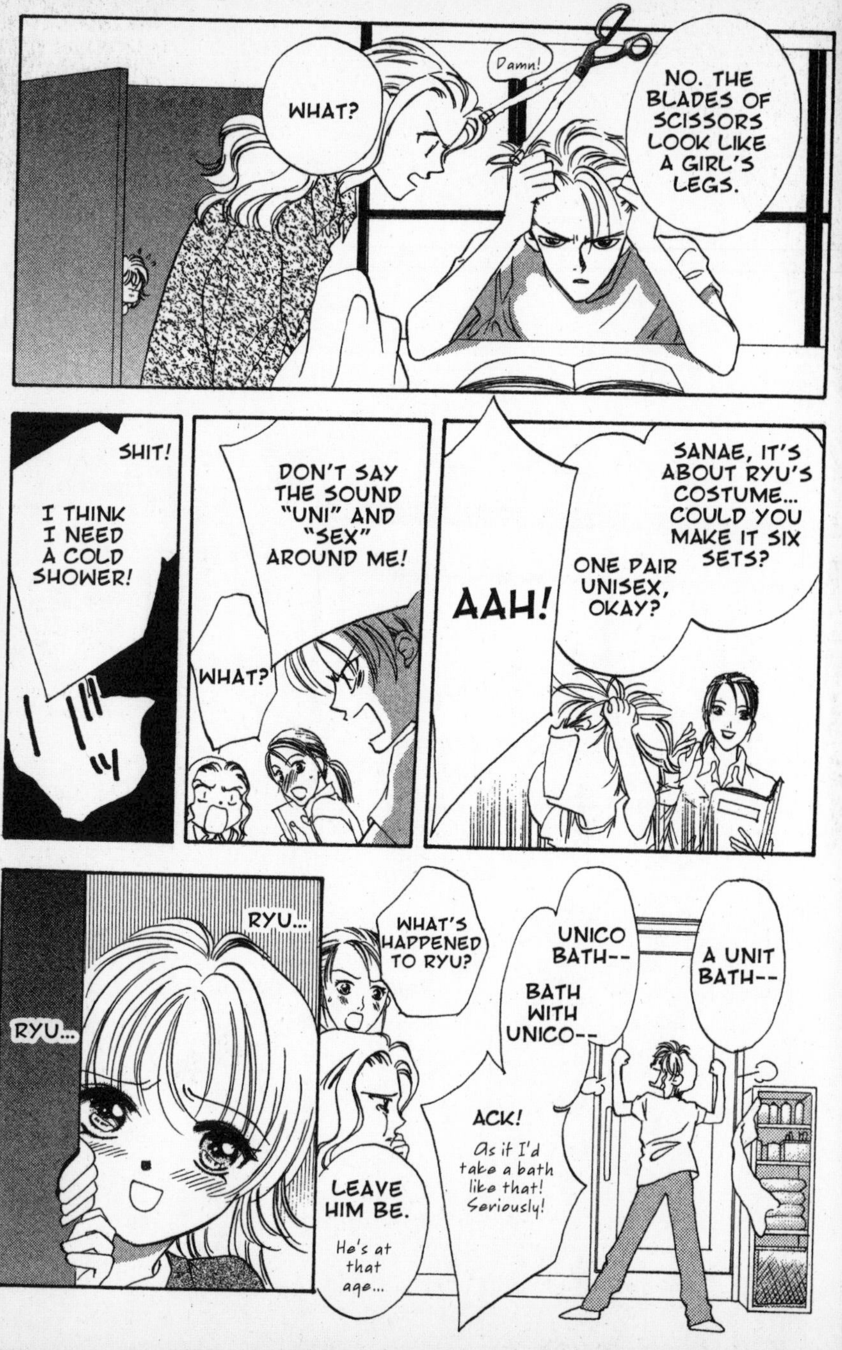
NO. THE BLADES OF SCISSORS LOOK LIKE A GIRL'S LEGS.
Damn!
WHAT?
SANAE, IT'S ABOUT RYU'S COSTUME... COULD YOU MAKE IT SIX SETS?
ONE PAIR UNISEX, OKAY?
AAH!
DON'T SAY THE SOUND "UNI" AND "SEX" AROUND ME!
WHAT?
SHIT!
I THINK I NEED A COLD SHOWER!
A UNIT BATH--
UNICO BATH--
BATH WITH UNICO--
WHAT'S HAPPENED TO RYU?
ACK!
As if I'd take a bath like that! Seriously!
LEAVE HIM BE.
He's at that age...
RYU...
RYU...

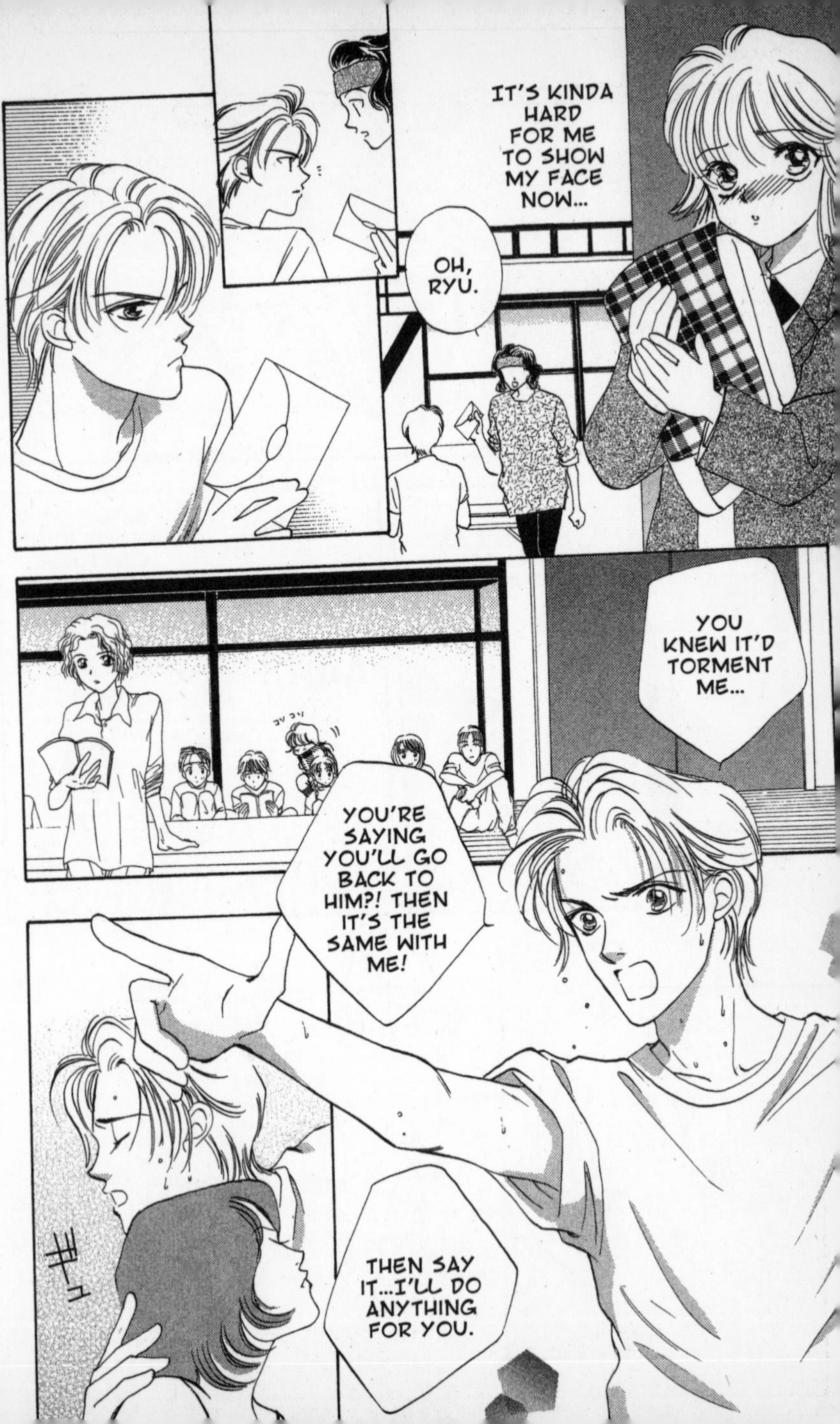
IT'S KINDA HARD FOR ME TO SHOW MY FACE NOW...
OH, RYU.
YOU KNEW IT'D TORMENT ME...
YOU'RE SAYING YOU'LL GO BACK TO HIM?! THEN IT'S THE SAME WITH ME!
ギュ
THEN SAY IT...I'LL DO ANYTHING FOR YOU.

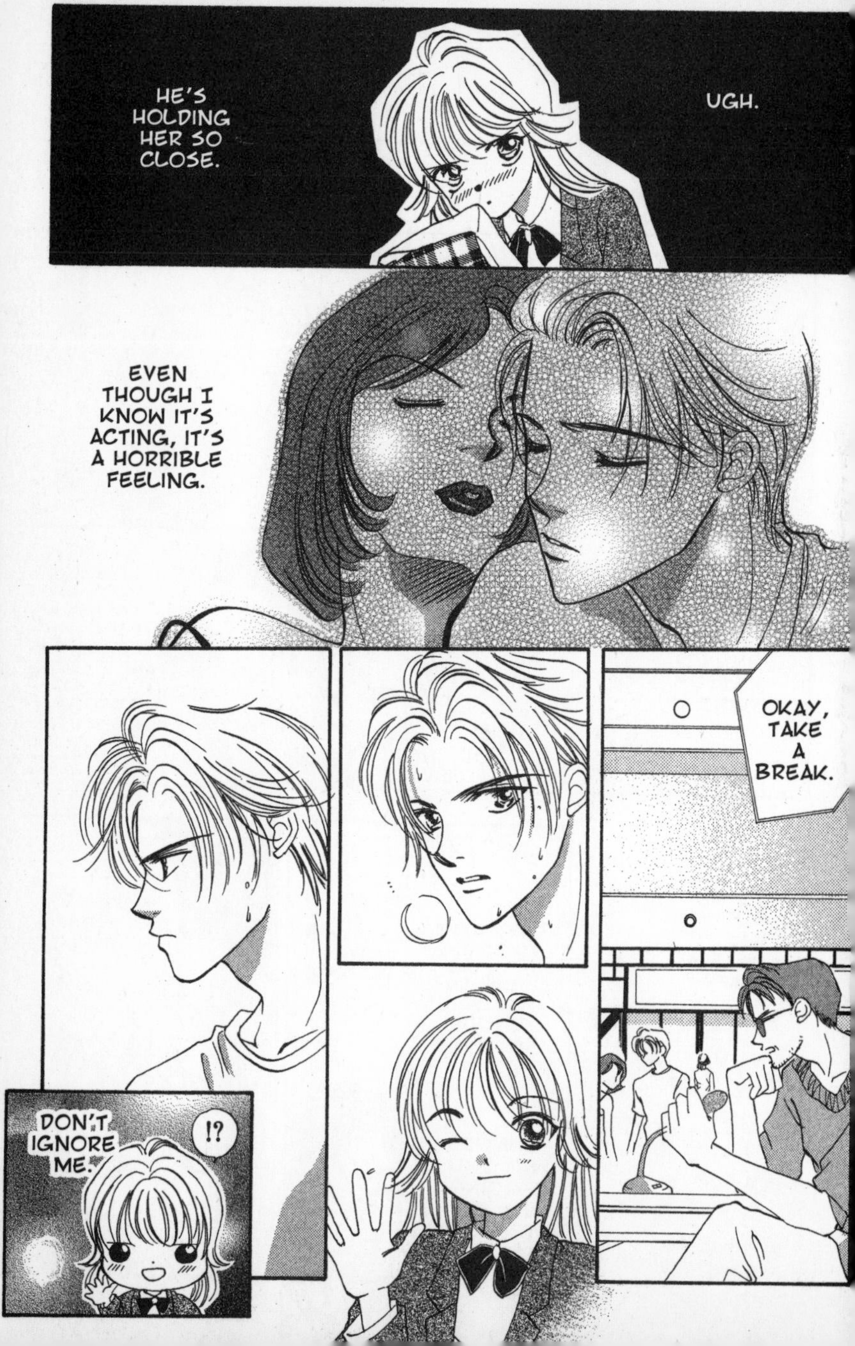
UGH.
HE'S HOLDING HER SO CLOSE.
EVEN THOUGH I KNOW IT'S ACTING, IT'S A HORRIBLE FEELING.
OKAY, TAKE A BREAK.
!?
DON'T IGNORE ME.

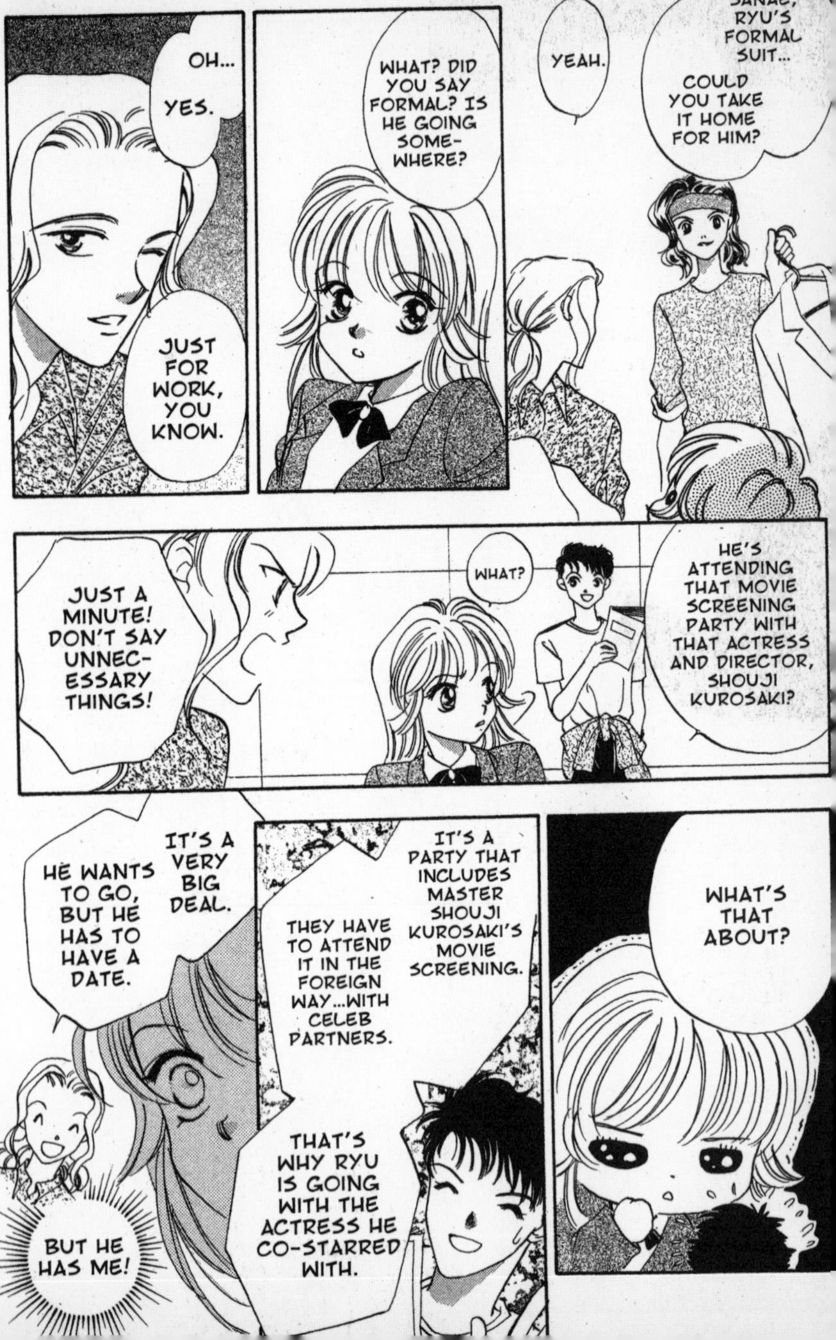

SANAE, RYU'S FORMAL SUIT...
COULD YOU TAKE IT HOME FOR HIM?
YEAH.
WHAT? DID YOU SAY FORMAL? IS HE GOING SOME-WHERE?
OH...
YES.
JUST FOR WORK, YOU KNOW.
HE'S ATTENDING THAT MOVIE SCREENING PARTY WITH THAT ACTRESS AND DIRECTOR, SHOUJI KUROSAKI?
WHAT?
JUST A MINUTE! DON'T SAY UNNEC-ESSARY THINGS!
WHAT'S THAT ABOUT?
IT'S A PARTY THAT INCLUDES MASTER SHOUJI KUROSAKI'S MOVIE SCREENING.
THEY HAVE TO ATTEND IT IN THE FOREIGN WAY...WITH CELEB PARTNERS.
THAT'S WHY RYU IS GOING WITH THE ACTRESS HE CO-STARRED WITH.
IT'S A VERY BIG DEAL.
HE WANTS TO GO, BUT HE HAS TO HAVE A DATE.
BUT HE HAS ME!

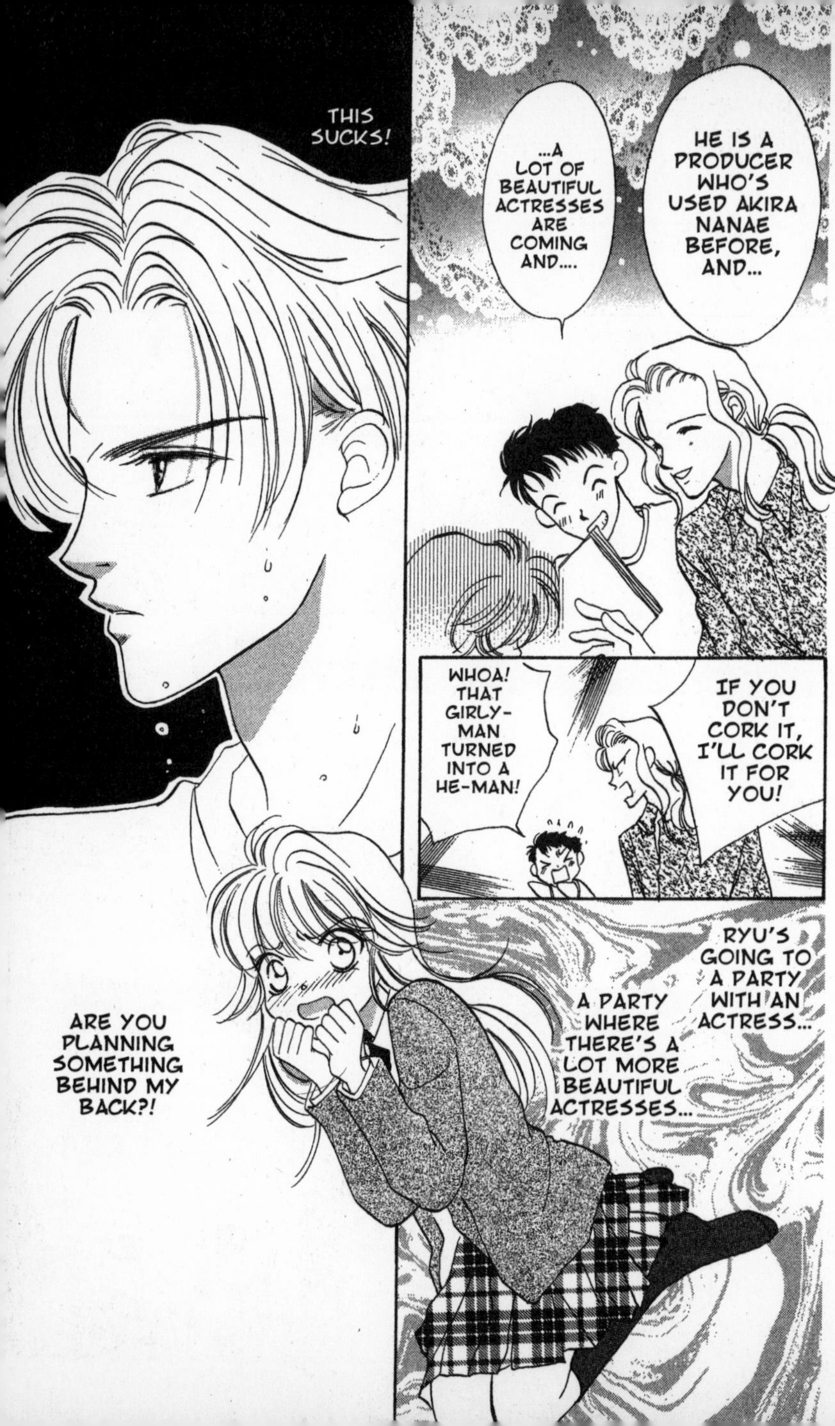
HE IS A PRODUCER WHO'S USED AKIRA NANAE BEFORE, AND...
...A LOT OF BEAUTIFUL ACTRESSES ARE COMING AND....
IF YOU DON'T CORK IT, I'LL CORK IT FOR YOU!
WHOA! THAT GIRLY-MAN TURNED INTO A HE-MAN!
THIS SUCKS!
RYU'S GOING TO A PARTY WITH AN ACTRESS...
A PARTY WHERE THERE'S A LOT MORE BEAUTIFUL ACTRESSES...
ARE YOU PLANNING SOMETHING BEHIND MY BACK?!

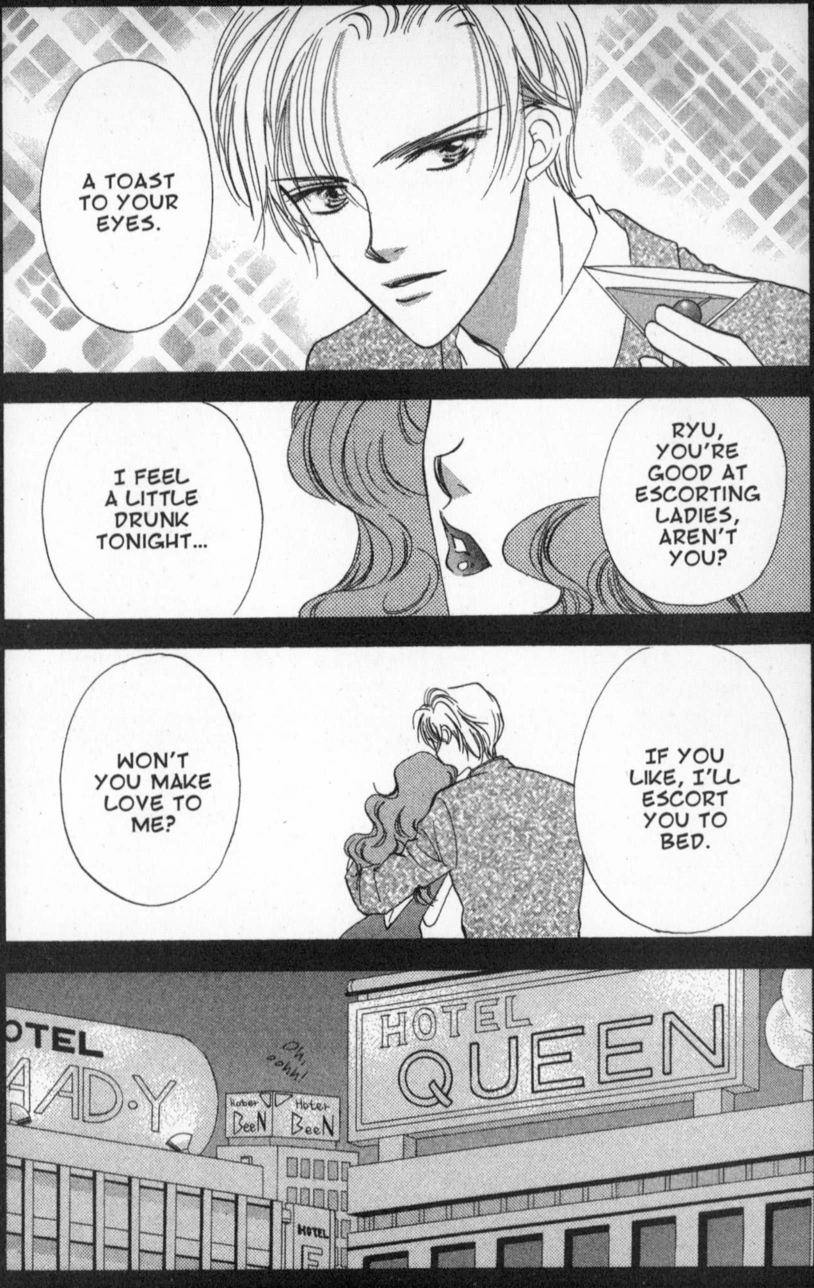
A TOAST TO YOUR EYES.
RYU, YOU'RE GOOD AT ESCORTING LADIES, AREN'T YOU?
I FEEL A LITTLE DRUNK TONIGHT...
IF YOU LIKE, I'LL ESCORT YOU TO BED.
WON'T YOU MAKE LOVE TO ME?
HOTEL QUEEN
Oh, oohh!
Hoter BeeN
Hoter BeeN
HOTEL

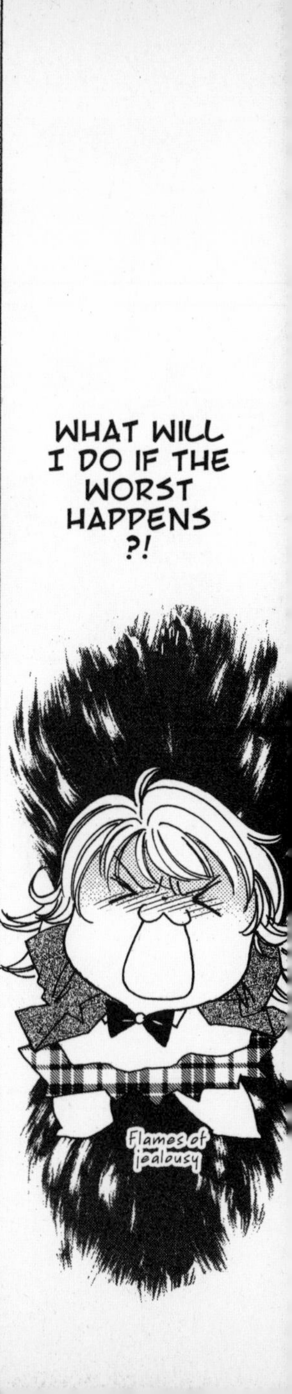
WHAT WILL I DO IF THE WORST HAPPENS ?!
Flames of jealousy

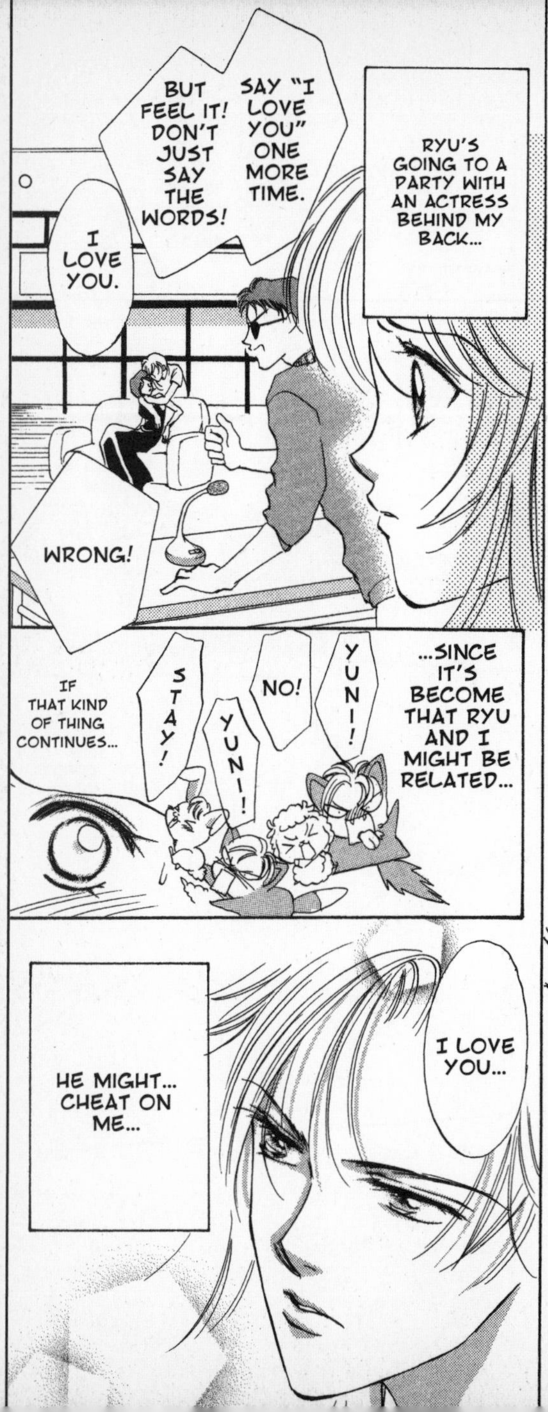
RYU'S GOING TO A PARTY WITH AN ACTRESS BEHIND MY BACK...
SAY "I LOVE YOU" ONE MORE TIME.
BUT FEEL IT! DON'T JUST SAY THE WORDS!
I LOVE YOU.
WRONG!
...SINCE IT'S BECOME THAT RYU AND I MIGHT BE RELATED...
YUNI!
NO!
YUNI!
STAY!
IF THAT KIND OF THING CONTINUES...
I LOVE YOU...
HE MIGHT... CHEAT ON ME...

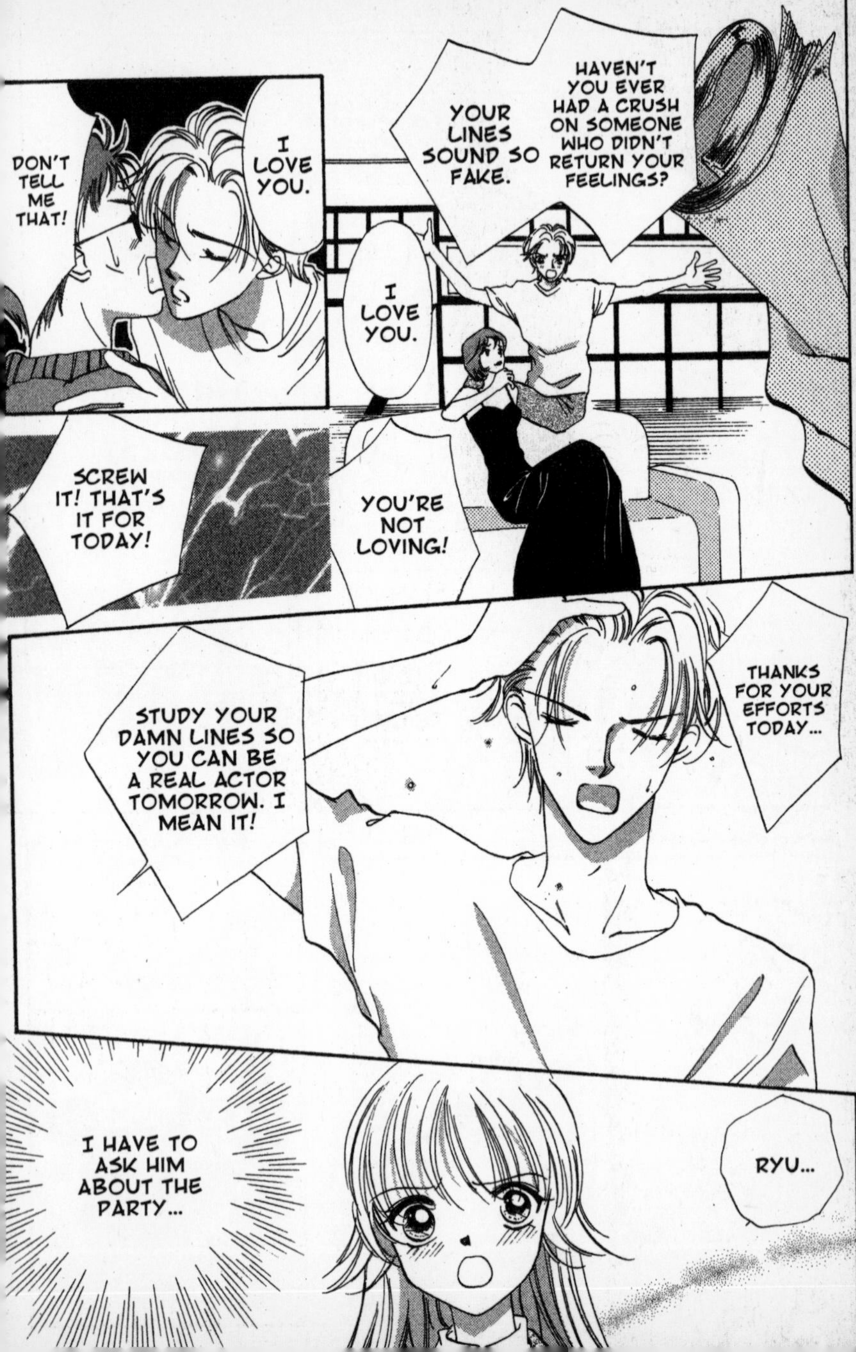
HAVEN'T YOU EVER HAD A CRUSH ON SOMEONE WHO DIDN'T RETURN YOUR FEELINGS?
YOUR LINES SOUND SO FAKE.
I LOVE YOU.
YOU'RE NOT LOVING!
I LOVE YOU.
DON'T TELL ME THAT!
SCREW IT! THAT'S IT FOR TODAY!
THANKS FOR YOUR EFFORTS TODAY...
STUDY YOUR DAMN LINES SO YOU CAN BE A REAL ACTOR TOMORROW. I MEAN IT!
RYU...
I HAVE TO ASK HIM ABOUT THE PARTY...

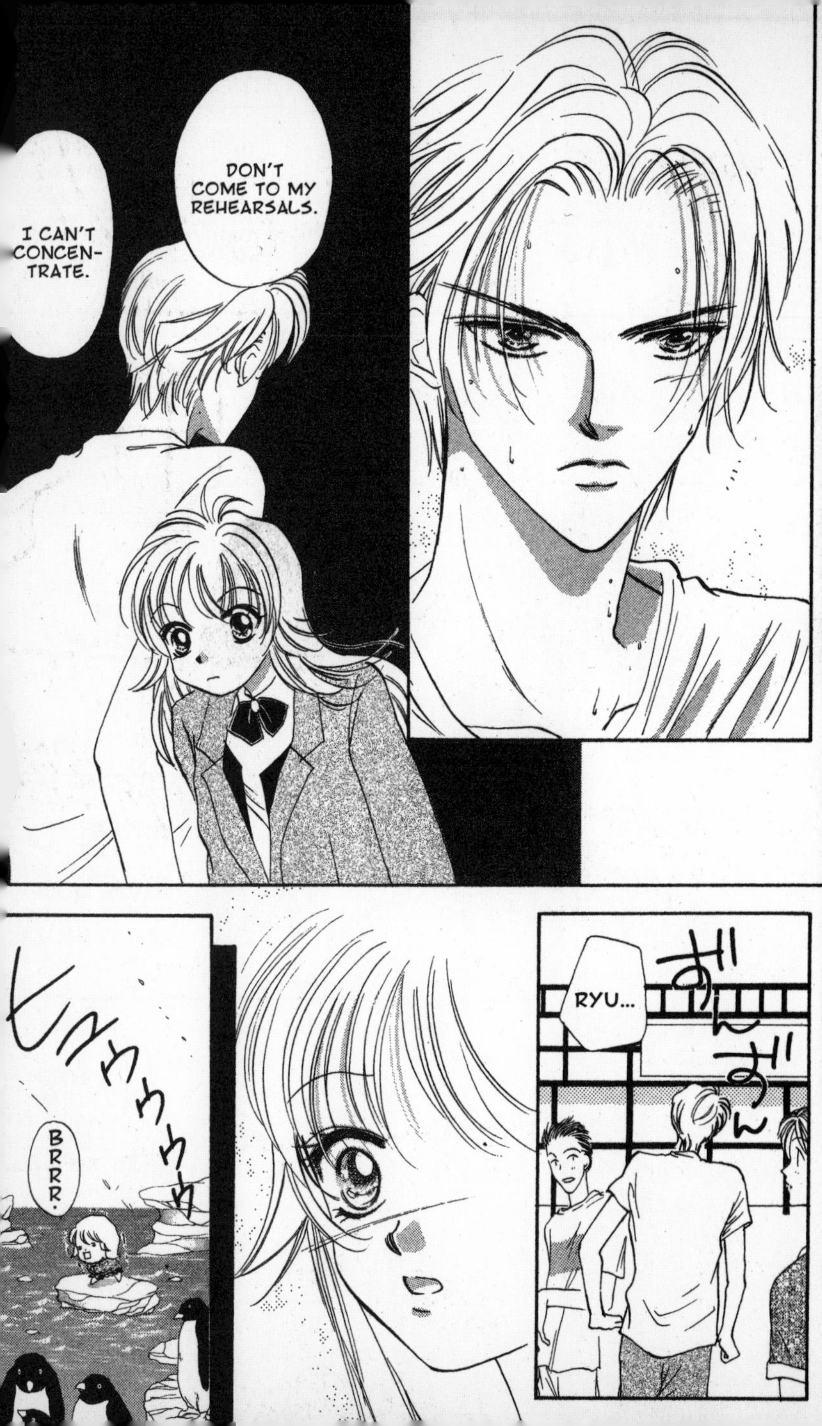
DON'T COME TO MY REHEARSALS.
I CAN'T CONCEN-TRATE.
RYU...
BRRR.

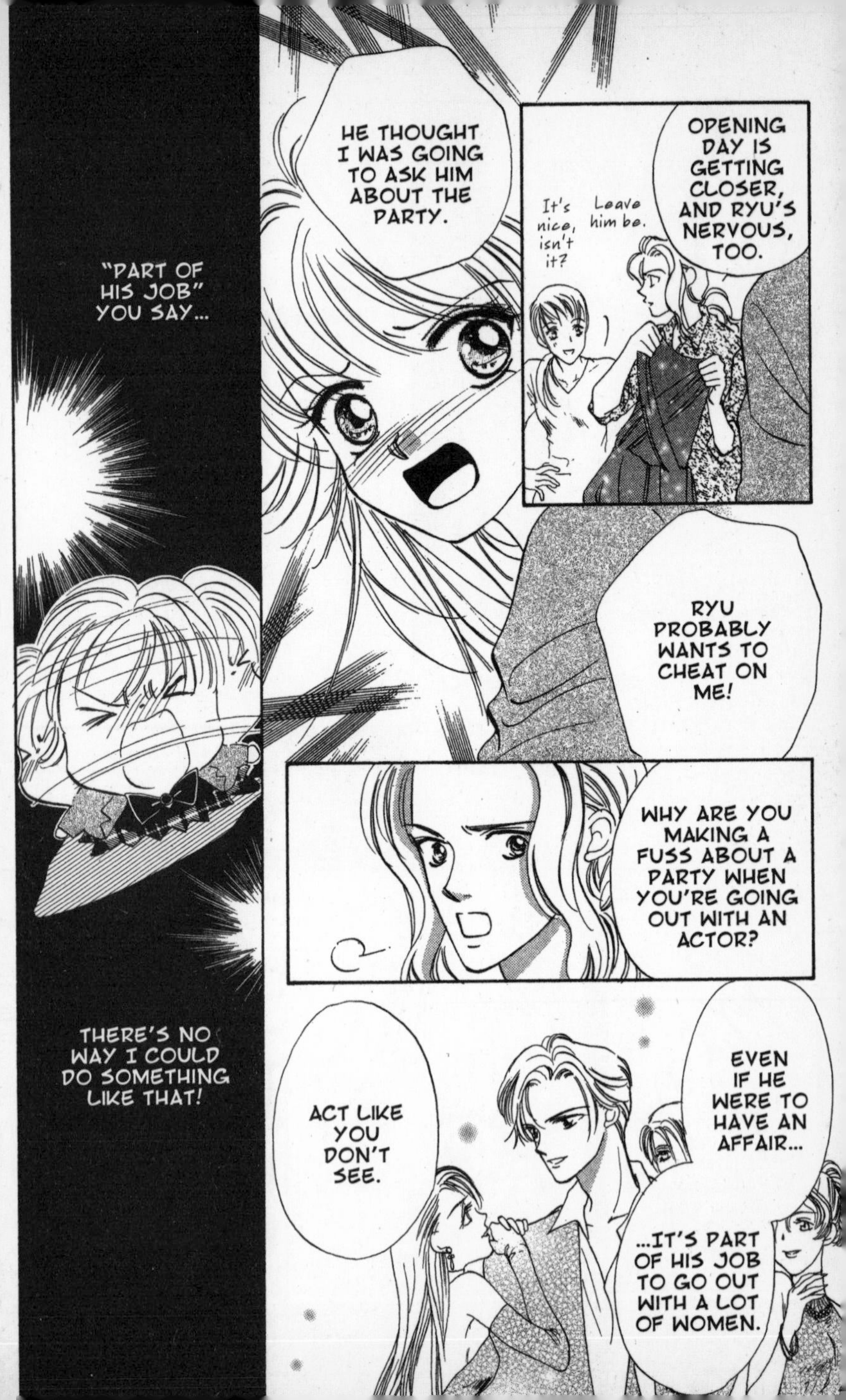

OPENING DAY IS GETTING CLOSER, AND RYU'S NERVOUS, TOO.
Leave him be.
It's nice, isn't it?
HE THOUGHT I WAS GOING TO ASK HIM ABOUT THE PARTY.
RYU PROBABLY WANTS TO CHEAT ON ME!
WHY ARE YOU MAKING A FUSS ABOUT A PARTY WHEN YOU'RE GOING OUT WITH AN ACTOR?
EVEN IF HE WERE TO HAVE AN AFFAIR...
...IT'S PART OF HIS JOB TO GO OUT WITH A LOT OF WOMEN.
ACT LIKE YOU DON'T SEE.
"PART OF HIS JOB" YOU SAY...
THERE'S NO WAY I COULD DO SOMETHING LIKE THAT!

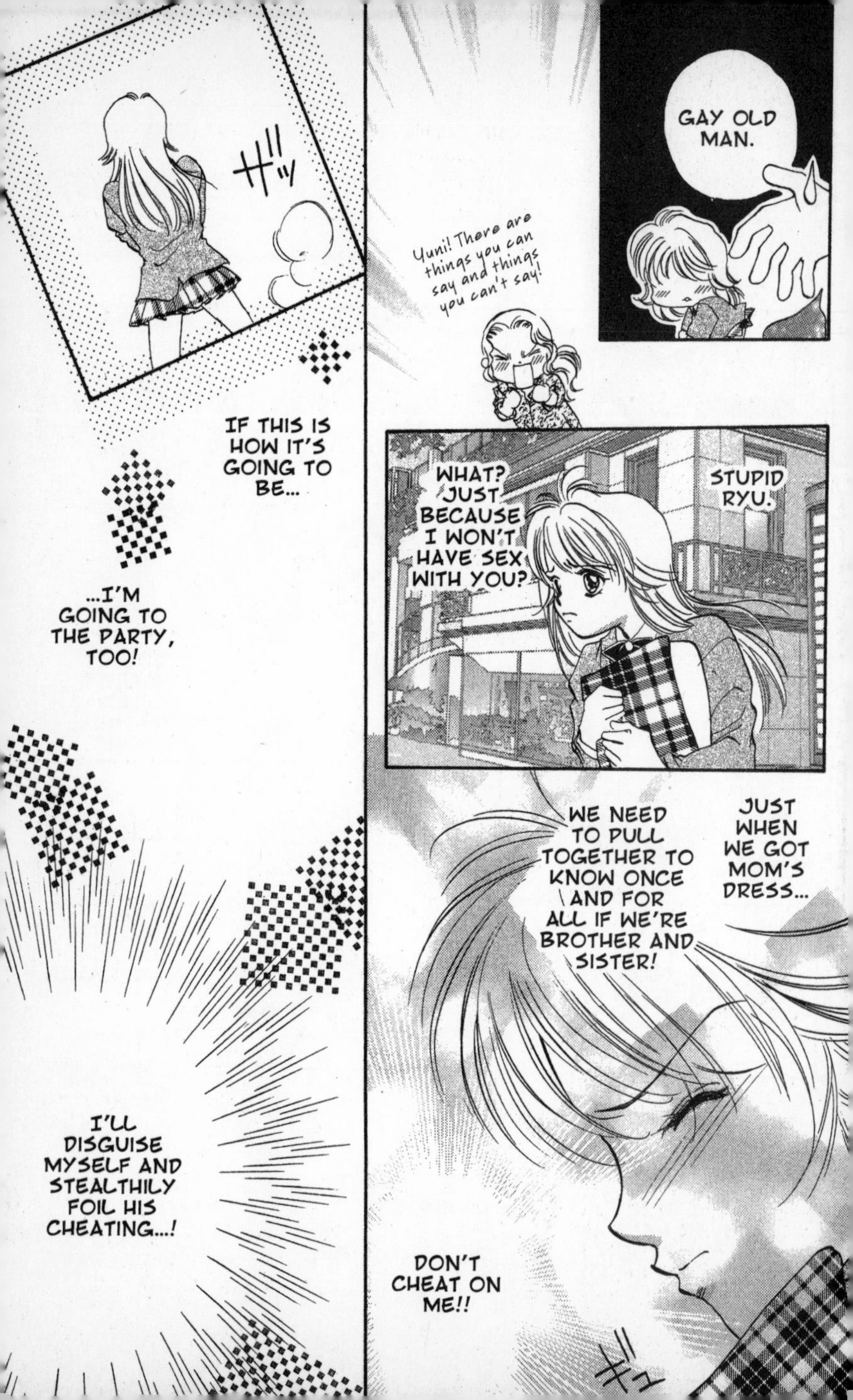
GAY OLD MAN.
Yuni! There are things you can say and things you can't say!
STUPID RYU.
WHAT? JUST BECAUSE I WON'T HAVE SEX WITH YOU?
JUST WHEN WE GOT MOM'S DRESS...
WE NEED TO PULL TOGETHER TO KNOW ONCE AND FOR ALL IF WE'RE BROTHER AND SISTER!
DON'T CHEAT ON ME!!
ギュ
ザッ
IF THIS IS HOW IT'S GOING TO BE...
...I'M GOING TO THE PARTY, TOO!
I'LL DISGUISE MYSELF AND STEALTHILY FOIL HIS CHEATING...!

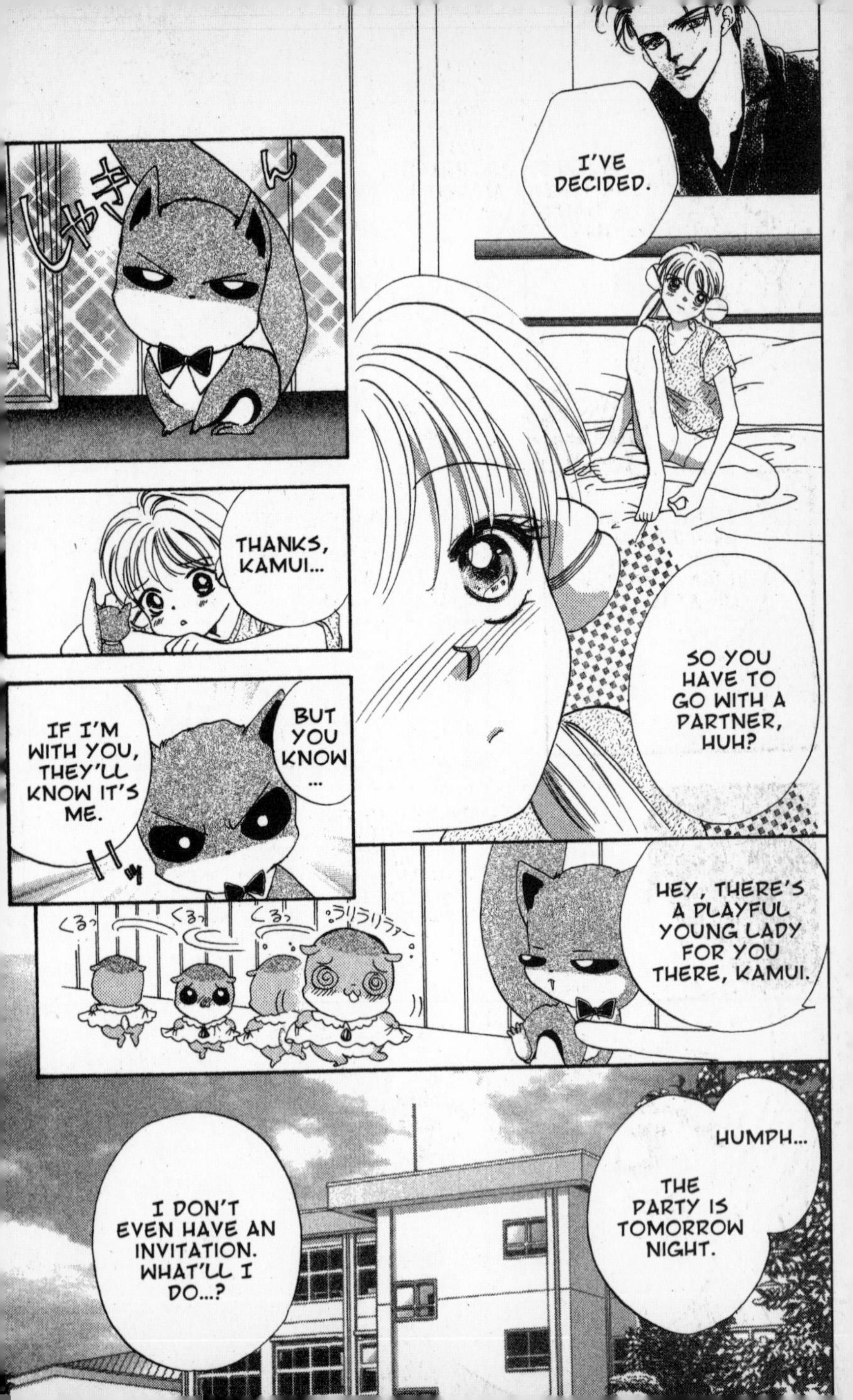

I'VE DECIDED.
SO YOU HAVE TO GO WITH A PARTNER, HUH?
しゃきーん
THANKS, KAMUI...
BUT YOU KNOW...
IF I'M WITH YOU, THEY'LL KNOW IT'S ME.
HEY, THERE'S A PLAYFUL YOUNG LADY FOR YOU THERE, KAMUI.
うりうりラァー
くるっ
くるっ
くるっ
HUMPH...
THE PARTY IS TOMORROW NIGHT.
I DON'T EVEN HAVE AN INVITATION. WHAT'LL I DO...?

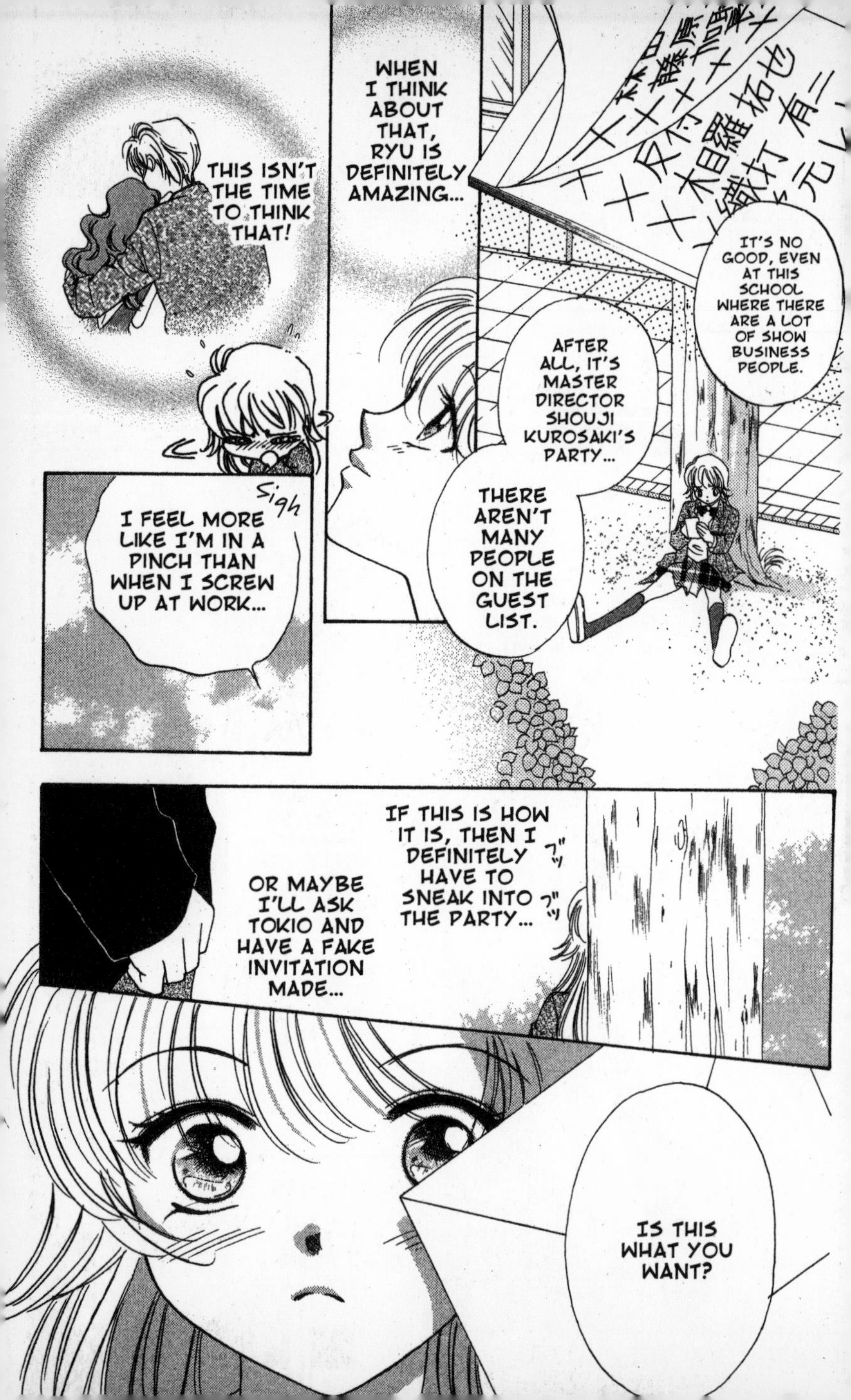
IT'S NO GOOD, EVEN AT THIS SCHOOL WHERE THERE ARE A LOT OF SHOW BUSINESS PEOPLE.
AFTER ALL, IT'S MASTER DIRECTOR SHOUJI KUROSAKI'S PARTY...
THERE AREN'T MANY PEOPLE ON THE GUEST LIST.
WHEN I THINK ABOUT THAT, RYU IS DEFINITELY AMAZING...
THIS ISN'T THE TIME TO THINK THAT!
Sigh
I FEEL MORE LIKE I'M IN A PINCH THAN WHEN I SCREW UP AT WORK...
IF THIS IS HOW IT IS, THEN I DEFINITELY HAVE TO SNEAK INTO THE PARTY...
OR MAYBE I'LL ASK TOKIO AND HAVE A FAKE INVITATION MADE...
IS THIS WHAT YOU WANT?

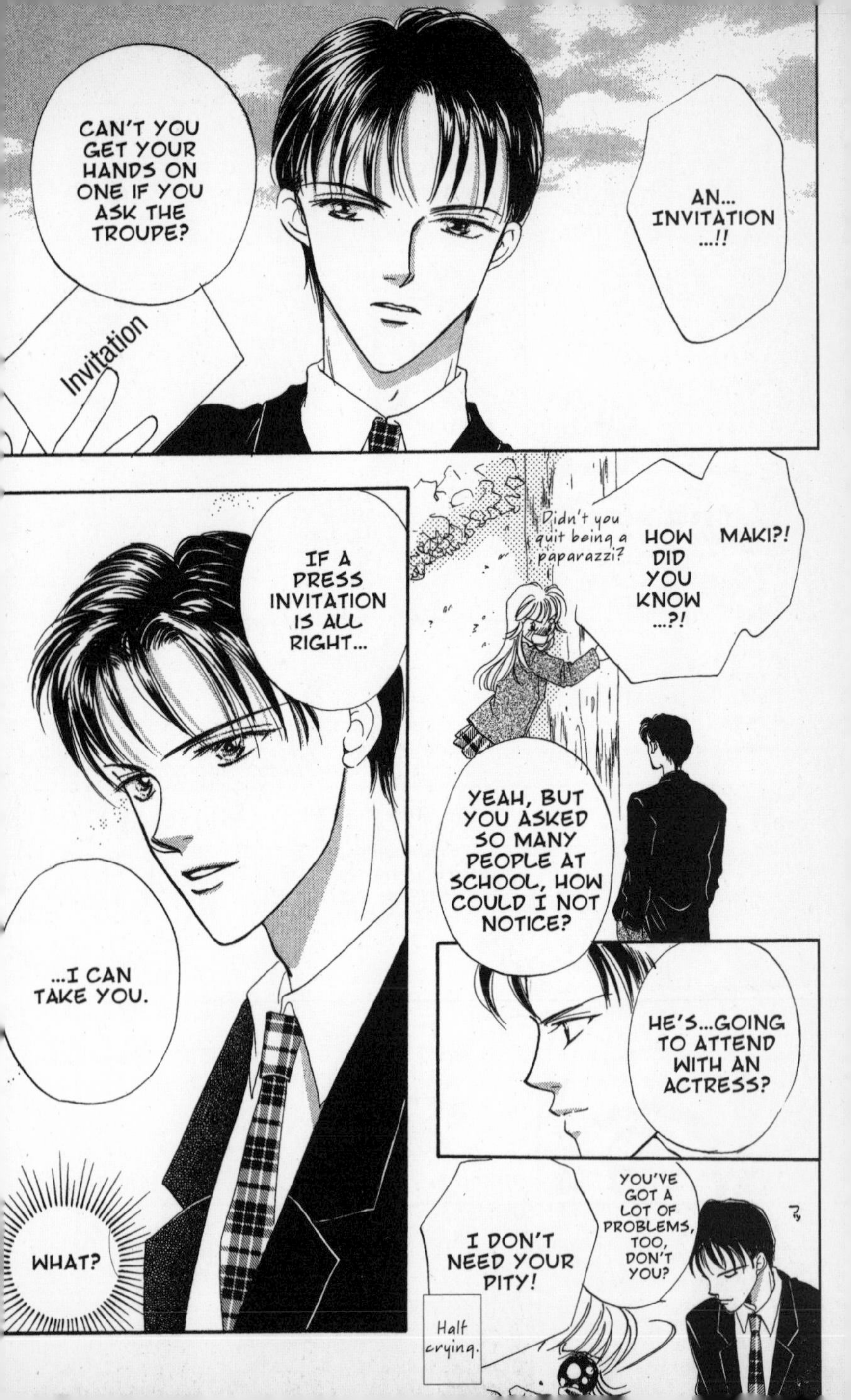
AN... INVITATION ...!!
CAN'T YOU GET YOUR HANDS ON ONE IF YOU ASK THE TROUPE?
Invitation
MAKI?!
HOW DID YOU KNOW ...?!
Didn't you quit being a paparazzi?
YEAH, BUT YOU ASKED SO MANY PEOPLE AT SCHOOL, HOW COULD I NOT NOTICE?
HE'S...GOING TO ATTEND WITH AN ACTRESS?
YOU'VE GOT A LOT OF PROBLEMS, TOO, DON'T YOU?
I DON'T NEED YOUR PITY!
Half crying.
IF A PRESS INVITATION IS ALL RIGHT...
...I CAN TAKE YOU.
WHAT?

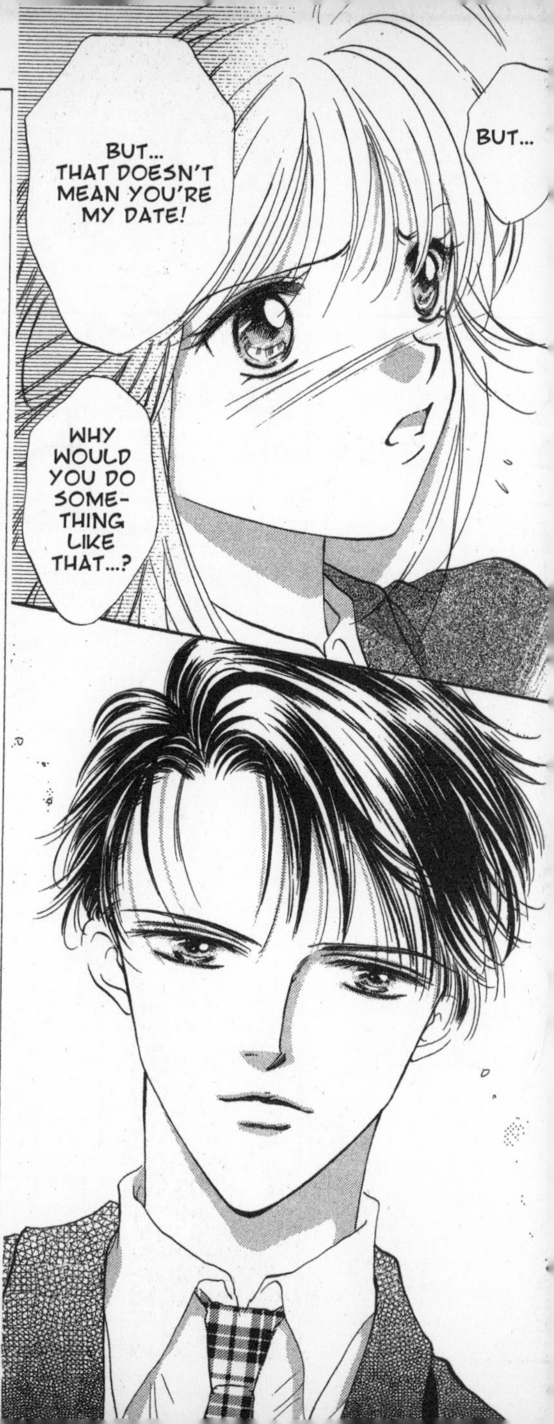
BUT...
BUT... THAT DOESN'T MEAN YOU'RE MY DATE!
WHY WOULD YOU DO SOME-THING LIKE THAT...?

Volume 5 and Garbage

When I wrote about Higata in Volume 4, I received a letter from someone who said that they might make a garbage processing plant in their neighborhood. So this time, I've decided that the last space topic would be "Garbage Issues."
I have a feeling that from the time I was in school they've been telling us to create less garbage and that it was already a problem, but maybe you can say that (our) realization of the garbage issue didn't change, or that we don't feel the sense of emergency.
But it's really bad, you know, and the Greenhouse Effect is finally bad, too. So I say, but most of my readers are students. Why don't the adults get a grip?! That's how it is, isn't it?
So, for now, I'll introduce the garbage counter-measures that I'd implement.

- I bring "my bag" when I go shopping.

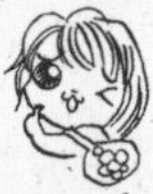
Yay!
Shopping bag? No thank you!

- I bring trays to the supermarkets that collect trays.

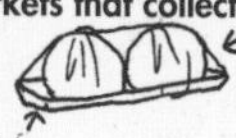
This.
That Styrofoam that they usually put vegetables and fish on.

- When the clerk at the mini-mart asks me, "Would you like chopsticks with that?" I answer, "No."

It's a slow and steady thing. While it's slow and steady, if this impacts the rest of the country, then the garbage will...decrease a little!
For the rest, I do stuff like choose products that are recyclable, and use both sides of copier paper. To tell the truth, I aggressively recycle even small bits of garbage, but there really isn't a system for that, is there? I think that for those of you who are students, by the time you become adults, the division of garbage will be more intense. So how about starting now?

Please tell your Mom that I recommend "My bags"

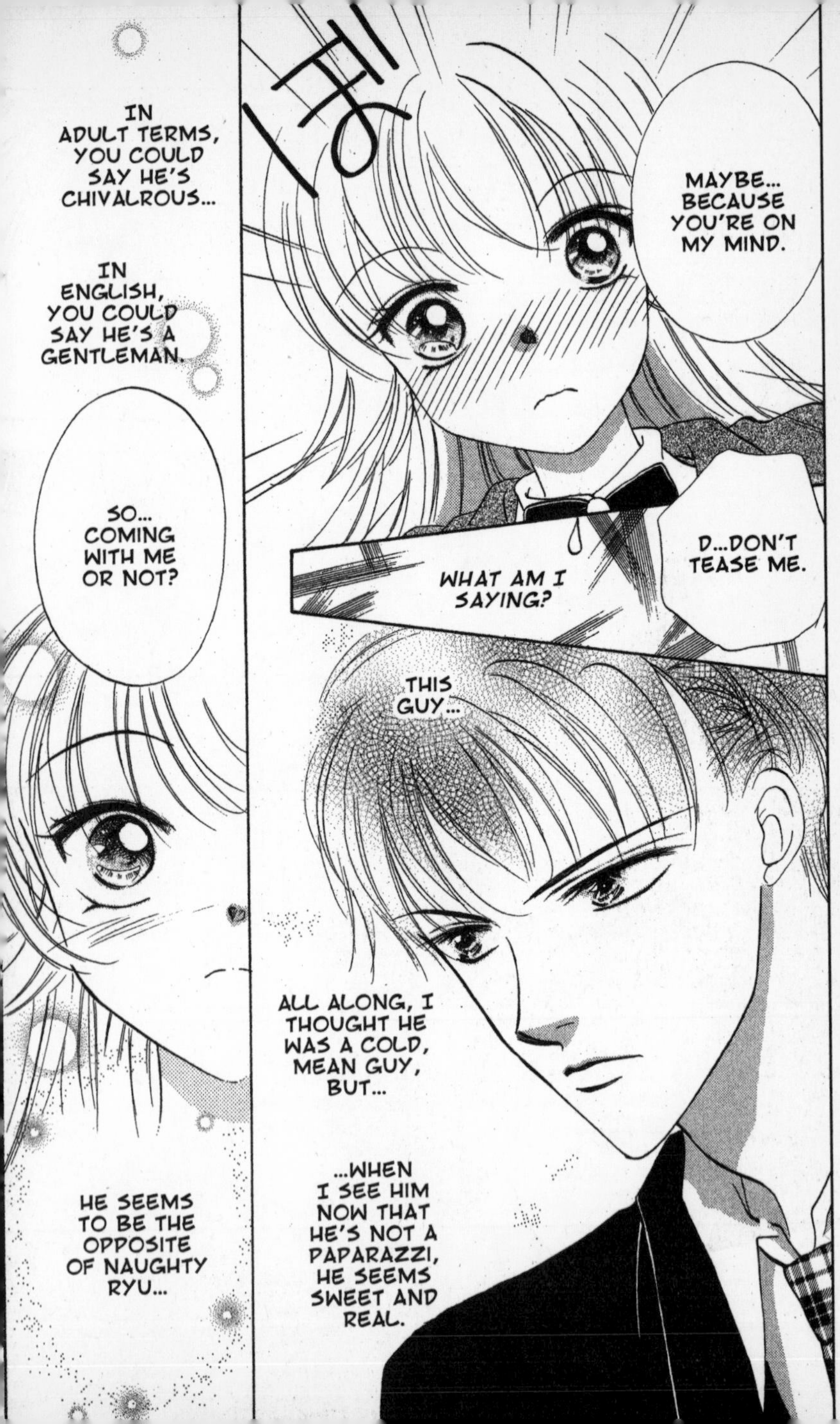
ぽ
MAYBE... BECAUSE YOU'RE ON MY MIND.
D...DON'T TEASE ME.
WHAT AM I SAYING?
THIS GUY...
ALL ALONG, I THOUGHT HE WAS A COLD, MEAN GUY, BUT...
...WHEN I SEE HIM NOW THAT HE'S NOT A PAPARAZZI, HE SEEMS SWEET AND REAL.
IN ADULT TERMS, YOU COULD SAY HE'S CHIVALROUS...
IN ENGLISH, YOU COULD SAY HE'S A GENTLEMAN.
SO... COMING WITH ME OR NOT?
HE SEEMS TO BE THE OPPOSITE OF NAUGHTY RYU...

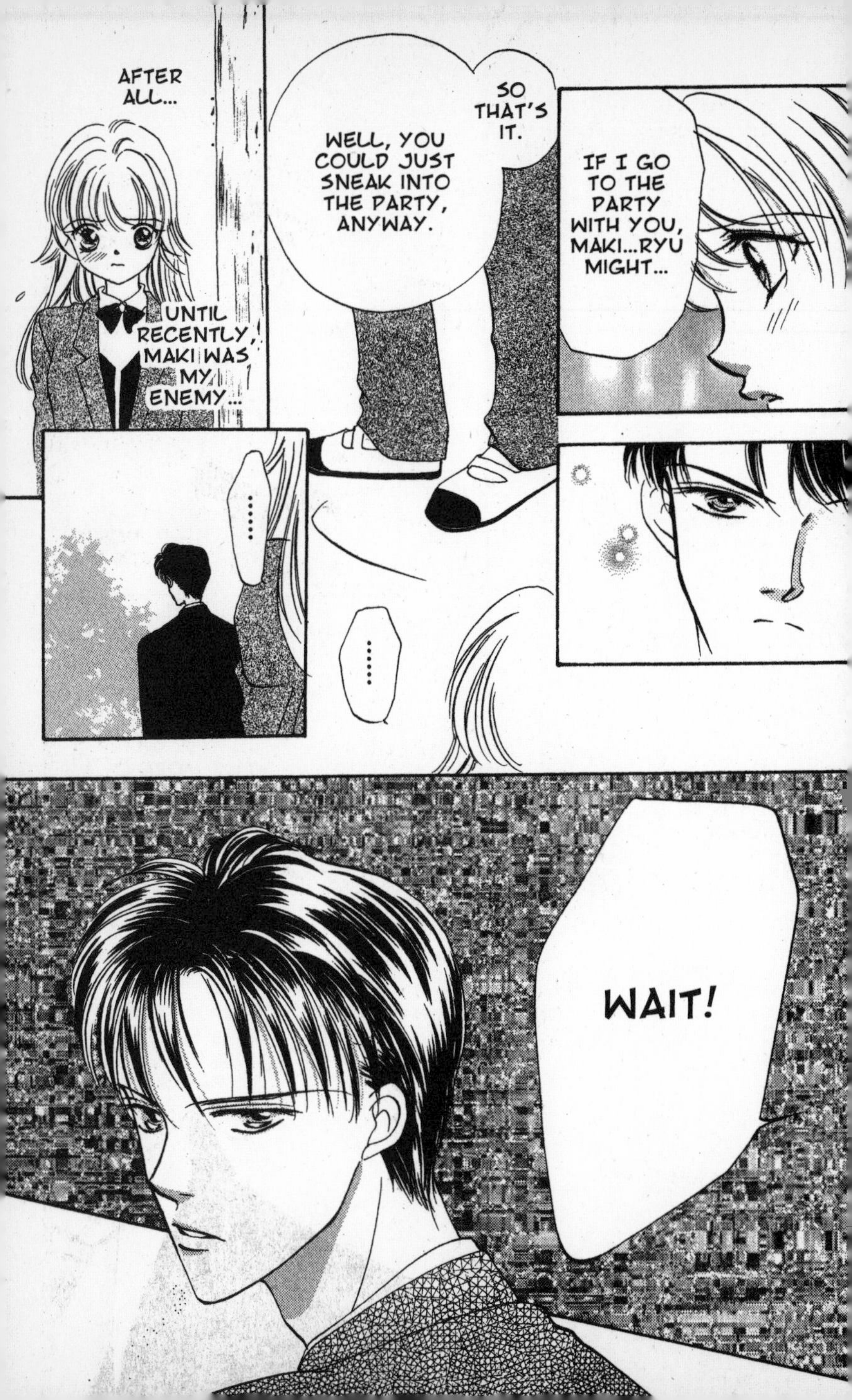
IF I GO TO THE PARTY WITH YOU, MAKI...RYU MIGHT...
SO THAT'S IT.
WELL, YOU COULD JUST SNEAK INTO THE PARTY, ANYWAY.
AFTER ALL...
UNTIL RECENTLY, MAKI WAS MY ENEMY...
......
......
WAIT!

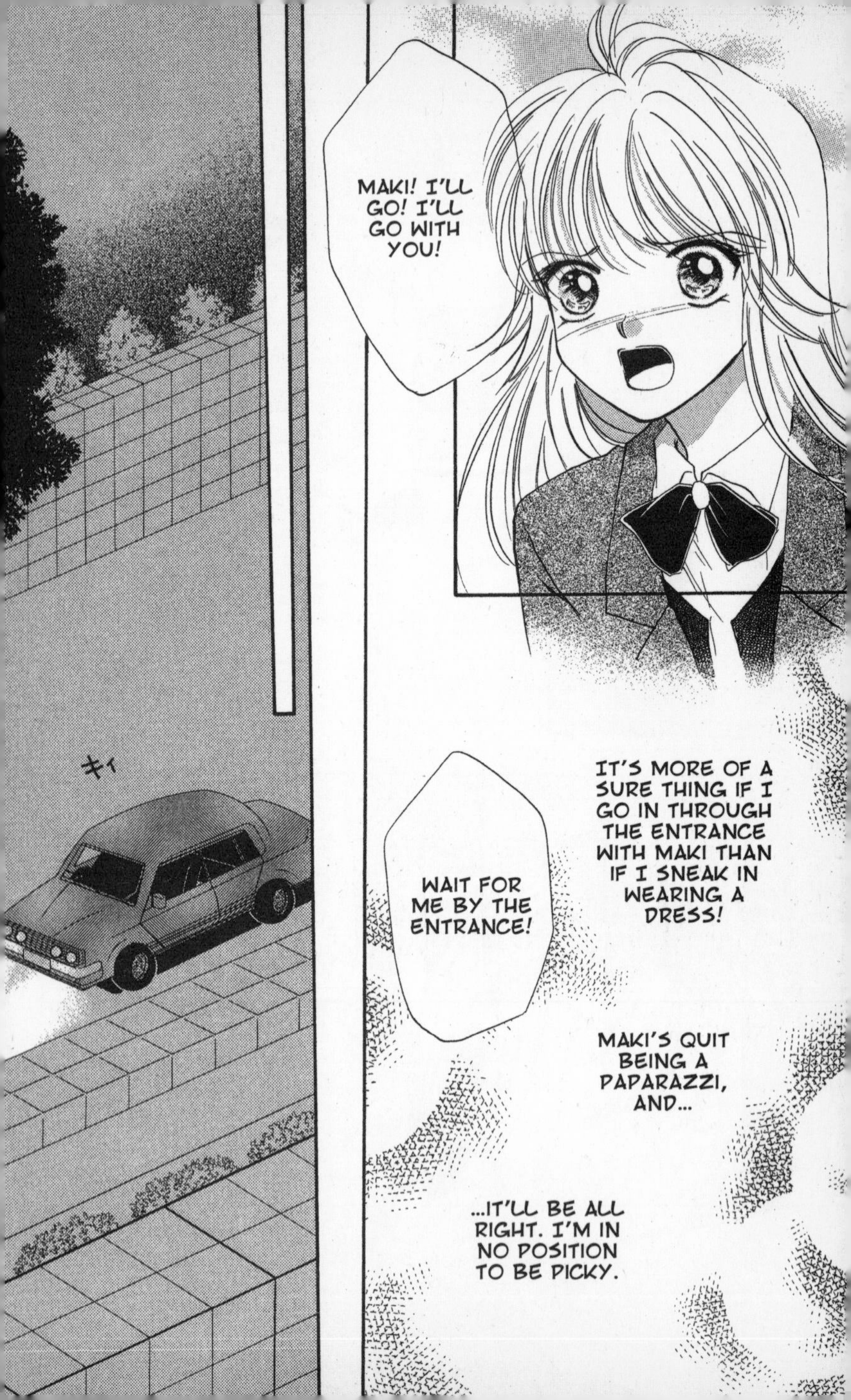
MAKI! I'LL GO! I'LL GO WITH YOU!
IT'S MORE OF A SURE THING IF I GO IN THROUGH THE ENTRANCE WITH MAKI THAN IF I SNEAK IN WEARING A DRESS!
WAIT FOR ME BY THE ENTRANCE!
MAKI'S QUIT BEING A PAPARAZZI, AND...
...IT'LL BE ALL RIGHT. I'M IN NO POSITION TO BE PICKY.
キィ

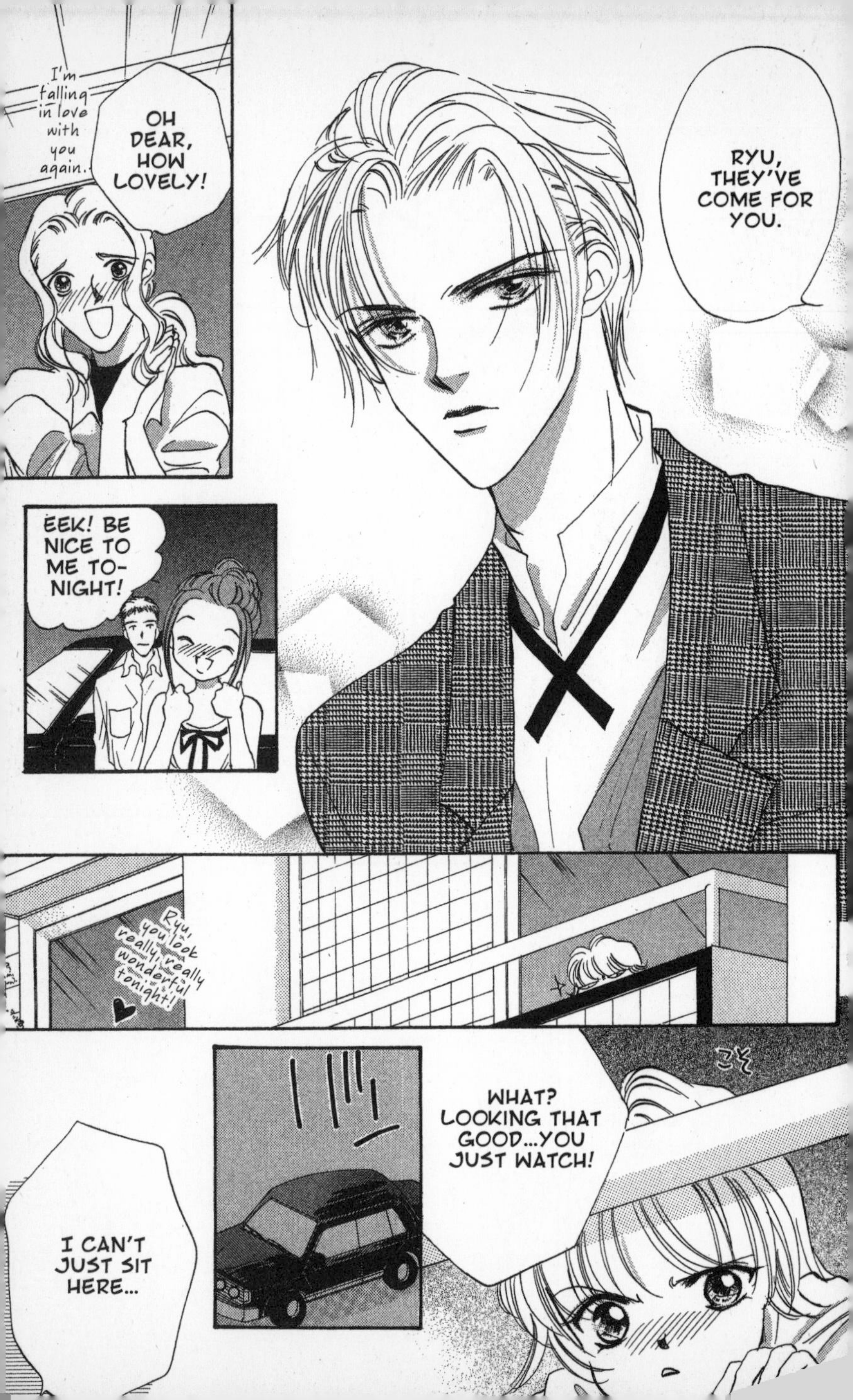
RYU, THEY'VE COME FOR YOU.
OH DEAR, HOW LOVELY!
I'm falling in love with you again..
EEK! BE NICE TO ME TO-NIGHT!
Ryu, you look really, really wonderful tonight!
こそ
WHAT? LOOKING THAT GOOD...YOU JUST WATCH!
I CAN'T JUST SIT HERE...

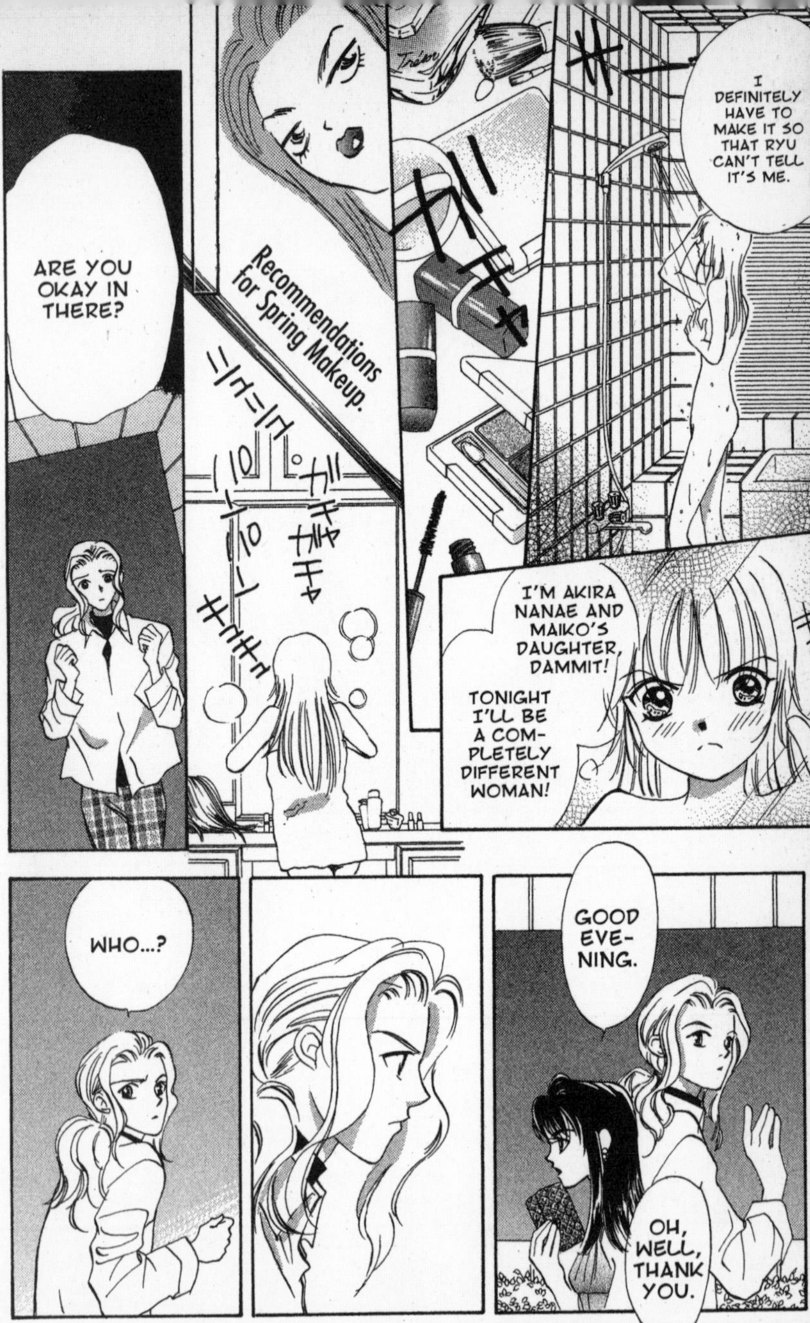
I DEFINITELY HAVE TO MAKE IT SO THAT RYU CAN'T TELL IT'S ME.
Recommendations for Spring Makeup.
I'M AKIRA NANAE AND MAIKO'S DAUGHTER, DAMMIT!
TONIGHT I'LL BE A COMPLETELY DIFFERENT WOMAN!
ARE YOU OKAY IN THERE?
GOOD EVENING.
OH, WELL, THANK YOU.
WHO...?

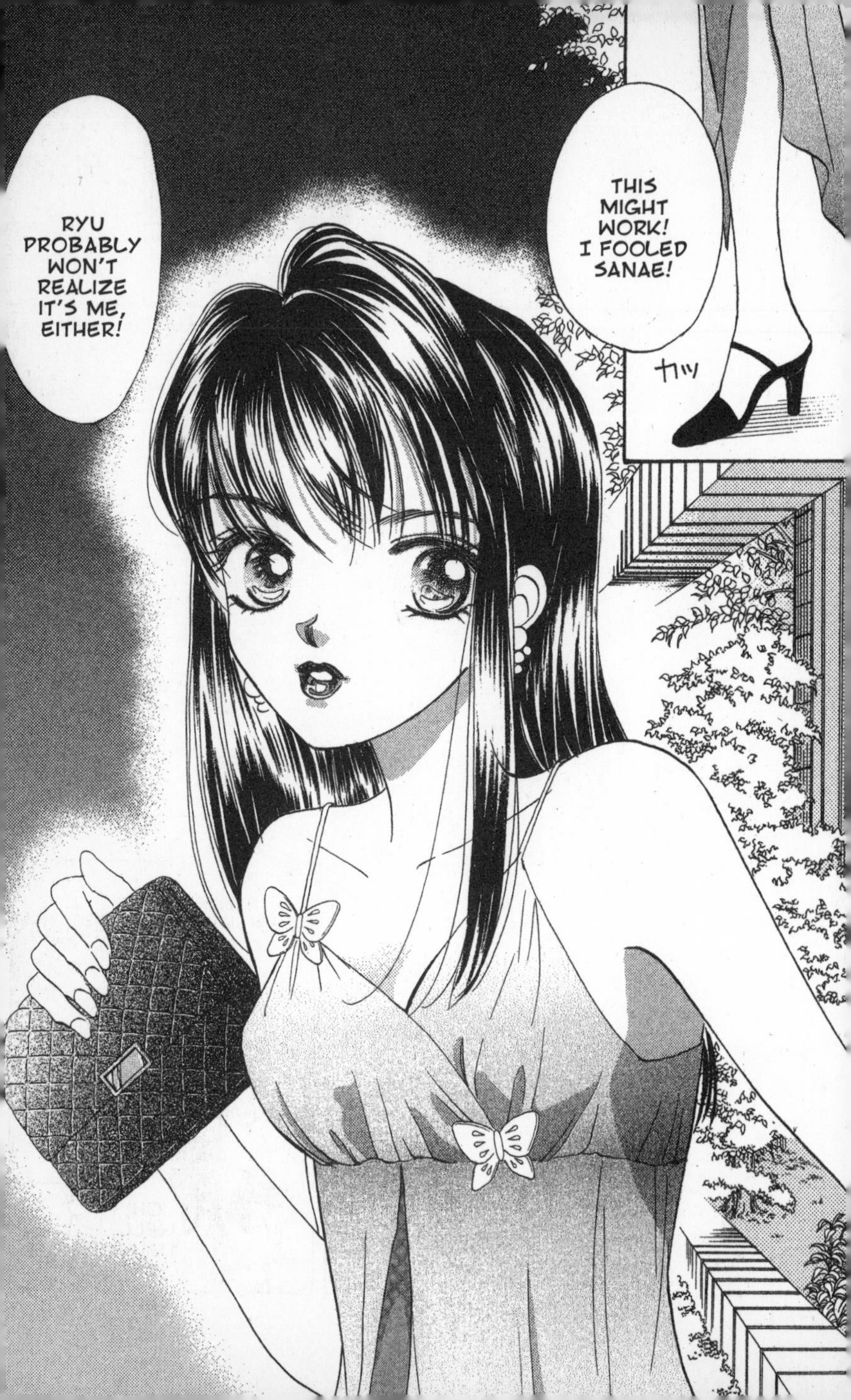
THIS MIGHT WORK! I FOOLED SANAE!
カッ
RYU PROBABLY WON'T REALIZE IT'S ME, EITHER!

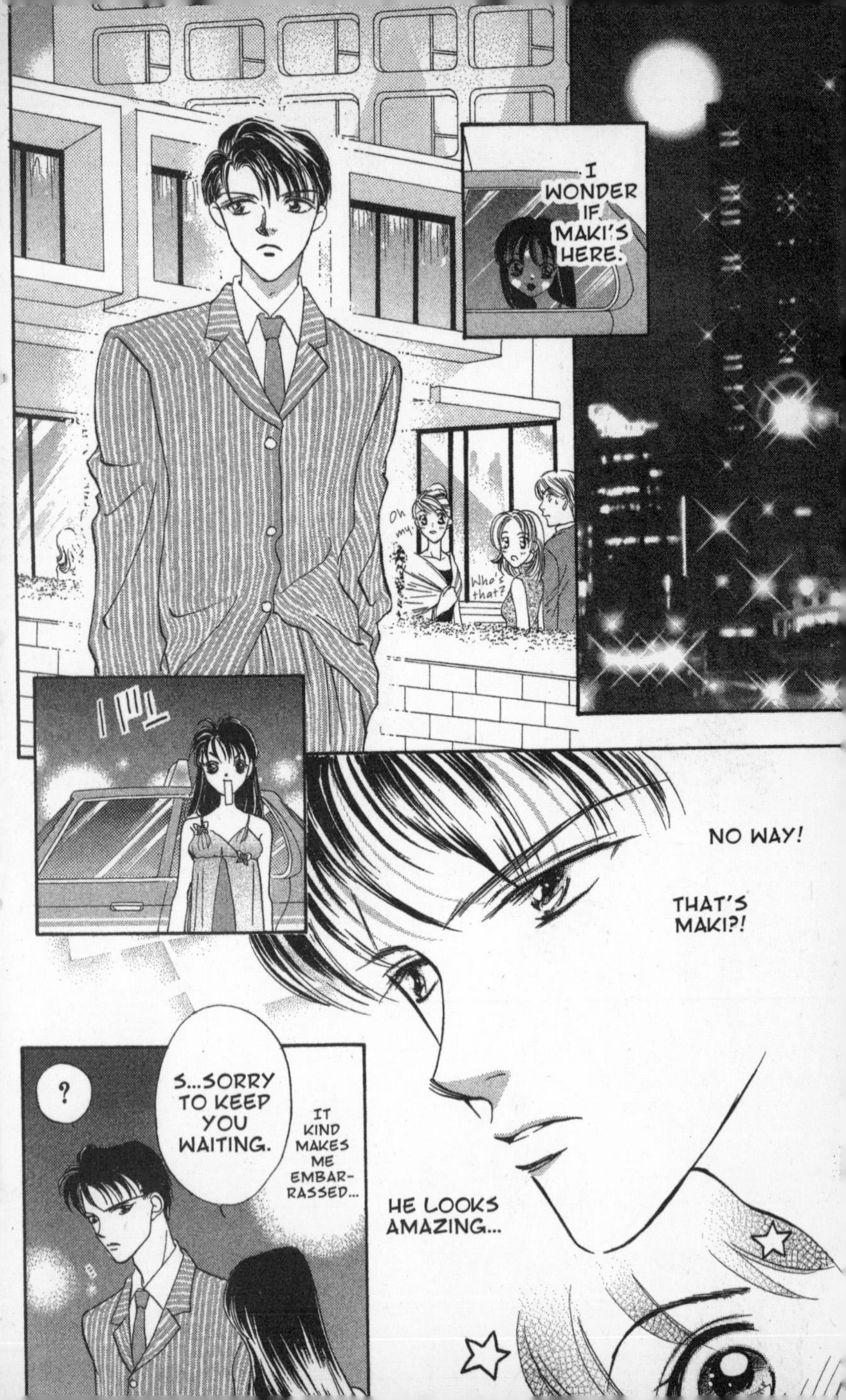
I WONDER IF MAKI'S HERE.
Oh my.
Who's that?
NO WAY!
THAT'S MAKI?!
HE LOOKS AMAZING...
?
S...SORRY TO KEEP YOU WAITING.
IT KIND MAKES ME EMBARRASSED...

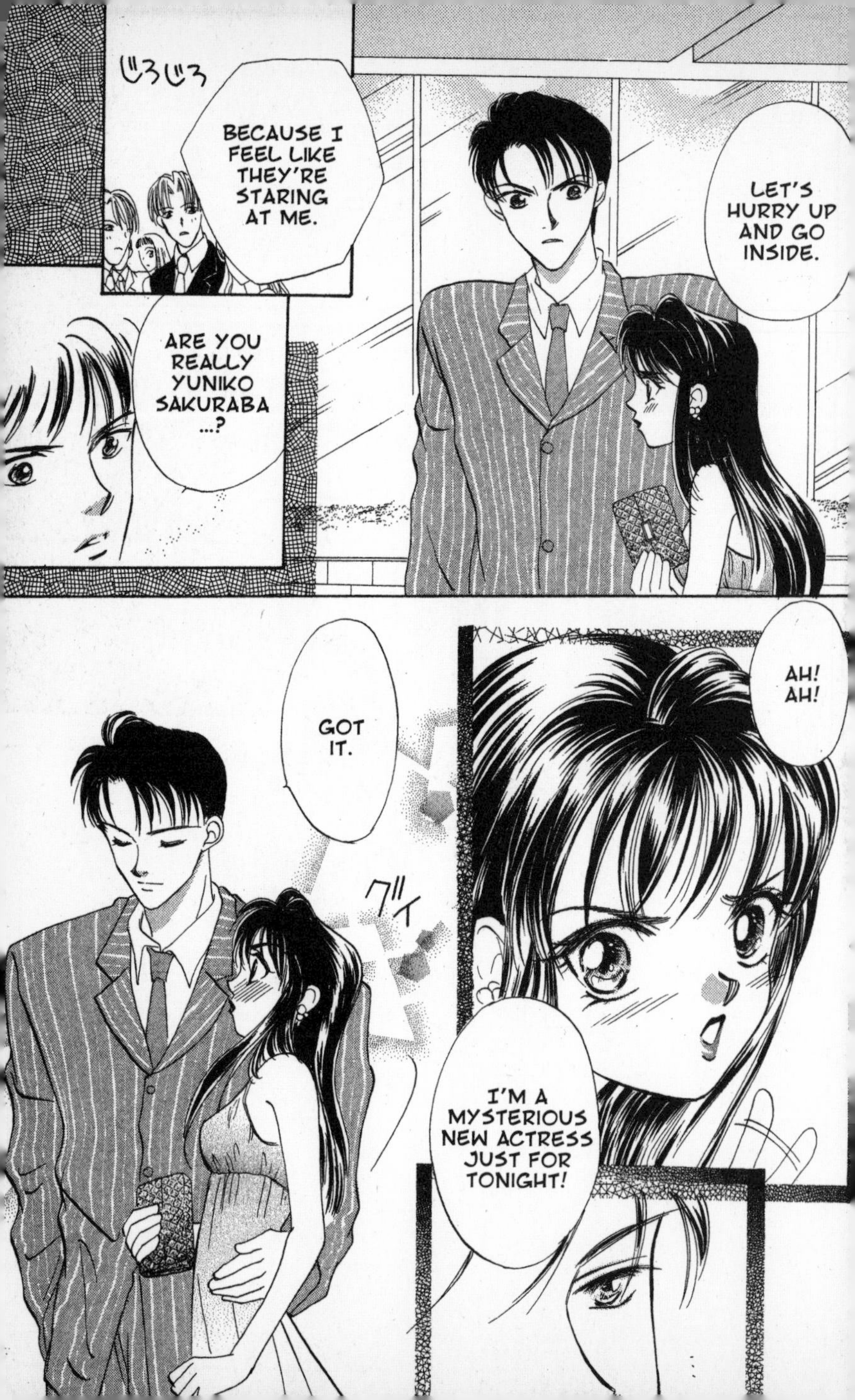
LET'S HURRY UP AND GO INSIDE.
じろじろ
BECAUSE I FEEL LIKE THEY'RE STARING AT ME.
ARE YOU REALLY YUNIKO SAKURABA ...?
AH! AH!
I'M A MYSTERIOUS NEW ACTRESS JUST FOR TONIGHT!
GOT IT.
グイ

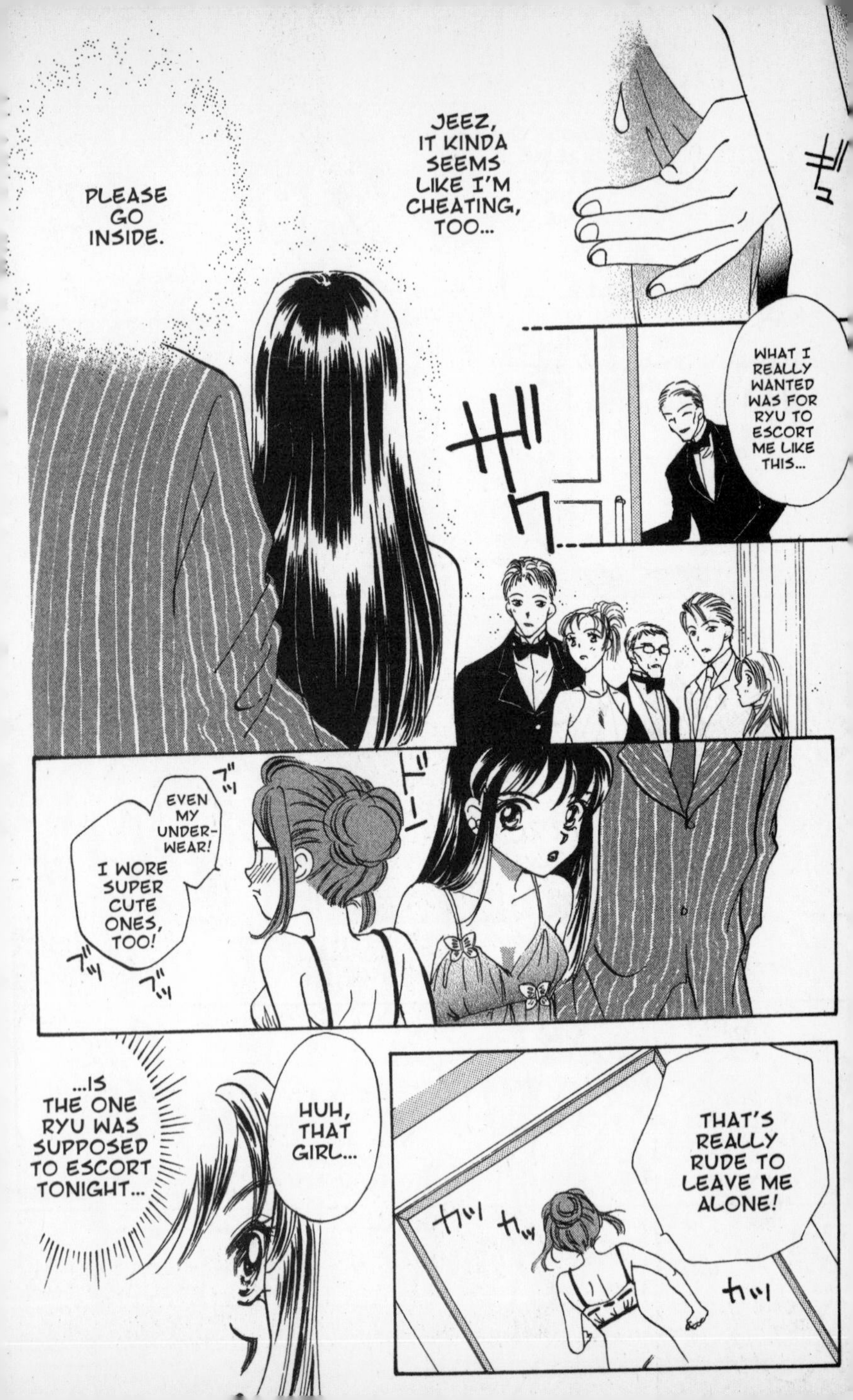
JEEZ, IT KINDA SEEMS LIKE I'M CHEATING, TOO...
PLEASE GO INSIDE.
WHAT I REALLY WANTED WAS FOR RYU TO ESCORT ME LIKE THIS...
EVEN MY UNDER-WEAR!
I WORE SUPER CUTE ONES, TOO!
THAT'S REALLY RUDE TO LEAVE ME ALONE!
HUH, THAT GIRL...
...IS THE ONE RYU WAS SUPPOSED TO ESCORT TONIGHT...

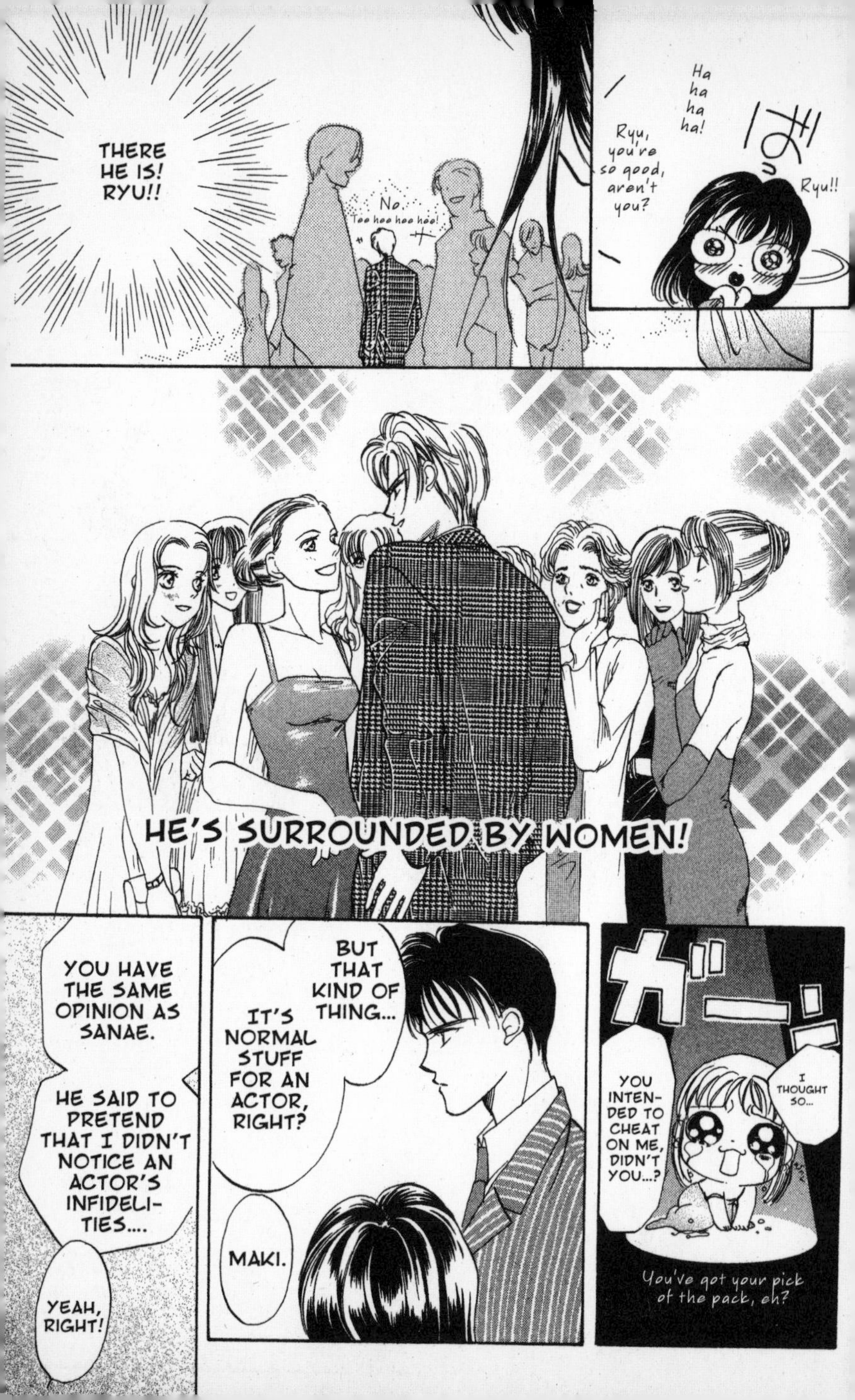
Ryu, you're so good, aren't you?
Ha ha ha ha!
Ryu!!
THERE HE IS! RYU!!
No.
Tee hee hee hee!
HE'S SURROUNDED BY WOMEN!
ガーン
YOU INTENDED TO CHEAT ON ME, DIDN'T YOU...?
I THOUGHT SO...
You've got your pick of the pack, eh?
BUT THAT KIND OF THING...
IT'S NORMAL STUFF FOR AN ACTOR, RIGHT?
MAKI.
YOU HAVE THE SAME OPINION AS SANAE.
HE SAID TO PRETEND THAT I DIDN'T NOTICE AN ACTOR'S INFIDELITIES....
YEAH, RIGHT!

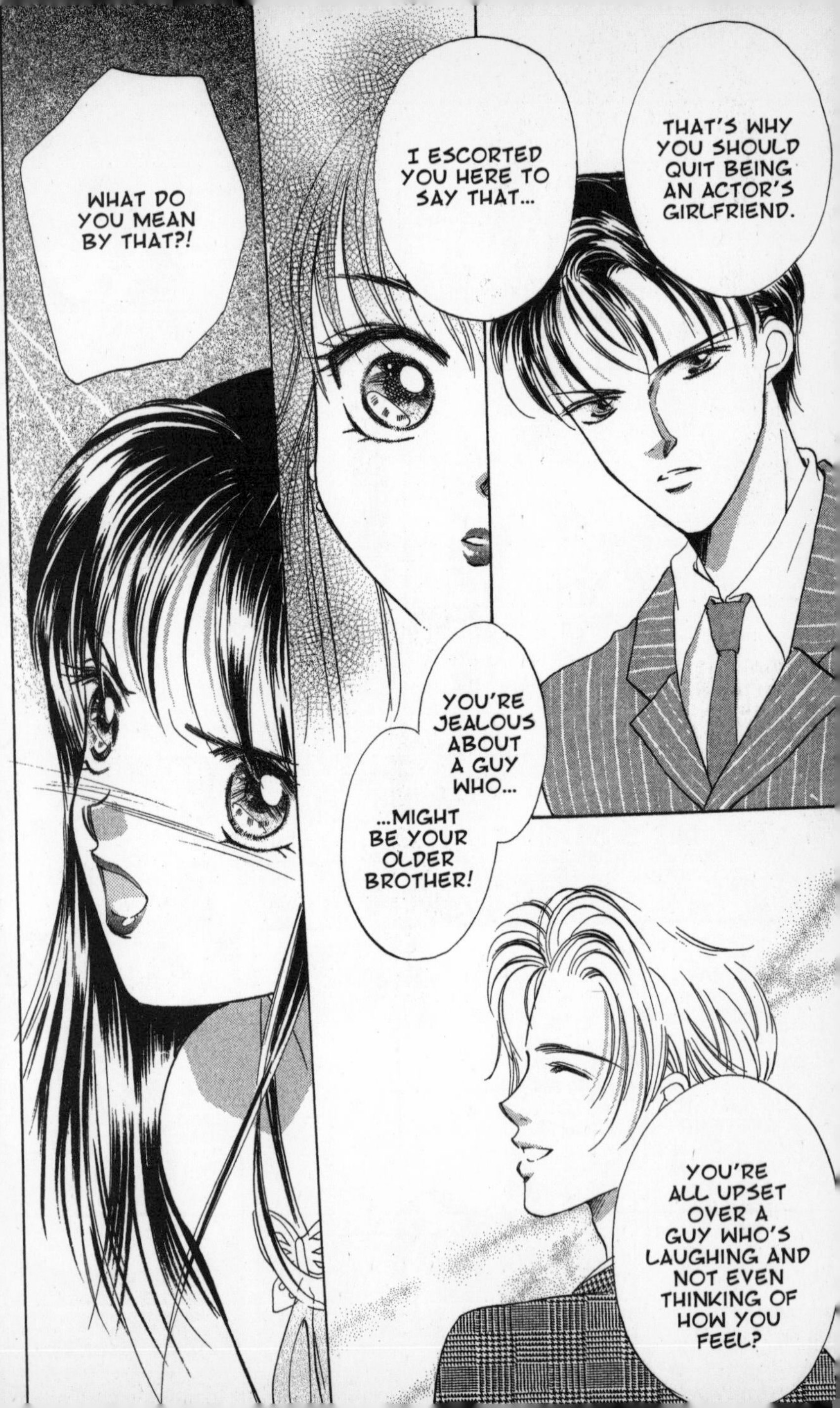
THAT'S WHY YOU SHOULD QUIT BEING AN ACTOR'S GIRLFRIEND.
I ESCORTED YOU HERE TO SAY THAT...
YOU'RE JEALOUS ABOUT A GUY WHO...
...MIGHT BE YOUR OLDER BROTHER!
YOU'RE ALL UPSET OVER A GUY WHO'S LAUGHING AND NOT EVEN THINKING OF HOW YOU FEEL?
WHAT DO YOU MEAN BY THAT?!

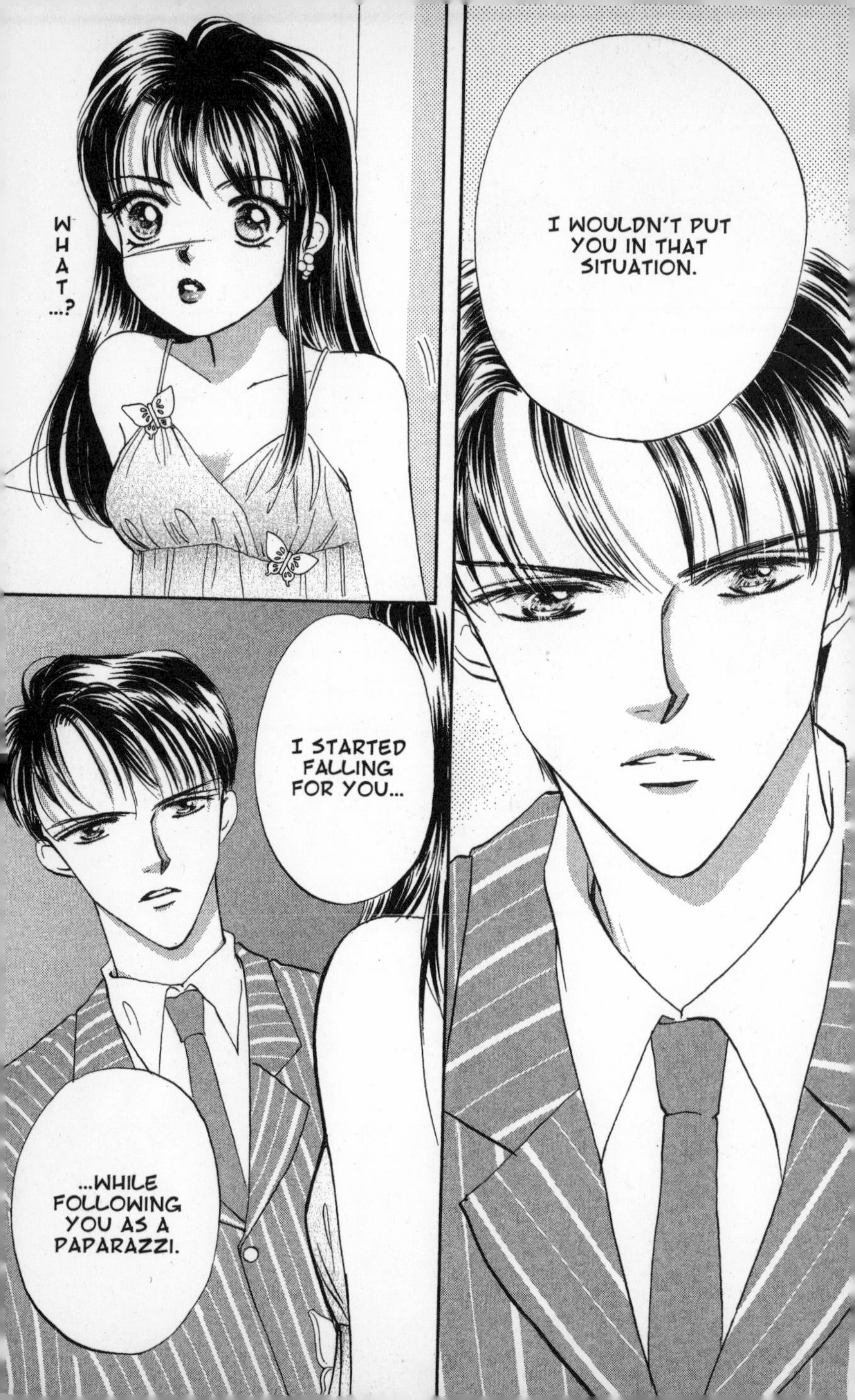
I WOULDN'T PUT YOU IN THAT SITUATION.
WHAT ...?
I STARTED FALLING FOR YOU...
...WHILE FOLLOWING YOU AS A PAPARAZZI.

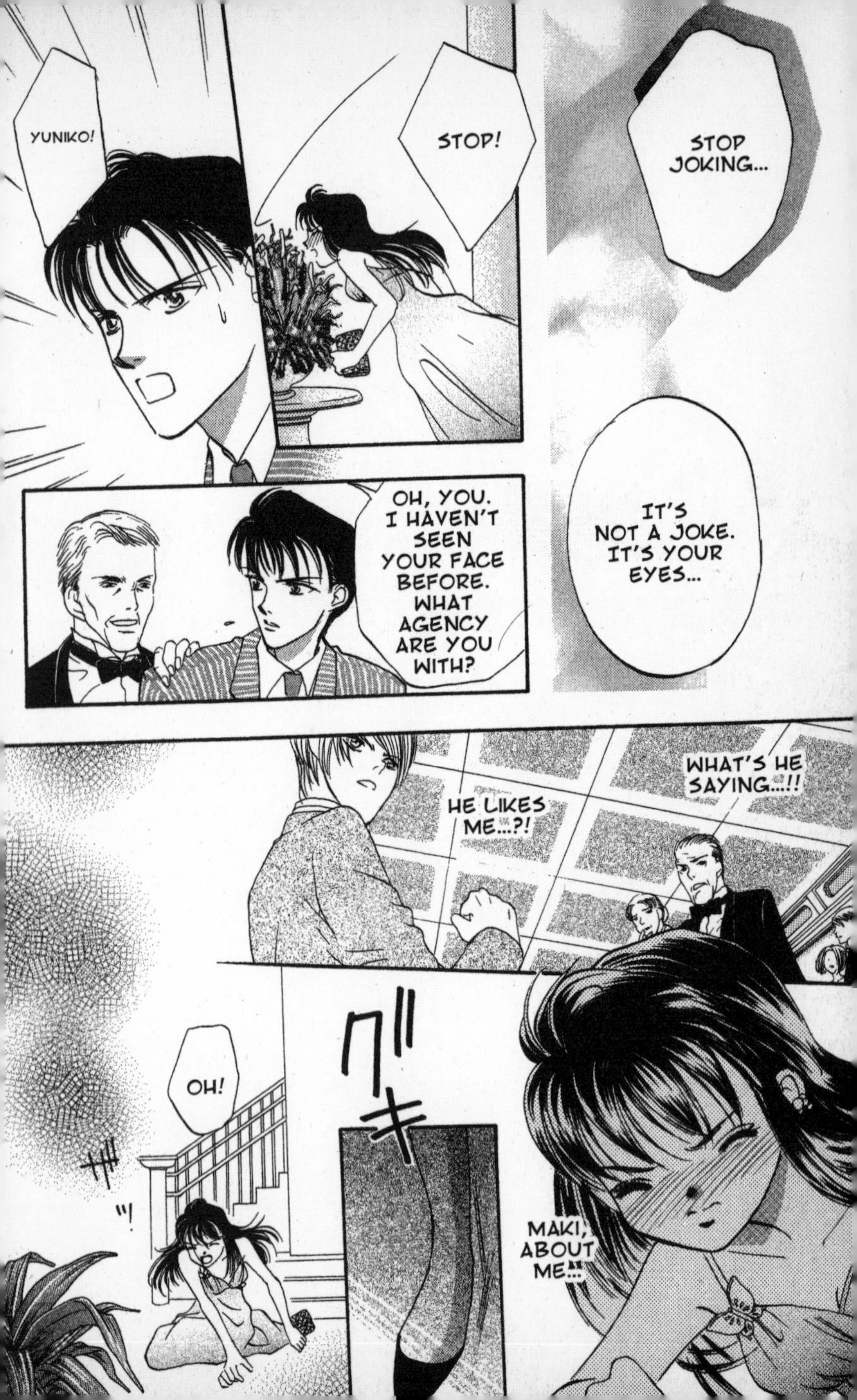

STOP JOKING...
IT'S NOT A JOKE. IT'S YOUR EYES...
STOP!
YUNIKO!
OH, YOU. I HAVEN'T SEEN YOUR FACE BEFORE. WHAT AGENCY ARE YOU WITH?
WHAT'S HE SAYING...!!
HE LIKES ME...?!
MAKI, ABOUT ME...
グキ
OH!

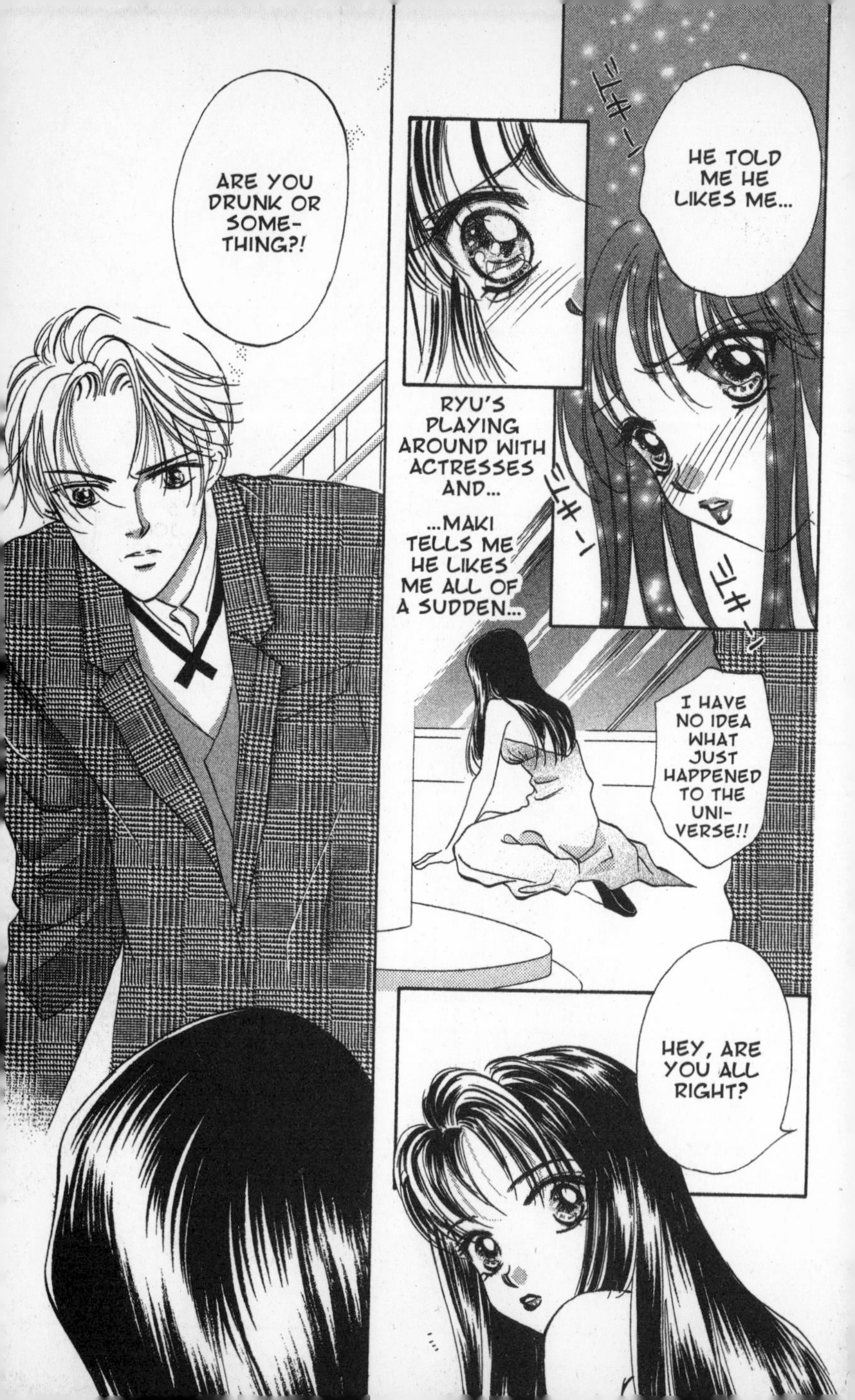
HE TOLD ME HE LIKES ME...
RYU'S PLAYING AROUND WITH ACTRESSES AND...
...MAKI TELLS ME HE LIKES ME ALL OF A SUDDEN...
I HAVE NO IDEA WHAT JUST HAPPENED TO THE UNI-VERSE!!
HEY, ARE YOU ALL RIGHT?
ARE YOU DRUNK OR SOME-THING?!

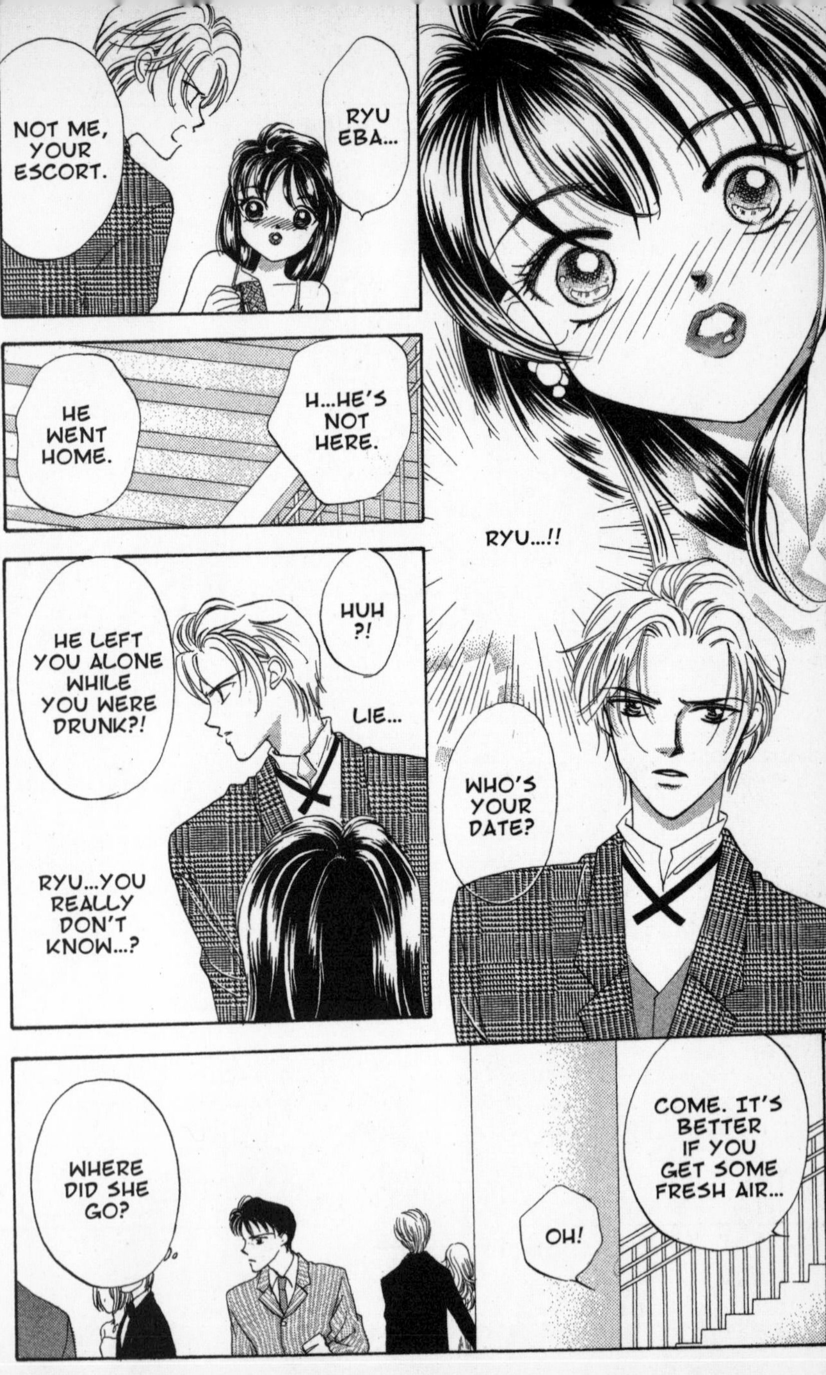

RYU...!!
WHO'S YOUR DATE?
RYU EBA...
NOT ME, YOUR ESCORT.
H...HE'S NOT HERE.
HE WENT HOME.
HUH?!
HE LEFT YOU ALONE WHILE YOU WERE DRUNK?!
LIE...
RYU...YOU REALLY DON'T KNOW...?
COME. IT'S BETTER IF YOU GET SOME FRESH AIR...
OH!
WHERE DID SHE GO?

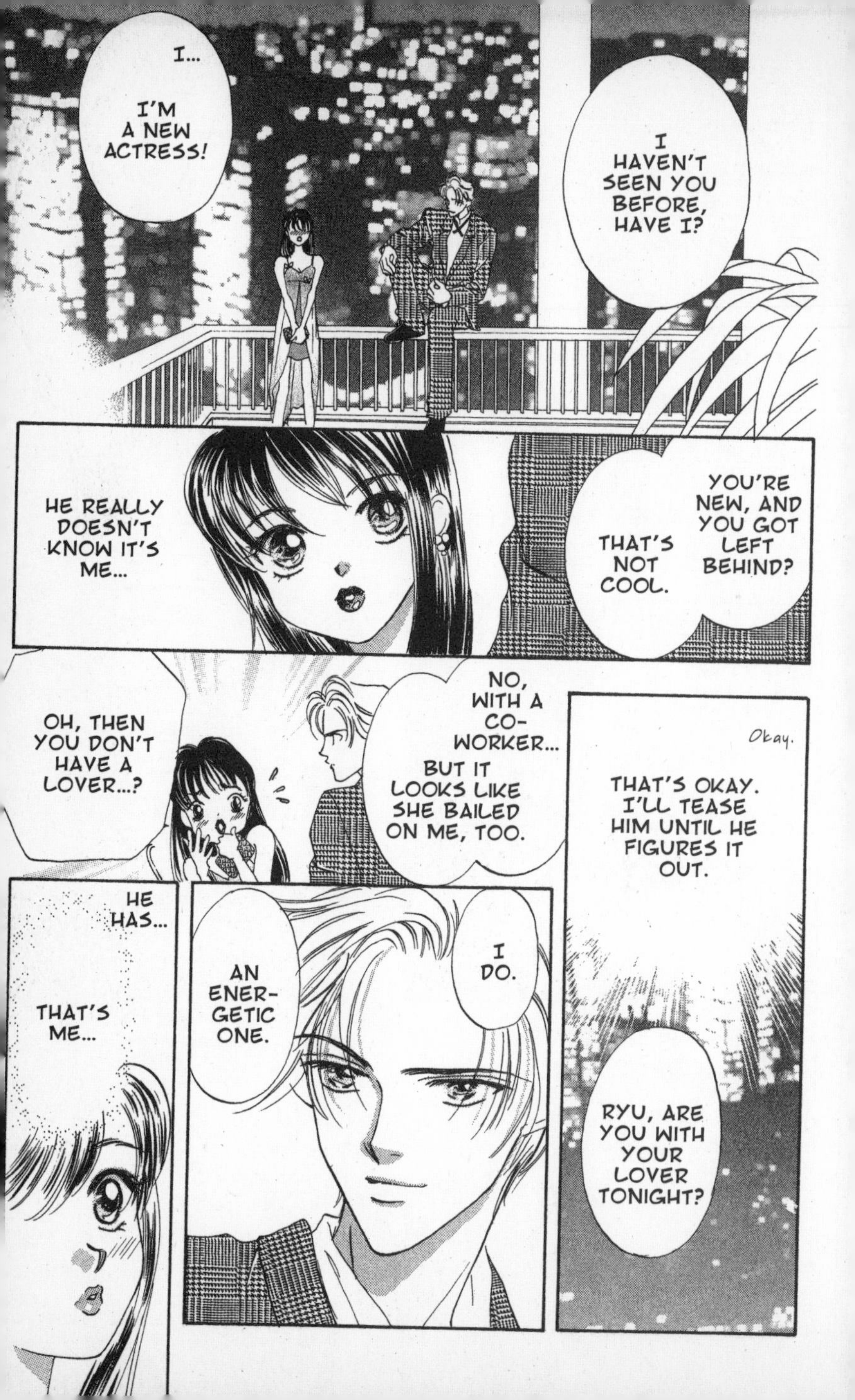
I HAVEN'T SEEN YOU BEFORE, HAVE I?
I...
I'M A NEW ACTRESS!
YOU'RE NEW, AND YOU GOT LEFT BEHIND?
THAT'S NOT COOL.
HE REALLY DOESN'T KNOW IT'S ME...
Okay.
THAT'S OKAY. I'LL TEASE HIM UNTIL HE FIGURES IT OUT.
RYU, ARE YOU WITH YOUR LOVER TONIGHT?
NO, WITH A CO-WORKER...
BUT IT LOOKS LIKE SHE BAILED ON ME, TOO.
OH, THEN YOU DON'T HAVE A LOVER...?
I DO.
AN ENERGETIC ONE.
HE HAS...
THAT'S ME...

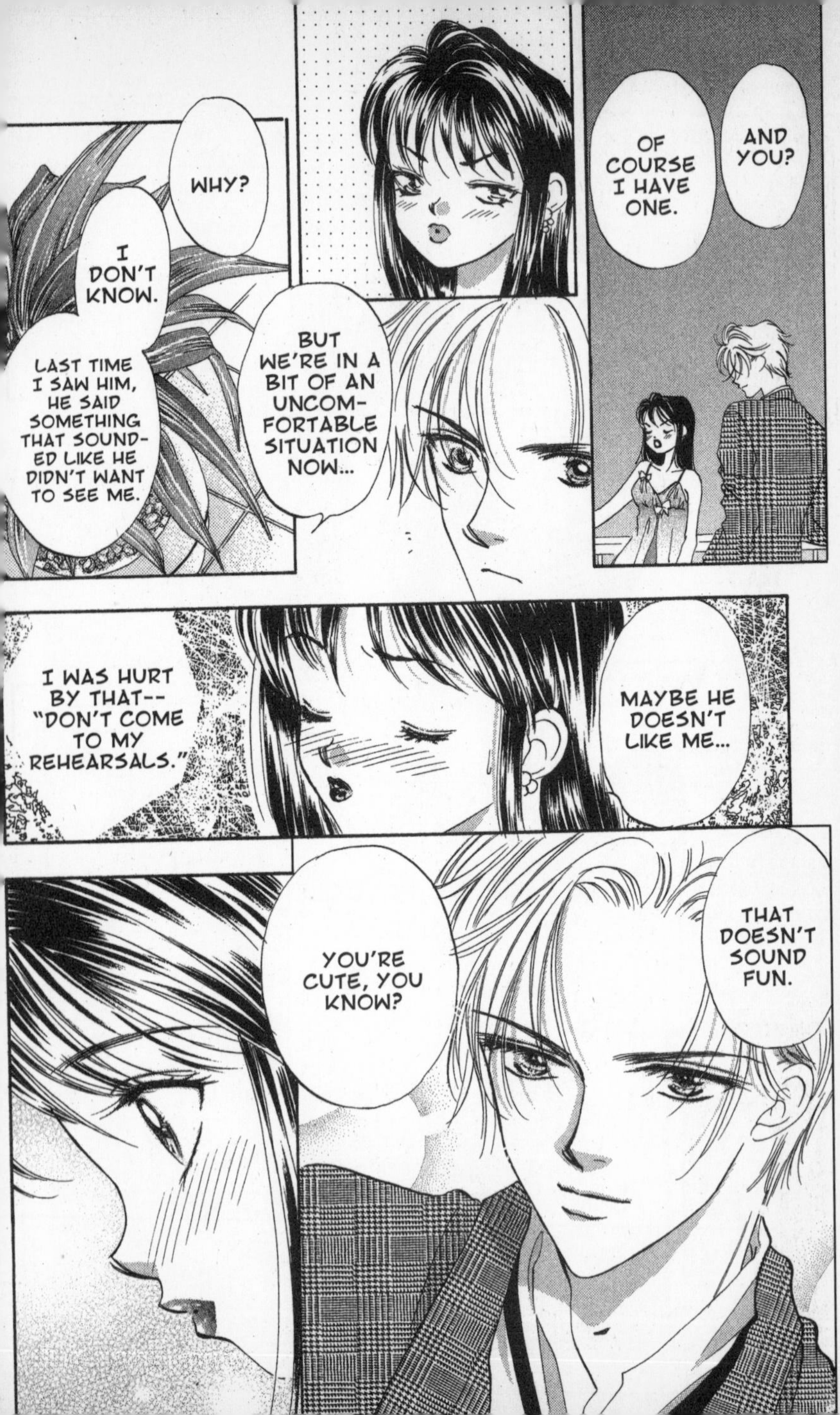
AND YOU?
OF COURSE I HAVE ONE.
BUT WE'RE IN A BIT OF AN UNCOM-FORTABLE SITUATION NOW...
WHY?
I DON'T KNOW.
LAST TIME I SAW HIM, HE SAID SOMETHING THAT SOUND-ED LIKE HE DIDN'T WANT TO SEE ME.
MAYBE HE DOESN'T LIKE ME...
I WAS HURT BY THAT-- "DON'T COME TO MY REHEARSALS."
THAT DOESN'T SOUND FUN.
YOU'RE CUTE, YOU KNOW?

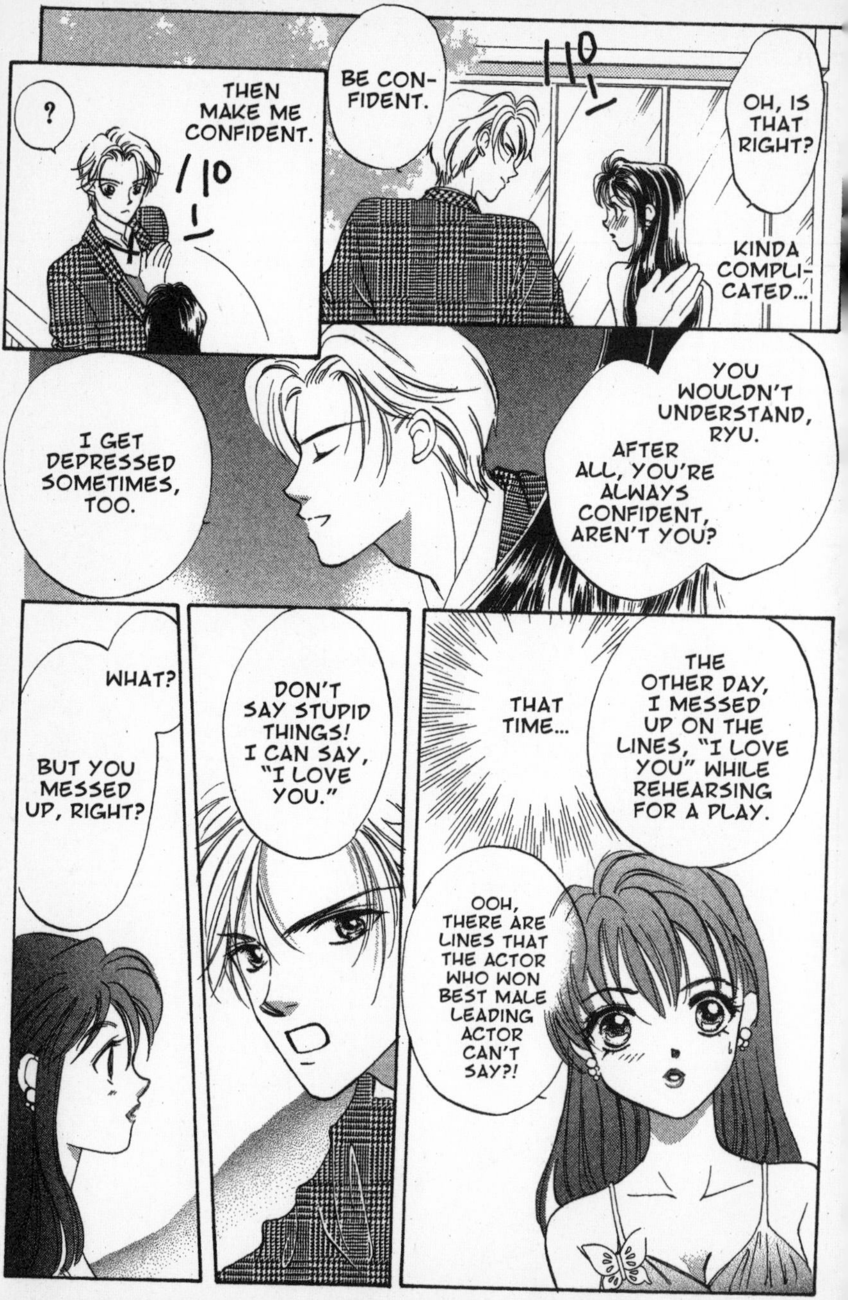
OH, IS THAT RIGHT?
KINDA COMPLI-CATED...
BE CON-FIDENT.
?
THEN MAKE ME CONFIDENT.
YOU WOULDN'T UNDERSTAND, RYU.
AFTER ALL, YOU'RE ALWAYS CONFIDENT, AREN'T YOU?
I GET DEPRESSED SOMETIMES, TOO.
THE OTHER DAY, I MESSED UP ON THE LINES, "I LOVE YOU" WHILE REHEARSING FOR A PLAY.
THAT TIME...
OOH, THERE ARE LINES THAT THE ACTOR WHO WON BEST MALE LEADING ACTOR CAN'T SAY?!
DON'T SAY STUPID THINGS! I CAN SAY, "I LOVE YOU."
WHAT?
BUT YOU MESSED UP, RIGHT?

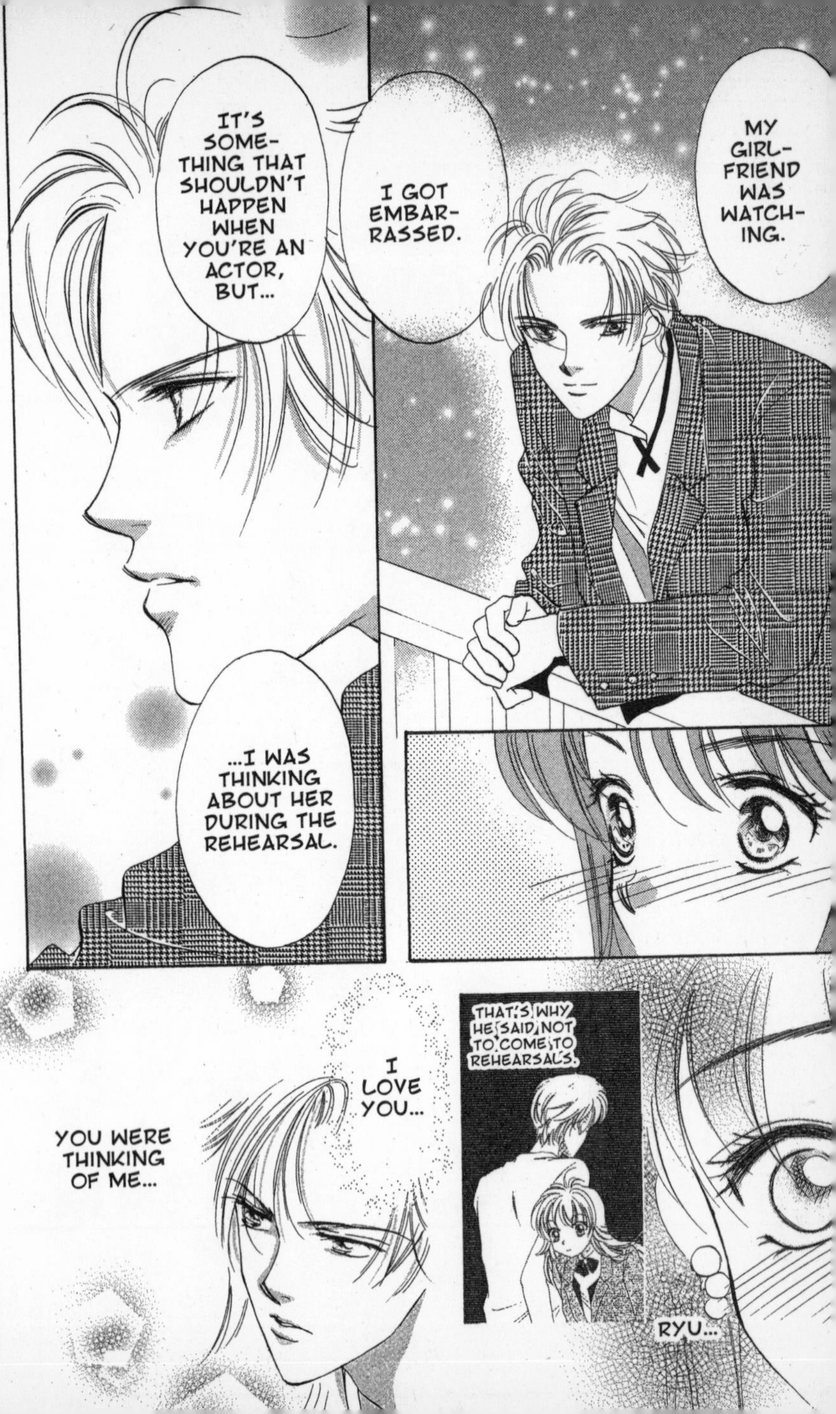
MY GIRL-FRIEND WAS WATCH-ING.
I GOT EMBAR-RASSED.
IT'S SOME-THING THAT SHOULDN'T HAPPEN WHEN YOU'RE AN ACTOR, BUT...
...I WAS THINKING ABOUT HER DURING THE REHEARSAL.
THAT'S WHY HE SAID NOT TO COME TO REHEARSALS.
RYU...
I LOVE YOU...
YOU WERE THINKING OF ME...

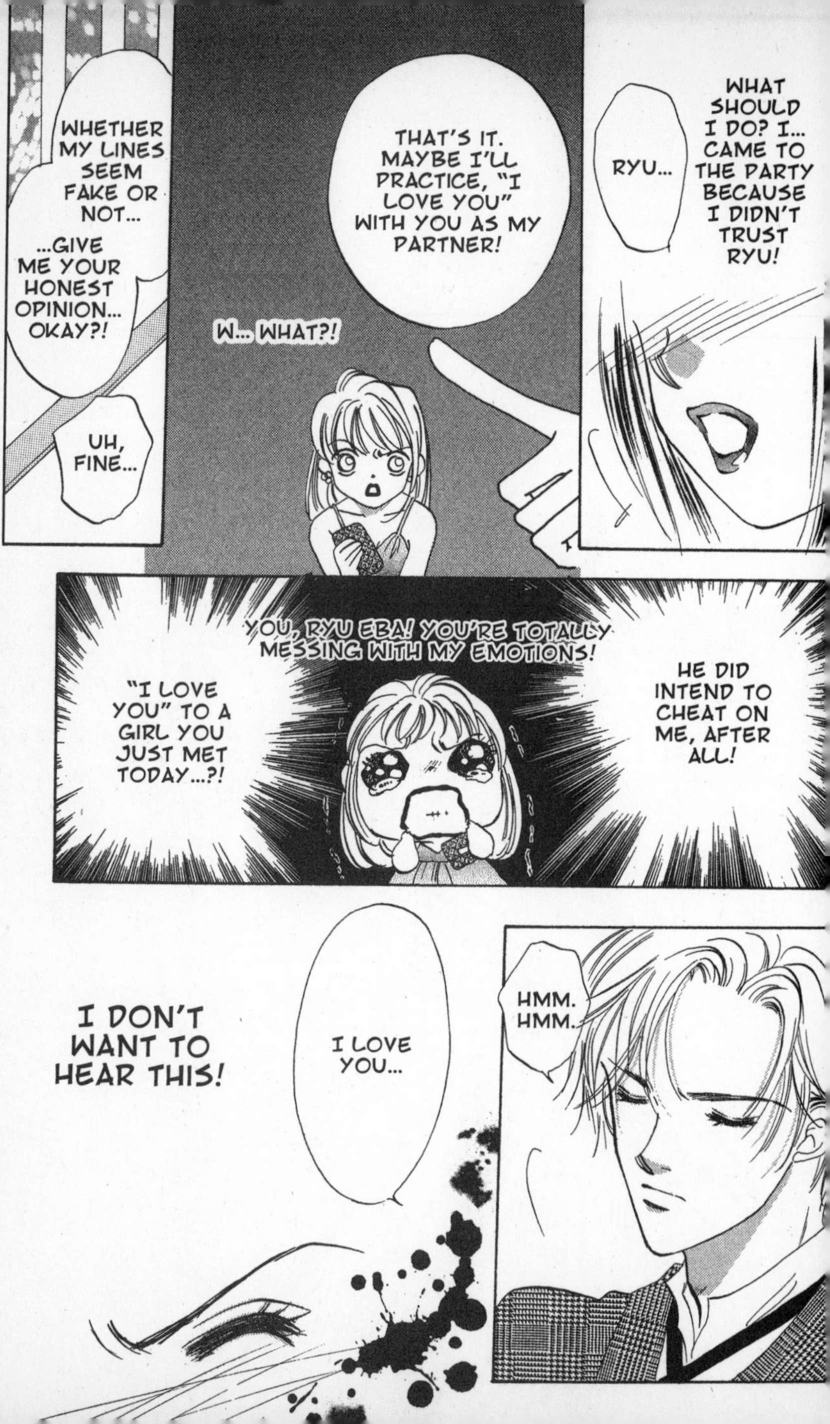
WHAT SHOULD I DO? I... CAME TO THE PARTY BECAUSE I DIDN'T TRUST RYU!
RYU...
THAT'S IT. MAYBE I'LL PRACTICE, "I LOVE YOU" WITH YOU AS MY PARTNER!
W... WHAT?!
WHETHER MY LINES SEEM FAKE OR NOT...
...GIVE ME YOUR HONEST OPINION... OKAY?!
UH, FINE...
HE DID INTEND TO CHEAT ON ME, AFTER ALL!
YOU, RYU EBA! YOU'RE TOTALLY MESSING WITH MY EMOTIONS!
"I LOVE YOU" TO A GIRL YOU JUST MET TODAY...?!
HMM. HMM.
I LOVE YOU...
I DON'T WANT TO HEAR THIS!

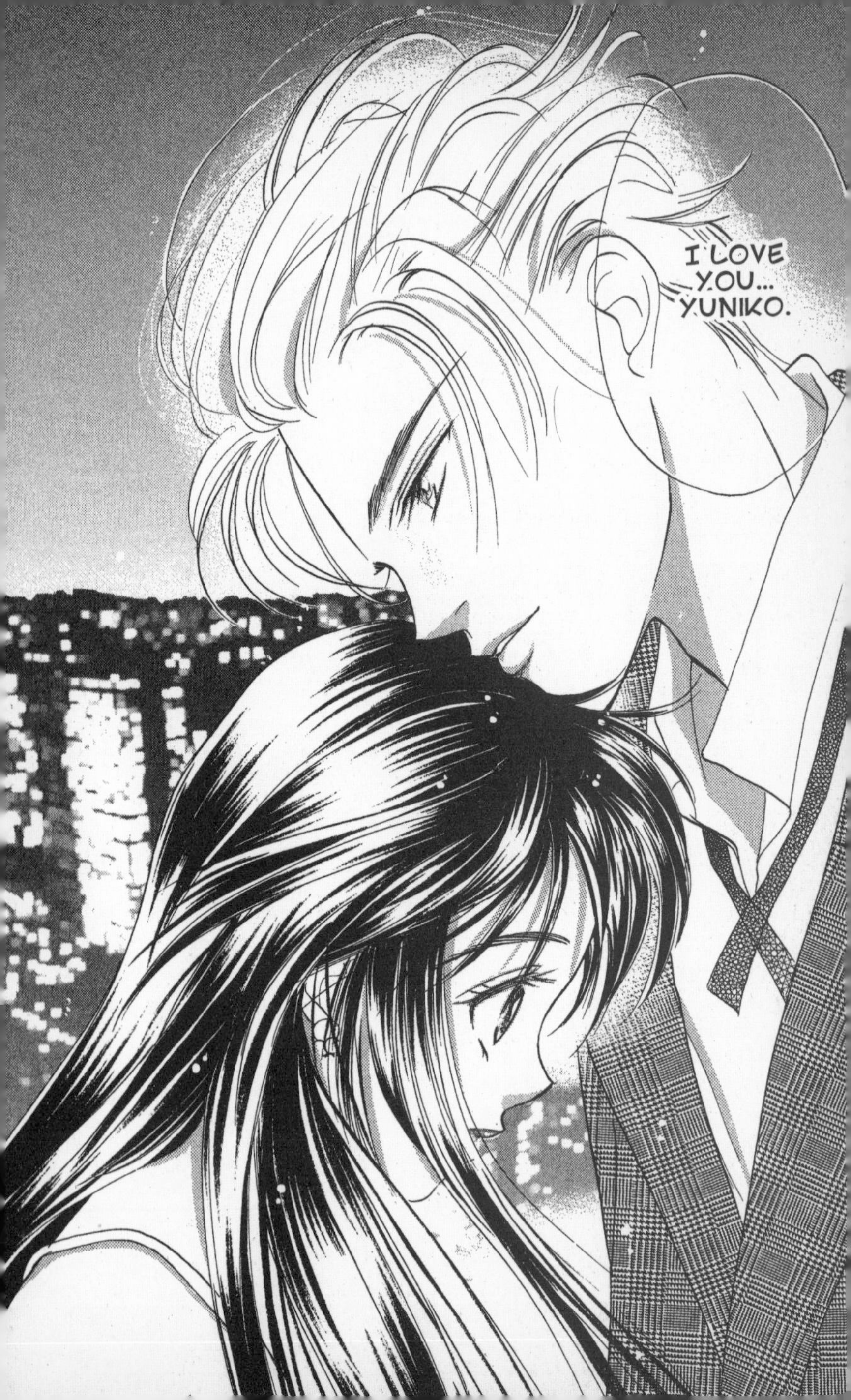
I LOVE YOU... YUNIKO.

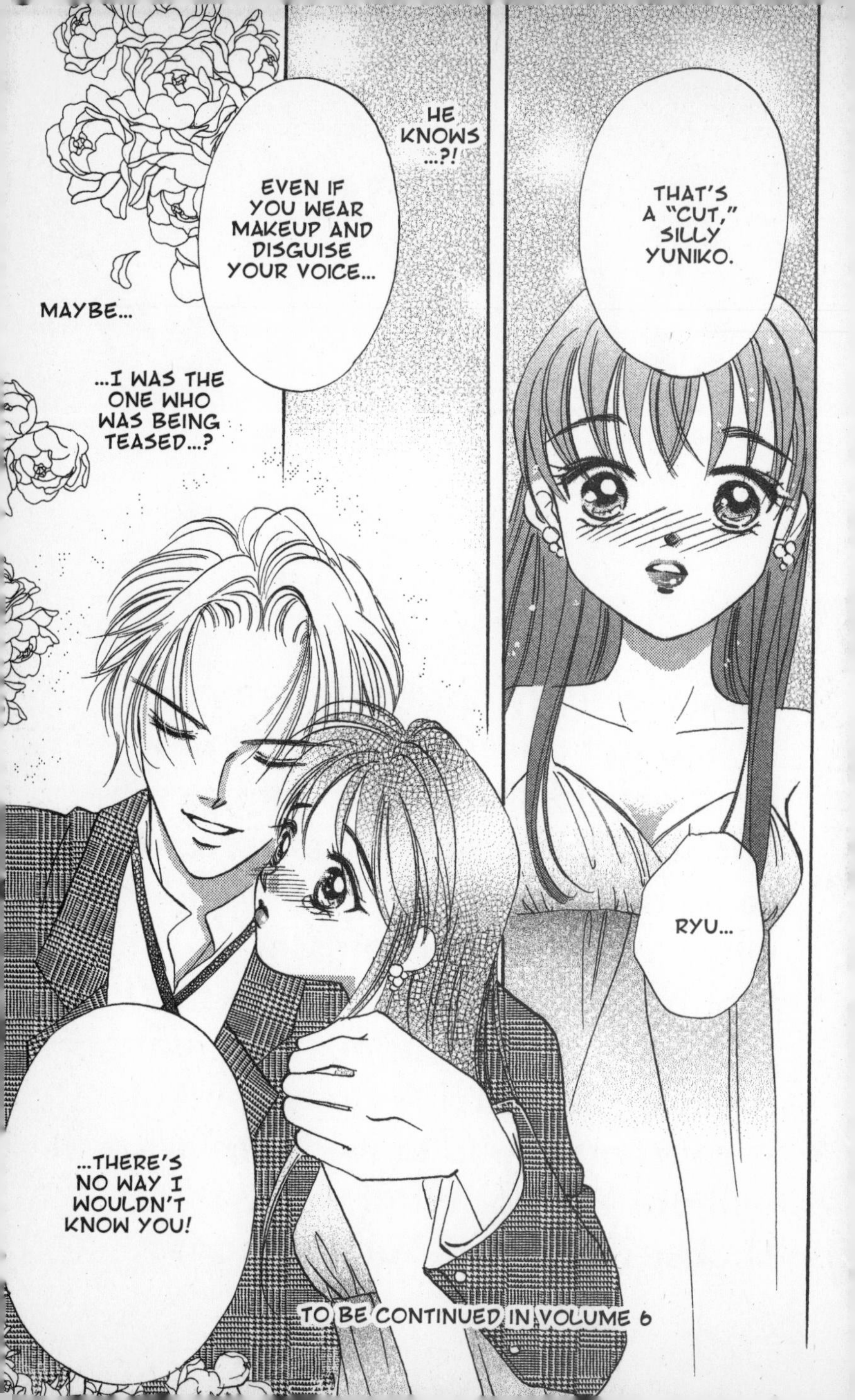
THAT'S A "CUT," SILLY YUNIKO.
RYU...
HE KNOWS ...?!
EVEN IF YOU WEAR MAKEUP AND DISGUISE YOUR VOICE...
MAYBE...
...I WAS THE ONE WHO WAS BEING TEASED...?
...THERE'S NO WAY I WOULDN'T KNOW YOU!
TO BE CONTINUED IN VOLUME 6

COMING SOON

VOLUME SIX

Yuniko and Ryu are determined to find out once and for all if they're brother and sister. Suddenly, ex-paparazzi Maki offers to help steal the remaining Akira Nanae belongings—why? When Maki confesses to Yuniko that his offer is only because he wants her, Ryu is furious and jealous and...distracted?! A Hollywood agent is courting Ryu to move to America... without Yuniko! What will Ryu choose? Who will Yuniko choose?

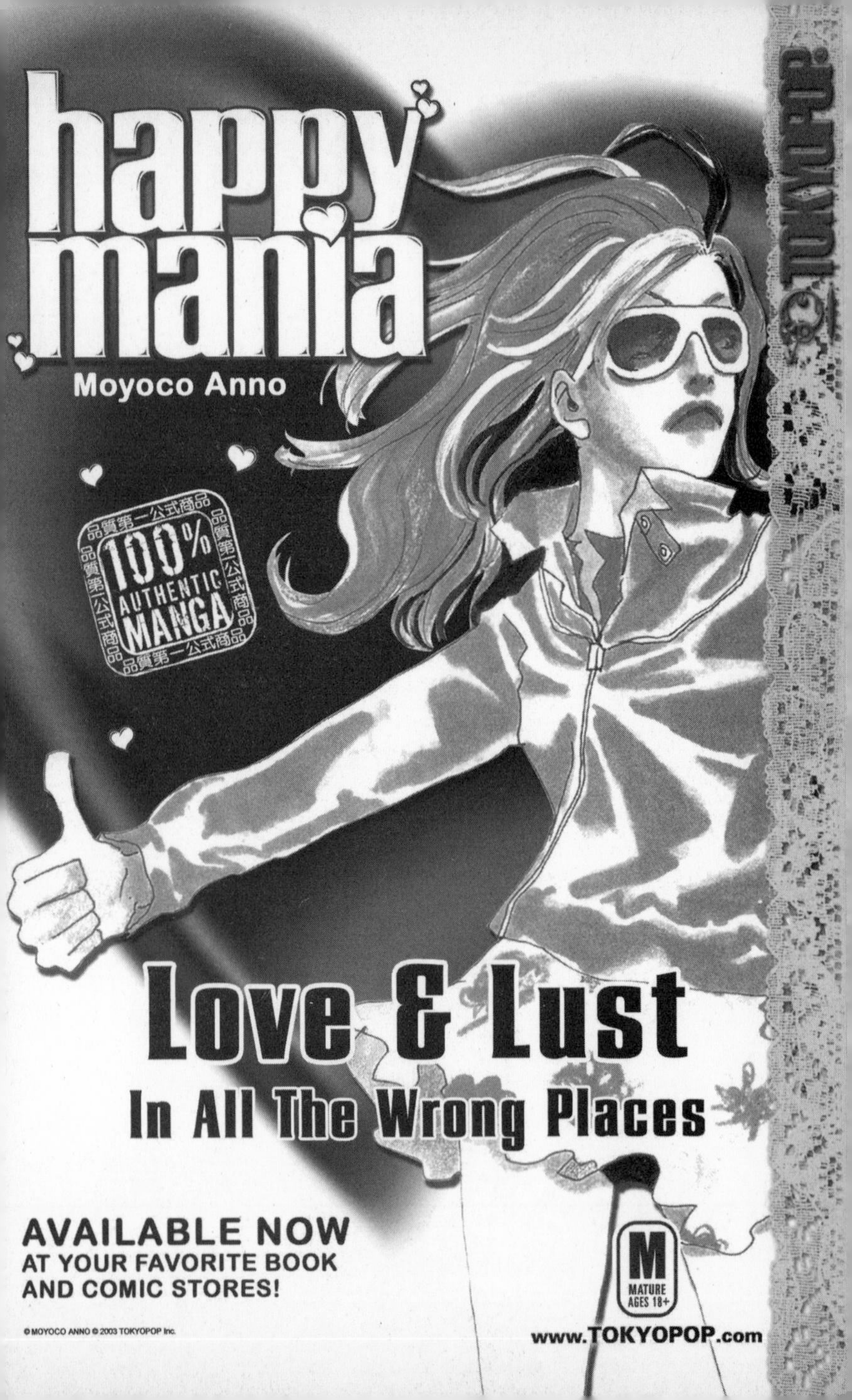
happy mania
Moyoco Anno
100% AUTHENTIC MANGA
品質第一公式商品
Love & Lust
In All The Wrong Places
AVAILABLE NOW
AT YOUR FAVORITE BOOK
AND COMIC STORES!
M
MATURE
AGES 18+
© MOYOCO ANNO © 2003 TOKYOPOP Inc.
www.TOKYOPOP.com
TOKYOPOP

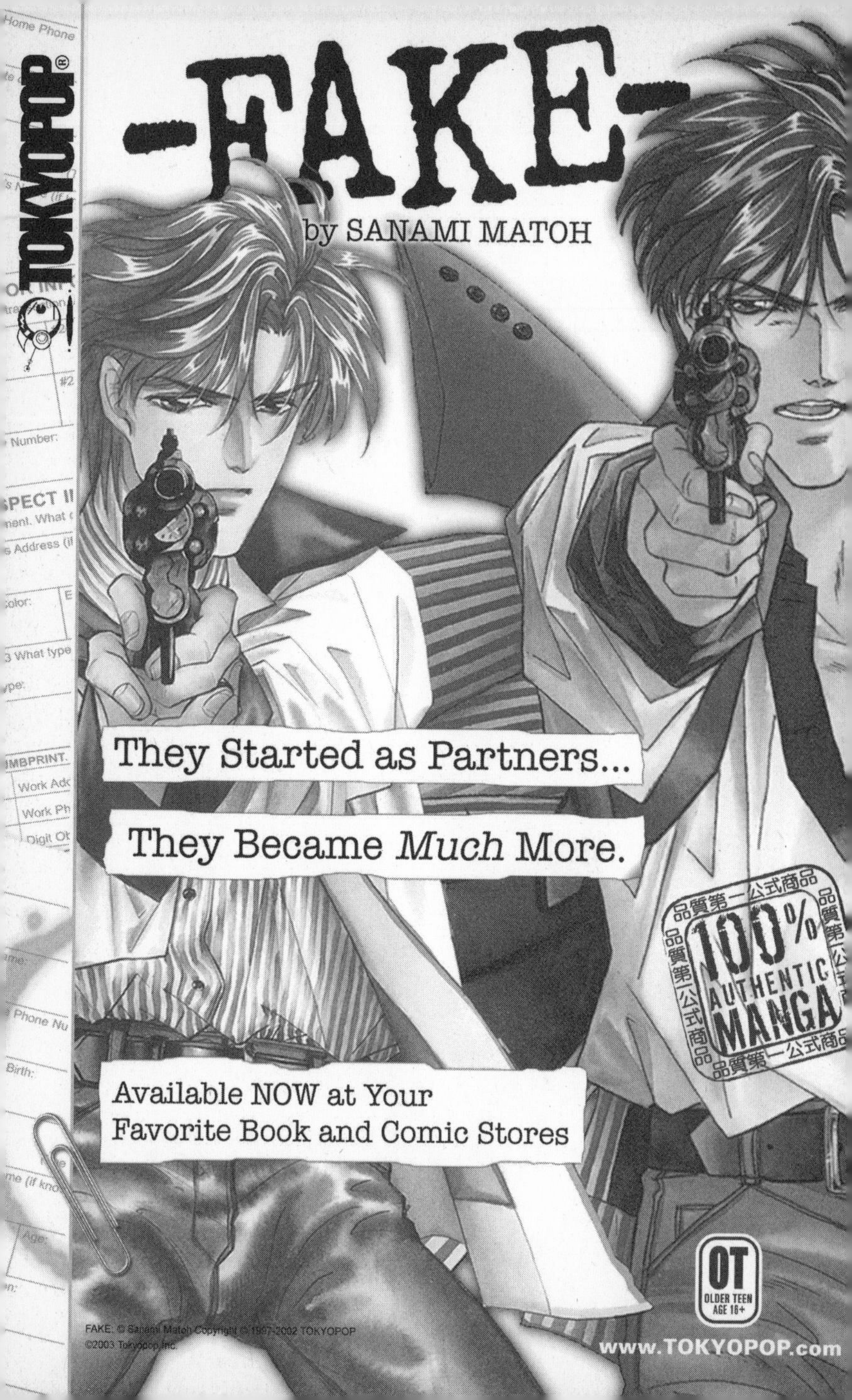
TOKYOPOP
-FAKE-
by SANAMI MATOH
They Started as Partners...
They Became *Much* More.
100% AUTHENTIC MANGA
品質第一公式商品
Available NOW at Your
Favorite Book and Comic Stores
OT
OLDER TEEN
AGE 16+
FAKE: © Sanami Matoh Copyright © 1997-2002 TOKYOPOP
©2003 Tokyopop Inc.
www.TOKYOPOP.com

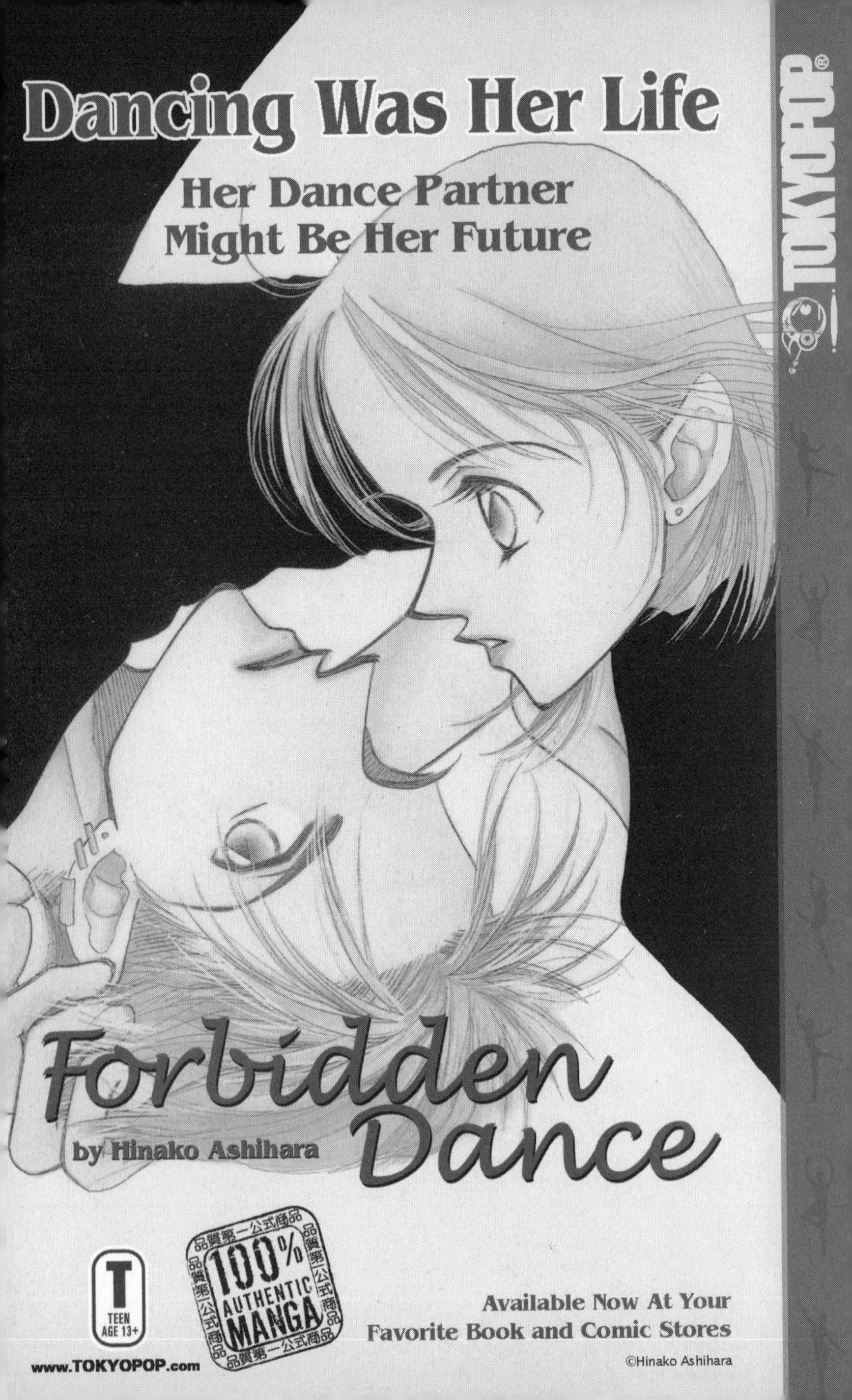
Dancing Was Her Life
Her Dance Partner
Might Be Her Future
TOKYOPOP®
Forbidden Dance
by Hinako Ashihara
T
TEEN
AGE 13+
100% AUTHENTIC MANGA
Available Now At Your
Favorite Book and Comic Stores
www.TOKYOPOP.com
©Hinako Ashihara

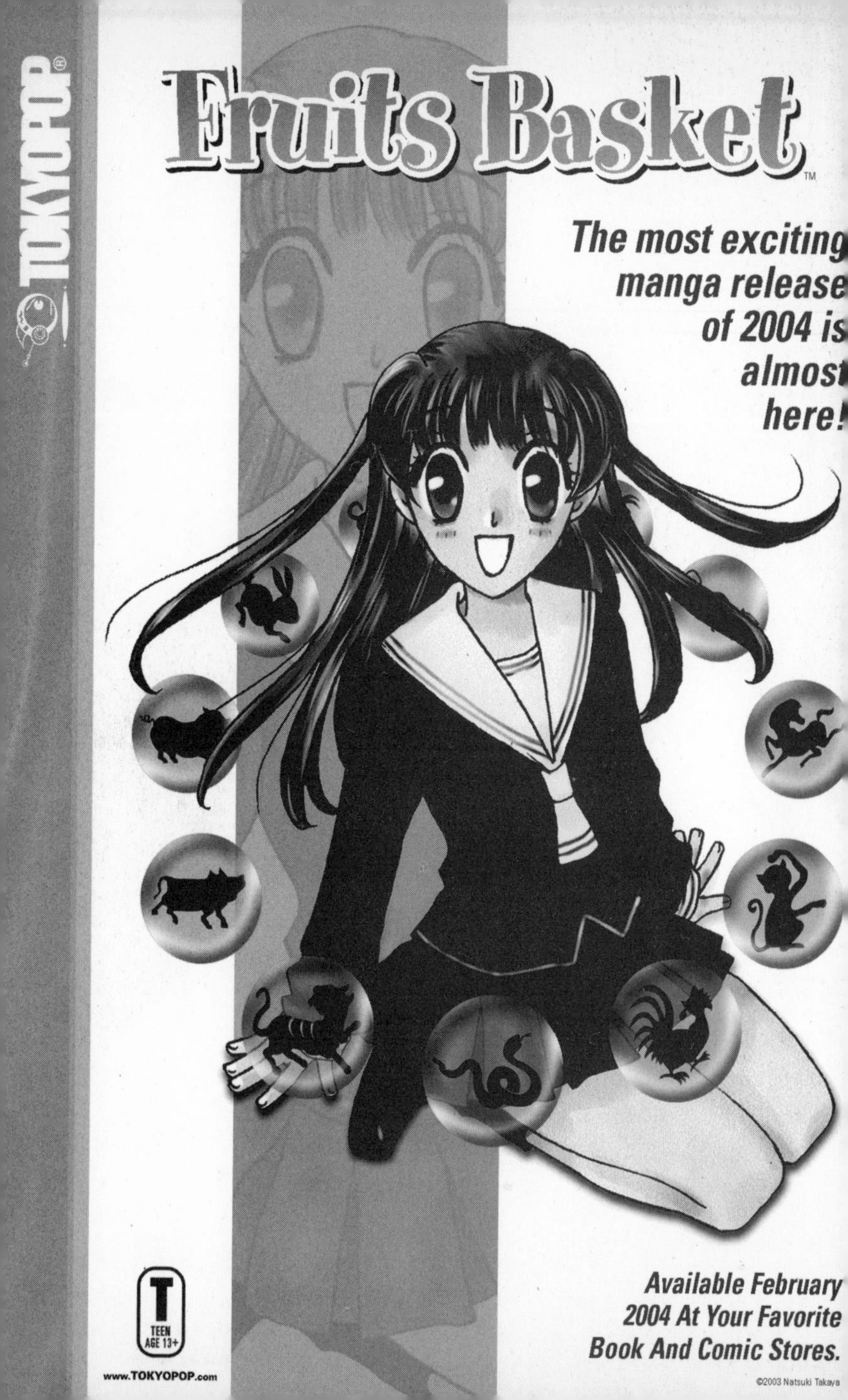
TOKYOPOP®
Fruits Basket™
The most exciting manga release of 2004 is almost here!
T
TEEN AGE 13+
Available February 2004 At Your Favorite Book And Comic Stores.
www.TOKYOPOP.com
©2003 Natsuki Takaya

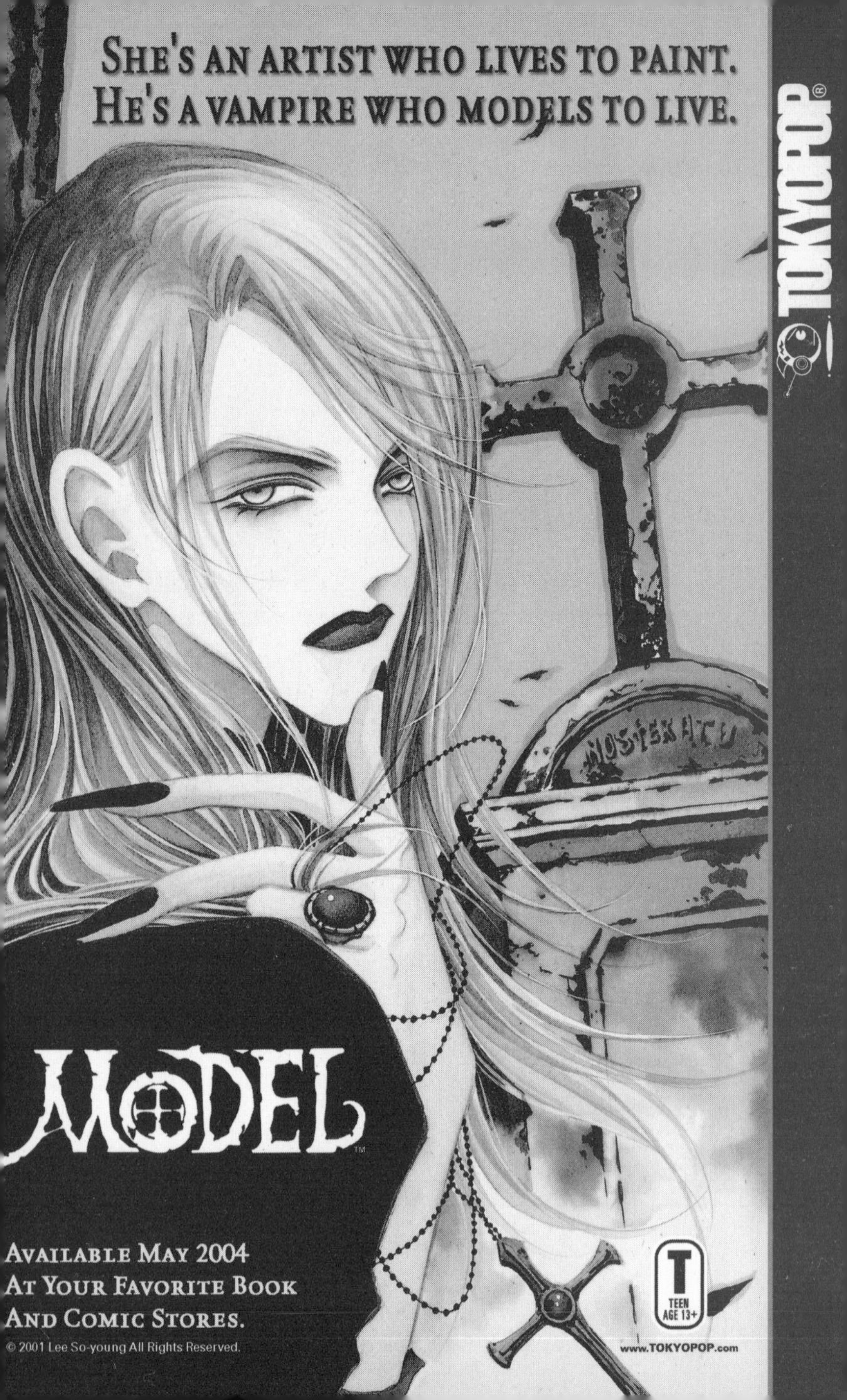
SHE'S AN ARTIST WHO LIVES TO PAINT.
HE'S A VAMPIRE WHO MODELS TO LIVE.
TOKYOPOP
MODEL
AVAILABLE MAY 2004
AT YOUR FAVORITE BOOK
AND COMIC STORES.
© 2001 Lee So-young All Rights Reserved.
T
TEEN
AGE 13+
www.TOKYOPOP.com

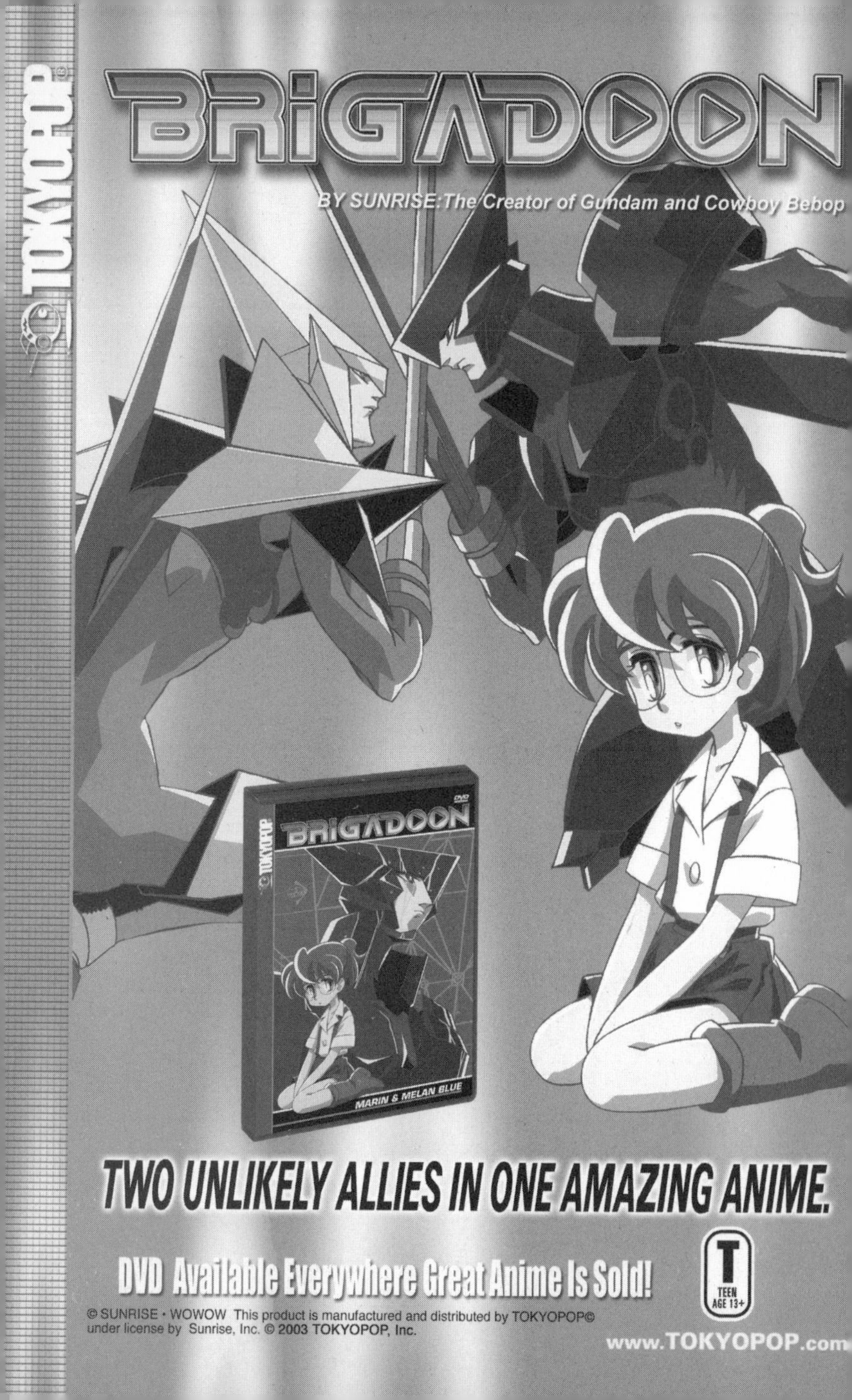
TOKYOPOP
BRIGADOON
BY SUNRISE: The Creator of Gundam and Cowboy Bebop
DVD
BRIGADOON
TOKYOPOP
MARIN & MELAN BLUE
TWO UNLIKELY ALLIES IN ONE AMAZING ANIME.
DVD Available Everywhere Great Anime Is Sold!
T
TEEN
AGE 13+
© SUNRISE • WOWOW This product is manufactured and distributed by TOKYOPOP© under license by Sunrise, Inc. © 2003 TOKYOPOP, Inc.
www.TOKYOPOP.com

STOP!

This is the back of the book.
You wouldn't want to spoil a great ending!

This book is printed "manga-style," in the authentic Japanese right-to-left format. Since none of the artwork has been flipped or altered, readers get to experience the story just as the creator intended. You've been asking for it, so TOKYOPOP® delivered: authentic, hot-off-the-press, and far more fun!

DIRECTIONS

If this is your first time reading manga-style, here's a quick guide to help you understand how it works.

It's easy... just start in the top right panel and follow the numbers. Have fun, and look for more 100% authentic manga from TOKYOPOP®!